*Your views of Revelation should not promote skepticism but be shaped in an understanding of God and his Son Jesus Christ. That should develop spiritual insights and beliefs when you exercise your intellectual understanding of end times. It must be grounded in the reality of God and Jesus Christ, and not humanism.*

# Understanding the Book of
# REVELATION

## DR. ANDERSON HENRY RUFFIN

Dr. Anderson Henry Ruffin/Book Baby Publishing
7905 North Route 130
Pennsauken, NJ 08110
www.website-books@bookbaby.com

Print ISBN: 978-1-66783-232-6
eBook ISBN: 978-1-66783-233-3

Publisher's Notes: The book will focus on, "The Understanding of Revelation," sharing
views of traditional and contemporary authors. It will focus on the aspects of the last
book of the Bible, through conventional investigative and spiritual practices. The Book of
Revelation will offer an assortment of writing, questioning, and critical thinking about the
essence of end times.

# CONTENTS

# ACKNOWLEDGEMENTS

I am grateful to family and friends for giving ideas that enabled the conception of this book and the understanding I received during research and writing. I thank those who shared their time, emotions, and knowledge with me because they believed that doing so would make a difference. Their input, support, and interest kept me going. I appreciate and acknowledge their contributions and support.

Special thanks to all who inspired me along the journey: Dr. Charles L. Lett and Dr. Aaron Dobynes, Dr. Liz Cotton and Dr. Allam Baaheth (mentors), Carolyn Flanagan Ruffin (wife), Andrell and Thanya Ruffin (son and wife), Arissa Ruffin (daughter), Taylor and Tyra Ruffin, Jeffery Ruffin, Davell Jackson (pastor), Robert Hudson (pastor), and Joe and Clementine Johnson.

They willingly sacrificed their time, contributed resources, intelligence, patience, encouragement, and motivation, during the challenging times of engagement in the writing of this book. All these beautiful people shared my desire to pass knowledge and wisdom to the present generation, especially my granddaughters.

Many sacrifices and offerings of prayers and the mercy of God enabled me to complete this book to God's glory and for the advancement of His Kingdom. The intention behind drafting this book is to bring attention to the many problems of understanding the Book of Revelation. All praise and glory belong to God.

# INTRODUCTION

A pastor stood at the door of his church and passed out an assignment for the group to read the Book of Revelation for the next six weeks of Wednesday night Bible class. He asked the group to read the chapter from the beginning to the end. He asked the class to write a summary of the Book of Revelation. Take your Bible and write down the information you can conclude from the Bible about Jesus. When each student began to examine his Bible, they started to see things they have forgotten or ever noticed before. They began to realize that Jesus represented a significant figure important to Biblical history. Some needed to be reminded that the Lord had delayed his coming for everyone to be saved. They realized that reading Revelation inspired a kind of discernment, appreciation, and understanding of the whole book. It is time for the Old and New Testament together, improving the perception of the present and the future's anticipation. By examining the Book of Revelation, the reader's understanding is engraved.

I have had many conversations on the Book of Revelation. Everyone has their view and personal belief system, even atheists. Regardless of who is speaking, how did they develop considerable thoughts and ideas about Revelation? Revelation views should not promote skepticism should be shaped around God and his Son Jesus Christ on spiritual insights when exercising an understanding of end times. It must be grounded in the reality of God and Jesus Christ, not men.

The Book of Revelation is one of the most fascinating books in the Bible. It is viewed as mysterious, indisputable, and inscrutable. Many scholars refuse to be challenged by its contents. The Book of Revelation is a book of symbols, apocalyptic prophecies many see as more challenging to interpret than any other book of the Bible. Many terms like four horsemen, locusts, dragons, and beasts have challenged writers and commentators since John wrote the book. The Book of Revelation is apocalyptic; however, not all of it is. The book contains detailed prophecies, letters giving advice and encouragement. The book inspires believers to overcome obstacles and hold on to their faith (1:4, 11, 2:1 – 3:22). God is in control of history, and He is coming back again in judgment and to reward those who have remained faithful (22:7, 12, 13, 20). (22:7, 12, 13, 20). The Bible says that it is a blessing to read and teach from Revelation.

The Book Revelation has a different structure than other books. There are four different schools of interpretation used to interpret the Book of Revelation: Preterist, Historicist, Futurist, and Idealist. The Preterist school of thought sees the book as already been fulfilled by AD 312 with the conversion of Constantine. 'Preterist' is a Latin word meaning "*past*" and pertains mostly to history rather than being prophetic of coming events. The Preterist review has the most merit because it was written to the seven churches in Asia (modern Turkey).

The Historical view the book is a panorama of the church's history from the days of John to the end of ages or Christ's second advent. The Historical view sees the book as local persecution experienced by the churches reflecting Nero's reign in the late AD 60s, but some writers agree that it was during the reign of Roman Emperor Domitian AD 81 to 89. The Idealist views the book as an extended term and regards the conflict of the age-old principles of good and evil with no historical element. The Futurist, beginning with chapter four, addresses prophecies yet to be fulfilled. The author of this book shares the thought and position of the Futurist.

The Book of Revelation uses apocalyptic literature to include the use of highly symbolic figurative. Revelation incorporates fascinating sights, images, lightning, thunder, lampstands, creatures, angels, singing, claims, plagues, horses, trumpets, fanfares, bowls, vials, and chorus praising God and His Son Jesus. It explains why the righteous suffered, and God's judgment will be delayed. It offers the believers hope. Widespread attention is given to events displaying God's power against godlessness and evil. God will destroy a hellish world and create a new heaven and earth for the believers.

The main character in the Book of Revelation is God, the Creator of the universe. Jesus Christ is the Son of God, and the message is given to Him. Jesus Christ gives the message to angels, and they deliver it to John in a vision. He is an apostle of Jesus Christ. John investigates the issues of the Church's human history through the eyes of God, establishing a need for the world to be saved. The unbeliever will face a catastrophe of events to convince them to seek God and Jesus Christ for consolation. Jesus gives a Revelation to an angel. The angel gives the Revelation to John, a faithful servant. John is told to write down what he sees and give it to the Church. The message is given to the followers. God wants us to know His Son, Jesus. It is commanded of John to draft what he sees. What John sees is the Revelation of Jesus Christ (Rev. 1:1). If we want to know God, we need to learn about Jesus. God gives John a message to carry to churches of Asia.

John, Apostle and Evangelist, the Beloved Disciple whom Jesus loves, and is often referred to as the Theologian or Divine is the author of Revelation. He was a son of Zebedee, a master fisherman. Peter, James, and John held a position of distinction among the apostles witnessing many of Jesus's miracles. John took a permanent part with Peter in the founding of the Church.

After Pentecost, John made a pillar in the church at Jerusalem. Later, he settled in Ephesus, where he is remembered for his valuable service for the cause of Christ. He was banished to Patmos in the reign of the Emperor Domitian (81–96 AD).

The Book of Revelation is God's word to the believers to encourage them at the end times. The term *'revelation'* here means 'uncovering, unveiling, and uncovering something hidden about Jesus Christ.' 'Apocalypse' was the word for a 'crisis,' and for 'a crisis which bordered on the end.' The word *'apokalypsis'* sometimes called an *'apocalypse,'* means 'unveiling, uncovering, or unwrapping' (Rom. 16:25; Gal. 1:12; Eph. 1:17; 3:3). *'Apokalypsis'* is a Greek word meaning 'revelation,' applied chiefly to the Book of Revelation by John. A style of writing, to the Jewish circles, immediately preceding and following a life of Christ. It is also a style of writing made by a prophet familiar with the Biblical symbols and written at a time of persecution, in the style of a revelation marked using symbolic numbers, animals, and other creatures. A permanent feature is its telescoping of past, present him, and future events giving hope that God's saving acts will endure. Apocalyptic writers like Daniel and John focus on revealing what has been hidden with regards to end times. Some features as described by Leon Morris in his book, *Apocalyptic,* are included:

The writer tends to choose some great man of the past and make him the hero of the book.

1. The hero often takes a journey, accompanied by a celestial guide who shows him interesting sites and comments on them.

2. Information is often communicated through visions.

3. The visions often make use of strange, enigmatic, and symbolism.

4. The visions are often given with regards to human interventions in present or future situations.

5. The visions usually end with God bringing the present situation to a cataclysmic end and establishing a better situation.

6. The writer often claims to write in the name of a chosen deity or a hero.

7. The writer often takes history and writes it as a prophecy.

8. The focus of apocalyptic is on comforting and sustaining a righteous remnant.

In the New Testament, the revealing of the sons of God (Rom. 8:19), Christ's incarnation (Lk. 2:32), and his glorious appearing at His second coming (2 Thess. 1:7; 1 Pet. 1:7). In all its uses, "Revelation" refers to something or someone, once hidden, becoming visible. Revelation is the unveiling of Jesus Christ. Webster tells us *apocalypse* means, "The complete final destruction of the world, as described in the biblical Book of Revelation, but the Greek meaning is opening." God wants the contents of the book open. God's Revelation focuses on Jesus and His majesty. Jesus will bring all nations into subjection as the Kings of kings. The source of Revelation comes straight from the Triune Publishers in heaven (Rev. 1:4-5). It is designed to explain what happens before Christ's return, during, and what He will do at the end of human history. The book is constantly moving toward a grand finale focusing on the end of human history and the beginning of a utopia.

The churches of the 21st Century are nevertheless God's design for fellowship, discipleship, ministry, the deliverance of the saints, and a cherished house for generations to grow until the end of times. There are five purposes behind the writing of Revelation:

1. To encourage, counsel, and warn the churches of Asia Minor.

2. To encourage, counsel, and warn every generation to proclaim Jesus Christ.

3. To encourage, counsel, and warn the world of things coming upon the earth. Humanity must repent and receive the salvation of Jesus Christ.

4. The book reveals how Christ will judge the world for rejecting God and persecuting His people.

5. It is a book designed to warn and comfort (Rev. 1:3; 2:7; 3:21; 14:13; 22:14).

Many believers have misunderstood the Book of Revelation because they refuse to accept the contents of saving the unbelievers, and the book challenges anyone who has not accepted Jesus Christ as their Savior to do so before it is too late. It is a book of comfort and peace. The end times are coming, and humanity must prepare for a historical ending. God is continuously warning humanity to come to a sense of repentance or face the wrath of God. John has been given the task of inviting humanity to view what God has in store for the believers and the unbelievers.

The Book of Revelation does not paint a beautiful picture of what is to come, but it offers us time to get ready for the end of time. We can see beyond the present and investigate the future to see the eternal punishment of Hell. God will destroy the earth one day, but the Apostle John speaks of a great day to come where believers will escape the judgment. A thorough examination of Revelation will encourage eternal life. Therefore, the promise is, "Heaven and earth shall pass away, but the words of God shall not pass away" (Matt. 24:35). Revelation 21:1 tells us, "And I saw a new heaven and a new earth, for the first heaven in the new earth were passed away, and there was no more sea." Revelation encompasses three sections:

1. The past—the things which have been seen (Chapter 1).

2. The present—the things which are to come (Chapters 2-3).

3. The future—the things that shall occur after these things (Chapters 4-22).

From Genesis to Revelation, Satan is constantly plotting to see humanity's downfall. He conquers the souls of men who turn from God and Christ. He is called the prince of the earth who was tossed out of heaven for his disobedience (Rev. 12:7-10). Satan is a deceiver. When he came to Eve in Eden, he was called *"subtle"*. The word means making use of clever and indirect methods to achieve something crafty and shrewd. He has been deceiving people ever since. He will continue to weave his web of lies and half-truths until he is cast into the Lake of Fire. The world has become ungodly and evil and has hindered a relationship between God and humanity. Contemporary times are mutilated with an escalating disorder, abortions, terrorism, assaults on different religious systems, and people of color. Moral constraints have eroded morality. There is little collaboration on these matters.

God will invariably defeat the evil forces in the world and establish a new heaven and earth. Judges 21:25 tells us, "In those days, there was no king in Israel: every man did that which was right in his own eyes". The world is becoming a place of disorder, and humanity will not turn back to the principle of God's word. John will see Jesus scrutinize the Church, and he will be instructed to write down what he sees in a disoriented world. He will see the plan of God's delight and wrath leading to the end of human history.

An Apostle is sent forth as a messenger or delegate. The word used in the New Testament is unique to the Twelve chosen by Christ to witness His life and Resurrection and then preach His Gospel. John the Apostle, the writer of Revelation, was a disciple, or follower, of Jesus and was responsible for spreading the message of Jesus, as his title of *"apostle"*. He is not to be confused with John the Baptist, the forerunner of Jesus. He has the incredible task of writing God's Revelation to awaken a spirit of renewal in developing an opportunity to live with God in eternity.

John was a man sent from God. He came to testify concerning the knowledge of God and His Son so that through Him all might believe. John was not the light; he came only as a witness to the light (Jn. 1:6-8). Who is the light in Revelation?

1. the faithful witness (Rev. 1:5)

2. the firstborn from the dead (Rev. 1: 5)

3. the reading of the kings of the earth (Rev. 1:5)

4. the Alpha and the Omega (Rev. 1:8; 21:6; 22:13)

5. someone like a Son of Man (Rev. 1:13)

6. the First and the Last (Rev. 1:17; 22:13)

7. the Living One (Rev. 1:18)

8. him who holds the seven stars in his right hand and walked among the seven golden lampstands (Rev. 2:1)

9. him who died and came to life again (Rev. 2:8)

10. him who holds the sharp, double-edged sword (Rev. 2:12)

11. the Son of God (Rev. 2:18)

12. him who holds the seven spirits of God and the seven stars (Rev. 3:1)

13. him who is holy and true, who holds the keys of David (Rev. 3:7)

14. the Amen (Rev. 3:14)

15. the faithful and true witness (Rev. 3:14)

16. the ruler of God's creation (Rev. 3:14)

17. the Lion of the tribe of Judah (Rev. 5:5)

18. the Root of David (Rev. 5:5; 22:16)

19. the Lamb (Rev. 5:6) mention thirty-two times in Revelation

20. Lords of lords and King of kings (Rev. 17:14; 19:16)

21. Faithful and True (Rev. 19:11)

22. the Word of God (Rev. 19:13)

23. the Beginning and the End (Rev. 21:6; 22:13)

24. the Offspring of David (Rev. 22:16)

25. the bright and morning star (Rev. 22:16)

26. the Lord Jesus (Rev. 22:20, 21)

John gives a charge to the Church to carefully examine God's mission and plan to fight the enemies until He returns. Jesus sees some severe concerns about the Church, "You have lost your first love, faithfulness, accept the teaching of Balaam, tolerate the woman Jezebel, walking unworthy, deny Jesus's name, and you have become lukewarm" (Rev. 2:4, 10, 14, 20; 3:4, 8, 16). It must continue to develop a true loyalty and adherence to Jesus, and that it agrees and embrace Him without amends. It must invariably produce faithful obedience and rekindle the charges which Jesus has appointed without mental reservations or purpose and fulfill the obligations, design, and mission forever. "And upon this rock, I will build my Church, and the gates of hell shall not prevail against it" (Matt. 16:18). John received this vision while in the spirit on the Lord's Day (Rev. 1:10). It is considered the first day of the week (Sunday) as meeting together, breaking bread, communicating, and receiving instructions, laying up offerings in store for charitable purposes, and occupation in holy thoughts and prayers. The Lord's Day is a reference to the Day the Lord deals in judgment and sovereign rule over the earth.

Revelation is written in times of persecution, usually depicting the conflict between good and evil. It is not just another book. It is a book of prophecy, and it is written to the seven churches in the Roman province of Asia. Given to John as a vision, the book records a picture of future events concisely. The Book of Revelation blesses the man who reads, teaches, and obeys the message. Revelation. 22: 18-19 tell us, "It must not be tampered with," and some solemn warnings are given to the guilty:

1. A person must not add to the word of this book.
2. A person must take away from the words of this book.

If a person tampers with the Word of God or adds to the words, He will suffer the plagues covered in Revelation. If anyone adds or takes away from God's words:

1. A person will not have the opportunity of eternal life. They will not have the privileges of entering the new heaven and earth.

2. Jesus will take away the privilege of entering the Holy City, the heavenly Jerusalem.

3. Jesus will take a share out of all the glorious promises of the Book of Revelation (1 Cor. 2:1-5; 1 Thess. 2:2-5, 2: 13; Rev. 22:19).

The Book of Revelation encouraged the First century Christians to stand firm and avoid paganism under the Roman authorities. Despite the threat of diversity and martyrdom, they were to wait patiently for His return. Jesus promised, "Behold, I am with you always, until the end of time" (Matt. 28:20). Revelation closes with the greatest of all assurance. The assurances are twofold:

1. Jesus Christ is the one who reveals and testifies to the things written in Revelation. They are not the imagination and words of men. They are the words of the living God, the son of God himself.

2. Christ declares: Yes—it is true. He is coming soon (Rev. 20-21).

We do not know when Jesus Christ will return. Amen! (Rev..22:21, Phil. 4:5, James 5: 8; Rev. 3:11). The Book of Revelation began with a promise (Rev. 1:3) and closed with a promised blessing (Rev. 22:7).

# CHAPTER 1

## *The Revelation Of Jesus Christ*

---

The Revelation of Jesus Christ is considered a letter to the seven churches in seven cities in the Roman Empire in Asia Minor. John is given a vision of unveiling or disclosing what will happen before, during, and after Jesus Christ's return to earth at the end of human history.

The number "seven" is used throughout Revelation and often serves as a key to actual events. The number seven is often used in the Bible to refer to completeness and fullness. It speaks of the seven churches of Asia Minor (Chapters 2 and 3). The number seven speaks of blessings (Rev. 1:3, 14:13, 16:15, 19:9, 20:6, 22:7, and 22:14). Seven angels (8:2), seven seals (Rev.5:1), seven trumpets (Rev. 8:2), and the seven plagues (Rev. 15:1) depict God's judgment in Revelation. The seven spiritual figures are revealed:

1. A woman clothed with the sun (Rev. 12:1)

2. The dragon (12:3), that ancient serpent of Genesis is called the devil and Satan (Rev. 12:9)

3. The male child, destined to rule all nations with an iron rod (Rev. 12:5)

4. Michael (Rev. 12:7)

5. The sea beast (Rev. 13:1)

6. The land's beast (Rev. 13:11) who implanted the mark of the beast

7. The Lamb of God (Rev. 14:1)

John lived in Ephesus preaching gospel belief in Jesus Christ (Rev. 1: 9). He is the only Apostle left at this time. The Roman government exiled John to the island of Patmos for proclaiming the gospel of Jesus Christ. He is an older man in exile on the small, barren island of Patmos imprisoned because of his faithful.

The island of Patmos is one of the Sporades islands located in the Aegean Sea (modern Turkey). Patmos was a Roman penal colony about 50 miles from Ephesus. Patmos is 40 miles from Ephesus, 10 miles long, and 6 miles wide. John was banished during the reign of Domitian for witnessing to the world about Jesus, AD 94, and liberated AD 96. According to Eusebius, a Christian historian, Nerva released John from Patmos, AD 96-98.

Under the Roman government, prisoners lost all civil rights, and their property was confiscated. A prison term had no end unless the emperor who had banished the citizen died. John survived Domitian, and he returned to Ephesus and lived until he died a natural death.

The message of Revelation evaluates the spiritual heartbeat of the churches and offers some encouragement during times of persecution. The seven churches of Asia Minor are experiencing a spiritual decline. John receives a vision from Jesus, and he is instructed to write a letter to the seven churches of Asia (Rev. 1:10) in the Roman province referred to today as modern Turkey. The seven Churches include Ephesus, Smyrna, Pergamum, Thyatira, Sardis, Philadelphia, and Laodicea. Each Church becomes a recipient of John's message. Troas were other churches in the area (Acts 20:5, Colossi (Col. 1:2, Hierapolis (Col. 4:13), but the seven churches were the most important ones when John authored the Book of Revelation.

Verse 1

Why did Jesus choose John to author the Book of Revelation? John loved Jesus more than the other disciples. John was always clinging to Jesus. John was the best candidate for recording the events in Revelation. He knew Jesus better than anyone else in humanity. John was an eyewitness to Jesus as the Messiah and Savior. The Messiah, 'the anointed one,' is God's Son who makes provisions for the recovery of humanity's sin and its penalty. God raised men to deliver His people from sins during Israel's history, but they could not and did not save from the spiritual bondage of the sin. Jesus did not meet the Messianic expectations of the Jewish leaders. Jesus recognized and confessed himself to be the Messiah. The Bible contains evidence of His Messianic office and the works that he did.

Jesus had great confidence in John because he was the only disciple who stood at the cross with Jesus's mother, his mother's sister, Mary, the wife of Clopas, and Mary Magdalene (Jn. 19:25). John's resume includes:

1. John had an early career as a fisherman in Galilee.

2. He was the brother of James, son of Zebedee (Matt. 4:21).

3. John left a profitable business to follow Jesus (Matt. 4:22).

4. He wrote the gospel of John, three New Testament letters, the Book of Revelation, and one-quarter of the New Testament.

5. Peter sees the disciple Jesus loved as the closest friend (Jn. 21:20)

6. He was present at Jesus's trial and the cross (Jn. 18:15 – 16; 19:26)

7. John was entrusted with the care of Jesus's mother, Mary (Jn. 19:25 – 27)

8. He was an eyewitness at the empty tomb of the risen Christ.

9. He was the only one of the original twelve followers of Jesus to die of natural causes.

John is called the "apostle of love". He is also called the revelator (Rev. 1:1, 4, 9; 22:8). He was a disciple and a part of Jesus's "inner circle" with Peter and James and was the only Apostle who died of old age. He authored five books of the Bible: The Gospel of John, the epistles 1 John, 2 John, and 3 John, and the Book of Revelation, although some scholars dispute if he wrote them. The other was martyred.

Verse 2

What John is going to write is the Revelation of Jesus Christ? The woman in Revelation means unwrapping or unveiling. The Greek word is *"apokalypsis"* or *Apocalypse*. In English, the word means the end of the world. Jesus wants us to know what will take place soon. The Revelation of Jesus Christ is a book of prophecy foretelling future events and proclamation of future events God will do through His Son. The book includes moral instructions to the lost and what they must do to escape the wrath to come. The words *"time is near"* suggest what must take place soon (Rev. 1:1). We live in a world of conflicting claims that are not true. The world is heading for destruction, filled with violence, scandal, failing governments, political disorder, depression, evil, and sin. John's vision shows that God will intervene.

John receives a vision and is instructed to write down God's program for humanity, understanding of end times, and spell out the second coming of Christ:

1. what he has seen (the vision of Jesus)

2. what is now (the message of Jesus to the seven churches in Revelation 2 and 3)

3. what will take place later (Rev. 4-22).

The Book of Revelation comprises the final book of the New Testament given to John by an angel dispatched as a special messenger from Jesus. John was instructed to bear witness to what he sees from God, the testimony of Jesus. He will see the events in a vision and be asked to record them. John is telling us who Jesus is. He does not want us to develop a false recognition or become confused about Jesus. He gives us a testimony of Jesus sent by an angel that:

1. Jesus is the risen, glorified Son of God ministering among the churches (Rev. 1:10ff).
2. Jesus is the king of the earth (Rev. 1:5).
3. Jesus is the one "who is and who was and who is to come, the Almighty" (Rev. 1:8).
4. Jesus is the one who was dead but now lives forever.
5. He is the beginning of the creation of God (Rev. 3:14).
6. Jesus is the Lamb in heaven, with authority to open the title deed to the earth (Rev.6:1ff).
7. He is the Lamb on the throne (Rev. 7:17), the Messiah who will reign forever (Rev. 11:15).
8. He will return in glorious splendor to conquer His foes (Rev. 19:11).

John knows that believing the right things about Jesus is critical to getting everything else right. Three descriptions of the Person and the work of the Lord Jesus Christ are mentioned:

1. Jesus is "the faithful witness and Son" to reveal the Father (Jn. 14:7-9, 12:45; Col. 1:15; Heb. 1:3).
2. Jesus has the right to bear the title of the world's Savior.

In the Old Testament, Israel was God's witness to the world (Isa. 43:10), and in the New Testament, Jesus is the witness to the world (Matt. 28:19-20; Acts 1:8). Jesus Christ was and is God in human flesh. He is more than a reflection, and He is God! Therefore, He was able to be a faithful witness" to the Person and work of the Father (Jn. 18:37; 1Tim. 6:13).

God is in control, and His justice will prevail. God gave his plan to Jesus Christ. He sent his angel to reveal the message. John and the servant in Revelation reveal the Word of God to lost humanity, to accept Jesus Christ. The warning is imminent, and we must keep our eyes on the future. Jesus may return at any moment. Revelation warns the unbeliever of God's justice, wrath, and judgment for rejecting Jesus Christ as Savior.

Verse 3

John tells the believers that the Word of God must be obeyed. He faithfully reports what he saw (Verse 1:2). Revelation will bless the person who reads, hears, and obeys the Church's message (Rev. 1:3). Seven John tells the believers that the Word of God must be obeyed. He faithfully reports what he saw (Verse 2). Revelation will bless the person who reads, hears, and obeys the Church's message (Rev. 1:3). Seven Beatitudes or promises are made to the reader of Revelation:

1. The reader will receive a blessing. Let the truths come into your heart (Rev. 1:3).

2. Believers will find rest and reward (Rev. 14:13)

3. Keep and observe; let the truths come into your life until Jesus returns and receive your blessings (Rev. 16:15).

4. The promise's benefit is an invitation to the marriage supper of the Lamb and the Church (Bride) in heaven (Rev. 19:9).

5. Receive eternal life (Rev. 20:6).

6. The relevance of the prophecy is true. Reading Revelation is a blessing to those who read, hear, and keep the teachings of Revelation (Rev. 22:7).

7. The reader who hears and obeys will receive robes of righteousness to access the Holy City (Rev. 22:14).

Paul admonishes Timothy to give attendance to reading (1 Tim. 4:13). In the First Century Church, God's word was read aloud in the assemblies. We have done away, except at the beginning of Sunday services. Responsive reading has been done away with today. Reading Revelation in public and private aloud or silently, the Lord promises a blessing. In Jewish culture, the Word of God is still read, whether the group is small or large.

Verses 5-6

The announcement is to the churches in Asia. They are representatives of the churches of Jesus Christ (Verses 4-8).

1. Grace and peace as mentioned (4-5).

2. Jesus Christ as Savior and Redeemer (5-6).

3. Christ is the Almighty (V. 8).


Jesus name in Revelation is given titles and descriptions in Verse 5 that are mentioned throughout the Book of Revelation:

1. the faithful and true witness (Verse 5, 3:14)

2. the firstborn from the dead (Verse 5)

3. the ruler of the kings of the earth (Verse 5)

4. He is Alpha and Omega (Rev. 1:8; 21:6; 22:13)

5. He holds the seven stars in his right hand and walks among the seven golden lampstands (Rev. 2:1)

6. His word is sharp as a doubled sword (Rev. 2:12)

7. He is the Son of God (Rev. 2:18)

8. He is the ruler of God's creation (Rev. 3:14)

9. He is the lion of the tribe Judah and the root of David (Rev. 5:5-6; 22:16).

10. He is the Lord of the lord and the Kings of kings (Rev. 17:14; 19:16)

11. He is the Lord Jesus (Rev. 22:20, 21).

The Church can receive grace and peace from Jesus Christ. Grace means favors and blessings from God through Jesus Christ. Grace and peace were a greeting the early Church used to declare that God had given the people as a reality. The Lord blesses and keeps you. The Lord makes his face shine on you and is gracious to you. The Lord turns his face toward you and gives you peace (Num. 6:24-26). The peace of God, which transcends all understanding, will guard your hearts and your minds in Christ Jesus (Phil. 4:7).

John writes to enlighten the servants of the Lord to continue to worship God because of his intimacy (Jn. 15:15), worthiness, sovereignty, and promises of a glorious future. Jesus Christ is the great Savior, Redeemer, and commander of the world. How do Christians determine what they believe? How are we freed from our sins? Jesus is the faithful witness who has risen from the dead. We must keep in mind that all Jesus says is true. John was writing to believers experiencing persecution. He assured that Jesus continuously cares and loves them no matter what may come their way. He set them free from their sins by his blood, through death on Calvary's cross, "To glory and power forever" (Rev. 1: 6). Five things are declared in Verses 5-6:

1. Jesus Christ is the faithful witness and person we count. He came from God, out of heaven, to reveal the truth (Jn. 18:37).

2. Jesus is whom we believe. He arose and conquered death for us. All believers will do the same to live with God eternally.

3. Jesus Christ is the present King of the earth, and He is the sovereign ruler over the earth. He is in control. He can handle the mess of this world. Jesus is delaying his return so that all men can repeat and be saved from God's wrath (Ps. 24:1, Rev. 11:15).

4. Jesus Christ has redeemed us (Rev. 1:5b).

5. Jesus Christ is the exalted king. He has the responsibility as the overseer, manager, supervisor, and governor of heaven and earth. We

shall share in the administration of the affairs with Christ throughout eternity (1 Cor. 6:2, Rev. 20:4). As priests means, we will have an open asset to God's presence anytime (e (Rom. 12:1, 1 Pet. 2:5).

After Jesus spent forty days on the earth, He ascended to heaven and is seated at the right hand of God the Father Almighty (Mark 16:19). He will come back in the same way you have seen him go into heaven (Acts 1:11). Luke Chapter 24 tells how Jesus leads the eleven disciples to Bethany, a village on the Mount of Olives. He instructs them to remain in Jerusalem until the coming of the Holy Spirit. "And it came to pass, while He blessed them, He parted from them and was carried up into heaven in full view of His disciples (Lk. 24:50-51, Acts 1:9).

The disciples wanted a sign to show the coming at the end of the ages. Jesus said, "When you hear wars and rumors wars, nations rising against nations, kingdoms against kingdoms, famines, and earthquakes in various places. These events devised worldwide grief and agony (Matt. 24). No one knows, neither the angels of heaven nor the Son, only the Father alone (Matt. 24:36), knows when Jesus is returning. He was taken up into heaven, will come in like manner as you saw Him go (Acts 1:11).

Jesus Christ is returning, and everyone will see Him (Verse 7). The theme of Revelation is Christ coming to execute justice and judgment upon the earth the second time. Three things are said:

1. Every person shall see him as a come in His glory with his host of angels (Rev. 21:23).

2. Those who reject him shall wail and mourn. They shall cry because they have cursed, rejected, ignored, neglected, rebelled, disregarded, and opposed Jesus Christ as the Son of God.

3. Jesus's return will prove that He is the Messiah, the anointed one, and the Savior of the world. He will come to execute justice against the evil works upon the earth (Matt. 24:30, 8:38, Rev. 11:15-18).

Verse 8

Jesus Christ is the person of deity (Verse 8). He is Almighty God. He is Alpha and Omega, the beginning, the end, and the last (Rev. 22:13). He is the creator of all things, and He will end history (Col. 1:16). There is nothing outside his knowledge. In Revelation, God's power is supreme over all the events of humanity. Jesus exercises sovereign control over every person, object, and event. Not one molecule in the universe is outside of his dominion. Jesus Christ controls all things. We will find peace, safety, and security in Jesus (Jn. 10:28 – 29, Eph. 2:4-7). Jesus Christ is the Lord who is, who was, and who is to come. He loves all of us. We will know his wrath (Ps. 135:14, 1 Cor. 6:9-10).

Jesus Christ is Almighty God. He controls the whole University. He possesses all power, omnipotent, can do anything, control anything, and every person in it. He controls atoms, protons, neutron electrons, space, and matter. He controls every circumstance and event throughout the universe (Rom. 8:28, 38-39; Col. 1: 15 – 17; Heb. 1:1 – 3).

The Bible tells us that Jesus Christ became flesh and dwelt among us, and we beheld his glory (Jn. 1:14). Jesus lived an extraordinary life teaching about life, death, and eternity. Jesus was the Messiah, God incarnate. He came to show the world God the Father. Many views Jesus with patronizing nonsense as a demon, a crazy man, a moral teacher, a lunatic, or merely a man. John does not see Jesus this way. He partners with Jesus in his suffering of the coming kingdom. He is blessed to receive a message to deliver to the churches.

Jesus is the Savior, the Redeemer, the supreme majesty, can provide, protect, assure, and secure. He is a judge and will do so at the end times. John wants the believers down through the centuries to know who has given this message to the churches.

Verse 9-10

John says three things about himself (Verses 9-10):

1. A brother of the churches, meaning he believes what they believe.

2. He endured trials and tribulations, afflictions, persecution, imprisonment, economic injustice, slanderous accusations by Jews, attacks from government soldiers, mobs, suffering, and pressure. He is looking for the same thing, seeking the kingdom of God (Matt. 24:13; Acts 14:22).

3. John was banished from society, loved ones, and friends, but Christ meets his needs (Heb. 13:5; Isa. 41:10; Matt. 28:20).

Verse 11

John is assigned an angel to receive the Revelation of Jesus Christ. "He was in the Spirit on the Lord's Day, and I heard a loud voice behind me like a trumpet saying, "Write on a scroll what you see and send it to the seven churches"." (Rev. 1:10-11b). Five times John is commanded to write what he sees and hears on the Lord's Day (Rev. 1:11, 19; 14:13; 19:9; 21:5). What is the Lord's Day? It is mentioned in the New Testament. It is the first day of the week when Christians gather to worship and celebrate the Lord's supper (1 Cor. 11:20).

John was isolated on an island in prison for preaching the Word of God (Verse 10). He says that he was in the spirit on the Lord's Day. The Lord's Day means Sunday, the first day of the week, the day when Christ was raised from the dead. John is not dreaming. "In the spirit" means being in union with the Holy Spirit and with Jesus Christ. John was in a holy trance when he received this spiritual experience. The Holy Spirit empowered his senses to receive a Revelation from Jesus.

The vision begins when John hears a voice that sounds like a trumpet. It is an overpowering and commanding voice to ensure he hears what God is about to reveal. John has been anointed to write down on a scroll the vision he is about to see and send it to the seven churches of Asia Minor (Rev. 1:11). The churches are to preserve their faith until Jesus Christ return. John is given a message for the churches to develop their faith for the great purpose of glorifying Jesus Christ.

John hears and sees in a vision someone like the Son of Man standing in the middle of seven gold lampstands (Verses 12-14). The seven candlesticks represent the churches in Verse 20. Why this symbol? Jesus is the light of the world (Jn. 8:12), and the churches are to proclaim his light. The church must make sure that the Word of God is studied, taught, and preached among humanity to the end of the world (Jn. 1:4, 8:12; 2 Cor. 4:6; Phil. 2:15).

Jesus's glory is so excellent that John cannot describe using earthly words. John describes Jesus this way. Jesus is seen in His Glory as God the Son. We must remember John had seen Jesus as a man, but now He is seen in His divinity wearing heavenly attire representing some of His royal attributes:

1. Jesus is dressed in a robe of prophets, kings, and princes clothed to his feet, symbolizing His ministry (Verse 13).

2. Jesus proclaimed the Word of God as a Prophet.

3. Jesus is Priest. He gives us access to the presence of God and makes us acceptable before God (1Pet. 2:9).

4. He will make us kings and princes sharing in the affairs of the universe. He will protect, provide, work all things out for the good of those who love and follow Him.

5. Clothed in a robe symbolizes a judge amid the churches. He will come in judgment over the earth with eternal dominion (Dan. 2:44, 1 Cor. 15:23-24).

John describes a picture of Christ:

1. His head hair was white as wool and snow (Verse 14). He is the eternal Lord of the universe like the, "Ancient of the Day (God)" (Dan. 7:9). White is representing purity. He never sinned. He never had

one evil or negative thought that came short of the glory of God (2 Tim. 3:16), represent Christ holiness.

2. Eyes like a flame of fire (Verse 14) represent Christ as all-knowing, symbolizing the piercing, penetrating power to see anywhere, even in dark places behind closed doors. His eyes search the innermost parts of the heart and know all. He is omniscient (Dan. 10:16; Jer. 17:10, 23:24).

3. His feet are like fine brass, refined in a fiery furnace (Verse 15). They are prepared to move around and preach the gospel and the glad tidings of peace. They also tread down the enemy and rush to rescue his people (Isa. 52:7; Dan. 10:6).

4. Jesus's voice sounds like many glasses of water (Verse 15), represent Christ's authority. It sends forth glorious messages of salvation, hope, joy, confidence, and comfort (Jn. 18:37; 2 Thess. 4:16 – 18). It thunders forth majestic rebuke, conviction, and judgment (Ps. 29:4; Jer. 25:30; Rev. 3:20).

5. Jesus's right hand holding seven stars represents the pastors of the seven churches and Christ's control of church leaders (Jn. 15:16; Matt. 28:19 – 20, and 2 Tim. 1:20, 4:18).

6. Verse 16-Out of his mouth, a sharp two-edged sword represents the word of God, his penetrating power, Christ's judgment on the church's enemies (2 Thess. 2:8; Heb. 4:12; 2 Tim. 3:16).

7. Jesus Christ has a countenance like the shining sun, which symbolizes the dazzling brilliance of his presence in all his majesty, honor, and glory. His glory and light shine from heaven because He is the light (Matt. 17:2; 2 Cor. 4:6. Acts 9:1 – 5).

8. Jesus has a golden breastplate stamped across his chest. It represents close to the heart. Christ poses people in his church so close to his heart (Rom. 8:38 – 39).

John fell to his feet, witnessing what he saw. The vision was real to John, and he reacted to Jesus was in fear. With his right hand, Jesus reaches out softly to touch John, assuring him that the glory of the Lord would not consume him. He assured John, and his fellow believers to not fear death. Christ said four things to him:

1. Fear not—do not be afraid. His appearance was not the judgment but giving a great mission to the church is to reach the lost (Isa. 41:10, 43:1-2).

2. I am the first and the last. I can be with a person when they are born, when they die, and all the days between (Jn. 8:58, 17:5; Rev. 22:13).

3. I am he who lived and was dead; behold, I am alive forever (Rev. 22:13; Jn. 1:3-4, 10: 10, 14:6; Rom. 10:9).

4. I have the keys of pale and of death (Verse 18). Jesus says I have conquered death, and I can deliver you from the judgment of death and hell (Hades). I have given you access to heaven. Jesus has the keys to unlock both and deliver us from the bondage of both (Christ alone has the keys to signify power, authority, and control over people's lives and death (Heb. 2:14–15; Rev. 1:4, Isa. 25:8).

John was commanded to write in detail what you are to see, which is the outline of the Book of Revelation:

1. He had seen the things in the vision of the glorified Christ (Chapters 1–2).

2. The things which are—state and condition of the churches (Chapters 2–3).

3. The things which shall be hereafter, the consummation of human history, which includes evens as they intertwined to the end the world (Chapter 4–22).

With the knowledge we have about lampstands or candlesticks, the King James translation said, "Jesus stands amid the seven candlesticks lampstands with the seven stars in His right hand. It is a clear message to the seven churches. The seven candlesticks or lampstands have been symbols of the churches. They hold a light to the world, receiving their glorious light from Jesus Christ (Matt. 5:14; Eph. 5:8; Phil. 2:15; 2 Thess. 5:5).

To assist in perceiving the candlesticks' identity or lampstands, we need to consider the seven lampstands you saw in the seven churches (Rev. 1:20). The seven churches receive the light from Jesus Christ. This light guides the footsteps of the leaders and members. The light represents the word of God to bring enlightened teaching to those in its presence. The Holy Spirit serves to bring the word of God to mind (Jn. 14:26) and helps us to understand.

Jesus stands as judge among the seven churches. He is walking among the lampstands and holds the seven stars in His right hand. Many scholars believe the seven stars, or seven angels are messengers of the churches.

Jesus is protecting and guiding the church leaders. The lampstands represent the messengers through whom the inspired word of God has been brought to the church by chosen men of God anointed to be messengers.

The lampstands are gold. Gold denotes value and purity. The church is precious to God, and it is pure in His sight because of His son's death. The lampstand carries light. Jesus is the light, and the church brings to light (the gospel) into the world.

# CHAPTER 2

## *Message To Ephesus, Smyrna, Pergamos, and Thyatira*

The message that God gives to John is to the seven angels of the Church. Jesus selects the seven churches that are representative of all churches on earth. The Greek word *"Angelos"* is translated as angels, which means a messenger in the seven churches.

They are the pastors who declare God's Word to the churches. The seven churches are congregations of Christian believers in Asia Minor, who worship Jesus Christ. Tony Evans, the Tony Evans study Bible, (Nashville, TN: Holman Bible publishers, 2019), 1512. Each leader is responsible to Christ because Christ chose them. He picked them out of the world, nurtured, nourished, cared, secured, and protected them. He set them aside to be used as an instrument of His pleasure. They became unique instruments used for the glory of God and were held accountable to Him.

Verse 1

The audience John is addressing is the seven churches of Asia Minor. John focuses on the Revelation of Jesus Christ. Jesus identifies himself with the individual churches in Chapter 2. The Lord more directly addresses himself with the Church at the Ephesus (2: 1–7), Smyrna (2: 8 –11),

Pergamum (2: 12–17), Thyatira (2:18–29), Sardis (3: 1 – 6), Philadelphia (3: 7 – 13), and Laodicea (3:4 – 22). The churches are listed in order along a trade route and were the natural centers of communication for the districts of Asia Minor. Traveling along the trade route, one goes from Ephesus to Smyrna and Pergamum. The traveler would return south through Thyatira, Sardis, Philadelphia, and to Laodicea.

The churches were founded and instructed by the apostles. John writes one letter to the Church. They all get the opportunity to read each other's mail. All churches were struggling with the same problem. We get a picture of contemporary churches struggling with the same issues as the early churches. Jesus expects the Church to be overcomers in any age of persecution. We think the Church is excellent, pure, and free from evil and heresy, but we are no different early ages. The Church has a mixture of good and evil, wheat and tares, sheep and goats, and unfruitfulness. The seven churches were struggling with the effects of a corrupted world. We see precious men and women holding on to the faith and who loved the Lord with all their hearts. We see virtue, faithful pastors, martyrs, rich and poor shining through the dark clouds of hope. The brightest light (Jesus Christ) of the world continues to shine in dark places. John uses the same pattern in writing the letters to the churches:

1. He addresses or greets the angels of the churches (the pastors-Verse 1).
2. These are the words of Jesus Christ, derived from the vision.
3. He speaks of commendation for the congregation because they neglected God's priorities. (Rev. 2:1-7).
4. The letter includes words of criticism, complaint, and commendations for spiritual deficiencies.
5. A warning or threat for churches of all ages (Rev. 2:7).
6. A word of exhortation or correct for what is right or wrong, and Jesus incites encouragement to the churches.

7. A unique promise to the overcomer.

Jesus has something to say to all the churches about their relationship with Him. They can take an inventory and check their spiritual condition. When he addresses the seven, He addresses all the churches on earth, a personal application to their situation. They tell us what Christ thinks of his Church, both as it is and should be.

Jesus Christ knows His Church, and He provides, protects, guides, and directs the Church (Matt. 16:17-19). Jesus knows every Church and its precise situation. He wants the Church to be the best it can be. Jesus has something to say to every individual Church in existence. The Church and the individual must be shaped in the character and likeness of Jesus Christ.

Verses 2-3

John dispatches the first letter to the pastor of the Church in Ephesus (Verse 2). Amid their struggles with evil, Christ speaks to the Church to encourage them concerning His character (Rev. 2:1b, 11, 17, 18b; 3:1b, 7b, 14b), and exalt them in faithfulness (Rev. 2:7, 11, 17, 26-29; 3:5-6, 12-13, 20-22). If the Church looks to Christ, it will endure suffering, evil and break forth in triumph.

Ephesus was located on a major Roman road, and it was known as the crossroad of civilization. It was the queen city among the seven churches of Asia Minor (30-100 A. D.). It was called the free city, and the people enjoyed the title "Supreme Metropolis of Asia." The Romans granted the rights of self-government within its limits, and they never had the indignity of having Roman troops quartered there. It was a commercial city and the center of trade among the coastal communities. It was rich in learning, art, wealth, and religion. However, because of the silt, the harbor became so bad that trade declined.

Religious cults influenced people's hearts and minds. The great Temple of Diana was in Ephesus was the goddess that focused on the sexual pleasures of the flesh. Individuals found their pleasure and satisfaction in prostitution with a host of priestesses. The temple of Diana was the pride of Ephesus and the people.

They made it is the most idol sacred thing in the world. It became the most significant business in Ephesus. As trade declined, the people depended more upon the business that came from their religion and superstitions. The city became a haven of the disease of sensual unrighteousness that corrupted the people. Ephesus was the center of the Pannonian games and ranked with the Olympic games. Everyone wanted to live in the Ephesus because a person could make it big. A person could become a powerful influence and have a good time.

John, in the first letter, tells them to repent and do the first works. The lampstand of Ephesus will crumble, and the light of the Church die out (Rev. 2:1-7). God charged the Church with misconduct because they began to tolerate evil and false doctrine. It became a dying city living on a past reputation as a religious and philosophical center.

The Church of Ephesus started with twelve believers when Paul visited the city. He gave instructions to the twelve, and he began teaching in the synagogue. Paul spent two years in Ephesus teaching at the school of Tyrannus (Acts 19:10). Ephesus was the home of Apostles John, Apollo, and Timothy. Aquila, Priscilla, Paul, Timothy had planted a church in Ephesus. Paul established the Church of Ephesus on his third missionary journey (Acts 20:16). John had a close association with the Church. He speaks of the one who has given him the message.

The Church at Ephesus represents the time between the Day of Pentecost and 100 AD. The Church had an outstanding reputation, but they became lethargic. The Church had a heart problem, lost its first love (Christ). No matter how good we think a church is, Jesus says, "I know your works" (Verse 2). They were an old-fashioned, fundamental Church doing the works of the Lord. Ephesus began to let the world influence their worship or their walk. They were once a rock-solid congregation.

Jesus Christ praised them for doing the business of the Church:

1. They work hard—refers to their accomplishments to do great things in the community. Labored refers to "intense work involving toil and pain" (Matt. 5:16; Rev. 2:2).

2. The "church patience" reminds us that they carried out their works for the Lord during great "persecution". The people of the cities around them hated the message they preached. Ephesus was a working church. They stood against all temptations and trials (James 1:12, Heb. 10:36).

3. The Church cannot not bear those who are evil. It cannot tolerate sin, shame, dirt, pollution, and filth (2 Cor. 6:17 – 18, Prov. 8:13).

4. The Church tested all the preaches, teaches, and rejected the false. There were loyal to Christ and the truth of God. (2 Jn. 4:1 – 3).

Each Church took on the character of its cities. Those who lived in city minds were formed by the character of his city in a way that offered no other parallel. The Church demonstrated a significant change in the middle of an immoral pagan society; the Lord complained against Ephesus (Verse 4). The Lord knew that this Church was going through the motions of serving Him. He knew that they had lost the love for Him they once possessed. If the churches were honest about their condition, their favorite hymn would be "Oh, How I Loved Jesus!"

As it was in Ephesus, many 21st Century churches are merely going through the motions. Many do not love Jesus like they once did, and it shows in the hearts and minds of God's people. We may ask some questions:

1. Do you love Jesus with all your heart, your soul, and mind?

2. Are you serving Jesus for His blessings or because you are consumed with love for the Lord Jesus?

Verse 4

The Church of Ephesus's most significant problems were the pagans around them and the persecution they faced. The Church was a center for Christian evangelism of Asia Minor (Acts 19). The Church had lost her feelings for Christ. Jesus was no longer first in their lives. The Church had lost a personal fellowship, the right belief, and had no urgency to fight for Christ, but other things became a priority. Ephesus had become a backsliding church, and Jesus condemned them for their lack of love for Him. He told them that there was a personal problem in their hearts with the Lord Himself. Their hearts were cooling, and the fire of devotion was going out. You must return to first love attitudes, and the first deed acts; they are darkening the life of the Church.

Jesus tells the Ephesians they had a personal problem. In Verse 2, Jesus tells them, "I know you have a problem with rightness, thou hast left thy first love." The word "left" means "to send away, expire, forsake, or abandon." Jesus is talking to believers who had walked away from Him. They have abandoned, disregarded, and forsaken His love like a husband divorcing his wife. They symbolically sent the Lord away.

The word "*first*" means "one in rank or importance". They still love their Church. They still love their doctrines. They still love their activities. They still love their busy schedules. They still love all they do. Jesus must be first more than the other things. We violate the greatest commandment (Matt. 22:37-38), and it open to breaking other commandments.

Jesus calls the contemporary Church back to its first love attitude and the first deed acts, or they are in danger of losing Christlikeness for the Church and people. The First-Century Church displayed a strong love for Christ, but the fellowship ruptured. The churches developed a sense of criticism, grumbling, jealousy, and a selfish mind (Jn. 13:34-35; 2 Cor. 1:10).

Verse 5

Jesus is counseling the Church to repent, reminding them where they had fallen. Something is consuming the Church's energy, mind, and heart. Many are attached to things that are not of Christ. Remember how meaningful your relationship and performance are in Christ (2 Chron. 7:14, Lk. 10:38-42; Matt. 3:2; Acts 3:19). They must repent and turn back to their first love and devotion to one another. Jesus reminded them to remember when their love for Him was powerful, all-consuming, and the essential thing in their lives. They must remember those early days of salvation when the love of God for them was overwhelming. They must remember how it felt to be saved and know that all their sins had been forgiven. They must remember what it felt like to know that they were no longer dead in sin but had been made alive in Jesus. They must remember the excitement that every new revelation from the Word of God brought to their hearts.

John's letter is the Revelation of God, including His will, His nature, His person, and the character of His Son. When we look at Christ are to look at God. Christ is an expression of God in the human form. The Word became flesh and dwelt among us (Jn. 1:14). The purpose of the letter is that they come to remember God in a personal way. Christ gives a prescription: remember, repent, and repeat:

1. Remember from where you have fallen.

2. Repent means changing the mind, having a different attitude, turning around in a different direction, and resuming a fervent love for Christ.

3. The Church must repeat the work they did initially, be obedient to the works, and depend on Christ to renew their hearts.

Christ is the Son of God, and by his incarnation took upon Himself the form of man and became a divine man who died for sin. God is concerned that everyone is saved or will suffer His wrath.

Every believer needs to remember that when sin rolled away, and Jesus moved in, those were the days of excitement and joy. We were ready to go to the battlefield for the Lord. That excitement has disappeared with age. When we remember what Christ has done, we see how far they have fallen. We recognize sins. When we see the depths of sin, we can turn from it and fall in love with Jesus again. Communion, praying, worship, and sharing become joyful again (Acts 8:22, Prov. 3:6).

The Lord challenges the Ephesians to repent and turn back to their first love. The greatest challenge to the modern Church is to fall in love with Jesus once again. The Church must return to God's will and a loving relationship with one another. The modern Church has lost sight of Calvary.

Verse 6

The first letter is to Ephesus—the faithful Church had lost their love to Jesus Christ and begun to struggle with the false doctrine and practice of the Nicolaitans. They were followers of Nicolaus, a heretic. Nicolaitans' teachings were like the heretical doctrine of Balaam and Jezebel of Thyatira. They taught that Christ had done away with the Old Testament laws (Matt. 5:17), instituted the laws of Christian liberty, and that the soul and spirit of man were more important than his body. They engaged in idolatry and sexual immorality and assaulted the Church with these sensual temptations, but the Ephesian Church had taken a strong stand against these heretics (Verse 6). If they refuse to repent, the Lord's will "remove thy candlestick out of place" (Verse 5). They will cease to exist as a church and congregation. They will cease to exist because the lack of love for Jesus threatens the existence of their Church.

Everywhere you look today, most churches are struggling in their present condition because they stopped loving Jesus with a passion. Worship has become lifeless and dead. The preaching has lost its power and the teaching its effectiveness. Young people are moving away, and the Church has begun to die from lack of attendance, talent, and financial support. Many are consumed with activities unrelated to Christ. Churches are closing their doors, and the lampstand has been removed. The Ephesians are told that they can avoid their fate and many 21st Century churches if they repent their sins. The modern Church is dying. The only remedy is repentance and restoration.

Verse 7

According to John's vision, only the overcomer (Verse 7) will have privileges. The promise is made to the victorious followers of Christ who personally desire to hear the warning and overcome:

1. They will be allowed to eat at the tree of life in heaven (Rev. 22:14; Ezek. 47:7, 12; 2; Jn. 5:4, 11).

2. The overcomer will be a citizen of the paradise of God. God's paradise in heaven, but very dwelling place of God (2 Cor. 12:4; Lk. 16:23; 23:43; Jam. 2:26). Historically, this Church did not repent, and their lampstand was removed. Muslims rule the territory now.

Verses 8-11

Smyrna was 40 miles from Ephesus (Verse 8) and was a tremendous wealth and culture (100-312 A. D.). It was sometimes called "the Ornament of Asia". *Smyrna* means bitter because its main export was myrrh, a spice used in embalming and perfume oil. Myrrh was used in making holy anointing oil for the priests (Exod. 30:23), embalming (Jn. 19:39-40), for purification of women (Esther 2:12), and for relieving and dulling pain (Mark 15:23). It was a gift of the Magi at Christ's birth (Matt. 2:11).

It was a proud city with an extensive library, stadium, and the most prominent public theater. Smyrna was like the city of Ephesus with a beautiful temple. At the end of the main street, paved in gold, stood the temple to Zeus, and at the other end, the temple of Cybele (a local goddess). There were other temples: Diana, Aphrodite, Apollo, and Asclepius. Emperor Domitian ruled when he required all Roman citizens to worship the emperor or receive the death penalty. The people were loyal to Rome. Each citizen was required once a year to receive a certificate proving their political loyalty and the fact that they had done their civic duty. The city became the cult of emperor worship. Today Smyrna is called Izmir, and it is the third-largest city in Turkey (population 300,000). It exports tobacco, grapes, figs, cotton, olives, and olive oil.

The Church suffered because it was socially unacceptable. It was a city that hated Christians. The Church was huddled in homes or hiding in the catacombs when they worshipped the Lord. Smyrna had a large Jewish population. It was also a famous religious center for Christianity. Christians refused to declare Caesar as Lord. Many were burned alive and suffered horrific deaths for political reasons. Christians were persecuted as traitors, killed, tortured, burned in boiling oil, or at stake. Many were thrown to the lions in the coliseum. Polycarp knew the Apostle John and others who had seen and believed in Jesus Christ. He was burned alive as the twelfth martyr of Christianity in Smyrna in 156 A. D. Christ described suffering with three words (pressure, poverty, and persecution) (Verse 9).

Christ praised the Church for remaining faithful to his mission slander and persecution. He did not have to warn the Church. The ministers stood fast against persecution, even if it meant martyrdom:

1. Christ says, "He is the first and last". Meaning the Church recognized Him as the supreme authority over their lives in times of trouble. The Roman government had political authority over their life, but Jesus Christ held spiritual authority over them. His presence covers all the problems, circumstances, and trouble they faced. He is first and the last (Jn. 8:58; Rom. 8:28, 35, 37 – 39).

2. Christ says that he is the one who is alive and dead again. The word "*was*" means became, Christ, became dead. He triumphed over it. Alive means he arose. No matter what happened to Smyrna, it is a passing episode if he is martyred (Jn. 3:16, 5:24; 2 Cor. 10:13; I Pet. 1:3-4).

Christ complimented them for their suffering, persecution, and poverty. He said, "I know your suffering and poverty" (Verse 10). Most of their affliction came from the Jews. Christ said four things about the Church of Smyrna:

1. They were faithful despite ridicule, mockery, abuse, cussing, property loss, imprisonment, and martyrdom (Matt. 24:9; Lk. 21:12; 2 Tim. 3:12; 2 Pet. 4:12-13).

2. Many were forced out of their jobs, and many had their property confiscated as lawbreakers despite having to make claims once a year to the state saying, "Caesar is lord." True believers can only say "Jesus is Lord" (Rev. 2:12; Matt. 8:20; 2 Cor. 8:9).

3. The Church was spiritually wealthy but outwardly poor (James 2:5). They shared agape love for Christ and one another. They depended on Christ to supply their needs. Living by the fruit of spirits daily (Gal. 5:22-23), they studied and taught the word of God, living righteous and holy lives (Matt. 6:20; Eph. 1:18-19; 2:4-7; Heb. 11:24-26).

4. The Jews stirred up trouble with ridicule, accusation, talking, mocking, backbiting, tearing down, lying, criticizing, discriminating, spreading rumors, murmuring, and dividing. The persecution lasted for ten days. It refers to the last and most severe persecution under the Roman emperors from 303 to 313 A.D., during the reign of Diocletian.

Jesus said the Jews were the synagogue of Satan, meaning they were serving Satan's purpose (Jn. 8:31-47). They killed the faithful followers of Jesus Christ. He promised overcomers should receive forever:

1. A crown for works (not salvation) James 1:12. Their reward is with Him: at the "Bema" seat.

2. A crown of Life (James 1:12; Rev. 2:10) for those who have suffered for His sake.

3. A crown of Righteousness (2 Tim. 4:8) for those who loved His appearing.

4. A crown of Glory (1 Pet. 5:4) for those who fed the flock.

5. Crown Incorruptible (1 Cor. 9:25) for those who press on steadfastly.

6. Crown of Rejoicing (1 Thess. 2:19) for those who win souls.

7. They will be transferred to heaven and crowned with eternal life (James 1:12, Jn. 3:16, 6:27; 2 Jn. 2:25).

8. The overcomer shall be delivered from second death and the lake of fire (Rev. 20:14; 21:8; 2 Cor. 4:17). (Rev. 20:14; 21:8; 2 Cor. 4:17).

9. Jesus promises in Isaiah 41:10, "Fear not, for I am with you; be not dismayed, for I am your God; I will strengthen you, I will help you, I will uphold you with my righteous right hand."

10. Every Church must hear John's message. The churches must remain faithful to keep their lampstands and the crown of life (Jn. 3:14-15, 36; 10:28).

Smyrna stood as a faithful church for Christ amid evil and the corrupted world (Matt. 10:32-33; Mk. 8:38; 2 Pet. 2:1). He tells them more persecution is on the way, but do not fear. There is a promise to the overcomer (Verses 10 and 11). The lesson we learn from the Church of Smyrna is to remain steadfast and faithful to Christ, no matter the cost. You will receive a reward in heaven that will make your sacrifice worth it.

Verses 12-17

After leaving Smyrna, the city of Pergamos lies forty miles directly north, about 10 miles inland (Verse 12). The city was on a mountain that could be seen fifteen miles away. Pergamos means "*Citadel*" in Greek. It was a beautiful commercial city of temples and groves. It was a place where parchment was first used. Pergamos had become the capital of the Providence of Asia and the center of Asian culture. It was a university town. It had a library that rivaled Alexandria. It was famous for medical schools. Four great temples were built in honor of the pagan gods: Zeus, Atene, Dionysus, and Asclepius. Each temple had its variety of corresponding ideologies, which the Lord summarized into Balaam and Nicolaitans (Verse 15). The Balaam is covetous and refers to he who hires himself to do religious work for gain (2 Pet. 2:15). Nicolaitans' teaching was getting the Church to conform to worldly standards.

The Romans capitalized on Pergamos' religion in support of imperial worship to the leader of the state. A citizen had to show his loyalty to Rome, going to the temple once a year, pledging his allegiance to the emperor. A written certificate was required to be in his possession to be shown on demand.

The Church of Pergamos was lenient in compromising their faith and engaging in the sexual immorality of pagan worship. The city became a center for the imperial cult. Christ describes himself to the Church as he who has the sharp, double-edged sword. Pergamos was noticed for its superior quality of sword manufactured in its precincts. The sword to Rome was a symbol of authority and judgment, to take away life and give death. Christ's double-edged sword represents God's ultimate authority and judgment to save lives from death.

Christ describes himself as one who has a sharp two-edged sword in his mouth. It represents the word of God, the Old and New Testament (Eph. 6:17; Heb. 4:12):

1. The word of God is sharp. Cut through most hardened hearts, separating sinners from his sin. One side proclaimed living a righteous life, or the other will receive judgment and destruction. The word proclaims the loving grace for those who follow Christ ((Eph. 6:17; Heb. 4:12).

2. Some government officials misused the sword to execute innocent people, those who refused to deny Christ. Those who do evil are now warned of judgment and destruction (Rev. 2:16; 2 Tim. 4:18; 2 Sam. 22:2).

Jesus commanded the Church for three things:

1. The Church was loyal despite the environment. Christ refers to the city as a seat of Satan. The people were worshiping the emperor as a god. They continued to meet despite ridicule, contempt, opposition, and death. Many believers confessed to Christ as their Savior (Matt. 10:32-33, 8:38; Rom. 10:9-10; 2 Jn. 2:22-23).

2. The Church was pure in doctrine after being in a cesspool of worldliness (pleasures, possessions, and comforts of the world). They believed in the word of God. They confessed Christ in all their affairs. Every week, the word was being taught and studied (2 Thessalonian 2:2-6; 2 Tim. 4:1-2; Titus 1:9).

3. The Church was standing fast in persecution. They held on to Christ who could save them. One believer had been a martyr for witnessing for Christ (Antipas). Christ gave this dear man a title, 'my faithful one' (Rev. 3:14).

Jesus had complaints against the Church at Pergamos (Verses 14-15):

1. The Church was guilty of teaching the doctrine of Balaam (Num. 22-23 and 31).

2. The teaching is still around today—eating food sacrificed to idols and sexual morality.

3. The Church had baptized people who had never repented over the ways of the world.

4. Allowed worldly to be taught in the Church.

5. Mixed membership of believers with unbelievers (Num. 22-25, 2 Pet. 2:15; Jude 11).

6. Some Christians were living holy sacrificial commitment, and others sought worldly pleasures and possessions of this world. However, they allowed the Church to engage in fornication, sexual sin, drunkenness, participation in feasts, and make sacrifices to idolatrous worshipers (1 Cor. 5:11; 2 Cor. 6:14, 10:14-11:1; 2 Thess. 3:6).

7. They were guilty of making the false profession of the Nicolaitans (Rev. 2:5-6). Pergamos became a compromising church.

Jesus Christ's counsel to the Church of Pergamos was that everybody needs to repent because they had compromised Christianity to the world, which disfigured and debauched the Church. Believe in the gospel and get rid of those who refuse. Stop conveying false hope. The warning was that too many worldly members reject Jesus Christ (Heb. 2:3; 2 Pet. 3:17).

The modern Church has problems. Many in the body of Christ think that after being saved, they can live like the world. The Church becomes a powerless institution in society and has lost respect. Christians are to live as good characters changing the world into the image of Christ. We walk differently, talk differently, and have a different set of standards than the world. The Church avoids a worldly attitude about substance abuse, sex, music, and other pleasures. When Jesus saves a soul, he creates a new creature (2 Cor. 5:17). He changes everything about that saved person's life.

Manna came from heaven to sustain Israel and Jesus came from heaven (the living bread) to provide for the world (Verse 17). The bread Israel had to gather daily was corruptible (Exod. 16: 14-36). Those who accept Christ as living bread will never hunger again spiritually (Jn. 6:51). He will provide spiritual nourishment better than manna. The promise is twofold:

1. The believer is given the right to feed upon Christ (Jn. 6:32-33, 35, 58). The bread is spiritual food for the soul (Eph. 3:1; Matt 6:24; Jn. 6: 50-51). The very purpose of the bread is to give life.

2. The Pergamos promises to Christians of this era, Jesus promised to give them a white stone as a reward.

The Greeks and Romans had a custom of perpetuated friendship utilizing a white stone divided into halves in ancient times. Each person inscribed his name on the flat side, and the parts were exchanged. When they met, even after many years, they could place the halves of their stones together, signifying their lasting relationship.

1. The stone assured aid even for the descendants. The stone became a mark of identification and was also used to signify citizenship and allegiance to the city.

2. It was a symbol of victory given to those who had won in one of the ancient games. The stones were called "*tessera*," a small tablet (as of wood, bone, or ivory) used by the ancient Romans as a ticket, tally, voucher, or means of identification. They allowed free access to all public entertainment

3. A courageous gladiator would be given a white stone with the initials "*s.p.*" on it. It stood for "*spectatus*" and meant that "his valor had been proven beyond all doubt".

4. The guests at the great Supper of Lamb would have a white stone placed at their seats. In ancient times a white stone was placed at the seat of the guest with a message.

5. The host shared an intimate thought with each guest.

The overcomer will be honored with a white stone as a token of Christ's reward. It allows admission into heaven and God's presence. The person who has the white stone with Christ's name on it can get into heaven. The overcomer has access to the banquet of all times: the marriage supper of the Lamb (Rev. 19). Jesus promises special privileges enjoyed by the overcomers of Pergamos and the New Testament believers. A privilege only known to the one who receives it (Verse 17). The white stone held special meaning to the people of that day. They believed the black stone rendered evil and judgment. Jesus speaks to this fact:

1. The white and black stones indicate judgment in ancient courts. A judge rendered his verdict by placing stones in a container, and at the appropriate time, he would roll the stone out, thus rendering his

judgment. A black stone indicated a judgment of guilt, while a white stone indicated a judgment of innocence.

2. Jesus tells the world they might ban the believer, but they were innocent in his eyes. He had taken away all the black stones that were against them, and he had washed them clean.

3. A white stone signifies an acquittal, whereas a black stone proclaimed the defendant guilty. Overcomers of the Tribulation will be given a white stone with a new name on it.

4. He promised the overcomers a new name which no man knows.

5. The guests at the great Supper of Lamb will have a white stone placed at their seats. It was customary in that day for guests at a dinner to have a white stone placed at their seat. When they were seated, they could look at the stone and underneath a private message from the host. It was a way for the host to share an intimate thought with each guest.

The lesson we learn from the Church of Pergamos is that they do not compromise with the world. People sell their souls for possessions, power, and pleasures of this world.

Verses 18-29

The Church of Thyatira was the smallest of the seven churches and was located forty miles southeast of Pergamos. It is the fourth of seven churches that receive a spiritual evaluation directly from God through Jesus Christ. The apostle Thyatira means "unceasing sacrifice."

Thyatira was known for its brass works and woolen industry and the dyes produced there. Thyatira was known for its brass works and woolen industry, especially for the dyes produced there. Thyatira manufactured the expensive purple dye from shellfish valued by the wealthy. Divers brought up this little creature that could not be reproduced anywhere else on earth. A main trade route went through the city. Merchants from around the world bought and sold there.

A woman named Lydia, who is called "a seller" of purple, lived in the city of Thyatira (Acts 16:14). Lydia met Paul at Philippi and was the overseas agent of Thyatira manufacturers arranging dyed woolen goods.

The very life of the community was centered on trade and guilds. These were like the ancient unions of the day. Workers from various industries, bakers, wool workers, dyers, bronze workers, potters, and others, banded together to set prices and guarantee work. To refuse to join a guild was to give up all prospects of work. These guilds would often have meetings in the pagan temples around town. Such meetings were often immoral affairs involving drunkenness, drug abuse, and sexual immorality. These meetings would also involve a meal and either begin or end with sacrificing a pagan god.

When an animal was sacrificed in a pagan temple, often only a tiny portion was sacrificed. Sometimes, just some hair clipped from the head of the animal might be all that was used. The rest of the animal was then divided between the pagan priest and the worshiper. The worshiper could sell meat in the marketplace or throw a feast for his friends, and they would eat the sacrifice.

When the pagans in Thyatira were saved, they were faced with a problem. Should they refuse to join the guilds and be unemployed, or should they participate in the pagan rituals and compromise their testimonies? The mind of God in this matter is found in Acts 15:29. The newly converted gentiles are commanded to abstain from meat sacrificed to idols, among other things (1 Cor. 8-10).

The believers had to participate in their pagan idolatrous feast to the gods to secure a job. Christians lower their standards to participate in these meals and make a sacrifice to the gods. Thyatira was also a center of occult worship. There was a temple in the city dedicated to fortune-telling. It was presided over by a female oracle named Sambathe.

The Church at Thyatira had a heart problem—it looked good on the outside, but it was corrupt at its core. Jesus came to confront their sin. John dispatched a letter from Christ telling the Church of Thyatira, "I know all the things you do" (Verse 19). Thyatira is suffering from apostasy. *Apostasy* is defined as a falling away, a withdrawal, a defection or abandonment of the faith in Christ. It is the complete refusal repentance of the Christian faith. Paul warns that a great apostasy will be a prelude to the Second Coming of Christ (2 Thess., 2, 3). Jesus introduces Himself to this Church in Verse 18 and presents himself in three ways. Jesus comes as the saving one and the Son of God (Verse 18). He reminds these people that he is the Savior and that He alone is worthy of worship. People are to believe, follow, obey, become attached, and love Christ (Lk. 14:26-27; 1 Jn. 2:15-16).

Christ declares he is the searching one. His "eyes are like unto a flame of fire" (Verse 18). He sees the works of the hands, motives, and thoughts of the heart. He sees when a person is compromising, doing things in the dark, behind closed doors, in parked cars, in the offices and houses of the world. He sees those leading people lie, steal, cheat, commit immorality, become intoxicated, and take drugs. He rewards according to their works (Job 10:14, 16; Jer. 2:22; Amos 5:12, 1 Cor. 4:5).

Christ is the sovereign one with "feet like fine brass" (Verse 18). Brass, or bronze, in the Bible, is symbolic of judgment. He introduces Himself as one able to see all; He comes to the Church of Thyatira as a judge. His feet shall crush all those who compromise with the world.

Thyatira was a working church, faithful, loving, loyal, and long suffering, involving all kinds of services including ministries that showed love: Evangelism: reaching out to the lost, adults and senior adults, the needy, orphans, the hungry, homeless, shut-ins, foreigners, prisoners, and the poor.

The word "*service*" represents a spirit to ministry (1 Thess. 1:3) to serve God and Christ as a living sacrifice (Rom. 12:1). The person is to serve and worship Christ and God, to serve and worship in the Church, and to offer service to humanity in a Godly way:

1. They were motivated by agape love. Agape love is "unconditional, unceasing love that knows no boundaries and is not influenced by the worth of the object being loved." It is God's kind of love (1 Cor. 13:1-3; 1 Jn. 3:18).

2. Facing opposition, they sacrifice time, money, possessions. The Church does not backslide but goes forward in love, faith, service, and patience.

Too often works needed to be done in the Church, and no one wanted to do that work. That was not a problem in Thyatira. There were chores to do, and plenty of people were willing to do the work. Jesus praised their works. The outreach ministry was ever on the increase.

Jesus says every Church should be like the Church of Thyatira. Thyatira was described as dynamic, vibrant, alive, meeting all the community's needs. It was a church crowded with people ready to serve the Lord. The Church was far from what it should have been. It was a compromising and corrupt church.

We should be active in the Lord's work, but we should see that everything we do is motivated by either edifying the Church, evangelizing the sinner, and exalting the Savior. Those three tasks comprise the church business, and we should be actively engaged in them for the glory of God.

Christ revealed the cancer that was present within this beautiful Church (Verses 20 – 21). His penetrating eyes revealed a cancellation of morality. Satan used worldly sin to conquer the Church. A prophetess Jezebel exposed people to false teaching (sexual immorality and food sacrificed to idols (Verse 20), had gained leadership in the Church, and was guilty of leading the people away from the true worship of God. Jezebel was no follower of Christ, but a false prophet leading God's people astray. The people of Thyatira tolerated her teaching and promoted sexual promiscuity in the name of religion.

Jezebel was the wife of wicked King Ahab (1 Kings 16:31). She was a devoted worshipper of Baal. Baal was a fertility goddess, and his prophets and priests were temple prostitutes who engaged in sexual acts and gross wickedness. She led Israel away from worshipping Jehovah God (1 Kings 21:25). After Elijah's great miracles, she threatened the Lord's prophets. He ran away in fear (1st Kings 19:1-3).

Jezebel is identified with wickedness and idol worship. The teaching influences the individual to believe they could be saved by grace and indulge the fleshly appetite of sin. Some people believe that the soul and the flesh were not connected. In other words, they taught that what a person did in their body had nothing to do with their spiritual life.

The woman of Thyatira is not the Jezebel of the Old Testament, but her teaching was like Jezebel's. The Spirit of Jezebel had been revived in the prophetess. Jezebel's teaching convinced people in this Church that they could hold on to their pagan beliefs and practices and still serve Christ. They could sin and still be saved, and that one thing had nothing to do with the other. Many pagans of Thyatira came to the Church (Verse 20). Christians were indulging in immoral practices. The Church of Thyatira:

1. Tolerated a false prophetess' teaching. She claimed that God called and gifted her to proclaim the truth. The Church gave her the right to teach.

2. The Church tolerated false teachings, seduction, fornication, and idolatry.

3. Contrary to the word of God, the Church was allowing her to spread false teaching.

4. She could seduce the Lord's servants: by arguing, presenting reasonable arguments, deceiving, misleading, and beguiling the Christians.

5. Allowing believers to commit fornication. The Church had to participate in some of the world's functions to be friendly, keep their jobs, secure promotions in the temple precincts of false gods.

God's standards were compromised, and it attracted the world into the Church. They were saying, "Come just as you are! Do not change a thing. Keep living as you have always lived. We will accept you just as you are. God loves you, and we do too." The Church allowed no time was to repentance. The Church was allowing her to spread false teaching, seduction, fornication, and idolatry. She refused to repent, and God's judgment will fall on the Church (Rom. 12:2; 2 Cor. 6:14; 2 Thess. 3:6; 1 Jn. 2:15-16).

What they were doing was not godly behavior. The Lord called this place "the depths of Satan" (Verse 24). The prophetess had seduced the people of God. The word "*seduce*" means to entice (someone) into sexual activity. The word "fornication" comes from the word "*pornia*". We get the word "*pornography*" from it. It refers "to any sexual sin". The word "*prostitute*" speaks of people, nations, or organizations that engage in some form of idolatry while claiming to be worshippers of God or to sell one's body to the lusts of another". It can refer to sexual sin, or it can be used as a metaphor for idol worship. The Church was engaged in these activities.

Anything a person worships before God is an idol. Idols can be a job, money, position, possessions, pleasure, sports, business, family, self, sex, knowledge, power, acceptance, recognition, and honor. Believers must separate from a lifestyle consumed with these things and live a lifestyle of committed repentant love of Christ (2 Cor. 6:17, Jn. 3:3, 1st Jn. 2:9-10).

In contemporary society, some members of the Church are putting these things before God. They need to repent (Jn. 15:19; Rom. 2:21-24, 12:2, 1 Jn. 2:15-16). In the letter to Thyatira, Jesus says, "I will give to each of you whatever you deserve" (Verse 23). Jesus tells the people, "Because I, the LORD, do not change" (Mal. 3:6). "I am the same yesterday and today and forever" (Heb. 13:8).

Jesus gives a warning to those who compromise and are corrupted in the Church (Verses 22 – 23):

1. Judgment will match her sins. Jezebel will reap what she sowed (Matt. 7:2; Gal. 6:7-8).

2. There is a warning to those whose lifestyle rejected Christ. Separate yourself from the world or receive great tribulation.

3. There is time to repent. Christ said his judgment would happen if they failed to repent of their deeds (Acts 3:19, 8:22; 2nd Chronicles 7:14). They will serve Christ in the new heaven and earth (1Cor. 6:2; Lk. 22:28-29; Rev. 20:4).

4. Christ will judge their sins (Ps. 62:12; Matt. 16:27; 2 Cor. 5:10).

Jezebel and followers will face God's wrath. God is still giving them space to repent! If they refuse, they will be judged "according to your works" (Jer. 19:11). Salvation is based on God's grace; judgment comes based on man's works. There is a promise to the overcomers (Verses 26-27):

1. The overcomer refers to believers who overcome the challenges of Satan and remain faithful to Christ.

2. Christ promises them that if they remain faithful to him, they will rule with him in his kingdom one day (Verse 27). The overcomers will be given dominion and splendor like the Lord. They will be given unique positions throughout the new heaven and earth (Rev. 3:21, 14:13, 20:4, 21:24-27; Lk. 19:17).

3. The overcomer will be given the morning star (Rev. 22:16). Christ is telling the Church of Thyatira to hold on. It is mighty dark now, but there is a glimmer of hope in the heavens. I am coming to expose evil with the light of truth and bringing the promised reward (Num. 24:17).

Is your Church like the Church of Thyatira? I believe that every church's trouble is covered by John's letters, and through them, the Church can be examined, diagnosed, and a remedy prescribed. We must pray for this Church and other churches to hold out against the rising tide of compromise and evil. Anyone willing to hear should listen to the Spirit and understand what he is saying to the churches (Rev. 2:29). Contemporary churches need to listen and comply with what the Spirit is saying to us.

# CHAPTER 3

## *Message To Sardis, Philadelphia, And Laodicea*

---

Sardis was the capital city of Lydia. It was founded about 1,200 BC, on top of a 1500-foot-high plateau that made the city impenetrable by invading armies. It was defended on three sides and could only be approached by an isthmus so narrow that only a handful of men could defend against thousands leading into the city.

Sardis was the home of Aesop. Legend has it that gold was discovered just lying around the rivers that flow through the city. It was a city of wealth in the production of dye used in cloth making. Dyeing was invented at Sardis.

Sardis reached its zenith and fell under Croesus. He and the city's people became complacent in their wealth, power, and city's apparent invincibility. Cyrus the Persian ruler defeated Sardis. One night, one of the Persian soldiers saw a Sardinian soldier drop his helmet over the city's wall. He watched as that soldier followed a hidden path down the side of the mountain to retrieve his helmet. When nightfall came, Cyrus and his troops followed the hidden path up the side of the mountain, entered the city while the guards slept, and conquered Sardis. The Romans defeated

Sardis. By John's Day, the people had become lazy, degenerate, immoral, and complacent. Sardis was dying through apathy and indifference.

Verses 1-2

John is commanded to write a letter to the angel of the Church of Sardis. The Master's appraisal of the Church of Sardis was that it was a dead and dying Church completely lifeless. It had an excellent reputation, highly respected by the community, but the Church was dead and lifeless. The Church was satisfied with itself, resting on his past achievements. The people were lethargic and complacent, believing that they were safe from any enemy. A lifeless and dying Church needs to seek:

1. The Spirit of God.

2. The fruit of the Spirit (Gal. 5:22-23.

3. The guidance of the Spirit (Jn. 16:13; Rom. 8:14).

4. Revival (Matt. 3:11).

5. The witnessing power of the Spirit (Acts 1:8).

6. The Spirit of wisdom, might, knowledge, and fear of God.

The Church at Sardis was not under Jesus' control. The Church was living but not in the truth. They had a form of worship but to deny the power thereof (2Tim. 3:5). The Church focused on rituals, ceremonies, and worship instead of Christ. Its works are only made-made activities and social services (Matt. 15:8; Mk. 7:6). Christ says, "I know your works, that you have a name, but you are dead" (Rev 3:1, 2). We see the reputation of what men thought and see.

The Church was full of programs, just as churches are in America today. The Church was full of carnality with fine choir, expensive organ, good music, hymns, and psalms with elegance, why the mind is separated from relationship with God. They were devoted to temple worshipping where no worshiper could approach the temple of God with soiled or unclean garments.

The Church became complacent and lethargic in studying God's word and in prayer and spiritual growth. There were no preaching and teaching to win and grow people in Christ (Matt. 7:21, 15:8; Ezek. 33:31-32). The Church needed the Holy Spirit to awaken them.

Verse 3

The members of the Church in Sardis were doing things they were supposed to do, but they were sitting in service half-asleep, allowing their thoughts to wander about instead of hungering for the word of God (Verse 2). The Church needed to seek the Spirit of remembrance and righteousness. The Church was in sad shape, but not all was lost! Jesus gives two-fold counsel:

1. Remember how you received and heard the Gospel. Be watchful, translated this to mean "arouse, wake up, to stir your minds and thoughts, and become alive in Jesus Christ" (Eph. 5:14-18). The believer is a watcher and ensures he is alive spiritually (Matt. 24:42-43; Rom. 13:11; 1st Pet. 5:8).

2. Strengthened the things that remain, which means to make stable, firm, "Get back to God's plan" (Matt. 7:26-27, Lk. 12:47; Jam. 4:8; Ps 119).

3. Hold fast to the original spirit that gripped their lives. Be submissive to the control of the Holy Spirit (Rom. 8:11). Jesus's spirit has all the power the churches need. His word has the direction the churches need to accomplish the mission in this world.

4. Hold fast to the word of God. The Church to obedience and the word of God. Repent of their sin. If they want to renew their fellowship with Jesus Christ, they must repent (Verse 3).

Jesus is speaking the same message to the modern churches today. Confess wrongs, turn away from errors and increase prayer life. Men are trying every method under the sun to reach sinners and do the Church's work. The Church's power is found in the fullness of Jesus Christ and the holy ghost and the word of God. What we need is not a new method but a new desire to seek the fullness of the Holy Spirit and do everything according to the teachings of the word of God.

Verse 4

What are some signs visible in your Church?

1. A dying church rests on its past accomplishments and is satisfied with its present state.

2. A church is more concerned about its rituals and formalities than it is about spirituality.

3. A church is more concerned about social change than about seeing people changed by the power of God.

4. A dying church is more concerned with material growth than it is with spiritual growth.

5. A dying church is more concerned with pleasing men than it is with pleasing God.

6. A church that clings more tightly to its creeds and confessions than it does to the word of God.

7. A dying church loses its conviction that the Bible is the word of God.


A Church that is alive in a church shows some signs:

1. Is characterized by growth.

2. Demonstrates that life exists through spiritual growth.

3. Continues to develop spiritually.

4. In a Church that is alive and well, there will be unity and harmony in the fellowship.

When the Church is infected with sin, it is headed for disaster and death. A living church is full of laughter, joy, weeping, shouting, singing, hurting, and praying together. When there is life in the Church, there is emotion. One sure sign of the dead Church is the absence of emotion. The Church will be in motion actively engage in doing the work of the Lord. Most churches are dead or alive.

Verses 5-6

Christ commanded the Church to return to the faith and remember what you received and heard (Verse 3). If you refuse, "I will come unexpectedly like a thief, and you will not know at what hour I will come" (Rev. 3:3). Jesus may be alluding to His second coming, but to the seven churches of Asia Minor, the warning to the Church is He will take away their lampstands. As bad as things were in Sardis, some were saved and seeking to serve the Lord. Jesus makes promises to the faithful believers who walked daily:

1. The victorious will be clothed in white—the garment of righteousness, purity, and perfection because he trusts Christ (Matt. 22:11, Lk. 15:22, 2 Cor. 5:21, Rev. 7:9, Isa. 61:10). White is a symbol of purity, victory, and festivity. Jesus made this promise to all those who are saved by his grace.

2. Their names will not be blotted out in the Book of life (Lk. 10:20; Rev. 20:15; Exod. 32:33; Dan. 12:1).

3. "I will not blot his name out of the Book of Life" (Verse 5). There will be absolute security for all those who believe in Jesus. The Lamb's Book of Life contains all the redeemed names (Rev. 21:27). It will not be removed when a person is saved (Matt. 10:32-33, Lk. 12:8; 1 Jn).

There is always the danger that any church can die because they have undertakers for ushers, embalmers for elders, and morticians for ministers. Their pastor graduated from the cemetery. The choirmaster is the local coroner. They sing, "embalmed in Gilead". They will be the first churches taken at the rapture, for the Bible says, "The dead in Christ shall rise first" (1 Thess. 4:16).

The great physician has his finger on the pulse of this Church and on that of every member. He is always faithful to reward His people for their faithfulness. What does his touch reveal about us? I want to challenge each of you to examine your heart and the life of your Church. If he has spoken to you about any need, the altar is open for you to pray for its success.

Verse 7

John continues to do as he is commanded to write a letter to the seven churches of Asia Minor. Philadelphia is the sixth Church located on the hillside about thirty miles southeast of Sardis. It was situated on the border of Lydia, Mysia, and Phrygia, earning the name gateway to the East. It was founded in 190 BC by Attalus II, Philadelphus of Pergamum.

The city sat over an earthquake fault and was constantly devastated (Verse 7). When this happened, the pagan temples fell and had to be rebuilt. In fact, in 17 BC, an earthquake destroyed Philadelphia, and many of the people refused to move back into the city. No such problems will affect the temple of God!

The city was filled with many pagan temples. It was a practice for citizens to have their names engraved on pillars that were placed in temples. Jesus tells his people that they will be honored by being made a pillar in His temple (Rev. 3:12). The Church of Philadelphia was in an insecure area. The pillar symbolizes strength, durability, permanence, immorality, a monument, stability, steadfastness, and security! He is promising to establish his people in absolute security in his presence one day!

The city had a Jewish synagogue within the city limits. They claim to be the true follows of Christ. The city was great influenced by Greek culture. It represents all churches that are alive and faithful through the ages. The Church of Philadelphia focuses on teaching people to love Christ and one another. It was a faithful church. It represents all churches that are alive and faithful through the ages. The Church remained alive as it taught, preached, exhorted the believers, studied the word, prayed, witnessed, and faithfully minister. The church ministries reached the lost, built up the believer, ministered to the needy, and reached out to the world by supporting worldwide missions.

The word 'Philadelphia' means, "Brotherly love or one who loves his brother." Christ had no words of rebuke for the small Church.

They claim the keys of David mean the right to open and close the door of God's kingdom. Jesus said, "I am the door; you can come into the kingdom through me" (Matt. 16:13-20). He is the only one who is trustworthy (Jn. 1:14, 14:6, 18:37).

The key of David is a symbol of authority. He alone opens and shuts, determines who lives in heaven with God, holds and shuts the door to eternal life (1 Tim. 2:5; Heb. 9: 24, 12: 24). Jesus gives the Philadelphian church the keys because they accepted Jesus Christ. What keys? Jesus gives the keys that grant authority, access, and availability. Jesus comes to this ancient Church and says, "I have the keys!" He is telling us today that "He has the keys". What kind of keys does Jesus have?

Jesus alone is the Master of death:

1. He has the key to death. You cannot stay dead if you know Him (Jn. 11:25-26).

2. Christ has the keys to suffering. Only He can open heaven and shut hell. Jesus is the key to Heaven (Rev. 1:18).

3. He has the Keys of Salvation. Christ can open the door into eternal life for those who will come to Him (Jn. 4:12; 10:9, 14:6).

4. He has the Keys of Service. He decides when we serve, where we serve, and how long we serve (1 Cor. 16:9).

5. He has the Keys of Safety. No one can touch those who are locked away within Jesus Christ (Col. 3:3).

Verse 8

Jesus now moves to offer commendation to the Church. He tells them that he knows what they have been doing (Verse 8). The Church had little strength, but they open the doors for evangelism and mission to reach people. They were witnessing and bearing testimony to the salvation of Christ for eternal life. He commends the Church for reaching out and not denying His name (Matt. 28: 19-20; Mk. 16: 15; Jn. 20:21; Acts 1: 8; Rev. 3: 8). The world will ridicule, mock, pock fun at, reject, ignore, bypass, curse, imprisoned, abuse, backbite, attack, kill, tempt, and take advantage of the Church. A church must never cave in (Matt. 10:32-33, Lk. 12:38). A church that obeys Christ means studying the Word of God, living the Word of God, and proclaiming the Word of God to the world (Jn. 8:51; 2 Tim. 2: 15, 3:16; Jn. 14:23). Christ would not allow anyone to close the Church because they kept His word and obeyed His commandments. No one can keep you out of heaven when you have the keys to enter. No one can keep you out of heaven.

Jesus makes it clear there is a reward to the faithful. A true believer believes in Christ (Rom. 4:11). It has nothing to do with race, creed, or color. It has nothing to do with the claim of racial dissent (Rom. 2:11). A true Jew is not a person of an earthly race (Rom. 9:6-9).

Verses 9-10

The synagogue of Satan refers to the Jews who say that they follow the true God, but they do not (Verse 9). They reject Christ as rejecting God and the promises of the Messiah. Many of these Jews were persecuting the believers in Philadelphia. They rejected the Son of God. They claim to reveal God, but they were lies. The great hope given to the Church of Philadelphia from Christ is twofold:

Believers shall be vindicated before all their persecutors and come worship with the Jews at the end times (Isa. 45:14, Ezek. 37:28). Israel (the Jews) will be worshiping the Messiah right along with Gentile believers. Christ gave this promise to the Church of Philadelphia (Ps. 22:27-28).

The believers shall experience a great deliverance during the hour of the Great Tribulations (Matt. 24:21, 1 Thess. 5:9). The Great Tribulation will involve persecution of the antichrists (Rev. 13:7-8) and judgment of God against all believers who reject Christ (Jude 14-15, Rev. 19:1-3). The believers will be protected from God's wrath and judgment (Verse 10). Noah receives God's protection during the Great Flood (Gen. 7:1, 16). Lot receives protection when God destroys Sodom (Gen. 19:12-22). God will not touch the earth in judgment until the Bride of Christ (New Testament Church) is seated with Jesus at the marriage supper of the Lamb (1 Thess. 4:13-18, Rev. 19:7-10).

Verses 11- 13

Jesus Christ encourages the Church that He is returning soon at the twinkling of an eye (Verse 11). Hold fast to your crowns. Crowns are rewards:

1. The incorruptible crowns (1 Cor. 9:25).

2. The crown of rejoicing (1 Thess. 2:19).

3. The crown of righteousness (2 Tim. 4:8).

4. The crown of life (James 1:12).

5. The crown of glory (1 Pet. 5:4).

Why is it so important for the Church to look for Jesus to return? We will live pleasing to Him and not be ashamed when He comes. We are obliged to worship and do His works faithfully until He returns. Why? Because the Church may lose its crown (Matt. 24:15, Lk. 12:37, Rev. 3:11). Believers will be marked with the name of Jehovah, the name of the New Jerusalem. He has already placed a mark on us, and we are destined for home (2 Pet. 1:4, 1 Jn. 2:25). It symbolizes possession and ownership to neither man nor Satan (Rev. 3:21, Isa. 56:5, 62:2, Rev.3:12).

Jesus closes the letter to this Church with promises of hope for the future. Repentance. Jesus closes the letter to this Church with promises of hope for the future. The overcomers will be made pillars in the Temple of God (Verse 12). In the pagan temple of Philadelphia, the highest honor for an individual was his name written on a pillar. His name and the reason for the honor would be inscribed.

Jesus says to these saints, "You will be known in heaven" (Rev. 3:12). They were weak in many ways, but they were pure and strong in their doctrine belief in Jesus Christ. God puts his name on believers striving to be holy in the Philadelphia church to establish ownership in a corrupt and sinful world (Verse 12). He redeemed them, and they are His forever!

We live in an age of substitutes: sugar substitutes, salt substitutes, and meat substitutes. We have fake fur, leather, rent-a-dates, virtual reality, and surrogate mothers, and fake pretenders surround us. Jesus is not a substitute. He is the real thing: salvation, prayer, grace, heaven, his presence, word, and power are real! Jesus is the real thing. The Church has the tremendous responsibility of lifting the name of Jesus. He must be the centerpiece of every church worship and praise. Jesus will bless that Church just as He blessed the Church of Philadelphia 2000 years ago. The day is coming, "Every knee should bow, of things in heaven, and things in earth, and things under the earth; and that every tongue should confess that Jesus Christ is Lord, to the glory of God the Father" (Phil. 2:10-11). He is in control of the universe. In the New Testament era, his name is Jesus.

In heaven, the believer will have a new name! They will receive the name of the city of God, the New Jerusalem, as citizens (2 Pet. 3:10-13, Rev. 21.1-5).

Old-fashioned churches are not famous today. We speak of the modern or contemporary Church with all the conveniences to make things comfortable. They preach an entertaining word. They live as they please. They evangelized the lost and exalted the Lord for gain. The day is coming when accountability will be required. Just because a Church has the Christian name on its front does not guarantee it will do the Lord's will. The closing of this John letter is the same as the others. He tells the churches,

"Anyone willing to hear should listen to the Spirit and understand what the Spirit is saying to the churches" (Rev. 3:13).

Churches in the 21st Century need to be like the Philadelphian kind of Church. Jesus gives much praise to these churches and makes promises to the overcomers. Christ makes the same promises to us today. He examines the churches and sees nothing worthy of praise. Some churches showed half-hearted commitment, and were useless, worthless, lukewarm, complacent, lethargic, self-satisfied, half-hearted, and neutral. Jesus praised the Church of Philadelphia for their continual commitment to never deny Jesus Christ.

John continues to write, "To the angel of the Church in Laodicea, these are the words of Amen (Verse 14). Amen means to be firm, stable, sure, established, and trustworthy (Isa. 65:16). It is used of the Lord as the True One. With Jesus, there is no further search needed for the truth, and all the treasures of wisdom and knowledge, are true without subtractions or additions (Col. 2:3).

John circulated the letters to the seven churches in Asia Minor. Jesus stripped the churches of false appearances and pretentiousness, rationalizations, and excuses. Jesus warns the Church against the deadening and lukewarm effects of trusting material wealth rather than pursuing a vital relationship with Jesus Christ. The Church had lost its impact trusting in worldly things and left Jesus standing on the outside.

Verse 14

Laodicea was located forty miles from Ephesus. It was the chief city in Phrygia in the Lycus valley on the west coast of Asia Minor. It was a highway for commercial trade connected to important cities like Ephesus, Smyrna, and Sardis, but it was a center of textile production and banking. The wealthy combined to build theaters, colossal stadiums, lavish public bathhouses, and shopping centers.

The city was a manufacturing center of wool garments, medicinal eye salve, powders, and tabloids (Rev. 3:17-18). The city had a plentiful water supply through an aqueduct coming from a spring four to south. The neighboring city of Hierapolis provided water from hot springs in contrast with the water from the springs of Colossae, which was ice cold. The water reaching Laodicea was lukewarm.

The people were immersed in Greek culture and learning. The local Church was wealthy. Nothing is known of the ministry of this Church in preaching the Gospel throughout the region around it. Laodicea represents an apostate church or people church (1900 to the Tribulation). They demonstrated a self-sufficient attitude that determines their spiritual life and relationship with the Lord. Since much of Laodicea's wealth depended upon trade, the Christian merchants cooperated with the imperial cult. They maintained their trade associations, or would they renounce Domitian and reaffirm their faith in Christ. Many of the Laodicean Christians compromised their faith in such ways that the writer of the apocalypse says, "I will spit you out of my mouth" (Rev. 3:16). The Church of Laodicea did not trust Christ as their Master, the King of kings (Rev. 1:5).

The Church of Laodicea did not understand that Jesus Christ is the maker and sustainer of all things in the universe. He is the source of wealth and satisfaction, purpose, meaning. No matter how the Church prospers is meaningless and useless apart from being centered in Jesus Christ (Rev. 3:14, Jn. 1:3, 10:10, Col. 1:16, Heb. 1:1-2).

Verse 15

What does the Lord see in this Church at Laodicea? Jesus says to this Church as He said to all the churches, "I know your works or deeds" (Verse 15). The Church cannot run and hide their works like Adam and Eve. The Church had problems that were like the water in the city. Lukewarm reflected the Church's character. Jesus tells the Church that he wants them to be either "hot or cold." Hot is *zestos*; a word that means boiling (Rom.12:11). The word zest comes from *zestos*. Cold water is refreshing for the weary, and hot water has a healing or soothing effect on the body. Laodicea had neither; it was nauseating.

Jesus wants the Church to be zestful and show zealousness for the things of Christ. He wants the Church to be a place where His worship and presence can refresh people and sinners come for spiritual healing. Christ describes the Church as a lukewarm church. It meant the church believers were:

1. Half-committed to Christ. The church stressed rituals, ceremonies, and programs to become acceptable to please God (Rom. 12:1-2, 1 Jn. 4:1-3).

2. Half-committed to proclaiming that Jesus Christ is the Son of God (1 Jn. 2:22-23).

3. Half committed to teaching the word of God (2 Tim. 3:16, 4:2-4).

4. Half-committed to evangelism and mission (Matt. 28:19-20, Acts 1:8).

5. Half-committed to stressing holiness and pure living for Christ (2 Cor. 6:17-18,1 Pet. 1:16).

6. Half-committed to self-denial and sacrificial living. People must deny self and live holy (Lk. 9: 23, 18:29-30).

7. Half-committed to the Church (Heb. 10:25).

8. Half-committed to attending and staying awake and learning in the service of the Church (1 Tim. 4:13, Heb. 10:25).

9. Half-committed to supporting the Church (1 Cor. 16:2, 2 Cor. 9:7).

10. Half-committed to witnessing (2 Tim. 1:8, 2:2, 1 Pet. 3:15).

11. Half-committed to studying the Bible and prayer (2 Tim. 2:15., 1 Pet. 2:2-3).

12. Half-committee to daily devotions (Rom. 15:4, Deut. 17:19).

Most people profess Christ attend Church only to appease their consciences to fill the good about Lord. Jesus comes to this Church with a single word of commendation, "The Church is lukewarm. The other churches received a word of commendation, but not this Church. There is nothing to commend. You have no commitment or zealousness of good works. He comes to them and lays out the problems in Laodicea. Most churches look at witnessing, rituals, baptism, church membership, ordinances, services, ceremonies, fellowship, and worship attendance to make them acceptable. The Laodicea church is missing the faithful witness of God (1 Tim. 6:13, Rev. 1:5, Jn. 3:11, 8:14).

Verse 16

Jesus gives the Church a warning, "I will spit you out of my mouth" (Verse 16). The word "*spit*" means to gush or eject something from the mouth. We get the English word "*emetic*," which makes you want to throw up or vomit. Jesus tells the Church, "They are like drinking lukewarm water, and it makes me want to throw up (Verse 16). Because of your wealth, you became self-sufficient, independent, self-centered, prideful, conceited, boastful, and confuse prosperity with spiritual blessings. So, they focused on their capability, ability, and resources instead of Christ (Rev. 3: 17, 2 Cor. 10:12, Gal. 6:3, Prov. 3:7, Ob. 3-4). The Church was wretched, miserable, and spiritually blind. They could only see the world; money and human ability (Isa. 53:6, Eph. 4:18).

Verses 17-19

The Church was spiritually naked. They failed to see the need for the righteousness of Jesus Christ. They felt their gifts and works to the Church would secure God's approval (2 Cor.5:3, Rev. 16:15). They rejected their genuine spiritual needs. They needed repentance. They needed to be purified in the fire (Holy Spirit). Jesus said, "You are poor" (Rev. 3:17), meaning without spiritual insight or discernment. What they need was spiritual gold, the richness of Jesus Christ (Isa. 55:1-3). The Church needs more than money; crowds; buildings; recognition in the community; more than many things we place on great value (Matt. 6:20, 19:21, Gal. 5:22-23). The Church needs Christ's power, presence, and humanity obedient. When a church stops progressing, it loses its vision and passion for Christ.

Jesus says, "You need white clothes to wear, to cover your shameful nakedness; and salve to put on your eyes so that you can see" (Verse 18). They needed three things:

1. They need spiritual gold or spiritual fruits (love, joy, peace, goodness, faith, assurance, confidence, security, and hope in Jesus Christ (Matt. 6:20, 19:21, Gal. 5:22-23). Goal purified points to the divine righteousness of God; wisdom, sanctification, and redemption (1Cor. 1:30).

2. They needed white garments or spiritual clothing to be clothed in the righteousness of God in Christ. God counts that person as being in Christ. He covers the believer's sins. Without this process, the person will appear to be naked on the great day of judgment (2 Cor. 5:17, Eph. 4:24, Col. 3:3).

3. The Church needs to buy eye salve to see the light of the world instead of Jesus Christ. Eye slave is for spiritual discernment. They saw little of Christ. Eye salve means the God-given ability to see spiritual truths of Jesus Christ (Jn. 1:4, 8:12, 9:29; 2 Cor. 4: 6).

Laodicea was proud of their material possessions; it made them feel confident, satisfied, and complacent:

1. They did not realize that possessions did not award them a relationship with Christ. They failed to realize true riches in Christ.

Verse 20

The Church of Laodicea had become complacent, like most 21st Century churches. There was a second chance for this Church. They needed to be zealous and repent because of their sins. They would lose their lampstands if they did not repent. Jesus extends an invitation. He stands at the door pleading for humanity to let him enter. Jesus knocks and keeps on knocking at the door to come in (Ps. 34:18, Jn. 3:13, 6:33, 38, 8:

42). He will never force his way into any home, Church, or persons. The Church must heed Jesus' warning or be chastened. *"Chasten"* means "to correct with blows". The word *"rebuke"* means "to convict, or to correct".

Jesus may touch any area of life to get your attention; He might even use death (1 Cor. 11:30). Faith comes by hearing and hearing by the word of God (Rom. 10:17).

The knocking symbolizes the seeking of Jesus Christ. He knocks at the door of man's heart. He knocks so much that a person must open or deaden his ears to the knock (Matt. 18: 12, Lk. 19:10). When a person opens his heart, Jesus Christ enters; He penetrates the life of the person. The life-changing presence and power of the living Christ symbolize radical change, the person to be born again (Jn. 3:3-5). He makes a new creature out of the person (2 Cor. 5:17) He makes a new man (Eph. 4:24; Col. 3:10). He changes the person's corruptible nature into an incorruptible nature (1Pet. 1:23). He gives the person a new nature on God himself (2 Pet. 1:4).

Christ coming into your life symbolizes fellowship. He is looking to care, talk, share, lead, guide, strengthen, empower, and meet your needs. He will work all things out for your good with love, joy, and peace forever (Jn.17:23; 1 Cor. 3:16, 6:19-20). What makes Jesus sick is when the churches rely on themselves and their good works. Jesus is calling, "Behold, I stand at the door, and knock: if any man hears my voice, and opens the door, I will come into him and will sup with him, and he with me" (Rev. 3:20). Come to him and take whatever steps it takes to have fellowship with Him."

Do you care less whether you go to Church? Do you lack the desire to read the Bible, pray, share the Gospel, or serve the Lord? Jesus makes a powerful promise in this Verse 21. He makes promises that all the benefits of salvation will be given to the person who overcomes them. The converted person will become identified with Jesus and reign with Him in heaven someday. The promises are made to those willing to understand what Jesus is saying to the churches (Verse 22).

The Laodicean Church represents the churches of today. Christ is Lord, a master, who possesses supreme authority from God. There is no honest confession of Christ as Lord. The word "*Lord*" appears 433 times, while the word "*Savior*" 24 times is given to Christ (Lk. 22:25, Rom. 6:9, 14, 7:1, 2 Cor. 1:24, 1 Tim. 6:15). The Church is full of believers that do not believe and receivers that do not receive.

# CHAPTER 4

## *The Things Hereafter*

Chapter 4 begins with John's second vision as a personal message to the Church. The book shifts from the Churches of Asia Minor to a universal Church established by Jesus Christ. Jesus addresses the Church with a greeting, a descriptive title of the Lord, a commendation, a criticism, a complaint, condemnation, counsel, a warning or threat, an exhortation or counseling, and the promises of heaven to the overcomers if they correct their failures. The Church is encouraged to persevere amid evil because of Jesus Christ. Chapter 4 introduces the things in the future: the seals, the trumpets, the vials, and other end-time activities. The three primary cycles of sevens in the book: the seven seals (chapters 6-7), the seven trumpets (chapters 8-14), and the seven bowls, the unbelievers will receive the wrath and judgment of God for rejecting Jesus as Savior. (Chapters 15-19). John is now introducing the reader to "after these things" of chapter 4.

Verse 1

John is invited into heaven to witness a sequence of visions depicting the things that must take place in the future. "Must" refers to what is necessary and binding for God's holy purposes or appointment. We follow a chronological order of the Tribulation judgments on the earth because humanity rejected God's Son as the world's Savior. The New Testament Church will not be here during the Tribulation. The true Church is caught out, and the lukewarm Church is spued out. John records the things that happen after the Laodiceans are spued out (Rev. 4:1). The Church will be caught up to meet Jesus in the clouds in the air. Once the Church is gone, Satan will attempt to rise and control the world's governments and bring about a world system of evil and destruction of humanity. It is time for the Church to see the future events that are coming upon the earth, "The things which shall be hereafter (Rev. 1:19)." It refers to the Church age between Christ's ascension and his rapture. All events will occur following the rapture. John shifts from earth to heaven. John was told to write down these things:

1. Write down what you see in the vision. The things which thou have sent (the vision of the glorified Christ).

2. Write down the Lord's message and send it to the seven churches, their state, and condition. The things which shall be hereafter (the future events that are to Chapter 4-22). Jesus Christ has pointed out the Church's failures and warned and counseled them to correct their failures.

3. He has also given them the great promises of heaven if to the overcomers.

4. It is time for the Church to see the future events coming upon the earth. The time is Jesus Christ is coming back. He is going to establish the kingdom of God forever in a new heaven and earth.

In the second vision, great things are seen. John shifts from earth to heaven. He sees a door standing open in heaven (Verse 1). Jesus opened the way to the throne of God when the temple curtain was torn from the top to the bottom for believers (Matt. 27:51). The door is considered a door of opportunity.

Verse 2

Jesus opens the door, and John hears an authoritative voice speaking like a trumpet. The voice tells John to come up here and see the world's history. The Spirit immediately transports him to heaven (Verse 2a). First, the throne of God is seen, which was a special throne for the Tribulation (Ps. 9:7; Dan. 7:9). Second, God is seen sitting on the throne, where God reigns (Verse 2). The throne is the center of the heavenly scene. God's throne is eternal, and it is where John is transported in the Spirit.

Humanity may not give God the time of day, but they will bow one day before the throne (Phil. 2:9-11; Rom. 14:12). It portrays that God is in control and that He is the supreme ruler of the universe. God deserves our worship and praise. John sees that all images in Chapter 4 are centered on the throne. A "*throne*" speaks of "sovereignty and authority". It is used as the throne of God from which grace proceeds (Heb. 4:16, Matt. 19:28).

John allows us a view of the one who occupies the place of absolute authority over all the affairs of heaven and earth (Ps. 47:8; 103:19). The word "set" speaks of "stability, firmness, durability". He attempts to describe what he sees, but the glory of God is indescribable. So, he attempts to let the Holy Spirit assist in the description of these celestial events. He describes God as being like a "jasper and a sardine stone".

Light from above, circling the throne, from the throne, in front of the throne, and surrounding the throne reflects God's glory. Worship becomes perpetual. Worship is significant for every Christian. We sing, write, and witness to an Almighty God of the universe.

Jesus is seen holding a book that contains the destiny of the world in the end times. The book is sealed, and no one is found worthy of opening and revealing the contents. John is discouraged. The book contains what will happen in the world and throughout eternity. John attempts to describe the impossible. The one on this throne is God the father. How do we know? God, the son, takes the seven-sealed books out of his hand in Revelation 5:5-7.

Verse 3

God is described in terms of light, precious jewels, and stones of that day (Ps. 104:2; 1 Tim. 6:16, 1 Jn. 1:4; 12:35-36). They symbolize God's glory, awesome holiness, and majesty (1 Tim. 6:16):

1. The jasper stone (sparkling white) portrays God's purity and reflects His brilliance and holiness. It calls attention to God as the light that unmasks darkness and evil.

2. The Sardius stone (fiery red) represents the justice of God. He will judge, but his compassion and mercy will temper it. He is the Lamb of God who came to take away the world's sin through His death on the cross.

3. These stones had a special relationship to the tribe of Israel (Exod. 28:17-21). The "Sardius" represented the tribe of Reuben (the first tribe), which means "Behold a Son." In Chapter 4, the Sardis was a blood-red, speaking of the sacrifice of Jesus on the cross for the remission of sin (Jn. 1:29).

4. The "jasper" represented the tribe of Benjamin (last tribe) and means "Son of my right hand". These two stones represented all twelve stones and reminded that God always kept His covenants with His people. In other words, these stones were a constant reminder that God would keep His word and do everything He had promised to do.

5. The throne is encompassed or encircled by an emerald rainbow (various shades of green). The rainbow is a sign that the storm has ended. It was a sign given to Noah that God would never again destroy the earth by a flood (Gen. 9:11-17). The encircled rainbow symbolizes God's absolute sovereignty, the power, and the mercy of God. It is a signal that reminds the children of God that we have received His mercy and will arrive in heaven to live forever. The rainbow speaks to them as being saved from the wrath to come.

Verse 4

Around the throne of God are 24 elders clothed in white raiment with golden crowns on their heads (Verse 4). Who are the elders?

1. They are angels and redeemed representatives of the Church of all ages, including the Old Testament and New Testament saints. Show them surrounding the throne God. They are honored and resting in God in a permanent place forever (Rev. 4:4, 14:3, 19:4).

2. They are clothed in white, representing the purity and holiness of God and Christ (Rev. 3: 18-20).

3. They have crowns of gold on their heads, meaning they hold positions of authority. They serve God by overseeing some rules and dominion over the universe.

4. The elders cast their crowns before the throne of God as they fell and worship Him (Rev. 4:10, 11, 5:8-11).

Who are the elders of Revelation? John speaks of the twenty-four elders as part of the vast array of heavenly beings who worship and serve God and Jesus Christ. He did not identify these twenty-four elders, but scholars share some thoughts:

1. David divided the priesthood into 24 orders as a course of duty. They were to serve as officers and leaders in the Church of Jesus Christ.

2. They could be functioning representatives of the Church as a royal priesthood (1 Pet. 2:5, 9).

3. They could be a combination of the twelve patriarchs and the twelve apostles of the Church, both the Old and New Testaments (Rev. 21:12, 14).

The elders shared in ruling the universe as Christ promised the believers to reward them (Rev. 2:26-27; 3:21):

1. One elder encourages John when he weeps (Rev. 5:5).

2. One elder brings the progress of saints to God (Rev. 5:6).

3. One elder explains part of the vision to John (Rev. 7: 13-14).

John sees the one standing amid the candlesticks. It shows that Jesus is the head of the New Testament church. He is the one being worshipped by the 24 elders. Jesus is the son of God, the begotten son from the day yet from the dead, the one who loves and washes us of our sins in his blood on Calvary's cross. He purchased us with His blood (1 Cor. 15:20 – 23, 1 Jn. 4:9, 1 Pet. 1:18 – 20, Col. 1:20, Rev. 1:5). Christ is the only hope of escaping the wrath to come.

Verse 5

Lightning and thunder in the Bible are often used to reflect God's majesty and power (Ps. 77:18) the seven lamps represent the seven Spirits of God, the Holy Spirit. The seven lamps or torches signify the unique role of the Holy Spirit in executing judgment. The events will be dreadful storm that is about to occur in the coming judgment on earth: the seventh seals, the seventh trumpets, and the seventh bowl. Man has been in rebellion against God's righteousness and has ignored His holiness throughout history; God is about to put an end to humanity's insurrection. Around the throne of God, the twenty-four elders are praising and worshipping the Lord (Verse 5). What does worship do? Worship allows us to focus on God and give Him praise and honor. We can appreciate God's character as the creator of all things, including heaven, earth, and humanity.

Verse 6

John sees a sea of glass like unto crystal. It was stretching out from the throne. When the tabernacle was constructed on earth, a "sea of brass" called "the laver" was outside the tabernacle tent. Before the priests entered the tent, they were required to wash in the laver (Exod. 30:18-21). It symbolized cleansing and forgiveness of sin. In heaven, that sea of brass has become a solidified sea of glass. It does not look like the sea we know on earth today, driven by storms.

There will be no more need for the saints to come to God for cleansing. This sea reminds us that it has become too late for repentance. Judgment is set and fixed. Man has reached his limit, and God is about to pour out his wrath on a lost and sinful world. What horror awaits the "earth dwellers"! John witnesses a crystal sea calm and peaceful, symbolizing an eternity of perfect peace (1 King 7:23 – 45). The sea of glass symbolizes three things:

1. The value and preciousness of God's presence—it was almost impossible to make pure glass in the old days. It was as valuable as gold (Job 28:17).

2. Show how God can see through everything. Nothing is hidden from him.

3. Show the purity of God.

Verse 7

John saw in the center of the throne were four living creatures of Revelation (Verse 6):

1. The lion king of the beast denotes power among the animal kingdoms. He denotes supremacy, majesty, and power (Gen. 49:9, Dan. 7:4, Amos 3:8).

2. A cow or an ox denotes strength, faithfulness, humility, patience, and the beasts of labor (1 Cor. 9:9, 10; Prov. 14:4).

3. The beast had the man's face, denoting reason and intelligence (Isa. 1:18, Job 9:24, 1 Cor. 2:11).

4. The flying eagle is the wisest of all birds. He flies the highest and is swift, denoting swiftness and sovereignty of God in relationship to the earth.

They are created for a purpose:

1. Notice their position. Angelic beings are posted in the middle and on each side of the throne. They are guardians of the throne (Rev. 4:6; 5:6; 14:6).

2. They always were near the throne of God (Rev. 4:6; 5:6; 14:3, had six wings and full and of eyes (Rev. 4:6-8), and function has to do with holiness the wrath of God (Rev. 6:1, 7, 15:7).

3. They declare the holiness of God Day and night and never cease to declare his holiness (Rev. 4:8).

The New Testament denotes these creatures:

1. The lion pictures Jesus as he is portrayed in the gospel of Matt.—the lion of the tribe of Judah. Like a lion, Jesus possesses majesty, power, and authority.

2. The calf pictures Jesus as portrayed in the gospel of Mark—the suffering servant. As a servant, Jesus demonstrated service and strength.

3. Jesus is portrayed in the gospel of Luke—the Son of Man. As the son of Man, Jesus possesses perfect intelligence and absolute moral righteousness.

4. The eagle pictures Jesus as he is portrayed in the Gospel of John—the Son of God come down from heaven. As the Son of God, Jesus possesses majesty and transcendence.

The early church fathers saw the four creatures representing the Gospels in the New Testament. Matthew is representing Jesus' royalty. Mark was representing Jesus as an ox (servanthood). Luke was representing Jesus as a man (His humanity) and John as an eagle (Jesus' deity). Many interpreters rejected the idea of this Christian writing.

Verse 8

The creatures' function is to glorify and honor God day and night (Verse 8). They show us the supremacy, strength, intelligence, and swiftness of God. They show us that all creation owes its worship to God. The four living creatures crying out to him day and night, holy, holy, holy, Lord God Almighty, which was, and he is, and is to come (1Pet. 1:16; Isa. 6:3; Rev. 15:4; Matt. 19: 26; Ps.115; Deut. 33:40, 33:27; 2 Pet. 3:8, Rev. 1:8). As the creatures cry out holy, holy, the response of the twenty-four elders is the same (threefold doxology). They begin to praise the Lord. We have an indictment against humanity that we worship Him without stopping day and night.

The four creatures will be used for judgment and wrath. Four represents the number of creation and the earth, including tribe, tongue, people, and nation. The great division of the earth is the four corners: north, south, east, and west. When God sends judgment on creation, it will be by four sore judgments: the sword, famine, noisome beast, and pestilence (Ezek. 14:21). All creatures are waiting to be delivered from the bondage of corruption and evil (Rom. 8:19-23).

Verses 9-11

The excellent message from this is that Jesus stands at the door, knocking to come in and offer the nonbelievers salvation. The living creatures are not the gospel, but they lead humanity to the one that will be praised and worshiped. They worship the one who lives forever (Verse 9). He is worthy of being praised and the beasts:

1. They cast their crowns before the Lord to show him worthy (2 Sam. 22:4; Rev. 4:11, 5:12). Five crowns in Scripture: the incorruptible crown (1 Cor. 9:25), the crown of glory (1 Pet. 5:4), crown of righteousness (2 Tim. 4:8), the crown of life (Jam. 1:12), and crown of rejoicing – soul-winners (1 Thess. 2:19).

2. They will take the crowns they have been given, and they cast them at the feet of the Lord. They owed everything to Him. They are not concerned about their glory, but they are lost in his glory.

3. They open their mouths and loudly proclaim their love and adoration for the Lord:

    a. Declare his worthiness.

    b. Declare his power.

    c. Declare his right to rule and reign.

    d. Declare the fact that he made the world and all that is in it.

    e. Declare their agreement with what he is about to do in the world.

6. They boldly declare his worthiness and praise to Him. The creatures never worship, only the Creator (Gen. 1:1; Neh. 9:6; Acts 14:15; Heb. 11:3).

7. They fall before Him and offer visible, open, unabashed praise as heaven is filled with the praises of God.

When humanity enters the presence of God, they must always fall in worship (Isa. 6:5; Ezek. 1:28; Dan. 7:15). What is wrong with praising the Lord? The only thing wrong is rejecting Him! Your praise should be volitional, visible, valuable, and vocal.

Utopia is coming, and the evil of the world will exist no more. The animal kingdom and all creation will be delivered from the curse. When Adam sinned, creation was cursed (Gen. 3). Jesus will take over, and Satan is bound in the abyss forever. Redemption is about to occur. If you want to escape God's judgment, you must be saved today. I want you to know that you will face the Lord in judgment. You need to come to Jesus for salvation. If you are saved, and you want to thank God, bow, and praise him now. O Lord our God, you are worthy of receiving glory, honor, and power (Matt. 5:5, Rom. 10:9-13, Rev. 4: 10b-11).

# CHAPTER 5

## *The Lamb And The Scroll*

---

As we enter the fifth chapter, John is caught up in heaven. Chapter 4 is connected to Chapter 5. John sees God sitting in heaven preparing to unleash his wrath on the inhabitants of the earth. The Lord is about to judge the world. Heavenly business is about to be transacted. The chapter sets the stage for the judgments and wrath that will come during the tribulation.

Chapter 5 contains the secrets that follow.

John notices the one sitting on the throne, and in his hand is a little book. The Greek word for a book is translated as a scroll, a roll of attachment sealed with seven seals. The little book accounts for God's past dealings with man, angels, saints, Israel, and creation (1 Pet. 1:18 – 23, 1 Jn. 3:1 – 2, Roman 8:18 – 23).

Christ is the only one worthy of removing the seven seals held in the setter holding a sealed book in his right hand. The seven seals are messages containing the history of the professing Church, pre-written and pin by the Holy Spirit, representing periods in the Church's history, Israel, and Pentecost to the Rapture. The scroll represents the title of deed to the earth. It depicts God's ownership of all creation and the accountability of those who misuse it or dishonor the creation and the Creator. Adam's sin and lost his right to Satan. Satan has promoted evil, darkness, sorrow, and death upon the world. The scroll represents the right to rule, and when the seal is broken, the things of the end can come to pass. God reveals his program for the end of time. he seven scrolls

God did not reveal the end of time to Daniel. He was told to seal the scroll (Dan. 12:8-9, 24). The scroll is a book of the last days of human history, and the climactic events that will take place are about to be unfolded. We see the book itself and a search for one worthy of opening the book of destiny (Verse 1).

The book is written on the front and back of the pages. It is a roll, or a scroll written on papyrus, with a ribbon around the roll. They were seldom written on both sides. It shows us that events of the end time are many and will take time. God will deal with the event and reclaim His creation, which had plunged into sin in Gen 3 when He can find someone worthy enough to open the book. It is sealed with seven seals and shows three things:

1. The book is large: seven seals are required to bind and hold it together.
2. The seven seals show us the secrecy of the book.
3. The last will of God. It contains a curse for those who reject and reward for those who have accepted and worship him.

Jesus shows us the conditions necessary to take back humanity and return it to the proper owner. In this, we see the paradise lost regained.

Verse 1

John in the throne room sees God holding the book in the palm of his right hand. The picture is that He is poised to hand it to someone who is found worthy enough to open it. The search begins. God holding the book in his right hand shows us several things: God is the supreme authority over the world. He governs all the events of history on earth and throughout the universe. He holds the future in his hands, the destiny of the world (1 Tim. 1:17; Exod. 15:18). God is ready to execute the events of Revelation.

Verses 2-3

The scroll is written within and without, broken before the contents are revealed (Rev. 5:1). Two-sided scrolls are called *"opisthographs"*. It was made of papyrus or leather from sheep or goats. The inside of the scroll reveals a tragic story of sin, death, failure, and defeat. On the outside are the terms of redemption. We discover that the Redeemer is willing to redeem anyone worthy of redemption.

When the book is open, the positive proof or seal is open. There is no trace of a title deed; it is a series of prophecies and judgments set in motion by Christ. Revelation focuses on redemption. It is an important truth. His seven-sealed book contains prophecies and judgments necessary to bring rebellious humanity to defeat and restore the earth's kingdom under God's authority and reestablish humanity as God had originally intended before the fall (Gen. 1:26-28). The seventh trumpet will defeat Satan and his followers and establish God's kingdom through Jesus. They are broken in broken to be read.

John saw a strong angel. He shouted out the most penetrating question in history. Who is worthy of opening the book and breaking the seals? The search fails because:

No saint or angel in heaven or earth qualified, not Abraham, Moses, David, or Paul was found worthy. Gabriel, Michael, and all the hosts of heaven were not worthy of taking that book.

No one living on the earth, king, president, ruler, billionaire, no politician, scientist, preacher, no one was worthy of taking the book.

No one in hell, no demon, doomed sinner, not even Satan himself, was worthy of taking that book.

Heaven had seen no one worthy enough to open the book. No one to restore dominion and end the onslaught of Satan. Man's inability to end evil, tyranny, and injustices is a reality. No one qualified on earth, but the Lion, the Sovereign Savior, has all the qualifications in heaven.

Verse 4

John broke down and cried bitterly. Why? Because he saw no one worthy before God to open the book. He weeps because he thinks he will not see one who was worthy of opening the book. Creation is doomed because of sin since man fell in Eden. John weeps for humanity.

A person who is worthy of opening the book must understand what is in God's hand. History is in God's hand. A plan of redemption is in God's hand. Therefore, someone must be qualified to reclaim the lost inheritance, someone who was true to humanity and free to redeem: not a sinful man, not an angel (Heb. 2:9, 14 – 17).

The Greek word "*dunamai*" means doing something by ability, strength, power, authority, or permission. The English word is "dynamic." "Dunamis" distinctly describes the power of God. The idea is that Christ alone is worthy in all creation to open the seals on the scroll in God's hand (Rev. 5:9-10). John weeps because of humanity's inability to solve the problem, but He rejoices when he sees that God has the answer. So, he is commanded John to stop weeping. God will bring history to a climax and establish righteousness throughout the earth through Jesus Christ (Jn. 14:2-3, Tit. 2:12 – 13):

1. We should bow in humility and dependency on God. We should praise and worship Him day and night while we have breath (Ps. 95:6, 96:9, Rev. 14:7).

2. We should pay attention to the Book of Revelation, study, and live in the message while we have the ability. The event is yet to take place (Eph. 3:5, 2 Tim. 3:16, Acts 20:32).

Verse 5

Notice one of the elders' words, "Weep not, behold; he points John to Jesus! The message of Jesus has been preaching for 2,000 years. Jesus is worthy. Jesus Christ is the Lion of Judea. As a lion shows that he is the most vital member of the tribe of Israel. Judah was the strongest tribe of Israel. God had prophesied through Jacob that His Son would be a lion whelp (young cub). Judea being the young cub, the Messiah is like the king of beasts, the Lion. The Messiah would possess the strength and power of a lion, the king of the beasts, will redeem us from Satan and the sin curse (Gen. 49:9-10), Matt. 1:17, Lk. 3:23). The Book of Genesis prophesized that out of Judah the Redeemer would come. It is Jesus who is the offspring of David and who possesses divine and humanity (Rev. 22:16). He is worthy of opening the seals.

"Jesus is the Lion" refers to His second coming, His majesty, sovereign, judge, and the government of God. Jesus as the Lamb speaks of His first coming, His humility, as Savior, judged, and the grace of God. He is the Root of David and the kinsman-redeemer (Isa. 11:1, Jer. 22:24-30). The future Ruler of the earth will rise like a shoot or stem of a cut-down tree. He will come from David's line as the Messiah.

Israel was looking for a king, a military leader, who would give them liberty—someone to lead them to victory over their enemies. When Jesus comes, He did not fulfill the expectations. Instead, he went around healing, preaching, and performing miracles. As a result, the Jews rejected and crucified Jesus.

1. He is the Messiah King of the world (Isa. 11:1).

2. The title reflects both the humanity and the deity of the Messiah who was to come (Gen. 49:8-10).

3. He is the one who has prevailed and conquered sin, not the kind of kingdom the Jews were looking towards (Eph. 1:7, 1 Pet. 3:18, 2 Tim. 1:10).

4. He has conquered death (2 Tim. 1:10, Heb. 2: 14 – 15.

5. He has conquered this evil world (Gal. 1:4, Jn. 16:33.

6. He has conquered Satan and all evil forces (Jn. 12:31, Heb. 2: 14 – 15).

7. He has conquered all rule, authority, and power (1 Cor. 15:24. Roman 8: 34 – 39).

If we are to inherit the new heaven and earth, then Jesus must become King. The person who opened the book would execute God's plans. Christ is worthy. The message of the book now can be open.

Verses 6-7

When John turns around, he sees amid the throne four beasts, elders, and Jesus. The Lamb that takes away the sin of the world is Jesus, who has been slain. He takes the book out of the hands of Him, who sit on the throne (Isa. 53). Jesus ascended into heaven and sat down on the right hand of his Father (Heb. 1:1 – 3)

God sent one worthy enough to open the book of destiny, one who gave His life as a ransom for our sins. John sees the one who dries up our tears, turns our pain and sorrow into joy. Christ takes the book out of the right hand of God, who sits on the throne and breaks the seven seals one at a time. John expected to see a great and powerful lion. Instead, he saw a crucified Lamb of God (Col. 1:12-13, 2:14-15, Heb. 2:14):

1. Every eye is upon him. He is the centerpiece of both heaven and earth.

2. He is the sacrificial Lamb of God who has been slain (Exod. 12:3, Isa. 53:6 – 7, Jn. 1:29, 36). He is the centerpiece of heaven (Heb. 9: 12 – 14, 1 Pet. 2: 24, 3:18).

3. The Lamb and Lion speak of His omnipotent power of the universe and His majesty.

4. He is the supreme intelligence of the universe.

5. He is sovereign. He walks over and takes the book of destiny. Therefore, he alone is worthy of carrying out the plans of God (Rev. 1:1).

6. The Lamb and Lion speak of His government.

Verse 8

Jesus the Lamb takes the book out of the right hand of God. Heaven breaks out with musical instruments in an anthem of praise, and they sing a new song. What is the point of music sounds in praise? Heaven is about to praise Jesus for His redemptive work.

The Lamb that John sees has seven horns, which is a symbol of power and government. The number seven represents perfection showing that Christ's government is perfect (Isa. 11). Seven eyes symbolize Christ's omniscience, wisdom, knowledge, and insight (Col. 2:3). The seven spirits of God include His Spirit (Isa. 6:1, Matt. 3:16, Jn. 3:34), wisdom (1Cor. 10:38), understanding (Isa. 11:1), counsel (Isa 11:1), might (Isa. 11:1), knowledge (1 Cor. 12:8), fear of the Lord (Isa. 11:1). All the Spirits are symbolic of the Holy Spirit, which denotes his perfection and fullness.

Verse 9

He is worthy and deserves worship. It begins with the four living breasts around the throne, followed by the twenty-four elders:

They fall before Christ and praise him with harps because he is worthy (Ps. 33:2; 147:7).

They offer up golden bowls of incense to the Lord, symbolizing believers' prayer (saints).

They sing a new song and focus upon the worthiness of Christ. Jesus steps forward and takes the book because He purchased our redemption with his blood.

They praise him because he was slain for man and redeemed him (Rev. 5:6-7, Roman 5:9, Gal. 3:13, Eph. 1:7, 1 Pet. 1: 18 – 19). Without the cross, there will be redemption concerning the bride of Jesus and no promises.

They praise him because of his universal salvation. He saves people from every tribe and language and every nation. He is no respecter of a person (Rom. 10:13, Tit. 2:11 – 12, 2 Pet. 3:9).

They praise Christ because He makes believers kings and priests, and they shall rule on new earth serving the Lord forever (Rev. 14: 13, 21:24 – 27, Matt. 25:23, Roman 8: 16 – 17, Rev. 20:4).

### Verse 10

Jesus Christ's sacrifice on Calvary for salvation has made us God kings and priests. We are a royal priesthood to serve and reign with Him. Christ has made us part of royal priests right here on earth (Lk. 1:30). We are also kings. Because He shed His blood at Calvary's cross, if we confess with our mouth and believe in the heart, we are redeemed. Heaven rejoices and praises Jesus for what he has done.

### Verses 11-12

There is majestic worship by the angels, living creatures, and the 24 elders. In Revelation 4, there are four beasts on the throne. Some scholars believe they are anointed cherub. In Hebrew, the word for "*anointed*" is messiah. Anointing was the sacred use of oil for persons, and things consecrating them to God. The Lord's anointed was a phase used to designate the king chosen by God. Christ is in the New Testament and is the anointed king worthy of praise. Heaven is joined by a host of angels, 10,000 x 10,000 and all creatures heaven and earth, under the sea and in graves, and in the seas—all creation breaks loose in a song of praise to He who is worthy (Rev. 5:11-14, Dan. 7:10).

They worship and praise Jesus Christ, who is in the center circle of the throne. All creation gives recognition to the worthiness of the Lamb and gives praise for His accomplishments. Every creature in heaven and on earth worships and praises Jesus Christ to the one who sits on the throne.

All creatures, the host of angels, the beast, the elders added their Words of praise. Let everything that has breasts praise the Lord (Ps. 150: 6).

1. Jesus's omnipotent power can open God's book of destiny and carry out and execute God's will throughout the universe (Matt. 28:18, Jn. 17:2).

2. possesses the wealth to meet any needs throughout the universe (2 Cor. 8:9, Eph. 1:7, Phil. 4:19).

3. praise him for wisdom (omniscient), seeing and knowing all things (1 Cor. 1:30, Heb. 4:15 – 16, Ps. 28:7).

4. his strength (Lk. 1:37, 1 Cor. 10:13, Eph. 3:20, Jude 24 – 25).

5. his honor (Phil. 2:9-11, Ps. 34:3, Rev. 19:7).

6. his glory (Matt. 5:16, 1 Cor. 6:19 – 20, Ps. 29:2).

7. his blessing (Colossian 1:2, Duet. 8:10, Ps. 100:4).

Verses 13-14

The whole universe worships the Lamb, Messiah, and Savior because He is worthy of being praised for blessing, honor, glory, power, riches, and His deity.

The four creatures shouted "A*men*". When all of this takes place, the four beasts say, "*Amen!*" The twenty-four elders cannot contain themselves, and they fall before the Lamb in spontaneous, open worship and say, "amen." "*Amen*" means "to be firm, sure, true." It is a further affirmation of the promise of the God. Praising God should never cease. It is the Lord's will. Let us continue to praise the Lord.

He is worthy of opening the book of destiny. He is worthy enough to rule and reign over creation and the last days throughout eternity (Roman 15:6, 1 Cor. 6:20, 2 Thess. 1:12, Rev. 14:7).

Whatever we gain has come to the cost of Jesus' death. He sits in heaven on the right-hand side of his father alive. Heaven declares:

1. A declaration of the worthiness of Jesus. He is worthy of taking the scroll. Jesus the Lamb is worthy.

2. All creation sings praises to the Lamb throughout every generation

3. His works qualified him to be our Redeemer.

4. He has made us be kings and priests in our kingdom.

# CHAPTER 6

## *Opening the Seals*

John continues to give a message to the church. We are introduced to the beginning of the great day of God's wrath. Jesus stands and proceeds to break the seals, and the judgment begins upon the earth: the seven seals, seven trumpets, seven bowls, and plagues. Chapters 6-19 concern the judgments often referred to as the Tribulation, a period of seven years. The judgment follows in the first six seals, but not with the seventh seal's (Rev. 7:1-8). The breaking of the seven seals reveals the second coming of Christ.

The seals are a vision of John that show what God has in store for the elect. The seals are the end of history itself. The end of the world will not come at once. The future will be filled with war, natural disasters, persecution, and the claim of false deliverers. The judgment series identified:

1. The breaking will bring war, famines, death, martyrs, prayers, and great earthquake (Rev. 6:1-8:6).

2. Announcement of trumpets (the seven trumpets): a third of vegetation burned, a third of the sea judged, a third of freshwater judged, a third of the luminaries darkened, increased demonic activity, and a third of humanity killed.

3. Announcement of bowls judgments (the seven bowls): Malignant sores, the sea turned to blood, fresh waters to blood, men scorched with fire, darkness over the kingdom of the beast, invasion from the east, earthquakes, and widespread destruction.

As each seal is broken, it tells us the events that are going to take place. They are witnessing the end of time. The first four judgments seem to describe the Antichrists gaining control over the nations of the earth. He wages war (the red horse), gain control of the economy (the black horse) and having his opponent put to death (the pale horse). In the fifth seal, we see what happens to the soul of the Christian martyrs whom the Antichrist slays. The seventh seal brings a terrible period of God's judgment.

Jesus Christ breaks the first four seals, one of the four living creatures surrounding the throne is commanded to come forth. A series of divine judgments are poured out upon the earth. The four seals will be events that will take place during the first 3 ½ year portion of the Tribulation.

Humanity will witness a time of destruction, devastation, and death that our mortal minds cannot comprehend. The church has been removed with no gospel witness left without teaching, singing, or preaching, and no peace is available. The world will suffer terrifying judgments.

Verses 1-2

One of the four beasts invites John, "Come and see". He saw a rider sit on a white horse (Rev. 6:1, Ps. 45). He is not Jesus Christ. When he rides out of heaven, it will be on a mighty white horse and his host of other riders (Rev. 19:1-11). As John viewed this prophetic scene, it seems to merge into a theatrical audiovisual presentation rather than a vision, but as a factual occurrence. When the Lamb opens the first seal, a storm is about to be unleashed upon the world beyond description.

The four riders represent conquest, war, famine, and death. So, the riders represent the human lust of violence for gain. God revokes his providential care over humanity (God is responsible for folding up the

Monopoly board, but only when the arguments get out of hand after parental supervision is removed!).

The first seal reveals a white horse and its rider. John looks and sees a rider given a crown, and he rides off as a conqueror bent on conquest. Who is this rider? Some scholars suggest two views:

1. He summarizes the victorious Christ himself. It argued that the color white is always associated with Christ throughout Revelation. In addition, the rider is said to be crowned. Many argued that it is not Christ (Mark 13:10).

2. The second significant view is that the rider is on a conquest. He appears in white (Matt. 24:5, 2 Thess. 2:11). The crown he wears is different from the crown worn by Christ in Revelation 19. It represents a symbol of military power (Ps. 46:9, Jer. 51:51, Hosea 1:5) and a picture of the four riders of the apocalypse.

John tells us that when the Lamb opens the first seal, a rider on a white horse appears with a bow and a crown and rides out as a conqueror bent on conquest. Horses appear, representing God's judgment of people for sins and rebellion. The horses have a symbolic meaning. The rider has a bow and no arrows (Zech. 9:14, Num. 24:8). When wars were fought in the Bible, it was with a bow and arrows. Breaking the seals in chapter 6, Christ does not send disaster because evil already exists in the hearts of sinful humanity. Some believe that his rise symbolizes the good news that the rider is Christ himself. The rider is a counterfeit Christ. Three facts support the idea:

1. The rider is given a crown. Christ is not given a crown.

2. The rider has a bow. Christ possesses no bow; a weapon of war is not a part of his being.

3. The rider set out to conquer.

John first witnesses a white rider released to ravage the earth; he carries a war bow and wears an imperial crown. Cavalry in full regalia may look glorious, but they bring death and destruction on their conquest—this cavalryman represents human lust for war let loose. The white rider may be a version of the legendary Minos, who rode on a white horse and carried a javelin with bow and arrows, but John's imagery is more Biblical than secular. The rider on the white horse's task is to deceive and oppress believers. The strongest argument points to the white rider being the Antichrist. He is setting out to conquer the world through deception. He is going to deceive people into sinning and becoming evil (2 Thess. 2:8 – 10). People rejected Jesus Christ. They will be cursed. God will allow the Antichrist to be a strong world ruler who can solve the world's problems and bring utopia to earth. Humanity will give the earthly kingdom to him by signing treaties and agreements that will allow him to rule over the nations and lives (2 Thess. 2:11; Rev. 17:17).

The white horse rider denotes peaceful victory. The rider comes on a white horse, brings a promise of peace to this world. The Antichrist will bring the world problems without peaceful solutions. The world will fall at his feet as the savior of the world.

The world will be ripe for this kind of leader. Humanity will turn the world government over to the Antichrist. We live in a world full of false messiahs claiming to have the answer to life will prepare the way for the Antichrist. Their claims of false. Man cannot create a utopia on earth (Matt. 24:5):

1. Violence, wars, and rumors of wars will prepare the way for the Antichrist. A devastated world will turn to any leader who can bring peace and restoration (Matt. 24:6-7).

2. Fear will drive people to a leader who can promise and provide financial and medical help and aid (Matt. 24:7).

3. Religious persecution and terrible apostasy and betrayal will seek the earth. Divisions between religion, family, and neighbors will

cause people to turn for help to bring about peace between religions (Matt. 24:9 – 10).

4. We live in a world full of false religion, and false preachers will prepare the way to the Antichrist (Matt. 24:11).

5. The world will experience increasing sin growth and love that grows cold. Humanity begs for help dealing with lawlessness, drunkenness, drugs, occult practices, crime, and evil. Society looks for someone who will bring genuine care and affection. (Matt. 24:12).

The Antichrist will be given leadership in the world during the last three and a half years of the Tribulation. The leaders of the nations will bow at the Antichrist's. However, the leaders of the nations did not grant that privilege to Jesus Christ. The Antichrist will portray himself to be one person when he is another person. The world will trust the man on the white horse who appears promising peace, safety, and prosperity. He will be the evilest leader the world has ever seen. Everything he is and everything he says will be lies and falsehoods. When we watch the news, we will soon realize that it is not always that the best and brightest rule the nations! The world is ripe for satanic deception. The world has already witnessed leaders who came to conquer. Most come with plans to conquer, claiming to be men of peace. Their deception was universal. The Antichrist will be the same and do the same, only on a worldwide scale. The world will be ripe for such a person to step to center stage.

Verses 3-4

The second seal is opened. John witnesses a second rider on a red horse who makes a thundering appearance. Who is the rider? He is the rider of strife, violence, assault, division, abuse, hate, uprising, murder, insurrection, war, and bloodshed. He will divide race against race, class against class, neighbor against neighbor, employee against employer, husband against wife, religion against religion, and nation against nation. He takes peace from the earth. The rider will bring peace a while, but there will be a break in behavior (Matt. 24:6-7). The red horse denotes slaughter and rivers of blood (Isa. 63:2, Rev.12:3). He symbolizes coming warfare with great bloodshed. Red is the color of fire and blood. Fire has the power to devour and destroy. When the destruction is unleashed upon this earth, there will be bloodshed on an unprecedented level. The seals unleash a time of war such as the world has never known. A rider on the horse has a great sword and is permitted to take peace from the earth.

He destroys every human relationship. Who is the rider upon the horse? John does not say, note what he will bring:

1. The rider in the last days will bring evil and truce breaking (2 Tim. 3:1-3).

2. The rider in the last days will bring war and rumors of wars (Matt. 24:6-7).

3. In the last days, the rider will be the great red dragon (Rev. 13:3).

4. The devil is a murderer and a great liar and deceiver (Jn. 8:44).

The Antichrist will be the supreme representative of the devil, and He will use his forces (sword) against God's people (Rev. 13:7-8, 17:15-18; 1 Thess. 5:3). The world will know no peace. Violence and war will rage. The Antichrist will attempt to institute peace, but it will be short-lived. Jesus warned humanity about putting too much faith in the cries of peace from politicians and rulers in this world (1 Thess. 5:3).

The rider is given a great sword. Great refers to the extent of warfare. It will be worldwide in its scope. The word "sword" refers to the short swords carried by Roman soldiers. These swords were used in hand-to-hand combat and were quite effective in putting the enemy to death.

When the Antichrist first steps onto the world stage, he will be hailed as a man of peace. However, after he is given the reins of power, he displays his true colors. After humanity allows him a place of prominence and power, he will demand absolute power. When this happens, many of the world's powerful countries will rebel, and the world will experience war on a scale that it has never witnessed. Millions of people will die worldwide. That number will fall far short of the millions who will die during the wars that will rage during the period. Russia and her allies will invade Israel in fulfillment of Ezek. 38-39. Their army will be defeated by divine intervention, and Israel will burn the weapons of warfare for seven years (Ezek. 39:9-10). The conflicts will not end here. However, the wars spawned by Antichrist will rage, one after the other, until Jesus, the Prince of peace, returns in power and glory! Nations, races, and religious wars will abound. Peace will be elusive for everyone everywhere! The world is ripe for these predicaments. It will be a time of war fought without God, without Jesus, and hope. Peace will return when Christ comes back. He will bring justice and restoration to his people.

Verses 5-6

John tells us that a rider on a black horse appeared when the Lamb opened the third seal. He has a pair of scales and brings famine and pestilence to the earth. The color black is associated with famine. It follows in the aftermath of war. Thus, worldwide hungry. Jesus said in Matthew 24:7 what is going to happen. The Antichrist has the world control of the economy and distribution of food. The rider on this horse appears with a set of scales indicating that the tribulation period creates a severe shortage in the necessities of life. Food and other necessities will be rationing. The world economy and distribution of food are control by the Antichrist.

The Antichrist set a scale to measure out the wheat. Wheat and barley were the primary food for people on John's Day. It used to cost a penny to buy three measures of barley. A penny was about a day's wages. Cabinets, refrigerators, and freezers are empty. We know nothing about having to do without or about having to make do with just a little.

A biblical "measure or unit of measurement" was used primarily by ancient Israelites to determine a fair measurement or wages for a day. A "penny or denarius" was a day's wage. Food like bread will be challenging to buy. People will begin to use barley primarily to feed livestock for food because they cannot buy wheat. The Great Tribulation will bring difficult conditions. It will be consumed by the poor.

We have the image of a man working all day to buy enough good food to feed him. He can work all day to buy enough food fit for an animal to feed a family. People will have choices to make. The rider will control food distribution. It is how he gains control of the world. It will cause terrible famine and starvation for the poor (Matt. 24:6-7; Lamentations 4:9, 5:10). Extravagant lifestyles will continue to exist for the wealthy.

The great divide already exists! Many people live in the lap of luxury compared to most people worldwide. Consider the facts:

1. Most Americans put enough food in the trashcan each day to feed developing nations. Many could eat a meal a day for five years.

2. During the 1990s, millions of children died from starvation. Those deaths could have been prevented if wealthy nations had offered economic resources.

3. The world spends $13 billion in United States dollars on its militaries in two days. We can satisfy the world's sanitation and food requirements with some of the money.

4. People of North America could feed the world hungry for years.

5. The dividing line between the wealthy and the poor will grow wider during the Tribulation.

6. During the Tribulation wars, the military's demand for certain goods increased dramatically, and there will be shortages.

7. Ration books will be handed out, and people will use the coupons to obtain the things needed. Sugar, coffee, butter, meat, cheese, canned goods, shoes, and gasoline will be carefully rationed.

8. During the height of the Tribulation war, sugar, gas, and coffee will be limited and rationed.

John shows us that God's justice will prevail. It will be difficult times to endure the Tribulation. One-fourth of the world's people will die, indicating that God limits His destruction and judgment against the unbeliever, giving them time to accept Christ as savior.

Verses 7 - 8

John tells us that a rider on a pale horse appeared when the Lamb opened the fourth seal. The rider is called death, and it has Hades with him. Together they are given the power to kill a fourth of the earth. "*Pale*" means yellowish green—the color of a corpse. It comes from "chlorophyll" and "chlorine". Two significant facts are mentioned in Revelation Chapter 5:

1. The pale horse has the name of death. It speaks of one waiting to the souls of unbelievers when they are taken by death in war.

2. He is given the power to cause unbelievable pain and suffering: he is responsible for killing one-fourth of the people on earth that would equal over one billion today.

3. There are four ways: the sword can help to kill many people. War and genocide, by deliberately setting policies to destroy certain races or groups of people, will become present.

4. The pale horse will create war, an atomic war on earth (Matt. 24: 6 -7). Hunger and starvation will follow, killing many people. The pale rider will cause a famine due to the rationing of food. Today, no one has ever experienced conditions such as these.

In many parts of the world today, the horror of starvation is devastating. Consider the statistics:

1. Thousands of children are dying daily (40,000) from starvation out of selfishness and greed.

2. Every 3.6 seconds, someone dies of starvation.

3. Every year 15 million children die of starvation and hunger-related illness.

4. Every year millions of people starve to death.

5. We have 1.3 billion people living on less than $1.00 of income per day. Another 3 billion must try and survive on less than $3.00 per day.

6. As horrible as those figures are, they will be dwarfed by the starvation problem this world will face in the Tribulation.

The brutality of this devastation from the methods death used will claim a significant number of people dying. The four methods mentioned are:

1. Warfare using weapons of destruction that are conventional and nuclear, biological, and chemical weapons as well. Famine resulting from starvation will become worldwide.

2. Death will occur from warfare and famine.

3. Animal attacks will account for many deaths.

In Matthew 24:7, Jesus tells us, "For nation shall rise against nation, and kingdom against kingdom: and there shall be famines, and pestilences, and earthquakes, in divers' places." The pale rider will continue to unleash horrible living conditions. Pestilence suggests diseases that will run rampant through humanity during this period resulting from unsanitary conditions of refugees and concentration camps. Diseases old and new never witnessed will happen. Bird flu, venereal diseases, flu epidemic, smallpox, polio, measles, aids, and diphtheria will leave millions of people dead. There will be few medical supplies.

The beasts of the forest and jungles will be hungry from the lack of food; they will attack humanity (Matt. 24:7). The word "beasts" can refer to animals like rodents (rats). Rats have been devastating around the world and bring on diseases. Consider this information concerning rats:

1. With warfare, death, and carnage, the rodents' population of the world will explode.

2. One breeding pair can produce excessive litters of offspring per year.

3. Rodents like rats are nasty animals, and they carry 35 known diseases.

4. They were responsible for killing a third of the European population during the Middle Ages as the bubonic plague raged.

5. Rats carry typhus, which has killed 200 million people in a 400-year period.

6. Rats destroy some $1 billion in food in the United States every year.

7. If you take today's population of six billion people, you are talking about the death of 1.25 billion people in a short period!

Peace will just be disturbed, still indicating that God is limiting his judgment. The unbeliever still has time to repent. God continues to show that he is merciful. The little punishment shows that God still loves humanity and is willing to be patient, giving people an opportunity to be saved before He brings final judgment. The judgment seals are going to happen. These judgments are just the seal judgments. The trumpets judgment and the bowl judgments are to come.

Verses 9-11

Living creatures and horses characterize the first four seals, and they ride away. Jesus breaks the fifth seal. Martyr souls under the altar are crying out to God. The martyrs beneath the altar are calling on God to avenge their deaths. They ask God how long it would take to wreak vengeance on your enemies.

All those who have died for Christ through the ages, their blood cries out for God's mercy. They have offered their lives as a supreme sacrifice. They are given a special place in eternity (Matt. 16:25, Lk. 9: 23; 1 Cor. 6:19 – 20). When the Rapture takes place, the Church and the Holy Spirit will go out and return as they did in the Old Testament. Believers will be severely persecuted throughout the Roman world (Matt. 25:14). They will be converted Jews (Matt. 25:40). Those who refuse the message of the gospel will listen to any message. The Antichrist martyred them because of their testimony. Two things exist here:

1. Believers will be slain for their beliefs in Jesus Christ (Rev. 1:9, 12:11, 17; 19:10, 1 Jn. 4:2 – 3).

2. They believe, live by, read, study, witness, teach, preach, and pray over it. Why? Because of their first loyalty to Christ.

The Antichrist will require first loyalty to the government state's religion. End times, people will reject God more, deny, ignore, neglect, disobey, and disbelieve Jehovah more. The earth will be hell on the earth after the Rapture. If you do not worship the God of the state, you will be killed (Acts 5:27 – 29). Laws will be created to serve the purpose.

The testimony of the people is not the testimony yet idea today in this age of grace and mercy. During the Tribulation, the testimony of people who will believe in the coming kingdom of Jesus Christ will cause persecution. The Bible tells us that you go to two destinations when death comes: heaven or hell. You either go to heaven or hell. There are no other choices! (Matt. 25:46; Rev. 20:12, Dan. 12:2).

Souls are not lying in the grave in a body awaiting a resurrection because of their testimony. They are in heaven. They are aware and talking. They are very much alive and in the presence of the Lord. The Tribulation saints will be hunted down like dogs for their beliefs in Jesus and executed for their testimony. The word 'slain' is used in Verse 11 instead of killing. The first group refers to the Jews and the Gentiles. John saw their souls under the brazen altar. Brass symbolizes the judgment of Almighty God.

The history of the church has been about persecution and martyrdom. The Bible is filled with examples of people put to death for their faith:

1. Stephen was stoned to death (Acts 7).

2. Millions were put to death in the ancient Roman coliseums to satisfy the bloodlust of the Romans.

3. Many Christians were tied to poles, dipped in wax, and fire to light dinner parties. Thousands were murdered like the Jews, who were put to death in German Nazi camps.

4. Today, thousands of Christians die every year because they believe in Jesus!

5. In Sudan, young Christian girls are taken as sex slaves by Muslim men and raped and beaten until they are used up, then they are killed.

6. In America, public opinion has turned against believers. Constitutional laws have changed, giving nonbelievers more ungodly rights.

Christian have been for the last 2000 years crucified, burned alive at stake, sawn in half, drowned, stoned, fed to wild beasts, released to them, shot, stabbed, sealed in their churches and burned alive, raped, humiliated and tortured. Many of these acts are a shadow of Tribulation. In Verse 10, John tells us the slain martyrs cry out for the justice of God because they desired to see God's name vindicated:

1. They address Him as the sovereign Lord, holy, pure, and trustworthy.

2. All their prayers are directed to him, for their lives.

3. He is the creator of all things in the universe.

4. They cry out for justice and vengeance against their persecutors. They cry for the vindication of the word of God and to avenge their blood. Why was their blood spilled? Why were they killed? Because of their faith and belief in a Holy God and Jesus Christ.

5. God keeps his word and promises.

6. They prayed for God's kingdom to come upon the earth (Rev. 6: 10, Ps. 74:10, 79:5 – 6, 94: 3– 4).

The martyr's souls in Verse 11 are wearing white, which signifies their purity and their saved condition of righteousness. The Lord gives each of these martyrs a white robe. They will be clothed in white and told to "rest yet for a little longer" until they know the company of fellow servants brothers should be killed as they were killed (Duet. 32:35, Rev. 1, Rom. 12:19). They sealed their testimony with blood after they are killed after the Rapture. They are told that more blood will be shed as they were until the Lord finishes his work upon the earth. God promises to bring justice to the unrepentant sinners at His appointed time. In this period, they should rest:

1. They will rest from the wicked (Job 3:17).
2. They will rest from all the trials and tribulations of life, free from all tears, sorrow, crying, pain, and death (Rev. 21:4).
3. The martyr's souls are resting in the perfection of a new life in Jesus Christ and the righteousness of Jesus Christ (2 Cor. 5:17, 21, Eph. 4:24).
4. They will rest in the peace of Christ (Heb. 4: 9; Rev. 6:11).
5. They are resting from all their exhausting labor on earth (Rev. 14:13).

More believers will be killed. More believers will die for their witnessing of Jesus Christ before the end comes. We must not fear being witnesses (2 Tim. 1:8, 2nd Pet. 3: 15, Acts 1:8). A Christian must remain faithful. Trust God and pray for strength to endure.

Verses 12-14

Jesus opens the sixth seal (Verses 12-17), and cosmic judgment falls on the whole earth, projecting the Lord's Day is near. The physical scene of the world will change to unbelievable disorder.

Astronomical events will happen:

1. Astronomical happenings will occur right before end times (Rev. 6: 13).

2. Events will occur right after the Tribulation when the Day of the Lord comes (Matt. 24:29-31; Ezek. 32:7 – 8; Joel 3:15 –16).

Earthquake beyond what man has ever seen. Destruction of property, life-gripping fear, and damage caused by aftershocks (Matt. 24:7; Rev. 6:12, 11:13, 16: 17 – 19; Joel 2: 10). The sun turns black, the moon turned blood-red, and the stars fall from the sky. Meteorites, volcanic eruptions, windstorms, and fire will catastrophically shower the earth. The believers are resting from all the trials and tribulations of life, free from all tears, sorrow, crying, pain, and death.

The heavens will disappear like a rolling up scroll, and the mountains will be moved out of their place. What does this mean? The devastation will cause humanity to cry for the mountains and the rocks to fall upon them (Isa. 34:4; Nah. 1:5; Jer. 4:24).

The world will be caught in the grip of a terrible cataclysm. Great clouds of dust and ash will be thrown into the atmosphere, dimming the sun's powerful light. Mourners will wear "*sackcloth,*" which refers to the wearing of black garments.

The moon will look like blood as it shines through a ravaged atmosphere.

The stars of heaven will fall from their sockets to the earth like the fruit of a fig tree shaken by a violent wind. Meteor will shower the earth for days causing death and devastation. The destruction will not compare with any other catastrophic events ever happening on the earth.

Verses 15-16

The effects of God's judgment upon people will cause fear for some people. The unbelief will not fear God because of their arrogance. However, many will fear God when they see Him sitting on the throne and face His wrath. Great fear will grip believers. They will not face punishment but receive a reward from Christ. Note the list of those who fear:

1. The wealthy of the earth will fear.
2. Military chiefs of the earth will fear.
3. The mighty and robust of the earth will fear.
4. Slaves and insignificant of the earth will fear.
5. Free and independent people of the earth will fear.
6. The great kings and rulers of the earth will fear.

The unbeliever upon the earth will be stricken with terror—a maddening terror. They will hide in dens, under rocks, crevices, and mountains. Humanity will beg for the mountains and rocks to fall on them. Panic will sweep the earth. God has no favorites, and there will be no partiality. The earth will know that God's judgment moves on the earth (Isa. 13:6, 8; Zeph. 1:14; Joel 2:1). They will cry for death. People will be rushing to find a place to hide, to keep from the face of God that is seated on the throne and from the eternal judgment (Lk. 23:30; Isa. 2:19; Hos. 10:8). No one will escape the hour of mortal fear (Rev. 1:7). Thank God, my beloved, that you are saved. Only the believers of Jesus Christ will go in the Rapture, and those not born again would be left behind to face the terrible times only upon the earth.

The earth is always stable. During the Tribulation, it will be shaken. The sun, moon, and stars will disappear. The millennia men have worshiped the natural world and suddenly find themselves in a world where nothing is stable. The world will come apart, and they are terrified!

Humanity will hide from the face of God and Jesus. His wrath will come as a sudden outburst of anger. It speaks of anger that slowly rises like water against a dam until the dam breaks and the flood comes. It has the idea of someone standing and clenching their fists for mercy and grace. It will be too late. The unbeliever will have nothing to receive but the judgment whose time has come (Duet. 32:39 – 43, Isa. 34:4, Joel 2:30 – 31, Matt. 24:29, Heb. 10:20 – 31).

Verses 16-17

There will be reasons for the panic on the great day of God's wrath. Instead of repenting, people will cry out to hide under rocks and mountains to bury them from the face of Jesus. The two verses tell us:

1. It is the day when humanity will stand before God, who sits upon the throne of the universe.

2. It is the day when humanity will face the wrath of the Lamb, the day when they must face the Son of God for having rejected, denied, cursed, disobeyed, disbelieved, ignored, and neglected Him.

3. It is the great day when humanity will face God's wrath.

4. It is the day when the unbelievers shall crumble and be subjected to humiliation and eternal guilt, condemnation, and punishment.

Remember, this is a picture of what is happening right before the day of the Lord comes. The end times have not happened. The events and catastrophe will frighten and panic people. When Jesus breaks the seals, the worst judgment is yet to come on humanity. The day of God's wrath is coming:

1. On the religious, who thought they could be good enough and do enough good to be acceptable to God.

2. On the rich and powerful, who thought they were self-sufficient.

3. On the poor, who thought they were too insignificant or thought their oppression would cause God to look upon them with mercy.

4. On the intelligent, who thought they were too knowledgeable to believe in Christ.

5. On the scientists and technicians, because they thought they had progressed, and could disprove God.

No one will be able to escape the wrath of God. How can the unbelievers escape the great day of God's wrath? (Jn. 12: 48, Rom. 2:5, Rev. 6: 17. Isa. 13: 9 – 11, Zeph. 1: 14 – 16, Mal. 4:1). Those who accept Jesus as your savior will receive a reward rather than punishment.

# CHAPTER 7

## *The Multipile Sealed*

---

John saw Jesus takes a scroll from the hand of God that had been sealed with seven seals. As Jesus broke each seal and unrolled the scroll a little further, events began to occur on the earth, and the time that we call the Tribulation began to unfold.

The faithful believers will be safe and sealed. The chapter contains two pictures: the sealing of 144,000 and the great multitude worshiping God before the heavenly throne. When the seven seals are broken, the seven-seal judgment is over; the period of history that would be known as the beginning of sorrows and woes will be finished. In chapter 7, God continues to show his incredible power. We will witness the most significant harvest of souls during the Tribulation.

Verse 1

Four angels are commanded not to blow their trumpets until the 144,000 Jews are sealed for protection as they go through the judgments. They are sealed before the seventh trumpet judgment. They will be protected and delivered from Satan and the enemies of God.

A storm is about to come, and God is about to unlatch the winds of judgments on the earth. God commanded the four angels to hold back the winds of judgment from the four main points of the earth. The sealing occurred between the sixth and seventh seals. The number four in the Book of Revelation has spiritual meaning. It deals with creation (Isa. 11:12) and refers to the four points of the compass: north, east, west, and south. The Bible references east wind. Other references to the number four in the Bible are the four world empires in all history, four seasons in the year, and if you multiply it by ten, you get 40 and still deal with the earth. Forty in the Bible deals with testing and trials. The use of numbers in this chapter lets us know that we deal with transpiring events on the earth. It is a picture of God controlling the whole earth. In his mercy, He has chosen to wait patiently for unbelievers to accept Jesus Christ.

The Angels are told to hold back the four winds for a time long enough for the message of salvation to be preached across the world. Every person can be saved by receiving Jesus Christ as Lord and savior. Those who receive the message will make up the great multitude that no man can number. They will have a seal on their forehead that will deliver them from eternal judgment and condemnation. (2 Pet. 3:7; Rev. 9:4, 14:1).

The seal or mark on the forehead represents your will, volition and God imprints on those who have chosen Jesus as Savior. It is God's Spirit in the believers to indicate ownership and control.

Verses 2-3

John watches a fifth angel rise from the east with the seal of the living God. The angel seals the servants of God in their foreheads. Satan imitates God by sealing his servants (Rev. 13:16-17). God will give a command. Delay the judgment until all servants of God servants can be sealed. The angel with a loud voice cries out to the four angels to hurt not the earth, neither the sea, tree until we have sealed the service of God (Rev. 7:3). The seal means the mark of possession, authority, power, protection, and preservation. In ancient times, king's ring was his seal. He would use his ring as an official mark on all documents showing his possession, authority, and power. The 144,000 will be sealed—protected and preserved by God (Gen. 41:42; Dan. 6:17; Matt. 27:66; Rev. 9:4, 22:4, Ezek. 9:4).

God permanently seals his people with the blood of the Lamb. The Lamb's blood sealed the children of Israel on the doorposts and lintels of their homes during the Passover in Egypt (Exod. 12:13). God will seal his servants from the tribes of Israel during the Tribulation period. The listing of the names of the original listing includes man, woman, family, and tribes (Duet. 29:18 – 21). Only one name is left out of the tribe of Dan for idolatry. They are sealed immediately after the rapture.

If you are saved today, you have been marked by God. He places his seal upon His possession! He claims you as his very own. God sealed the believers (Eph. 1:13-14) with the Holy Spirit. He paid the ultimate price to redeem humanity from sin (1 Cor. 6:19-20). We are safe in him until we make it to heaven. The demonic forces released on the earth doing the Tribulation will not hurt God's people (Rev. 9: 4). Only those who accept antichrists will not receive the mercy of God. He remembers His mercy throughout the history of humanity. In the last half of the Tribulation, God will pour out his wrath on the unbelievers (Rev. 7: 14; 2nd Pet. 3: 9; Jer. 17:10).

Verses 4-8

The Bible is clear where these 144,000 people originated from all the tribes of the children of Israel (Rev. 7:4). They are 12,000 Jewish believers from the twelve tribes. Israel is God's chosen people. The passage says:

1. The 144,000 Jews will be converted or saved doing the Tribulation. The answer is that both Jews and Gentiles will be saved verses 9–17.

2. The 144,000 is a unique body of Jewish believers dedicated to serving the Lord Jesus Christ during the Tribulation of the last days.

3. They are virgins that have never been married. It is a fantastic body who vows and commit their lives never to deny Christ. The

encouragers and ministers to the believers will be severely attacked and persecuted by the Antichrist (Rev. 14: 4 – 5).

4. Israel will be restored (Roman 11:23 – 24, 25 – 26).

Why are there precisely 12,000 from each of the 12 tribes?

The number 12 in the Bible is associated with Israel's history. There were 12 tribes, 12 loaves of bread on the table of shewbread in the tabernacle, 12 gates into the city of Jerusalem, and 12 stones in the high priest's breastplate. God has a plan for their future restoration and the redemption of Israel (Rom. 9-11). They will be to preach the gospel during the Tribulation. The Lord will raise an army of 144,000 converted Jewish evangelists who will take the Revelation message to the ends of the earth and fulfill the prophecy of Matthew 24:14. The Antichrist will try to stop them, but he will be powerless to hinder their ministry. He will not be able to silence them, kill them or stop them. God has sealed them, and they will be protected until their ministry has been fulfilled.

The Church has failed to reach the world. The Lord will provide an opportunity for the unconverted and the unreached to be saved. The most incredible evangelistic effort the world has ever witnessed. The 144,000 redeemed Jewish preachers will take the gospel to the world, and many will be saved. The twelve tribes symbolize all of God's followers, the Church (Gal. 3:29; 6:16; 1 Pet. 2:9). The Lord will redeem millions during the Tribulation, and the faithful will be sealed before the persecution comes. They will remain faithful until the end.

Verses 9-10

Who shall be saved during these times? One-fourth of the earth's population will be destroyed by famine, war, pestilence, hunger, and starvation. This period is called death and hell. Is there any hope? Can people be saved?

John saw a multitude, a vast crowd, too great to count. Who are they? They are people from everywhere (Rev. 5: 9):

1. from all nations

2. from all tribes—all tribes will have some people within them saved.

3. from all people saved—some people will not be saved

4. from all tongues—meaning from all languages will be saved

A great multitude of people will turn to Christ. It will be the most remarkable revival in the history of the world. The angels, elders, martyred, the redeemed, and living creatures. They will be shouting, "Salvation comes from our God on the throne and from the Lamb" (Rev. 7:10, 12). They have earned the privilege to stand before the throne of God, and the Lamb is the most glorious position:

1. to be near God and Christ

2. to be face to face with God and Christ

3. to be honored with the presence of God and Christ

4. to know God and Christ in all their fullness in being

Clothes in white robes of righteousness symbolize purity because of their salvation (Rev. 3:4-5; 4:4; 19:14). They will be made pure and free from the blemish of sin and all the corruption of the world. These people are saved by grace, and they have been rendered righteous. That is the promise of God to all who will come to Jesus Christ.

The believers hold palm branches in their hands as a symbol of celebration of their triumph over sin, evil, corruption (Verse 9). A multitude no man could number, of all nations, peoples, tongues stood before the throne. They celebrate the victory of deliverance, salvation, and joy to Christ. He is worthy of praise, worship, and adoration. God will celebrate with them forever.

Verses 11-12

All the creates around the thrones are praising God as they fall on their faces. They sing a song that contains seven words of praise: blessings, glory, wisdom, thanksgiving, honor, power, and might. The saints lift their voices to their redeemer for His redemption. They know that they are in heaven because of the grace of God and the shed blood of Jesus Christ. All saints share in praising Jesus because they have reasons for praise, shouting, singing, and testimony, for He is worthy of being praised (Lk. 10:20). We must learn to praise the way the angels, elders, and four living creatures are doing in heaven:

1. They praise God for his blessings. His perfect gifts and profound happiness.

2. They praise God for his glory, moral perfection, and splendor.

3. They praise God for his wisdom. He is omniscient. He plans all things, and it works out for good. He is praised for his plan of redemption.

4. They offer thanksgiving to God. They thank him for creation, life, salvation, redemption (pardoning of sin), and everything else.

5. They praise God for being supremely, majestic, and trustworthy. They praise him publicly for saving people.

6. They praise him for his power. He works out our salvation and redemption. He delivers us from evil, death, and corruption through the power of His actions.

7. They praise God for his might and strength. God is strong. He never gets tired or becomes weary. There is no weakness in him. He is always able to help his creatures. God never fails. He possesses perfect strength forever (Heb. 13:15, 1st Pet. 2:9, Colossae 1: 12, Ps. 67:3, 1st Thess. 5:18). They close their statement of praise with an "*amen*". To say "amen" means to say, "may this agree or according to you, God." Today, we must learn to praise God using the seven attributes.

Verses 13 – 14

John is stunned by the sight of this great crowd dressed in white robes. It means the crowd has no sin, evil, or corruption in them. They are clean, pure from all defilement. They are perfectly righteous but note a critical fact: no person on earth is sinless, righteous, perfect, pure, or incorruptible. Everyone has sinned and will end up in the grave. They are washed in the blood of the Lamb to get a white robe (verse 14). Six things are said about them:

1. The Antichrist will attempt to wipe out believers on the earth (Rev. 13:7, 2nd Thessalonian 2: 3-4)

2. Daniel predicts the times of trouble (Dan. 12:1).

3. Jesus foretold the Great Tribulation (Matt. 24: 21 – 22).

4. John says that the purpose of the Antichrist is to set up the worship of the state as the first loyalty of citizens of the world (Rev. 13:15).

5. A believer would have to deny Christ or be put to death. They will die by the millions because of their love for Christ.

6. They are those who "washed their robes and made them white in the blood of the lamb" (1 Cor. 15:3-4). During the Tribulation, souls will be saved by the simple preaching of the gospel.

Verses 15-17

Redeemed believers in heaven will serve God continuously day and night. The temple here means heaven itself. They will have direct access to the presence of God anytime, anyplace:

1. Believers will be perfect, so they never tire or become weary or need sleep. They will be able to serve and night continuously. All of heaven will be a sanctuary.

2. Believers will serve God: they will rule and reign throughout the universe, overseeing the new heaven and earth for Christ (Matt. 19: 28, 25:23, Lk. 19: 17, 19, Rev. 5: 10). The Lamb will be amid them.

Humanity will not have its physical needs met on earth. Hunger, thirst, suffering will exist. People will starve to death, be forced to flee their homes and belongings. The picture of a war-torn world will be seen on television. The Tribulation saints will be protected against the elements of nature's scorching heat and the frigid cold. They will be protected from all enemies, even from the sun and heat (Rev. 7:9 – 17).

The believers will have all their needs met in heaven. The Lamb of God himself shall shepherd the believers. The spiritual needs, the soul's needs for life, will be provided in heaven: love, joy, peace, security, completeness, fullness, confidence, and assurance (Ps. 23:1f). God himself will feed them and lead them. Those who have received the beast's mark will hide under the sun's heat by day and stars by night. They will be forced to steal, or beg, and suffer the hardships of the Tribulation.

In heaven, God will give directions and guidance to the saints. He will assign the responsibilities and tell believers what to oversee for him. They will receive the blessing of drinking from the fountain of living water. The living fountain will provide refreshments, meaning God will provide all their needs. No hunger or thirst. God will provide a perfect place for perfect people. Believers shall never suffer, not even a single pain or hurt. They shall be perfected forever (Jn. 4:14, 6: 35, 14:1-3, 2 Tim. 4:8, Rev. 21:4, Isa. 49: 10):

Before the Tribulation starts, humanity will have an opportunity to be saved. Here is the invitation:

1. If you are lost and want to be saved, come to Jesus today and get to know him.

2. Come right now and accept the love of Jesus as savior.

3. Jesus is waiting with outstretched hands. Do not delay.

# CHAPTER 8

## *The First Four Trumpet Judgments*

The seventh seal and the seven trumpets come as the last seal judgments needed to usher in the Lamb and the kingdom of God. No one knows when God will close the Monopoly Board (Matt.24:36), but the day is coming when he will. Jesus is recognized as the one worthy of opening the seals himself (the sacred book). The scroll has writings on both the inside and the outside, which includes three woes. John continues to receive his spiritual Rev. from heaven, and he is commanded to write it down. He sees Jesus as the beginning of birth pangs (Mark 13:8).

The beginning of birth pangs refers to the messiah's coming, and the dawning of the new age of the kingdom involves Tribulation, agony, illustrated by the pain of childbirth (Matt. 24:1-14). Such events do not necessarily herald the last day since they are "only the beginning" of the birth pains, the "first birth-pangs of the new age". The end is still to come.

The sounding of the trumpets is good and bad news; it heralds the day of judgment. The trumpets reveal judgment on those not marked with the inscription of the Lamb and God on their forehead. The interlude gives an insight into the state of the Church caught up in the day of judgment as believers wait for the invitation to ascend into heaven (Rev. 11:12). The gospel mission continues, and some repent.

Verse 1

Jesus breaks the seal, and the seventh trumpet judgment is unleashed upon the earth with horrible consequences because many people have denied and rejected Jesus as the Savior of the world.

When the seventh angel breaks the seventh seal judgment, Heaven's response is seen and heard in anticipation, "The kingdoms of the world become the kingdoms of our Lord" (Rev. 11:15). A picture of shattering silence just before a storm displays the tremendous reverence of what God is doing. It lasted for 30 minutes in anticipation of some terrible judgment to burst across the scene of human history (Amos 5:13, Hab. 2:20). When the seventh seal is open, we have a moment of silence before the outpouring of judgment. Believers on earth are still praying for God's divine grace.

Silence is a powerful thing. You can be asleep in service, and suddenly something gets your attention. Silence lets you know the time has come. If a preacher were to stop his sermon and remain silent for 30 minutes, it would seem like an eternity.

We need to learn that silence is good. Habakkuk 2:20 says, "But the LORD is in his holy temple: let all the earth keep silence before him." Some writers suggest that Heaven went so quiet that God could hear the prayers of his people (so God is hard of hearing?). I do not draw significant conclusions from the silence and argue that it is nothing more than a dramatic pause because the text does not give reasons.

Humanity rushes on in their sins and lives vain lives. Do we understand what God is about to do when his silence falls upon the earth? God's wrath calls for a moment of silence before the event. Heaven knows tragedy is about to strike before the storm in the face of impending judgment.

Verse 2

When we study the Bible, the seven angels designate a specific group. The Bible names several specific angels: Uriel, Raphael, Michael, Saragael, Gabriel, and Remiel. The names of the seven angels are mentioned in the Jewish book of 1 Enoch (1Enoch 20:1-8). In the Book of Revelation, the only angel named Abaddon is described as the king of an army of locusts. His name in Hebrew is Abaddon, translated to Apollyon. The seven angels who stood before the altar were given seven trumpets symbolizing God's intervention into human history. The trumpet is used to alert, announce, or warn that an event is about to occur. The seven angels receive the trumpets. Instead, John sees another angel with the golden incense in his hand. He offers prayers for all saints as the smoke ascends to God. He takes a censer filled with fire from the altar and casts it on the earth.

God is about to move against humanity's evil on the earth. Only those who follow the anti-Christ and have his mark of the beasts (Rev. 9:4, 16:2) will receive God's wrath and judgment. The silence is broken. The unbelievers will be crying out day and night to escape God's justice and vindication. Jesus is going to cast out the antichrists and those who follow him. He judges those who ridiculed, mock, curse, abused, and committed actions like attacking, and striking his people, arresting, imprisoning, condemning, and killing his people. Heaven will sound the seventh trumpet against rebellious earth, and God will release unstoppable wrath on sinful man.

Verses 3-4

Another angel takes a golden censer (1st King 7:50) filled with incense, and he offers it with the prayers of the saints on the altar before God. The censor is mentioned in connection with the high priest (Lev. 16:12; Heb. 9:4). The prayers of the saints ascend into the very presence of God. When the angels poured incense on the altar, the cloud of fragrant smoke rose. A censor was filled with coal twice a day (Exod. 30: 7 – 9). The smoke would rise upward, symbolizing believers' prayers ascending to God. The prayers were for justice and deliverance (Rev. 6:10).

The angel acts merely as an agent presenting the prayers of the saints to God. We wonder if God hears our prayers, or they disappear forever. The Bible tells us that God answers the prayers of saints: Some prayers cannot be answered until the time is right:

1. God collects prayer during a prayer session, and they will be answered. Jesus receives our prayers and offers them to God, as we see in these verses.

2. God keeps the prayers of saints (Rev. 8:3).

3. God answers the prayers of the saints that are made in faith, trust, and entire dependence upon Him (Mark 9:23, 11:24, Matt. 17:20; 21:22; Jn. 14:12-15, James 1:4-8).

The prayers of the saints have power in the name of Jesus. We have family rights to use the name of Jesus in prayer (Jn. 14:13-16, 16:23-26; 1 Thess. 3:10, 5:7).

Verse 5

The angels take fire from the altar, mix it with the suffering saint's prayers, and throw it on the earth. The prayers for vindication, justice, fire is mixed. Why? The justice of God is about to fall on the earth. There will be voices, thundering, earthquakes, and judgment on the earth never witnessed before.

The prayers that will be accepted in heaven produced a significant change upon the earth. Who is this angel? Some Bible scholars believe the angel is Jesus because he is the only word to receive the prayers of the saints (Rev. 5:8). The same angel takes his censor filled with the fire from the altar and casts it upon the earth, symbolizing the prayers of the saints being answered. God is about to act and answer:

1. We have an increase in violent thunderstorms with their thundering and lightning.

2. We have an increase in earthquakes.

3. The Great Tribulation is now being launched (Ps. 19:9, 96: 13, Mk. 6:11).

4. God is going to execute judgment (Jude 14, Roman 1:18).

Verse 6

The angels sound their trumpet for judgments. They blow one after the other as they take their turn proving successive events. The message of the trumpet is one of continuous hardship and suffering. The trumpet blast has three purposes:

1. To warn that judgment is inevitable.

2. To announce the return of Jesus Christ.

3. To call the forces of good and evil to battle.

Verse 7

Some scholars believe these verses suggest a symbolic interpretation of four and three. Many believe four the world and mark God's creative works: On the 4th day, God finished his work on the heavens and the earth (Gen. 1:14 – 19):

1. We have four divisions of humanity: nations, tribes, people, and tongues.

2. We have four directions or regions: north, south, east, and west.

3. We have four seasons: spring, summer, fall, and winter.

4. There are four kingdoms: animals, minerals, vegetables, and spiritual.

The first four trumpets bring devastation to the world, God's creation. The last three are aimed at humanity as a rebellious hardened people. The first angel sound is sounded, and destruction coming upon the specific area of nature. The calamities that follow are related to the plagues suffered in Egypt when Pharaoh refused to let God's people go (Exod. 9: 23 – 25). The first trumpet blast and judgment begin, and the ecosystem is impacted. The university laws of nature will be swaying with violent disturbances (Rev. 6: 12 – 14). Cosmic disturbances will create chaos on the earth, weather more violent than ever before. Hail looks like fire mingled with blood; fierce windstorms never seen by man will devastate one-third of the vegetation (grass and trees). The ability to plant will be interrupted by the lack of seeds creating a shortage of food. Desert land will be the result of the destruction of trees.

The oxygen levels will drop, and the quality of breathable air will suffer greatly. We will have a tremendous geological, ecological, and economic disaster. Fruit-producing trees will be destroyed. Hail as large as a boulder will fall from the skies and mingling with lava from volcanic eruptions will create cataclysmic events. Water will be contaminated as it will have the appearance of blood.

God's wrath falls upon the earth and burns up one-third of nature, all the trees on the earth, and wheat along with all the grass. The grass is used for grazing livestock.

The first judgment reflects the seventh Egyptian plague of thunder, hail, and lightings (Ex.9:13-26, Ps.105:32). The presence of blood is somewhat of a mystery; "Rome wants blood: God will rain it down until its people drown in it (Blount)." Smalley suggests the "blood" links the vision with the first plague upon Egypt, where the river Nile turns to blood. Blood will fall from the skies, and the seas will be turned to blood. I think God is sending humanity a clear message. Man has rejected the blood of Jesus as the sole means of salvation. God places the blood before their eyes as a constant reminder that nothing, but the blood of Jesus can wash away to stains of sin! Each judgment represents the spiritual concepts and the wrath of God:

1. Hail comes from above and naturally speaks of the source and the suddenness (Isa. 28:2).

2. Fire speaks of the consuming character of God's wrath.

3. These judgments consume and destroy the meaning and purpose of life on earth.

4. Blood is naturally descriptive of death. It only reminds humanity that the wages of sin are death and that the judgments will kill them.


Verses 8 -9

The second trumpet blast causes a third of the sea to be destroyed. Some scholars suggest this refers to a falling meteor or asteroid that looks like a giant torch. It will impact the ecology of the sea, creating destructive waves. As for the image of flying mountains, if the Revelation was written after the eruption of Mount Vesuvius in AD 79, we may well have an allusion to this catastrophic event. Pliny writes that the debris from the explosion filled the bay, making it impossible to land boats.

It is a great burning mountain that is seen falling into the sea. One-third of the sea life is contaminated and becomes blood. One-third of marine life dies, and one-third of all human ships are destroyed. One-third of living creatures will be destroyed. One-third of the sea is contaminated with the dead, rotting bodies of marine life. The results of the death and chemical composition of the meteorite turn the water into blood. It would also trigger massive tidal waves that would sink great number of ships. Their rusting hulks will choke shipping lanes and hinder the movements of men and materials.

The Bible has examples of plagues, storm, hailstorms, and volcanic explosion resemble what is coming when the second angel blew the trumpet:

1. the storm upon the enemy of Joshua and Israel (Josh. 10:11).

2. biblical hailstorms (Ps. 18:13, Isa. 28:2, Ezek. 13:11, Rev. 8:7)

3. the plagues upon Egypt by Moses (Exod. 9: 23 -24)

I believe John is alluding to the sea. Usually, as a reference to the sea that was prominent to the land of Palestine was the Mediterranean Sea. What appeared to John is a superb burning meteor that falls into the Mediterranean Sea, killing one-third of the sea creatures and destroying one-third of all ships.

The world sea trade will be interrupted. It brings panic, major natural problems, oil spills, waste disposal gas, chemical, toxic, and waste. There will be a shortage of sea life for food, the devastation of the fishing industries and businesses, the interruption of shipping commerce and trade. The financial loss and food supply will be crippled worldwide:

1. The destruction of fish will be like the plague upon Egypt (Exod. 7: 20 – 21, Hosea 4:1 – 3).

2. Destruction from the blast of the second trumpet will be forceful as an atomic explosion. Note these facts:

3. The explosion will be so forceful that the mass of the rock flying upward is so large that it looks like a great mountain.

4. The explosive mass will still be ablaze when it hits the earth.

5. The explosive mass will be cast into one of the seas. One-third of that sea will turn blood-red.

6. One-third of the sea life of that sea will be destroyed.

7. One-third of the ships in that ocean will be destroyed.

The world is coming to an end. It is time for people to repent. The judgment of God will be the worst to come. Nothing can save humanity but the blood of Jesus. It can wash away the stains of sin, and humanity has rejected Jesus!

Verses 10-11

Upon the third trumpet blast sound, John saw a great star fall from Heaven burning as if it was a lamp or torch exploding like giant meteors before they hit the earth, scattering over one-third of the world. Particles fall into the rivers and springs, affecting the water supply. It poisons the water and gives it a bitter taste, and many will die from drinking the water. The agent of destruction is a star/planet named after the bitter herb wormwood, so a third of freshwater becomes bitter and undrinkable (Jer. 9:15, 23:15). The image of bitterness in the Old Testament is linked to divine wrath and judgment, often associated with idolatry (Prov.5:3-4, Lam. 3:15, 19, Amos 5:7, 6:12, Hos. 10:4). The star is called Wormwood. Jeremiah speaks of the time of this judgment (Jer. 9:15). It is incredibly bitter and used in beverage manufacture and is more destructive and intoxicating to the body than alcohol. The results affect all the inland water. A third of the waters become wormwoods (a bitter taste), and men die from the bitter water. Wormwood is used in Scripture:

1. It becomes a symbol of idolatry because of its bitterness. Idolatry is a bitter taste for God to swallow (Jer. 9: 13 – 15).

2. Symbolizes the way people dismiss and treat God with disdain (Deut. 29:18, Jer. 23:15, Amos 5:6 – 7).

3. They are used to symbolize the bitterness that an immoral person brings into one's life (Prov. 5: 3 – 5).

Freshwater now gets the same treatment as saltwater, this time by a flaming star. All the rivers and springs are destroyed, whereas only a third of the rivers are destroyed. One-third of freshwaters are poisoned, and many die from drinking the tainted waters. What does it do?

1. Create thirst among people.

2. Create a shortage of fresh water.

3. Cause panic because of thirst.

4. Create mobilization of emergency aid needed to get water up to one-third of the earth.

5. Generate sheer terror, fright, and agony burning in the people's minds because of these three judgments.

Judgment will fall on the ungodly and the evil of the earth because they have abused, mocked, cursed, beaten, imprisoned, and killed the followers of Jesus Christ. God can only change bitter water to sweet water (Exod. 15:23-25). It will not be too late for unbelievers to repent.

The blast of the third trumpet will launch an astronomical eclipse (Joel 2: 10, Amos 8: 9). God strikes one-third of the light-bearing bodies of the universe, which hinders their light-giving capacity somehow. These events become evidence of God's sovereign control of the universe (Matt. 24: 29).

The cosmic judgment follows, affecting the light produced by the sun, moon, and stars. God is going to block out light from shining and allow darkness. The world's darkness is viewed as a sign of divine judgment. Light has always been the science of God's wisdom (1 Cor. 2: 6 – 13), his understanding (Ps. 119:130), and his word (Ps. 119: 105). Darkness indicates that man is living in a bad light, foreshadowing utter darkness and loss of the presence of God. Three things will happen:

1. One-third of the day will be blackened out, and likewise, the night.
2. There will be no light whatsoever for one-third of the day and night; the moon will be eclipsed for one-third of each night.
3. The day cycle is changed from 24 hours to 16-hours.

The picture is that God has had enough. He is ready to end the world and send Christ back to earth to establish righteousness upon the earth forever. God is using the force of nature as an instrument of judgment:

1. This judgment will be like the plague of darkness cast upon Egypt and Moses (Exod. 10: 21 – 23).

2. One such astronomical event has already happened in the seal judgments (Rev. 6: 12 – 14).

3. The Scriptures predict such an astronomical event of the latter days (Joel 2: 10, Amos 8:9).

4. Jesus Christ predicted such astronomical events for the latter-day (Lk. 21: 25 – 28).

Verses 12-13

When the fourth trumpet sounds, God controls the affairs of heaven and earth. The earth is plunged into darkness. God touches the planetary heavens because humanity had worshiped the sun, moon, and stars. Astrologers and fortunetellers rely on the plants and sun to predict the future. God demonstrates his superiority and sovereignty over His creation (Lk. 21:25-26). However, the results are the same, and the earth is plunged into darkness. The weather patterns, plant life, and temperatures will affect humanity's physical and emotional health. The growing seasons will be affected. It will be a time for people to repent.

God will be behind the event, striking fear in the ungodly and evil of this world. God will have two purposes: to lead men to repent and judgment if they refuse. The judgment of God worse is coming.

From the beginning, everything God made for man was for his good. He had plenty of trees, grass, water, food, and oxygen to breathe. Humanity has taken God's creation for granted and become progressively worse because of sin and evil. He was put out of the Garden of Eden. Throughout humanity's history, he has taken God's grace and mercy for granted. Now comes the Tribulation; God will be judged humanity for refusal to bow and acknowledge His Lordship. The weather patterns, plant life, and temperatures during the Tribulation will affect humanity's physical and emotional health.

Verses 12-13

The first four trumpets signify natural calamities God used against those who oppressed His people. The purpose of the judgments warns people and gives them time to repent before God's full wrath is poured out (Rev. 16: 1 – 21). These are minor judgments designed to serve as trumpets of warnings, giving opportunities to repent and turn to God. The misery would surpass anything unbelievers had encountered.

We now come to an interlude between the first four and the fifth trumpet. An angel cries out, "Woe! Woe! Wow," to those who dwell on the earth. The woes will be upon the inhabitants of the earth, those who refuse to hear the solemn warnings from Heaven. The angel is used as a sign of swift approaching judgment in the Old Testament (Jer.48:40, Hab.1:8). We are reminded of Jesus proclaiming "Woe" on the people of Israel for failing to respond to the signs of the gospel revealed in his miracles (Matt. 11:20-21). The same woe hangs over the Church, as it does over the whole of humanity, for failing to repent in the face of coming judgment.

The angel flies across the sky, giving an extraordinary warning. The idea is that it soars in height, right at the zenith of the noonday sun. Why? So that all can see and hear his voice cry out threefold woes on the ungodly and the earth. We have a symbolic language, stressing the strength, swiftness, certainty of judgments. The angel becomes a symbol of vengeance. He flies through the sky, pronouncing, "Woe, woe, woe to the inhabitants of the earth" (Rev. 8:13):

1. Plagues of demons come out of the abyss to torment men for five months (Rev. 9:1 – 12).

2. The plagues of demons come out of the abyss to slay a third of men on earth (Rev. 9:13 – 21).

3. Satan let loose on the earth to destroy men for 3 ½ years (Rev. 11: 14 – 13, 18).

Thank God for the Lamb. Amid the Tribulation, He sounds the alarm through God's written word, through ministers, by a man of conscience, and by the signs of times that God still loves, saves, and delivers. Perfect justice is going to be executed upon the ungodly and evil. They are to reap what they have sown. It is the beginning of a great tribulation that is coming up on the earth. Remember, God loves that all can repent and still be saved, no matter how ungodly a life he has lived.

Things are going to worsen. It is an excellent time to be saved. You will rejoice that you will miss these events, and if you are not saved, woe unto you. These things will happen in the future, and you may be here when they happen (Joel 1:15-2:11).

Humanity possesses nuclear power to destroy the world, but some of humanity may escape. Humanity will not escape the judgment of God. The best thing for unbelievers today is to be saved by His grace and be ready to meet Jesus when He comes so they can avoid tragedies.

# CHAPTER 9

## *The Fifth And Sixth Trumpet Woe*

---

Revelation 9 unbelievers must face God's judgments upon the earth never witnessed before. Chapter 9, the fifth trumpet sound of Apollyon, the Destroyer, was released. No wonder heaven was silent for half an hour. So, the seven angels who had the seven trumpets prepared themselves to sound. The seven angels sounded their trumpet one by one, and each trumpet is associated with a significant event. Therefore, all Heaven kept silent. Heaven knew what the seven trumpets meant. For instance, the seven trumpets will release the locusts from the bottomless pit. Demons are unleashed to attack the people on earth and torment them because they have chosen Satan. They had teeth like a lion, armor made of iron, and sound like chariots rushing into battle (Joel 1:6, 2:5).

Chapter 9 records the fifth and sixth trumpet judgments. Ironically, many people have not accepted Jesus Christ as their Savior. John draws us into this reality of choosing sides. The earth's environment has been shattered, and humanity is writhing from the awful judgments of God. The angel knows that the woes unleashed at the sounding of the fifth and sixth trumpets will be horrible as anything already witnessed.

In Chapter 9, God offers a graphic description of the last three judgments. He also offers grace and mercy to:

1. The Church is encouraged, no harm from the judgments.

2. He extends a warning to those who continue in sin and reject Jesus Christ.

3. The Church is motivated to share the truth of the Gospel with the lost. We live in a day when humanity does not believe in Hell as presented in the Bible. People joke about Hell. Eternity in Hell is not going to be pleasant.

Verses 1 and 2

When the fifth angel sounded the trumpet, the first woe begins. John sees a star that has fallen from Heaven. An angel had a key to open the bottomless pit. Smoke rose, and locusts come out of the smoke. They stink humanity like scorpions (those who do not have the seal of God on their foreheads). They are not given the power to kill but the power to torment humanity for five months. Humanity will seek death but be unable to find it.

Who is this star? The word *star* is used in is a symbolic way to refer to a person of fame or high position. The fallen star or Angel is Satan himself who has come down from Heaven to fulfill God's purpose and who unleashes the judgment on the world. Isaiah 14:12 tells us, "His name is "Lucifer." The name "Lucifer" means "Brilliant star; Light-bearer or Shining one." Satan is going around the earth devouring whom he can. God allows Satan to open this pit to release his demons and afflict the world. Presently, Jesus Christ has given him the key to the bottomless pit to afflict a world of evil men. God restrains and limits his destruction (Matt. 8: 29, Lk. 8:31, Rev. 1: 18; 3:7, Rev. 20: 11 – 15).

Job 1:6-12 tells us, "He still has access to the presence of God where he accuses the brethren. He is the "prince of the power of the air," cast out of Heaven and forced to confine his activities to the earth (Eph. 2:2). Note some facts about the devil or Satan:

1. He is said to be a star fallen from Heaven to earth. It means that he was already fallen when God gave him the key to the bottomless. The abyss will be where the Antichrist and his demon will come (Rev. 12:4, 9; Isa. 14:12; Lk. 10:18).

2. Satan falls from Heaven (Lk. 10:18).

3. He was the highest archangel created by God. He looked upon himself and chose his way. God did what he does to anyone who rebels against him: God had to cast Satan of Heaven out of his holy presence (Isa. 14:12-17; Eze. 28:11-19).

4. He is given the key to the bottomless pit, the abyss–the place where Scriptures say demons and the devil are kept (Rev. 20:1).

5. Satan is roaming His kingdom (the earth) (Job 2:2, 1 Pet. 5:8).

Satan's problem was pride, and he was cast out of Heaven. It is humanity's worst problem. He wanted to be God (Isa. 14:12-17; Eze. 28:11-19). Pride will cause one to think highly of oneself. It will cause you to refuse to bow to God. It causes one to walk in their self-righteousness. God says, "If you humble yourself under His mighty hand, He will lift you, (1 Pet. 5:6); but if you exalt yourself, He will bring you down (Lk. 14:11)." Pride goeth before destruction, and a haughty spirit before a fall (Pro. 16:18). It will take you to Hell. Believers are to humble themselves under the mighty hand of God (1 Pet. 5:6).

Satan still has access to the presence of God, where he accuses the brethren (Job 1:6-12; 2:1-7). He is the "prince of the power of the air" (Eph. 2:2). Satan is cast out of Heaven and forced to confine his activities to the earth. Humanity's enemy in this world is Satan. Jesus Christ delivers us from his grip (Jn. 8: 44; Jn. 12: 31; Eph. 2:2; Col. 2:15, 1 Pet. 5:8; 1 Jn. 3:8).

We are living in a day when the subject of Hell is viewed with much skepticism. People do not believe Hell is a place of torment. Many preachers and church members reject the notion of Hell, as it is presented in the Bible. People joke about Hell and use the word as a byword in everyday language. Hell is a real place! Real people are going to endure torment for eternity in a place called Hell. In these verses, Hell will visit the earth in the last days.

Presently, Jesus Christ has the key to the bottomless pit, but he gives Satan time to afflict humanity with his demons. Why? So that the world of evil men can reap what they have sown. God restrains and limits his destruction (Matt. 8: 29; Lk. 8:31; Rev. 1: 18; 3:7, 20: 11 – 15).

Verse 2

The abyss is a bottomless pit where demons are kept until the end of the world. John reveals this in his visit to Heaven when he is asked to come up here. Hell is a horrible place prepared for horrible people:

1. The word "*bottomless*" refers to "the *abyss*"—like a bottomless well. Satan is given a key to open the pit that leads into Hell itself (Lk. 8:26-31, Rom. 10:7).

2. It is a dark place where smoke ascends out of this pit and obliterates the sun's light. When the smoke clears, wired creatures appear locusts with the power to sting like scorpions.

3. Hell is a place where unbelievers will receive (Lk. 16:19-31; Rev. 14:10-11; 2 Thess. 1:8-9) anguish and torment. It is a place where nonbelievers will go by choosing not to accept Jesus.

4. It is a place where people will go unless they are saved.

5. It is a place where evil spirits and demons of Satan live. It is also where Satan and his angels will be bound and spent eternity in Hell after their work.

Many jokes about Hell and try to pass it off as silly superstition. God desires all men to be saved and come to the knowledge of Jesus Christ (1 Tim. 2:4). The saved will not go to Hell if you accept Jesus as your Savior. Many deny it; lost humanity denies it; human reason denies it, but Hell has a place. The souls of lost people will suffer in the fires of Hell at end times. The believers will escape the wrath to come.

When the fallen angel opens the bottomless pit, smoke arises, and evil spirits and demons are released. The smoke in the atmosphere became so heavy and thick that the sun was darkened. Out of the smoke will come locust-like demons from the abyss. They will be sent to afflict punishment upon the ungodly. Humanity will seek every way they can to escape; no pills, no potions, alcohol, or drugs will deaden the pain. What will happen to the ungodly and evil?

1. The underworld will attack them whom the Lamb does not save.

2. They will have the breath of life suffocated out of them.

3. They will experience horror after horror arising from the bottomless pit (Rev. 9: 1 – 3, 11; 11: 7-8; 20:1-2).

Why are these demons called locusts? Because locusts symbolize God's anger against the ungodly and evil of the world (Exod. 10:13, Joel 1:4). In the Old Testament, locusts symbolized destruction because they destroyed grass, trees, and crops (Duet. 28:42; 1st King 8:37; Ps. 78:46). Note eight facts about the locust:

1. The locusts will come out of Hell and be given scorpion-like tails to strike their victims. They will inject a poisonous fluid into the victim—it is not a fatal wound, but it will cause terrible pain but not death.

2. They are "reserved unto judgment" (2nd Pet. 2:4) and released to carry out their mission.

3. They will be restrained from damaging nature (grass, vegetation, trees). They are not earthly locusts, for locusts feed upon visitation.

4. They only agonize people who do not have the seal of God on their foreheads. God's people will be protected from suffering the judgment cast upon the ungodly and evil of the world. Many believers will be afflicted and die by the hands of the Antichrist, but the judgment of God will touch not a single believer (Rev. 7:2 –3; 8:13).

5. They attack people who do not believe in God to torment and not kill. They will sweep the earth. They may seem cruel, but we must always keep in mind what is happening: the ungodly and evil will be punished.

6. The locusts will torment millions. A torment equal to their faith. The torment is to last for five months. The pain inflicted upon humanity will tormenting, stinging, causing pain and suffering. There will be no escape! The idea is a continuous attack, even during this time. God will show mercy and give humanity a chance to repent (verse 20 – 21). As always, most will refuse.

7. People will suffer so much pain that they will beg for death (verse 6). They will not die. They wish to die but do not have the courage to go ahead and take their own lives. Men will pursue death and not be able to die any method they attempt to use.

8. The afflicted will be unable to gather the courage to kill themselves.

9. Death will be out of their reach to escape God's judgment. They will suffer.

10. Five months of agonizing pain. Five months is the typical lifespan of a locust (Rev. 9:6).

Verses 3-6

In Ezekiel 9:4, God commanded that the foreheads of the faithful be marked. Likewise, the Book of Revelation tells that 144,000 of God's servants will be marked with a seal on their foreheads (7:3). The seal will protect them from the torture that will be inflicted on the unfaithful (9:4). They would also be permitted to stand on Mount Zion with the Lamb and sing a new song (14:1-3).

The locusts are told not to hurt the grass, plants, and trees but attack the unbelievers (Rev. 9:4). We have a role reversal of locusts that destroy nature (grass, plants, and trees). God is going to use them for inflicting torment and suffering on humanity.

Verses 7-10

John gives descriptions of this demonic locust army:

1. They look like mighty horses prepared to battle, poised and ready to attack (Joel 2:4).

2. They have golden crowns on their heads—They come to the earth as conquerors symbolizing authority to afflict men. No medicine or act of science will conquer them.

3. Their faces are like men; this speaks of their intelligence, symbolizing the determination and intelligence of men.

4. Their hair is like a woman's—they are attractive and have some seductive charm.

5. Their teeth are like a lion's, and when they bite, they will cause an infectious wound to slow to heal. The bite of a lion causes infection, and bacteria in the wound rarely heal completely (Joel 1:6).

6. They will have breastplates of iron for protection. Humanity will not have the ability to kill these demons.

7. They will have wings that sound like chariots—which symbolize the ability to move with swiftness. Humanity will not be able to escape (Joel 2:4-5).

8. They will have stings in their tails and be ready to inflict pain.

9. They have a king over them who organizes and unites them in their attacks upon humanity. His name is "*Destroyer.*" Abaddon is the

Hebrew form of that word. Apollyon is the Greek form (Job 26:5-6, 28:22).

10. This demonic invasion will target all humanity.

Verses 11-12

Four things describe the king of the locusts:

1. He is an angel, a creature of immense beauty and strength.

2. He is the angel of the bottomless pit, a fallen angel whose home was in Heaven, and a servant of God. He is the fallen angel of the underworld of sin and evil, all ungodliness and unrighteousness (Rev. 9:11).

3. He is the King, the ruler, and the governor, of the bottomless pit.

4. His name means *Destroy*er, a powerful demon, and a commander in the hierarchy of demons. It is not Satan himself.

The first three woes have passed, but there are two more to come. Woes always refer to coming judgment and are also translated as destruction. Though carried out by demonic powers, these events are divine judgments. The two woes to come had a twofold purpose:

1. To warn non-Christians who refused to believe in God and his Son Jesus that they will be punished.

2. Time to repent and turn to Christ.

3. To renew hope in believers.

Verses 13-16

The four fallen angels are set loose that were bound at the great river Euphrates on the world, and terrible death and destruction follow. Four facts are given about there being loosed:

1. They are set loose by a command on the golden altar (Rev. 6: 9 – 10; 8:3-4). The golden altar is where the martyred souls were waiting for God's punishment to be executed on the enemies who had to kill them.

2. God launches judgment to vindicate the millions whom the Antichrist will slaughter during the Tribulation. He hears these prayers and executes justice against those who mocked, rejected, denied, disbelieved, disobeyed, and cursed the Creator.

These prayers cause God to release His vengeance in woes against nonbelievers. (8:10). The last two woes included:

1. The four angels have high military rank in Satan's Army of demonic horse riders of mounted troops numbering two hundred million ready for this period. God has already fixed the time for this judgment—the exact year, month, day, and the hour of the judgment.

2. In this woe, a third of humanity will be killed by God's great judgment. An army of this would be unbelievable on John's Day.

3. The head or spring of the Euphrates River flows out of the Garden of Eden. The world's great cultural, religious, and political systems came to life along the banks of this great river.

4. Here Satan first tempted to overthrow man. Sin, the first murder, and the first apostasy against God occurred here.

The first thing that resulted in the fallen human race occurred at the head of the Euphrates River:

1. The first murder took place, and the first organized rebellion against God took place.

2. Assyrians and the Babylonians carry Israel into slavery.

3. The deadly torment of locusts and plagues will not match the torment of this army, but some inhabitants of the earth will remain unrepentant (9:21). God is working out his plan.

4. They prepare to execute judgment on earth because humanity had given their total allegiance and support to the antichrist and his government's policies.

John showed that the four demonic angels would be released, and one-third of humanity will die. Humanity laughs at the facts because they do not believe demons exist. Believers are entangled in daily spiritual battles (Eph. 6:12). The reality of end times' spiritual battles will be made fundamental to humanity.

Verses 17-19

As described in Revelation, this King will lead a massive army numbering over 200 million soldiers. Today we have China with an army of this size. He will come from the East with a military superpower that neither fears nor respects the U.S. The Bible's word for "east" means "the sun rising," lets us know that it describes China. Many nations will take part. The ultimate conquest will be warfare against God. It will be a tumultuous time of wars, disasters, and divine judgment. God has it all under control (Ps. 2:2–6). The army will be:

1. An army of 200 million demonic spirits let loose upon the earth. Some have suggested that this is the human (Rev. 16:12) led by "the kings from the east". The Red Chinese Army could raise such a fighting force. No reference is made to the size of the Army led by the kings of the East (Rev. 16:12).

2. The riders will have breastplates fiery red, sapphire blue, and sulfur (brimstone) yellow to show who is identified with the army. The breastplate signifies that they will be indestructible, protected, and defended as they go to war against the ungodly of the world. Man will not be able to stop them.

3. The horses will be horrible and will create terror on the ungodly.

4. They will have he is like lions: ferocious, fierce, devouring, cruel, and consuming.

5. They will have mouths that spit out the fire: a brutal and fiery nature, vengeful and angry, and the destruction will have a wrathful nature (Rev. 14: 10, 19:20, 21:8).

6. The army will kill one-third of the ungodly and evil upon the earth. How? By the plague of fire, smoke, and brimstone. Weapons used are not given and observed how fire, smoke, and brimstone sound like an atomic explosion. Remember, all will be executed under God's judgment.

7. The power is in the rider's mouths, heads, and tails. The head symbolizes intelligence, the mouth symbolizes deceptive speech and a hunger to consume and destroy, and the serpent-like tails symbolize deadly strikes and wounds.

John sees the vision as the terrible times of destruction, death, and demonic activity that will happen. I praise the Lord not to be here when these events come to pass.

Verses 20-21

What is the purpose of the judgment? God wants to bring people to repentance. They will have a chance to turn from their evil ways and deeds, but they will continue to turn away from God. Many will continue to worship demons and idols. Several significant points are now made:

1. Two-thirds of the population will survive, not because they deserve to survive because God is merciful. God is merciful amid judgment. He speaks to them through judgment, but they will not repent.

2. There will be an increase in the gross sins—murder, witchcraft, immorality, and thefts will continue the worship of evil spirits (1

Cor. 10: 20, 1 Jn. 5:21, Rev. 9: 20, Exod. 20:4, Ps. 106: 36 – 39, Exod. 20:15, and Eph. 4:28, Titus 2:10.).

3. The antichrists will have worldwide support from humanity.

4. There will be an increase in the sin of sorcery. Sorcery includes all kinds of witchcraft, the use of drugs, or evil spirits to gain control over the lives of humanity. Sorcery includes astrology, palm reading, seances, fortune-telling, crystals, and other forms of witchcraft (1 Chron. 10:13, Isa. 8: 19 – 10, Mic. 5:12).

5. There will be an increase in immorality: premarital sex and adultery; it is abnormal sex, all kinds of sexual vice (Gal. 5:20, 1Cor. 6:18, Eph. 5:3, Col. 3:5).

The Tribulation will be a time marked by intense religious activity. Involvement with begins with entertainment, enlightenment, and enslavement. Humanity will be given choices to accept Jesus or the devil. They become trapped in an occult system and are unable to get free. Humanity will also worship Satan, making idols of gold, silver, brass, precious stone, and wood. Humanity will make idols gods that they will bow down to and worship: money, car, home, and materials possessions. He will love and adore these things. They are not a god who can see, hear, or move to help you. Humanity will turn to worship idol gods like those of ancient Israel (Psa. 115:1-8; Jer. 10:3-6). Amid trouble, plagues, disasters, and judgments, humanity will not continue to worship Jesus Christ. The reward will be a continued headlong plunge into the fires of Hell.

John let us know the day is coming. God has made a way for escape. What is that way? Casting your burden upon Jesus Christ and believe in your heart that He is the Savior of the world, you shall be saved (Heb. 2:3, Jer. 11:11, Amos 5: 18 – 19). Come to Jesus right now; the altar is open. It becomes the responsibility of humanity to come to Jesus Christ. Heaven is your home. No one will be left behind if they acknowledge Jesus, confess their sins, and get saved. They will avoid the horrible judgment to come.

# CHAPTER 10

## *The Seventh Trumpet or Third Woe*

---

God's wrath is poured out on an evil world, and He begins to make a righteous world during the Tribulation. Seven angels blow seven trumpets, releasing God's judgment on humanity. John reaches a point of discouragement. God encourages John to continue recording His works of wrath and judgment. John sees another mighty angel coming down from heaven robed in a cloud, with a rainbow above his head, his face is like the sun, and his legs are like fiery pillars (Rev. 10:1). The world has cut Jesus, the Son, out of the picture, and they have replaced Him with the faulty institutions on humanity. The result has been chaos.

Chapter 10 introduces the reader to the middle of the tribulation period, an interlude between the sixth and seventh seals. Jesus is back on center stage. Before the final storm, what is about to happen is announcing the final triumph—the seventh trumpet. God has chosen to explain but reveal His judgment upon evil and protect his own. Humanity cries out. Is there no hope? Is the Earth doomed? Is it to be a dead planet?

Verse 1

John sees a mighty angel come down and make a grand announcement to the earth. He will perform any specific mission having to do with the completion of God's plan. We are given the identity of the Angel. John sees who came down:

1. He comes down from heaven. He comes from the presence of God cloth in a deity. He is clothed with a cloud, crowned with the rainbow, and His face glows like the sun. His feet are like pillars of fire. He comes from the throne of God itself to announce the final judgment on the earth (Acts 1:8-11, Exod.19:9, 40:34, Nah. 1:3, Rev. 10:1).

2. He is clothed with a cloud which symbolizes a majestic, glorious, and heavenly appearance. The announcement is coming from the majestic and glory of heaven. Clouds indicate the unapproachableness of God toward sin, but He draws near to earth to offer mercy to the lost.

3. A rainbow is upon his head, which symbolizes God's glory and mercy (Ezek. 1:28). It is a sign of divine mercy amid divine judgment (Gen. 9:8-17).

4. God's mercy is shown to Noah (Gen. 9: 12 – 13).

5. The messenger has a face that shines like the sun (Rev. 1:16), symbolizes luster, brightness, brilliance, and splendor (Matt. 17:2). John sees the countenance of Jesus (Re. 1:16).

6. His feet are like pillars of fire which symbolize God's holiness, purity, righteousness, and strength (Exod. 14:20). The word "*pillars*" represents firmness, stability, and strength (Rev. 1:15), and is a metaphor for those who bear responsibility in the churches.

7. His glory is seen like columns of fire indicative of holiness and consuming power reflecting the glory of Christ.

8. He is holding a little book in his hand that is open. The little book is the message that must be proclaimed to the world, the message of Revelation.

9. The messenger stands with one foot on the land and one on the sea, which symbolizes the messenger's gigantic size, strength, and power. He is claiming both sea and land, the whole world for God. This message involves the whole universe (Ps. 24:1).

10. He has a voice that roared like a lion which symbolizes the voice of the lion of Judah, Christ himself (Rev. 5:5, Joel 3:16, Hosea 11:10).

11. The messenger calls forth with several thundering voices, which symbolize completeness, fulfillment, and finality. Thundering symbolizes the power and strength of God's voice.

Verse 2

The mighty Angel holds a book or small scroll that he had unrolled in his hands. The contents of the scroll are not indicated, but it contains a Revelation judgment. The messenger is Jesus Christ because he is worthy of opening the book and lose the seals (Rev. 5:5-7). The book is now open in the messenger's hands, the Mighty Angel who claims to take back land and the sea (Rev. 5:11-13). I believe the Angel is the same in Revelation 7:2, 8:13, and 10:1 is the Lord Jesus Christ.

Verses 3-4

When the Angel cries out with a lion-like voice, seven thunders uttered their voices (Ps. 29). Thunder represents the voice of the Lord in judgment (1 Sam. 7:10, Ps. 18:13) and is the voice of Lion of the Tribe of Judah. A roaring lion strikes fear in the bravest heart. An adult male lion's roar can be heard as far as five miles away. He usually roars just after sunset. They do so to proclaim a place in their territory. That is what we see in these verses. The Lord is staking His claim, and He is saying, "I am the Lion of the Tribe of Judah and keep your hands off what belongs to me!" The thunders are announcing the Lord's vengeance upon His enemies who at the time inhabit the earth (Joel 3:16, Rev. 14:14-20).

John is commanded to seal these things and forbidden not to write them down because the message had to do with God's indescribable judgments when He released them. The judgments were too severe. God has used some judgments throughout the Bible, including blood, tears, famine, heartaches and heartbreak, killing, misery, hail, fire, burning mountains, demon monstrosities, men begging to die and unable to do so. God has some things that He wants to keep concealed for the time being (Dan. 12:4). Sometimes the human mind cannot comprehend God. Paul says, "For now we see through a glass, darkly; but then face to face: now I know in part; but then shall I know even as also I am known" (1 Cor. 13:12). Trust the Lord to do right (Gen. 18:25; Rom. 8:28; 2 Cor 4:17).

To escape the judgment of God, you must be born again, receive his salvation, and you want to be on earth when the judgments are unleashed. The salvation of Jesus Christ notes what will happen to you (Jn. 1:11 – 12, Rom. 10:9 – 10, 10:13, 17, Eph. 2:8 – 9, 1 Jn. 1:9). When the voices utter that sound of thunder, you will be with Jesus.

Verses 5-7

The mighty Angel swears by God that there will be no delay when the seven angels sound his trumpet. God is going to release his judgment on humanity. He will bring about the end of human history. God will bring his plan concerning the earth under the authority of Christ everything in heaven and on earth (Eph. 1:9 – 10). All prophecies will be fulfilled. The time of final judgment has come. Satan will meet his final confrontation (Dan. 12:1). God's final plan is to remove all evil. The oath and announcement made are that time shall be no more. When the seven trumpet sounds, it blasts in the last events of human history that will take place against the ungodly and evil of the world will end for the last time. Governments, races, nations, and the Church had their chance. God has put up with humanity's insults. The time to receive God's wrath is about to take place. No further delay. Time does not end; it is not the beginning of eternal ages.

The only peace will come during the Millennium but is yet to come at the appointed moment. There will be no Millennium until Satan is chained forever (Rev. 20:1-3, 10). The oath and announcement must be heard by humanity. When the seventh trumpet sounds, the ungodly and evil of the world judgment is about to fall:

1. The antichrists are going to turn against the world.
2. The Lord God will destroy both the antichrists and his followers and the ungodly and evil upon the earth.
3. The kingdom of Jesus Christ will be established. His righteousness upon the earth and reign for 1000 years.
4. A new heaven and earth will be created to last forever.

The seventh trumpet will bring forth the last events of human history, finalizing the mystery of God. Jesus will create a new heaven and earth that will last forever (Roman 8: 18 – 22, but second Pete 3: 10 – 13, Rev. 21: 1-5, Isa. 65:17).

The devil is up to bat right now, but God is coming to the plate one of these days. There will be no more opportunities for the devil to score. Gabriel is going to blow his trumpet, and Jesus will return for His Church. Then, God will judge the earth, sin and the devil will be bound in eternity.

Why does God let Satan have his way? That is God's business. The business of the saints is to fear God and keep commandments: this is the whole duty of man (Eccles. 12:13, Roman 8:28). God has a plan, program, and it is on schedule. God has put up with sin and Satan long enough (Rev. 14:15). Evil will be punished, the devil cast into the pit, and Jesus reigns forever (Isa. 9: 6-7). Today, Christians know what will happen, and we must act upon it to escape God's wrath (verses 8-11).

Verses 8-11

John is commanded to take the book, which is open out of the hands of the Mighty Angel. The word of God is never handed to us. It is never forced on us. We must accept the message of the word. We are commanded to study the word to show thyself approved as a worker who need not be ashamed (Acts 17:11, 20: 32, 2 Tim. 2: 15, 3:16,1st Pet. 2: 2-3).

John is commanded to eat the book. "To eat" means John is to make the thing incorporate into one 's being. There is something special about this book! It was sweet in his mouth but bitter in his soul. Nothing is sweeter than the grace, mercy, and redemption for the saints. God's word is food for the hungry soul. It is a balm for the hurting soul. It is meat for the growing soul. If we are to be all that God wants us to be, we can grow strong in the things of the Lord. We must get into the Bible, for ourselves, every day! Are you feeding in the green pastures of this Word as you should? Remember, the word of God is sweet as honey (Ezek. 3:1, 3).

There is bitterness in the message of God's wrath: suffering, heartache, lamentations, woes, and judgments upon the unbelievers. There is bitterness in the judgment message that God's messengers deliver. Why? The book tells us about the horrible suffering of a Hell that awaits all the lost (Ezek. 3:1, 3). The Spirit of God will convict the hearts of sinners to be saved or receive God's judgment, wrath, and damnation (Eph. 2:8, Rom. 10:17, 1 Pet. 1:23). It is a bitter book when it refers to the judgment of God.

Eating is a picture of learning and assimilating the word of God (Ezek. 2: 9 – 10; 3:1 – 4). The Bible is spiritual food. Jesus said, "Man shall not live by bread alone, but by every word that proceedeth out of the mouth of God" (Matt. 4:4, Jn. 1:1, 14, 6:63). Jeremiah said, "Thy words were found, and I did eat them; and thy word was unto me the joy and rejoicing of mine heart: for I am called by thy name, O LORD God of hosts" (Jer. 15:16). Job said, "I have esteemed the words of his mouth more than my necessary food" (Job 23:12). Pet. said, "As newborn babes, desire the sincere milk of the word, that ye may grow thereby" (1 Pet. 1:22). The message of grace and mercy is sweet.

The word of God is sweet because the Church will triumph in the end, but it will be sour because the Church will face a terrible time of persecution. It also references the judgments (bitter) that are coming and salvation (sweetness) that are also coming. When you see the worldly conditions, the word of God is sweet to a lost soul. The word is sweet when we know the wage of sin is death. The word of God is sweet when we pass from death unto life (Jn. 5:24).

The book contains prophetic truth and Revelation from God that can be a blessing or unpleasant. What does this mean? The word of God contains:

1. sin and forgiveness

2. death and life

3. judgment and salvation

4. damnation and deliverance

5. heaviness is and joy

6. hell, and heaven

7. bondage and freedom

8. destruction and a new world

9. corruption and perfection

The mighty Angel, so massive that he straddles the whole earth with one foot upon the sea and the other foot upon the earth, lifts his hand toward heaven and wraps the significant announcement and most solemn oaths in verse one. He swears by God himself and declares the last events of human history.

When John saw the message's truth, he was told to prophesy to a world that had turned away from God. He must share the message with others. The same burden has been placed on the shoulders of believers today. We are to take the Bible with its blessings and burdens and share its message with a lost and dying world (Matt. 28:19-20; Mark 16:15). We are not to share God's Word for our benefit but with the world to tell the lost that "Jesus saves, believe on Him." You will have everlasting life. Do you need to be saved? Do you need faith in Jesus Christ? By grace, ye saved through faith (Eph. 2:8, Roman 10:17, 1 Pet. 1:23). Do you need to commit to reading your Bible and sharing the message of Jesus? If there are needs, the altar is open.

# CHAPTER 11

## *The Two Witnesses*

---

In Chapter 10, an Angel lays claim to the earth as God's representative. God's plan is moving to completeness. God instructed us to eat the scroll, which symbolized the sweetness and bitterness of God's word and encouraged us to keep proclaiming God's message.

Two prophets, or witnesses, arrived and gave additional messages from God. The Beast entered and began his evil attacks. God is about to take the earth back. He created it and for Him (Ps. 24). It had been under Satan's control since creation. Adam disobeyed God's command, losing dominion over the earth and creation. Jesus is preparing the way to regain the earth, create a new kingdom, and destroy the dominion of Satan forever.

Jesus is returning to the earth, whether you believe it or not. He is coming soon. Unbelievers need to prepare to leave this world (Lk. 21:28-32) and go to the new Heaven and earth.

John continues to share the heavenly vision with events related to the future of the world. The final triumph of evil over the great destruction of Israel and Jerusalem will come to an end. The mighty Angel shows John:

1. Rebuilding of the Temple in Jerusalem.

2. The Gentiles destroy the Temple at Jerusalem.

3. It ties in with the prophecy of our Lord and Scripture about the end times and the Antichrist.

4. It covers the great salvation of Israel and the coming kingdom of God. It gives a glimpse of how God will conquer evil and set up His kingdom.

5. Show pictures of the things that are yet to come in the Book of Revelation.

When we get to Chapter 11, John is instructed to measure the temple as the yardstick. Measuring is a sign of ownership. God measures what belongs to him. Two witnesses appear and announce God's judgment, and the Antichrist kills the witnesses, and God brings them back to life. John called them "witnesses" in Verse 3 and "prophets" in verse 10. They represent:

1. the law and the prophets

2. the old and New Testament

3. the words of God and the blood of Christ

4. they may represent the Church

5. martyrs who give their life of Christ

6. the divisions of the Church

7. Israel and the Church

8. Abraham's and Israelites (two nations descended from Abraham).

The seventh Angel blows the seventh trumpet. The events it not recorded until we get to Rev 15. Revelation 11 describes the last three and half years of the Great Tribulation. The Gentile will make their last stand to defeat God's plan and purpose for humanity's restoration from the Antichrist. The captivity began under Nebuchadnezzar (2 Chr. 36:1-7).

When Jesus comes in power, He will destroy the Antichrist and his armies (Rev. 19:11-21). John tells us, "Then I saw a new heaven and a new earth, for the first heaven and the first earth had passed away, and there was no longer any sea." (Rev. 21:1). With the Rapture of the Church, the unrighteous will be judged.

Verse 1

John is given a reed and asked to measure the temple of God, the altar, and those who worship therein. He is asked by the court outside the Temple to not measure, for it is given to the Gentiles. The reed was an instrument used in taking measurements and was ten feet long. He is not to measure the courts without the temple; this section is given to the Gentiles. The word rod can measure a place for destruction and punishment of correction and chastening (2nd Samuel 7: 14; 8:2; 2nd Kings 21:13; Ps. 2:9, Isa. 34:11, Lamentations 2:8).

John is letting us know that a new temple will be built in Jerusalem prescribed in the Law of Moses. The Temple of God John sees in his vision is the Jewish Temple.

David wanted to build the first Temple, and God appeared to Nathan, and in a vision (2 Sam. 7:13-17), explained the reason for His refusal for David to build the Temple. Solomon is the son of David. He is commanded to build the first Temple (1 Kings 6:1). It took seven years to complete the building of the Temple (1 Kings 6:38.) When it was finished, it was dedicated to the Lord with a great sacrifice. 1 Kings 8:63 says that twenty-two thousand oxen and one hundred twenty thousand sheep were offered to the Lord at the Temple dedication. The Ark of the Covenant was brought from the Tabernacle into the Temple. God demonstrated His approval of this house of worship by filling it with His Shekinah glory (2 Chron. 7:1-3).

The Temple building dominated the Jerusalem skyline until the Babylonian King Nebuchadnezzar destroyed it, and the Jews were taken into captivity in Babylon in 538 BC. Some could return to Jerusalem, and in 490 BC, the Temple was rebuilt by Zerubbabel. The Bible tells us five temples are mentioned:

1. Solomon's Temple (1 Kgs. 7; Ezra 3: 12).

2. Herod's Temple (Jn. 2: 20). Titus destroyed it in 70 AD.

3. The Temple of the Tribulation (2 Thess. 2:4; Rev. 11: 2).

4. The Temple of the millennium, the Temple of our Lord (Acts 15:16; Ezek. 40 through 43).

The Jews contest that this is sacred because they believe this is where Solomon's Temple was built. The original site of King Solomon's temple has been replaced by a new Temple (the Mosque of Omar, or the Dome of the Rock). The Arabs and Muslims believe that Mohammad ascended into Heaven from this rock, conferred with Moses, and returned to earth with the prayers that all Muslims should pray. They believe that all prayers ascend to Heaven through Jerusalem. So, they write their prayers on paper and stuff them in the cracks of the wall. Jews from around the world can e-mail their prayers to Jerusalem. These prayers are printed and taken to the Wailing Wall. It is the most contested ground in the world. The Arabs and Muslims goal are the annihilate Israel.

The Jews had a specific place to worship within the Temple. Currently, the Jews have no Temple, but that will change soon when Christ returns. It will be built in Jerusalem after the rapture of the Church. It will be a time of complete restoration of God's people (Jews). It will then be called the Holy City. What is the Holy City? Jerusalem is the Holy City (Neh. 11:1-18, Isa. 52:1, Dan. 9:24). The believers have no specific place of worship, but the Jews could not worship without the temple. Christians have no temple because the spirit of God is in them (Jn. 4: 21 – 24; Heb. 10:19 – 22, 1 Cor. 6:19, 2 Cor 6:16).

John becomes the leading actor. He is instructed to take the rod and measure the Temple, the altar, and the worshipers (Ezek. 40:3, Zech. 1:16):

1. The Temple, the altar, and the worshipers focus on the Jews and their place in the Great Tribulation.

2. The Temple, the altar, and the worshipers are symbolic and refer to faithful Israel, the Church, consisting of all believers in Christ.

The Temple and its worshipers will be saved, preserved, and not destroyed by the Antichrist (2nd Thess. 2:4). It is not a new temple; it will come down when the old Heaven and earth are replaced with the new (Rev. 21). God marks the true Jewish worshippers for protection and preservation. It is difficult to say that these things are not real things but symbols. God is telling John to measure the Temple for judgment and correction. They are as guilty as most others in rebelling against God: rejected him, disbelieving him, cursing him, neglecting him, denying him, disobeying him, ignoring him, and blaspheming him. Many Jews will be broken, and many by the thousands will be saved. Many are marked for judgment until this happened, just as all unbelievers (Matt. 7:21; 15: 8 – 9, 1Tim. 2:5, Heb. 8:6, 9: 2 9: 15 4; 12:24).

Verse 2

The Jewish Temple was divided into four courts, all surrounding a central building or Shrine called the holy place, all holy of holies. The courts moving out of the way from the holy place were:

1. Where the priests were where the altar of the burnt offering stood.

2. The courts of Israel or the Jewish men.

3. The inner court was for the Jews.

No Gentile was ever allowed within these court barriers. Surrounding these courts for Jewish worshippers was a huge outer court, the court of the Gentiles. Why were these courts not measured for judgment? Because they were already under the Antichrist and his government. True Jewish worshippers and Christian believers would have a problem contacting other people worldwide who have strong faith. The Antichrist will attack the nonbelievers with a vengeance never seen in the history of the world. It has already begun (2 Thess. 2:4, Rev. 13:1, Matt. 24: 15, Dan. 11: 40 – 45; 12:7).

Luke 21:24 prophesies that the Gentile will tread the Holy City until "the time of the Gentiles" is fulfilled. The period of forty-two months is the conclusion of "the time of the Gentile." Forty-two months or three and a half years will be the last part of the Great Tribulation. It is mentioned in Revelation 11:3 and 12:6 as 1260 days (Isa. 10:6). The Holy City will tread under foot for forty and two months, three and one-half years, the last half of Daniel's seventieth week (1260 days). The Gentiles will trample the people in Jerusalem for 1260 days (Isa. 10:6). Peter refers to this as the people being trampled (1 Pet. 2:5). Bible prophecies are always months of thirty days each The Antichrist will launch his terrible persecutions upon the world:

1. There will be the time the Holy City will be oppressed (Rev. 11:2).

2. The two witnesses will testify God to Israel and the world for 1260 days (Rev. 11:13).

3. The time and the Woman in the wilderness will be preserved for 1260 days (Rev. 12:6, 14).

4. The courts of the Temple in Jerusalem will be the trampling underfoot or destruction of Gentiles for three and a half years.

5. The time when the Beast will be allowed to blaspheme God for 42 months will be the conclusion of "the times of the Gentiles in keeping with the prophecy of Daniel" (Dan. 7:25, Rev. 13:5).

Christ and Daniel agree, "The abomination of desolation (the Antichrist) will launch the worst Tribulation the world has ever known" (Matt. 24: 15, 21, Rev. 9:3-11). It is called the beginning of sorrows (Matt. 24:8); the trials after the abomination of desolation are called the Great Tribulation, unparalleled in history (Matt. 24: 21). Daniel also gives a division of the time Jesus Christ does (Dan. 9: 27). He is also dealing with the end times just as Christ was:

1.  Christ was dealing with the end of Jerusalem and the end of the world.
2.  The fact that Christ said he was elaborating on Daniel's prophecy. This points to three and half years of great satanic power globally—a period known as the Great Tribulation.

God shows that He is building walls of protection around his people to spare them from spiritual and physical harm during the Tribulation (Rev. 13:7). The Temple will be a place of safety reserved for those who remain faithful to God while the Antichrist and the Gentile nation trod Jerusalem under their foot (Rev. 11: 2). The times of the Gentiles will end at the climax of human history when Jesus Christ returns in great glory and power and destroys the Antichrist and his governments and his followers (Rev. 19:11-21, Lk. 21:24). God will stop the judgment and have mercy upon those who turn to him for mercy (Hab. 3:2). It is the beginning of the takeover of Jesus rightfully regaining heir to His kingdom (Roman chapters 9 – 10).

God wants the temple and the Jewish people measured for judgment and correction; in the last days, they must be judged along with everyone else because of their unbelief, denial, rejection, and blasphemy against God's Son, Jesus Christ. They will worship under the old covenant, not recognizing the fact that Jesus is the Lamb who has come and shed His precious blood once for all to save the souls of humanity. They continue looking for a Messiah to come and save them. He has already been here. Jesus has shed His blood. He has paid for sin and will save those who call on Him by faith.

Scripture says that the Antichrist will walk into the temple and demand that the world give their first loyalty to him and the state. Jesus said that the Antichrist would stand in the holy place of the Jews (their temple) and make this proclamation. We also look at the fact that many were religious claim Jerusalem as one the centers of their religion—Judaism, Islam, and Christianity. Jerusalem is a good place for the Antichrist to launch his attempt to wipe out Christian believers (Matt. 24 15. 2nd Thess. 2:3 – 4). The Scriptures clearly say that the Antichrist is going to appear. Therefore, God will judge them just as he will judge all the ungodly and evil of the world. The Jews will be trodden underfoot by the Antichrist just as so many others will be.

Verse 3

God's people will suffer under the Antichrist, and he is going to give the two witnesses 1260 days with astonishing power. Who are the two witnesses? Some say that the two witnesses are persons and identify them as Enoch and Elijah, or Elijah and Moses sent back to the earth. The description of the two witnesses leaves their identity unknown. Bible scholars suggest that it might be Elijah and Moses because the two witnesses will resemble the miracles of these prophets.

Elijah represented the prophets, called fire down from Heaven, and stopped the rain for three years (second Kings 1: 10 – 14). Moses represented the law, turned the rivers and oceans into the blood, and sent plagues upon Egypt (Exod. 7 – 11). They appear with Christ in the Transfiguration (Matt. 17:1 – 7).

Some believe it is Elijah because Malachi 3:1 identified he would come again. Matthew 17:7-14 teaches us that Elijah had come back, and John the Baptist was Elijah. John denied that he was Elijah. It does not mean these two men came back from the dead. In the end times, they minister to Israel in the spirit of Elijah, Moses, Enoch, and John the Baptist would be significant to the Jews. They are not the two witnesses. Their identity is not revealed.

The two witnesses have a dual nature the law and prophet's division. Therefore, the lampstands represent the Old Covenant and the New Testament Church. The olive trees represent the law and the prophets. The lampstands attached to the olive trees are like the branches attached to the olive tree, an arrangement found in Revelation (Rom. 11:17 – 24, Jn. 15:1-8).

The two witnesses prophesied about Jesus Christ for a period when humanity rejected the word of God and will not find it for 1260 days (Amos 8:11 – 14). The following vision we are given is of two special witnesses. God sends two witnesses from Heaven as ambassadors to preach the Gospel message to the people in Jerusalem.

The two witnesses turn Israel back to God. Despite the Jews' unbelief and rebellion against God's Son as the Messiah. God still loves the Jews. He loves them for Abraham, Jacob, David, Paul, Pet., and the believer's sake. God is going to turn Israel. God is going to save Israel. God is going to save Israel and the two great witnesses. These two witnesses' messages will claim the salvation that is in the Lord Jesus Christ.

They are God's witnesses sent by Him. God commissions and empowers them (verses 3 – 4). They are raised only for the Tribulation period of history (Rev. 11:2):

1. They will be sent forth as true prophets who condemn sin and proclaim salvation in Christ Jesus. They will be dressed in sackcloth worn by the prophets of old. Because of this message, they are assassinated in the city where the Lord was crucified (verses 7 – 10). They are resurrected by God's breath and vindicated (verses 11-12).

2. They are clothed in sackcloth, a symbol of evil, calamity, and judgment. Sackcloth is *"sakkos"* referring to a dark cloth, often made of goat's hair and worn like a sack. It expressed mourning, repentance, and judgment.

Verse 4

The lampstands mentioned in Revelation 1:20 are the seven churches, but in this verse 4, they are as candlesticks. It becomes apparent that the lampstands in the Bible are symbolism used to represent the churches. The olive trees feed the Church (or churches) with olive oil. The lampstand converts the olive oil into light. The Church should continually feed upon the words of God to bring teaching to the churches. The Holy Spirit serves to bring understanding to the word of God should be viewed. The olive trees represent the inspired messengers who bring the word to the Church like Moses, David, Paul, and other witnesses.

The two witnesses are symbolically called "two olive trees and the two lampstands" Zachariah 4:1-14). The Jewish law requires two witnesses concerning law, religion, or dealing with a neighbor (Duet. 17:6, 19:15). Two angels were found in the tomb on the morning of Jesus's resurrection (Jn. 20:12). The seventy disciples of Jesus were sent out two by two (Lk. 10:1). God sends out his two witnesses, and they prophesy for 1260 days.

In Jeremiah 11, we see that both houses of Israel are called a "green olive tree". They were planted and named by *Yah* the Father Himself. We can be sure from Scripture that both the House of Judah and the House of Israel are symbolically labeled as olive trees. The lampstands here depict seven *ekklesiai,* the seven Asian churches (Rev. 1:11). The Greek noun *ekklesia* is the most common word used for Church, and it means "an assembly of called-out ones". The Greek word for Church is first found in Matthew 16:18 when Christ promised to give His power to the Church. Christ promised was of a singular Church.

In the Book of Revelation, we can see that a lampstand represents a called-out group of people, the House of Judah, and the House of Israel, who were first called out of Egypt together to be God's people. The two olive trees represent Zerubbabel and Joshua, the governor and high priest. At the end of this age, they will be called out once more to witness against the people of this earth when they forsake God and worship the Antichrist.

Scriptures make it clear that the wearing of sackcloth is a sign of mourning (Isa. 22:12, Jer. 6:26, Lamentations 2:10). These two witnesses are clothed in sackcloth because they are officially in mourning for humanity.

Verse 5

These two men will be killed, but not before they deliver the Gospel message. If anyone tries to kill them, fire flashes from their mouth and consumes their enemies because these men are under divine protection. They will kill everyone who tries to kill them. They will deliver God's message of repentance and will have the power to destroy their attackers with fire. Like Jesus, they will not be killed until they complete their assignment (Jn. 7:30). The Antichrist will not kill the two witnesses until they deliver the message of preaching Jesus Christ in the city of Jerusalem.

Verse 6

John describes the two witnesses. God sends the two witnesses to speak to the nation of Israel for spiritual and physical deliverance. They are called to prophesize in times of trouble. The Jews will be back in their homeland, and the temple will be rebuilt. The Beast will blaspheme God and all that is holy. They will have supernatural power, and the Beast will demonstrate like power (Rev. 13). When the two witnesses are here, Heaven and Hell will lock horns in the last great conflict. God's two witnesses will be able to use miraculous signs to prove the authenticity of their message. They will be able to shut up the heavens as Elijah did. It did not rain for three and half years, meaning 1260 days. They will be able to turn rivers and water that are left to blood and smite the earth with every plague they desire from Heaven as Moses did. They will have immense supernatural power to display that they come from God. The devastation already occurred in the early chapters: seals, trumpets alarms, plagues, earthquakes, and the suffering of those left on the earth. The two witnesses called on the people to turn to God and Jesus Christ for the world's last hope and be saved from judgment for their rejection of Jesus Christ.

The two witnesses represent spiritual and physical deliverance for the nation of Israel. They are prophets of encouragement bringing a message to Israel doing persecution. They also bring a message of discouragement to those who attempted to destroy Israel. They will speak, and miracles will happen:

1. Heaven will shut up, and no rain will fall for three years.

2. They speak, and rivers will turn to blood.

3. Plagues of sores and diseases will appear.

4. They will bring a prayer of supernaturalism from Heaven and the underworld.

5. When the seven angels sounded, the evil of the earth swiftly ends.

Verse 7

At the end of the appointed time, the two witnesses finished their testimony; they are persecuted and martyred. The spirit of the devil himself comes from the bottomless pit of Hell (Rev. 11:7; 13: 1 – 10, Matt. 24:15, 2nd Thess. 2: 4 – 9). The Antichrist will discredit the witnesses. After three and half years, when they finished their testimony, God will allow the Antichrist to go out and hush their testimony and successively assassinate them. Their death is not the end of their testimony.

Who is this Beast or Antichrist? Daniel describes the Beast as a "little horn" waging war against the holy people and defeating them (Dan. 7:8-27). John used the term to describe an opponent of Christ (1 Jn. 2:18, 22, 4:3). His goal is to terrorize believers (Mark 13:14). He will be a man of lawlessness who seeks to dethrone God and lead his people to destruction.

The Beast will be a man of evil who gains control of the world, forces people to worship him, establishes Babylon's wicked kingdom, and persecute those who opposed him (Rev. 13:16-17). He will be dictator or world leader of the Day (Rev. 13:11). He will be a world dictator who is head of the revived Roman empire and ten-nation confederation or a governmental system he will rule over. Some men have attempted to gain control of the world: Nero, Stalin, and Hitler failed.

The assassination of the two witnesses shows that their message has been compelling. The world will hate them, and the Antichrist will leave their bodies lying in the streets of Jerusalem for three days (Rev. 11: 9 – 10). The fact that he will not allow them burial is an outrage of common decency and humanity. The idea is for the whole world is to witness the scene on the media and television. Gifts will be rendered to them, but this will be a political payoff from the Antichrist.

The two witnesses ascend into Heaven. Four dramatic events will take place in Jerusalem:

1. Great earthquakes have shaken the city (Matt. 27:51, 28:2). God will shake the city again with a great earthquake.

2. A tenth of the city of Jerusalem will be destroyed.

3. Thousands of people will be killed.

4. The remaining population in the city will be terrified.

At end times, this describes the spiritual condition of Jerusalem:

1. An immoral city, and shameful sinful, a city that will reject the messages of God (Gen. 19: 4f).

2. A nation that is under the influence of the Antichrist and kills God's people (Exod. 1:7f).

Who is the Antichrist? He is a man of sin, a false leader, and a teacher (1 Jn. 2:22). He stands in opposition to Christ and persecutes believers. Evil men have been used by the Antichrist – the Neros, Hitlers, and the Stalins of human history. They were dictators of the world. Millions were killed signifying the name of the beasts. Scripture calls the Antichrist:

1. He is the abomination of desolation prophesied about Christ (Matt. 24:15).

2. He is the man of sin prophesied by Paul (2 Thess. 2: 3 – 4).

3. He is the little horn prophesied by Daniel (Dan. 7:25).

4. He is Satan himself, a man of lawlessness who comes out of the bottomless pit of Hell itself (Dan. 7:3, 7: 7 – 8, Rev. 17:8).

5. He is the world ruler who will make war against God and slaughter them (Dan. 7: 20 – 21, 25).

6. He is the world ruler who will conquer the world (Dan. 7:23, Rev. 17:12 – 13).

The Beast is the champion of every course of evil in the universe, which is opposed to God. The Beast that ascends out of Hell (abyss) itself is letting us know that he is demonically charged and controlled to kill the two witnesses. He will make war against the witnesses and kill them. Jesus Christ is the champion of God. Jesus Christ is the incarnation of God and goodness and will avenge the two witnesses.

The Antichrist is a dictator who comes into the modern world and breaks down the world systems as we know it now. He will be induced with the power of Satan and will claim God's entitlements. Assisting him will be the false prophet who will do the works in the dictator's name (Rev. 13:13 – 15, 19:20). He will come when there is a breakdown when there are financial and political disasters. He will claim to bring world peace, but he will be a counterfeit to Jesus Christ. He will draw people away from Jesus to worship him and the state. The spirit of the antichrist is now being taught in the institutions of humanity.

Verses 8-10

When the two witnesses finish their prophecy ministry, they are killed by the Beast and are left lying in the streets. It is where Jesus was crucified, the city of Jerusalem. This great city will become enemy territory, a place of immorality and persecution of God's people at end times.

According to the Old Testament law, the bodies of the two witnesses are left in the streets for three days and refused by the people a decent burial. Criminals were offered a decent burial the same day of the execution (Duet. 21:22, 23). The Beast celebrates after three and half days by mocking the two witnesses. There are victory parties, gifts are exchanged, and the whole city and world is expressing relief and joy.

It is a day of praise. The two witnesses are killed. It is a celebration of victory, but it is short-lived. God's program is about to regain its course of victory and judgment. On that day, we can imagine that the cable news channels like Fox News, CNN, MSNBC will broadcast the death of the two witnesses worldwide. The rebellious hearts of men against God are present again. (Ps. 2:1-6). These men have been preaching the message of judgment and condemnation that will come because they rejected Jesus Christ as savior. The world rejoices because the two witnesses are dead, and God's message is silent.

Satan has made the world blind to God's judgment; they think the two witnesses are dead and they can enjoy peace without Christ. The world continues to rejoice when the Gospel preaching is finally silenced. Many loves preaching that exalts the flesh and makes them shout, leaving the Church feeling good and not transform spiritually (Rom 12:1-2). They like to be entertained. The world hates preaching that exalts Christ and demands holiness. The world hates preaching that stands on Biblical principles. The world cannot stand preaching that sinner should repent of their sins and turn to Jesus by faith. We live in a world that hates preaching that magnifies Jesus as the only way to get to God. The message of the two witnesses will cause some people to turn to God. Many people will rejoice as children of perdition and head to Hell. Judgment is going to get worse as we approach the end of time. The triumph of the wicked has been brief (Job 20:5, Ps. 37:35, 36, Heb. 9:27-28).

Verses 11-13

After the death of the two witnesses, a miracle happens. John sees that God suddenly resurrects them. They stand to their feet and the world trembles in fear. After being dead for three days, they are alive again—it proves that they are from Heaven and men of God. The message of judgment and repentance is genuine. Jesus died and remained in the grave for three days, and the two witnesses are resurrected after three and a half days. The two witnesses will ascend to Heaven in a cloud (Rev. 11:12). One day believers, in a split-second, in the twinkling of an eye, will meet the Lord in the clouds (1 Cor. 15:52, 1 Thess. 4:17). The Antichrist will copy this resurrection (Rev. 13:3).

The men of God will receive vindication. God judges the city which has denied Christ. As the two witnesses begin their ascension, the third woe comes quickly, an earthquake will crumble the city to the ground, and seven thousand people will die. Many times, in Scripture God, send earthquakes (Matt. 27:51, Rev. 6:12, 16:18). A remnant of the Jews in Jerusalem becomes fearful and gives glory to God and asks for repentance. They see these events, repent of their sins, and call on Christ for salvation. God will use even these events to bring glory to His name!

Because of the mighty acts of God at the end times, the Jews will repent of their sins and give glory to God. Repentance means we get to the point that we ask God to forgive us of our sins and strive to be like Jesus Christ (Matt. 4:17, Acts 3:19, Rom. 2:5). What about you? Are you saved? If you want to escape the horrors of the Tribulation, accept Jesus as your savior and receive his mercy and blessings. You need to call on His name now, and Jesus will reach out to you and offer you eternal salvation. Let us ask Him right now. Lord, I believe you died at Calvary for my sins, and I accept you as my savior. In Jesus's name! Amen.

Verse 14

The first woe will be the demonic locusts like preaches swoop down and kill one-third of the earth's population (Rev. 9:1-12). The second woe will be demonic military horses-like creatures that kill one-third of the earth's ungodly and evil population (Rev. 9: 13-21, 11:1-13). The third woe, judgment, will bring the climax of human history and the end of times as we know it. Behold, the third woe comes quickly. God brings a quick end to humanity's wicked control of the earth without the use of bombs. God brings in earthquakes. God used earthquakes to bring destruction that has never been seen before (Rev. 6:12, 16:18).

Verse 15

The seventh trumpet judgment alerts are resume, and King Jesus is about to reclaim everything that belongs to Him. When the trumpet sounds, the ancient prophecies of Joel 2:1-2 will be revealed: the bowl judgments of God (Rev. 15:1).

John hears voices in Heaven saying, "The kingdom of this world has become the kingdom of Jesus Christ" (Rev. 11:15). The words "great voices" translate the Greek words "*mega*" and "*phonay.*" We get the word "*megaphone*" from these words. It refers to shouting and loud speech vigorous praise in glory (Rev. 11:15-16).

The scene turns to God and Jesus Christ ruling over the whole world. He is going to take back what belongs to Him (Ps. 24:1). He is about to sit on the throne of David in Jerusalem (Isa. 9:6-7, Lk. 1:3). All kingdoms of the world are done away with, and all people upon the earth live and work as citizens in God's kingdom. His kingdom will last forever. Presently, human governments involve:

1. Authority and rule and reign that are good and evil.
2. Laws that favor and that are unjust.
3. Unfavorable work to the citizenship.
4. A government that economy that is unhealthy for the citizens.
5. Protection: some earthly governments protect their citizens, abuse, or enslave them.
6. Provision: some governments provide for their citizens, and others do not.
7. Services: some earthly governments provide services for their people such as roads, sewage, water, jobs, and healthcare, or else they provide service.

All earthly kingdoms are imperfect, weak, and are unstable to bring utopia to humanity. They are flooded with the poor, hungry, homeless, sick, selfish, rich, proud, thieves, murderers, and evils and imperfections. They will focus upon pledges and possessions under the Antichrist. The glorious message of this world is that all kingdoms will become the kingdoms of God and Christ. He is going to bring Heaven to the earth. When?

During the millennium (1000 years), Jesus returns to the nations and people of the earth.

It will be a utopia on earth. It will be a physical and spiritual kingdom. The Church is safe with Jesus Christ, and all creation will be delivered from the curse of sin and evil. Peace and prosperity are coming. There will no longer be hunger, thirst, homelessness, diseases, war, murder, or any other evil upon the earth. Whatever is unfolding in Heaven will culminate on earth. Humanity has failed to establish a world of peace (Rev. 12:10,19: 6, 20: 4 – 6, Lk. 1: 32 – 33, Dan. 7: 13 – 14).

Verses 16-17

The twenty-four elders give praises to God. Praise. When they get a glimpse into the future, they praise him for four things. They praise God, calling him the Lord God Almighty:

1. He is Lord and Master, the ruler of all creation. He is the one who deserved to be worshipped.

2. He is omnipotent, all-powerful. He is and was, but no longer is to come because history has been fulfilled. Jesus comes as a tender Lamb the first time.

3. The second time He comes in great power and vengeance. He will roar out of Zion as the Lion of the Tribe of Judah (Joel 3:16, Rev. 5:1-7).

4. He is eternal.

5. They praise him for taking his great power back from Satan and reigning in his proper place. Man chose to follow Satan. But not all people. Some people did what God desired: freely chose to believe and follow him and love God supremely.

The twenty-four elders fell on their faces when Jesus took the seven-sealed book. The redeemed seniors of Heaven honor Jesus by offering Him their golden crowns. He was worthy of opening the book (Rev. 5). They knew that Satan is not destroyed, and the White Throne Judgment is on the way, and victory is yet to be won. The twenty-four elders witnessed the rule of God's righteousness upon the earth (Ps. 1:4-6, 24:10, 37:9-17, Lk. 1: 31 – 33, Rev. 15:3, 19:6, Exod. 15: 18).

The judgments of the seventh trumpet are the most intense and remarkable. Nothing can be compared to the witch's troubles in destruction among humanity when John heard of the seventh trumpet sound. God's manifestations upon the world are launched when the blast of the seventh trumpet sounded. The trumpet sounds in the ears of leaders, presidents, kings, and priests of the world. They are angry and will not be able to keep their throne, governments, and nations.

We will hear voices like many glasses of water, great thunder, harpers, and harps (Rev. 14:1-13). Heaven rejoices because God and His Son Jesus have taken possession of a world that was lost to sin and Satan thousands of years ago. Those who give their allegiance to Jesus Christ need never fear that He will be overthrown! He is and ever will be the King of Kings and Lord of Lords! He will never be defeated by any enemy (Heb. 2:8, Ps. 86:10).

I thank Jesus Christ that I will be in Heaven with the twenty-four elders to praise him one day. I thank Jesus Christ that I can praise Him today! He is King of kings and Lord of lords globally, but He is also the King of my heart (Rev. 19:16; Duet. 10:17; Ps. 136:3; Dan. 2:47).

Verse 18

Satan's final rebellion against God and will be destroyed and face the eternal judgment of God. The nations are angry. The time of God's wrath is upon the world's leaders, presidents, kings, and priests. The rulers, Antichrist, and his followers will plot against God and Jesus Christ. A great war will break out between God and Satan. All sin and unrighteousness will be removed. Note five points:

1. At the end of the millennium, the devil and his followers will try to defeat Christ and his followers to keep power upon earth. The results would be quick and catastrophic for the ungodly nations and people of the world (Rev. 20:7 – 10).

2. The wrath of God will fall on the ungodly (Jn. 3: 36, Rom. 1: 18, Eph. 5:6, Ps. 2:12).

3. The judge will be dead (Matt. 25: 31 – 32, 2nd Pet. 2:9, 3:7, 1 Jn. 4:17, Jude 14 – 15).

4. The godly will be rewarded: the believers, the prophets, and those who upheld God's name (Matt. 5: 11 – 12, 10: 42, 25: 23).

A final warning is given to the unbelievers, a warning of eternal doom:

1. A person who rebels against Jesus must face God as a rebel who stands opposed to God.

2. The wrath of God is going to fall against all who rebel against God.

3. The dead will face God. All the dead, every single person who has lived or ever will live—all shall stand face to face with God.

4. All who fear God's name will be significantly rewarded.

5. The ungodly and evil will be destroyed. All who destroy human life, their lives, or the lives of others, shall be destroyed.

The hatred of Jesus Christ in the world leads the unbelievers to eradicate his name from the community, schools, and public arena. Their hatred is expressed in attempts to maintain devilish principles. Jesus will have the final word (Ps. 2:4-9). He will have the final word, and all lost sinners will receive the due reward for their sins (Rom. 6:23). Again, the tragedy can be avoided if unbelievers accept Jesus as their savior and are saved! The invitation is always open and available. If you reject the invitation, you will open your eyes in Hell one day.

Verse 19

God's Temple will be reopened, and He will dwell in his temple (Rev. 21:2 – 22:5, Matt. 19: 23 – 24). At one time, Heaven and earth worship were close. Humanity will speak to him in perfect harmony and unity again. Jesus will restore heaven and earth union once again when His kingdom in Heaven comes on earth. The oneness will be restored (Rev. Chapters 21 and 22).

John sees a New Jerusalem come down from Heaven called the Holy City (Rev. 21). There is no need for the temple is a place of worship in Heaven. On earth, Jesus says, God is spirit: and they that worship him must worship him in spirit and truth (Jn. 4: 24). True worship is a matter of the heart.

When the temple of Heaven is open, John sees the art of covenant in the temple, which no ordinary person had ever seen inside, but it displays the glory of God fully. In the sacred casket, Israel had stored safety preserved under the safe hands of God. Now at the end of time, all promises are to be fulfilled. God's blessing went along with the treasure box or the sacred casket. Remember the Jordan River rolled back beneath, the enemies scattered when the Ark appeared, Jericho walls came tumbling down when they marched for seven days as the Ark was before them. The flashes of lightning, rumblings, peals of thunder, earthquakes, and a great hailstorm indicate God's signature on these events at the sounding of the seventh trumpet. They will appear again at the seven bowls event (Rev. 16:18-21).

The ark covenant reminds the people who have a special relationship with Him of God. It was the only visible throne of God on the earth (1 Sam. 3:3). This vision of the Ark reminds everyone that God is still on His throne! (Ps. 132:8). The Ark announces a solemn token of God's promise of presence and protection in the coming trails. Originally the covenant was with Israel, but the new covenant is with Jesus Christ with all nation who loves and believes in Jesus (Heb. 9:11-12, 10:19-20).

Whenever terror or destruction come, God will not break the covenant that he made with his people. It is a terrifying threat to the enemies of God but an uplifting promise to the people of God's covenant. Christ is our protection. He replaced the old covenant, nailing it to the cross (Col. 2:8-17).

Are you a part of that group that will be doomed and damned to Hell? If you are, you need to know that the wrath of God already abides on your life (Jn. 3:36; 3:18; Eph. 2:3; Rom. 1:18). You also need to know that you do not have to stay in that condition for another minute! Jesus will save you by His grace! He is calling you to come to Him. We are one heartbeat away from eternity. If you have come to where your soul is marked for Hell, accept Jesus Christ, and avert the tragedy!

# CHAPTER 12

## *The Woman and The Beast*

The middle of the Tribulation is a crucial unfolding of God's plan. John is making sure we gain knowledge about the major players and the key events that will take place. We begin this chapter with three primary characters: a woman with the child, the great red Dragon Satan, and the man child Jesus. John continues to see the unfolding of the future from the perspective of Heaven.

Revelation 12 introduced the vision of a woman clothed with the sun, moon, and stars (Rev. 12:1). The woman can be interpreted as Israel (Gen. 37:9). The faithful remnant of Israel is portrayed as God's virgin bride, is also contrast as an unfaithful prostitute. A rightful remnant is portrayed as giving birth to a child, symbolizing the future restoration of God's people (Isa. 66:7-10, Mic. 5:3). In Revelation, the woman's first child (Rev. 12:2-5) is often interpreted as Jesus and her "*offspring*" as Christian believers (Rev. 12:7). All descended of Adam was created to produce his kind (Gen. 1:26-28). In this sense we are the offspring of God. A familiar story of the conflict between the dragon and the woman would have been understood.

John saw this woman pregnant, and the child pictured being born in Verse 5 refers to Jesus Christ. He was born to rule all nations (Ps. 2:9). He alone was exalted to the throne of God. The mother is Israel as she cried out in labor pain as she gives birth to a man child whom Satan is ready to destroy. The woman not only suffers the pain of (Isa. 66:7).

Some scholars believe the man child cannot be Christ or the church because it is raptured out in Revelation 4:1 before the events of Revelation 4:22 which must be after the churches. The man child represents a company of all living people who we translated without sin and death.

The Hebrew word for *'pain'* encountered in this Scripture is commonly translated as *'torment'* or *'tormented'* in other verses. What are the differences between pain and torment? Torment is to cause severe suffering while pain is to hurt; to put to bodily uneasiness or anguish; to afflict with uneasy sensations of any degree of intensity. The pain we are suffering cannot be compared to the torment the unbelievers receive in Hell. They will go away into eternal punishment, but the righteous into eternal life (Matthew 25:46).

Verse 1

The symbolism we get from the 1,260 days binds the two witnesses and the woman's child and the dragon stories together. The woman is upon the earth. She represents Israel and the Church, the faithful people waiting for the Messiah (Isa. 9:6 – 7, Micah 5:2). In the Old Testament, the nation is pictured as the wife of God (Isa. 54:5 – 6, Jer. 3:6 – 8, 31:32). She is not identified, but John describes what he sees in the vision. Seven key figures describe the woman:

1. The woman is clothed with the sun, and the moon is on her feet; upon her head, she has a crown of twelve stars (Rev. 12:1).

2. The woman will birth a male child (Rev. 12:5 – 6).

3. Israel will birth the male child who is to rule with a rod of iron.

4. Israel will bring forth the Redeemer. John describes a child as born to rule the nations and have dominion over the earth.

Verse 2

The woman represents Israel, the very people who gave birth to Jesus Christ, the Son of God. The Church will reign with Him as He sits on the throne of David (Ps. 2). Three other women are mentioned in the book of Revelation:

1. Jezebel is representing the papal system (Rev. 2:20).

2. The woman we are now discussing is Israel, God's chosen people with earthly blessings.

3. The great harlot who corrupts the Church will be in power after the rapture of the true Church.

4. The Bride, the Lamb's wife, will be glorified in the city that John saw coming down from Heaven.

The woman will give birth to a male child who is destined to rule. The child is initially the nation of Israel, but the child is composed of the elect in the end time. Childbirth is a picture of the nation of Israel God used to bring His Savior into the world. Genesis 3:15 tells us, "And I will put enmity between thee and the woman, and between thy seed and her seed; it shall bruise thy head, and thou shalt bruise his heel." The woman is Israel, and the seed of the woman is the Lord Jesus. He is called both "the Son of David" and the "Son of Abraham." He will rule all nations with a rod of iron. The crown on the woman's head signifies dignity. The twelve stars speak of the twelve tribes of Israel's future glory.

Satan attempts to kill the child. Satan has always tried to kill Jesus (Gen. 3:15). Satan has left a trail of blood from Genesis to the cross to stop the woman's seed. Jesus has defeated all attempts. He paid the debt of sin with the shedding of his blood at Calvary's cross, conquered death, hell, and the grave. He is coming back again to bind Satan forever in the lake of fire.

Israel, not the Church, was the mother of Jesus Christ (Isa. 9:6, 66:7, Rom. 9:5, Jn. 4:22). The Church is the Bride of Christ. Israel is the mother of Christ, and the Church (Bride) is His wife. The false messiah is in power during the last three and half years of the Tribulation. He will attempt to destroy Jesus and His Bride.

The forces of evil angrily set out to destroy the woman and her other offspring. The woman (Israel) is granted special protection from the evil forces and is prevented from entirely wiping her out.

The child to be born is Jesus (Isa. 9:6, Micah 5:2, Rom. 9:5, Matt. 1, Jn. 4:22, and Isa. 66:7). She is in labor, and she brings forth this son with pain and suffering. Israel's pains and persecutions will suffer as Satan tried his best to short circuit the plan of God. When Jesus was born, the nation of Israel was writhing under the iron heel of the Roman Empire.

Verses 3-4

A red dragon appeared in Heaven, Satan. He is the devil. He is said to be a wonder or sign in Heaven. In his vision, John saw a red dragon with power over the world's kingdoms, signified by his seven heads, ten horns, and seven crowns (Rev. 12:3). His tail pulls down two-third of the stars of Heaven, and they cast them to the earth:

1. The stars are the angels who fell with Satan as he decided to over-throw God.

2. He has ten horns. They are instruments of destruction (Zech. 1:18 – 21) and are the number of evils.

The red Dragon represents the rider who will take peace from the earth. Red describes blazing heat and a bloody administration. He is represented by red because he has killed the saints of God. He is a murderer (Jn. 8:44). What are significant things about the red dragon? Scripture speaks of his evil work and appearance:

1. He is the highest and most glorious being ever created by God. He is so magnificent that he shines like the sun and possesses the glory just like God.

2. Satan has seven heads: seven represents the number of completeness and fullness. He is intelligent. He is not omnipotent, but his knowledge is complete. He will evilly use his head and authority over the nations he will control.

3. He has seven crowns, seven heads, and his ten horns (Dan. 7:7, Rev. 17:12) are not heavenly but symbolizing authority to rule the world.

4. The ten horns symbolize great power that pierces, rips, tears, and is ferocious and vicious.

5. Satan is the God of this world and he who blinds men's minds to follow (2 Cor. 4: 4).

6. He will be called the prince of this world (Jn. 12:31, 14:30, 16: 11).

7. He will be Prince of the power of the air (Eph. 2: 2).

8. He will be the king of a kingdom (Matt. 12:26, 4: 8 – 9).

9. He has his grip upon the whole world (1 Jn. 5:19).

Where will the red dragon come from, and where will he go?

1. His tail draws a third of Heaven's angels, and he is cast down to earth.

2. He draws, pulls, and drags a third of Heaven's stars (angels) with him.

3. He did cast them down long ago.

4. Satan has authority over one-third of the stars of angels of Heaven.

5. They were the stars of Heaven, but they were cast down from Heaven.

6. His name is Lucifer, which means star of the morning. He was a cherub who covered the throne of God itself. He was the angel put in charge of the glory of God's very own throne.

Satan began to look at himself and live as he wanted instead of like God wanted. He rebelled against God, and He was cast from his exalted position in Heaven. He became the archangel or enemy of God (Rev. 12:3-4,9, 2 Cor. 4:4, 1 Pet. 5:8).

Satan aimed to turn the hearts of the people away from God. He promised to send a seed into the world to crush the head and power of Satan (Gen. 3: 15, Rev. 12:4). He sends a Savior; Satan knew it and attempted to get rid of Jesus (Matt. 2:16). Satan appeared as the serpent who tempted Adam and Eve and led them to sin and hurt God. Satan's plan was and will be defeated because of God's love for humanity.

From the beginning, Satan tries to destroy God's plan, waging war against the seed, the Savior of the world, and God's promise to save the world. Satan has attempted to hurt God by doing all he can to devour Israel's line and keep the Savior from being born. Now that Christ has come, Satan does all he can to turn people away from judgment to come.

The war will wage on until the world ends. Satan will use all his resources to destroy the woman's seed, the followers of Jesus Christ. The Lord is not slow in keeping his promise, as some understand slowness. He is patient with you, not wanting anyone to perish, but everyone to come to repentance (2 Pet. 3:9).

Satan attempts to hurt God. Since Christ has come, Satan continues to do all he can to turn people away from God. It is a battle, a struggle that will continue until the world ends. Satan has twenty-one names and titles in the Bible. He is compared to:

1. A fowler (Ps. 91:3) who loves to entangle you and have you all tied up.
2. Fowls (Mathew 13:4,19) that snatch.
3. A wolf (Jn. 10:12) who creeps.
4. A thief (Jn. 10:10) that steals.
5. A serpent (Rev. 12:9; 20:3) that poisons.

6. A red dragon (Rev. 12:3-12) that drags with his tail.

W.A. Criswell traces some attempts of the devil to destroy God's plan for humanity's redemption. There was the line of Adam:

1. Satan led Cain to kill Adel, but God gave Adam another son, Seth (Gen. 4:1f).

2. Satan led humanity to sin, and both were cursed with wickedness that God had to destroy the earth.

3. He tried to corrupt the human bloodline by having the godly line of Seth intermarrying with the evil line of Cain. He did not know about Noah and the Ark. God raised Noah (Gen. 6:5f).

There is God's redemptive plan to create a line toward reinstating the original partnership beginning with Adam:

1. Next, there was the line Abraham, Isaac, and Jacob.

2. Satan led Esau to threaten to kill his brother, Jacob. God protected Jacob (Gen. 27:41f).

3. He did not know God would help Jacob escape.

There was the line of the children of Israel.

1. Satan tried to kill off the Jews in Egypt by having Pharaoh slay all the little boys. God would save a little boy named Moses who would lead the people out of Egypt (Exod. 1:8f).

2. Moses led the people to the Promised land. Moses people to lead the promised the and rearranged the ....

There was the line of David:

1. Satan led David's sons into sin and to murder, and they were disqualified. God always keeps at least one Son of David alive (2nd Samuel 13f).

2. Satan led Jehoram, one of Jehoshaphat's sons, to kill all his brothers. Sons were born to Jehoram later to carry on the line (2nd Kings 8:25f).

There was the line of Ahaziah:

1. Satan led Jehu to kill Ahaziah, and the queen's mother, Athaliah, took over the throne and killed all the sons. God led the wife of the high priest to save one tiny baby, Josh.

2. At this point, the line of the promised seed rested in the saving of a baby's life (2nd Kings 9:11 f).

There was a line of the chosen people:

1. Satan-related king Ahasuerus exterminated all of God's people. God gave him a restless and frightening night of sleep. The king, therefore, spent the chosen line (Esther).

There was a line of the promised seed, Jesus himself, at his birth:

1. Satan had worked from the beginning of time to prevent the birth of the Promised Seed of the woman. He intended to destroy the seed of the woman as soon as He is born.

2. Satan tempted Jesus to secure his loyalty and worship. Jesus rebuked Satan's will (Matt. 4:1f).

3. There was a line of the promised seed, Jesus himself.

4. Satan led the citizens of Nazareth to try to cast Jesus off the cliff of a hill, but Jesus escaped (Lk. 4:29).

5. Satan led the religionists to hate Jesus and plot his death repeatedly (Jn. 7:1). Jesus escaped time and again.

6. He failed in every attempt to stop the birth of Christ. When the time came for Jesus to enter the world, Satan did everything in his power to slay the Christ child when He was an infant. He moved Herod to destroy all the babies in Bethlehem under two years (Matt. 2:16-18). God warned Joseph and told Joseph to flee with the child (Matt. 2:1f).

7. Satan led the world to put Jesus on the cross and to kill him. God raised Jesus from the dead (Jn. 19:1).

8. Satan is a murderer, roaring lion, causes unrest and unhappiness, causes every tear that falls, energizes evil, and God destroys the body and soul (Jn. 8:44, 1 Pet. 5:8, Prov. 13:15, James 1:13 – 16, Rev. 7:17).

Verse 5

The woman gives birth to a boy. His name is Jesus. He will be born to rule all nations and rule *with a rod or iron scepter with no rebellion* (Ps. 2:9). The word "*rod*" refers to a shepherd's staff. Jesus will be not only be King over all the nations but also their Shepherd. It will be used to "destroy" what they strike, to break like smashing pottery. The Lord will strike the nations with the rod in meting out the fierceness and wrath of God to those that have it coming. He will use the rod of punishment to destroy the wicked. A time will come when the lion lays down with the Lamb as well as the wolf. It will not be like anything we have ever known or seen. The future rule of Jesus would be without any opposition.

Moses and Aaron used a rod against the Pharaoh to bring the destructive plagues upon Egypt. He also used it to part the Red Sea for His people (Exod. 4:2,17,8:16,9:23,10:13). In Matthew 25:31-46, the Lord separates the sheep from the goats using the shepherd rod and staff.

Jesus Christ is more than a match for Satan. God sent him to bring goodness and righteousness to the earth, use a rod of iron or judgment, and order to get rid of sin and ungodliness in the world. He did this on the cross to provide forgiveness of sins and develop a relationship for man to stand before God free of sin. Jesus Christ's death upon the cross will destroy the power of Satan (Jn. 12:31, Heb. 2: 14, 1 Jn. 3:8). He will use the rod of iron against all the ungodly and evil of the world in the end time. He shall bring the kingdom of God to earth- (Ps. 2:9, Rev. 2: 27, Rev. 19:15). When all these things happen, all believers will have a grandstand seat in Heaven. The Church will be caught up with Him before the Tribulation comes upon the earth.

He comes into the world, and He will one day rule the world because all things were created: things in Heaven and on earth, visible and invisible, whether thrones, powers, rulers, or authorities; all things have been created through him and for him. He is before all things, and all things hold together (Col. 1:16-17). Second, he has redeemed us to God by thy blood out of every kindred, tongue, people, and nation; He has made us kings and priests, and we shall reign on the earth with Him (Rev. 5:9-10). Third, you are worthy of receiving glory, honor, and power. You created all things, and by your will, they were created and had their being (Rev. 4:11).

John saw the child snatched away from the Dragon and caught up to God and his throne. The child is Jesus, who will live on the earth for thirty-three years. We have the Church ministry (1 Cor. 3:11), and the gates of hell will not prevail against it. During the Tribulation, the Antichrist will begin his reign. Israel will be forced to flee into the prepared place of protection. We do not know how many years until the woman will flee into her place of protection. Only God knows (Ps. 90:1-2).

Verse 6

The woman Israel flees for her life into the wilderness. The willingness represents a place of protection. John the Baptist, Jesus, and Paul travel into the wilderness for preparation (Lk. 1:80; 3:2, Mark 1:13, Jn. 11:54, Gal. 1:17). The Antichrist will attempt to kill the woman, and she will flee into the wilderness for protection. God will take care of her when evil controls the entire world for 1260 days.

John gives a picture of the terrible Holocaust of the end times. The Woman, Israel, is going to be severely persecuted by the antichrist (Rev. 11:2). The Jews will have to flee for their lives, flee to the wilderness of the mountains, hills, forests, and every hiding place to be found. The Holocaust is going to be large against the Gentiles as well as Jews (Rev. 7:9). The days will be great, a time described by Jesus (Jer. 30:7, Matt. 24).

We are living the days of grace. When the Tribulation occurs three and half years, Israel will be forced to flee into a prepared place. It will be a terrible time like the abomination of desolation (Matt. 24:15-23). The Tribulation will be a time of sorrow and woe to unbelievers. God's people will have nothing to worry about because you will be with Him in the air. He will save a remnant of believers, those who turn to him (Rom. 11:2, 15, 11: 23 – 24, 25 – 26, Isa. 43: 1 – 2).

The Jews will suffer, but they will survive because of the providence of God (Jer. 31:35-36). The hatred against the Jews is growing more potent as the Muslim nations of the Middle East cry for the destruction of Israel. Hatred will continue during the Tribulation period, and the Antichrist will continue to persecute Israel. When that persecution arises, Israel will seek God's plan for them. The Lord Jesus prophesied this in Matthew 24:15-22.

Satan hates Israel because she is a constant reminder to him that his power is limited. He attempts to destroy Israel because she reminds him of the glory he used to share.

Israel will find refuge in the wilderness. Some believe this will be in the ancient Edomite city of Petra. The city is surrounded by towering hills of rust-colored sandstone, which gave the city some natural protection against invaders. The entrance into Petra is through the Sig, a ravine enclosed by immense walls that reach hundreds of feet and provides an excellent place to hide and seek shelter.

God has a program for the unbelievers. He plans to accept Jesus as your Savior. Have you trusted Jesus as your Savior? Have your sins been washed away by the blood of the crucified and risen Lord? Are you saved? Are you living for Him as you should? Are you thankful that He saved your soul? Because God aided the woman's escape into the wilderness, we find security for all believers in Jesus. When Satan attacks God's people, the believers will be spiritually secured. As for those days, there will be no flesh saved, but for the elect. They may receive physical harm but will be protected from spiritual harm and the wrath of God.

Verses 7-9

What John saw was Satan. He is the great Dragon and the old serpent. His name is Lucifer. He was one of the highest angels ever created by God, but he failed because of selfishness and pride (Isa. 14:12, 1 Tim. 3:6, Rev. 12: 3 – 4; 2 Cor. 4:4, 11: 13 – 15; 1 Pet. 5:8). Scriptures describe Satan as:

1. He owns this world (2 Cor. 4:4)

2. Satan is the prince of this world (Jn. 12: 31, 14:20, 16:11. The Prince of power of the air (Eph. 2:2, 6:12)

3. Adversary (1 Chron. 12:1, Job 1:6, 2: 1 – 6, Zech. 3:1, Matt. 4:10, Mark 1:13, Lk. 4:8, Jn. 13:27, Acts 5:3, 26:18, Rom. 16:20)

4. The devil, which means the slanderer (Matt. 4:1, 5, 8, 11; Lk. 4:2 – 6, 13; 1 Pet. 5:8, Rev. 20:2)

5. Deceiver of the whole world (2 Cor. 11:3; Rev. 12:9)

6. Tempter (Matt. 4:3; 1 Thess. 3:5)

7. Evil one (Matt. 6:13; 13:19, 38).

8. The Father of lies (Jn. 8:44)

9. The accuser of the brethren (Rev. 12: 10)

10. A murderer (Jn. 8: 44)

11. Called Beelzebub (Matt. 12:24, Mk. 3:22, Lk. 11:15)

12. Belial (2 Cor. 6:15)

13. Abaddon (Rev. 9: 11)

14. The angel of the bottomless pit (Rev. 9:11)

15. Apollyon (Rev. 9:11)

16. The enemy (Matt. 13:39)

17. The gates of hell (Matt. 16:18)

18. The great red Dragon (Rev. 12:3)

19. Called a lying spirit (1st King 22:22)

20. That old serpent (Rev. 12:9, 20:2; Gen. 3:4, 14; 2 Cor. 11:3)

21. The power of darkness (Col. 1:13)

22. The prince of darkness (Matt. 12:24)

23. Called the ruler of the darkness of this world (Ephesian 6:12)

24. The spirit that works in the children of the disobedience (Eph. 2: 2)

25. Called the unclean spirit (Matt. 12: 43)

26. Called the wicked one (Matt. 13: 19, 38)

Satan's purpose is making war against God:

1. To receive power in worship of as much of the universe as possible (Isa. 14: 12 – 17, Ezek. 28:11 – 17. He goes about this in 3 ways:

2. He opposes and disturbs God's word in the world (Isa. 14:12 – 17; Ezek. 28: 11 – 17; Job 1:6; 2:1 – 6, Matt. 4: 10; Mark 1:13, Lk. 4:8, Rev. 12: 7 – 9).

3. To discourage believers through various strategies (Lk. 22:31; Eph. 6:10 – 12).

4. He arouses God's justice against people by leaving the old to sin and denying and rebelling against God. This justice led to judgment and eternal life with Satan (Matt. 12:25 – 26; Jn. 13:31 – 32).

5. He cut and hurt God. Why? Satan wants revenge against God. His strategies are to lead people into sin away from God (Rev. 12: 3 – 4, 7 – 9, 12:10 – 11).

Satan is our adversary. The word means *"adversary"* or "one who stands opposed." He opposes everything that has to do with God. He opposes everything God is trying to do. He opposes the people of God, the House of God, the Word of God, and the plan of God stands in open opposition to everything decent, holy, and right. Christ had defeated Satan when he died on Calvary (Jn. 12:31 – 32, 16:11; 8:44, Col. 2: 15, Jn. 19:28-30). Jesus never gave in to the devil's temptation (Matt. 4:1 – 11) and by never sinning (2 Cor. 5:21). Christ overcame sin. He was righteous; he was perfect. Christ defeated Satan by destroying physical and spiritual death (Heb. 2: 14 – 15; Roman 8:31).

A great war was fought in Heaven. When sin invaded the heart of Lucifer, he was cast out of Heaven, and his angels are now in a chain awaiting judgment. Satan is forced out of Heaven (Rev. 12:1-4). He led one-third of the angels of Heaven away from God in this rebellion. Satan's eviction from Heaven started a great war between God and Satan.

Michael and his angels defeated Satan. Who is Michael? He is the leading angel with the Jewish people and the guardian angel over God's elect (Dan. 12:1). Michael stands to see that Israel does not perish in the Great Tribulation, sometimes called the time of Jacob's trouble (Jer. 30:7). The war is between light and darkness, though invisible, it is still being fought on earth. The outcome of the battle, Satan and his fallen angels will be cast out of Heaven. Verse 9 tells us that Satan and his angels were "cast out into the earth". The words *"cast out"* mean "to let go of a thing without caring where it falls". Satan is forever driven from Heaven! The title, "Prince of the and power of the air," will be lost forever (Eph. 2:2).

After the Great Tribulation, Satan will never again have an asset to Heaven. He will never again accuse a believer before God. It will be the final battle between evil and good on earth. After this battle, Satan will be defeated forever (Dan. 10:14, 12:1). The Tribulation will be Satan's last effort to eliminate Jews and believers from the face of the earth. Why? Because that old Dragon, serpent, called the devil and Satan wanted to reign in Heaven (Rev. 12:9). Now Satan roams the earth going about on the earth, and from walking back and forth on it trying to defeat the believers with his tactics. God has countered the attacks. Several things happen for believers:

1. Scripture teaches that God has assigned angels to look after and minister to believers (Heb. 1: 1– 14).

2. Scripture teaches there are ranks and orders of angels. They have levels of authority. They rule as principalities and power over the spiritual world among good and evil angels (Roman 8: 38 – 39, Eph. 1:21, 6:12, Col. 1:6, 2:15).

3. Michael is one of the archangels who serve God. He is the prime administrator of God (Dan. 10:21; 12:1, 7 – 12, 1st Thess. 4:16, Jude 9). He is pictured as the guardian angel of God's people. He struggles against the fallen angels to control nations and people of the earth (Dan. 10:12,13, 21; 12:1, Dan. 10 – 12).

A spiritual war will be fought at the end of time between the spiritual forces of good and evil. Satan and his Angel will attempt to stamp out Israel and the followers of Christ. He will try to wipe out the believer. Why? Many people will not become worshippers of God.

We have a lawyer (Jesus) in Heaven (1 Jn. 2:1; Rom. 8:34; Heb. 7:25) who will defend the saints from the accuser. Jesus is an Advocate. The word "*advocate*" means "one who pleads another's cause before a judge" (1Jn. 2:2). He could be a comforter, consoler, or a defense lawyer. Jesus Christ is called our advocate. He stands up to declare us just and justified. He pleads our case by showing the nail prints in His hands and feet. He pleads the blood He shed on the cross as the perfect, eternal payment for humanity's sins. Christ represents us before the Father in heaven and He never lost a case. The Father cries, "Case dismissed!" Hallelujah!

Verses 10-11

Heaven praise for the victory of Satan being defeated by the salvation of Christ. A loud voice is heard; it comes from an angel (Rev. 19:10). Heaven explodes in praise and thanksgiving in a hymn of praise. The hymn has three stanzas. The tormentor, the accuser of the brethren, the archenemy of God, has been forever expelled from Heaven! So, the citizens of Heaven praise God and the Lamb for their power and glory in overcoming the devil!

Christ wins salvation for humanity's sin. Heaven rejoices with a great shout. Whom will this voice be? God's people. The voice refers to our brothers and sisters before God, day and night praising Him. It will declare the victory and salvation are now won once and for all. God will bring every person who has ever trusted him into eternity. The power of God's Christ and Messiah will be proven. Every true believer will now live with God forever, worshiping and serving him because of the power of God's Messiah (1 Cor. 4:20; Rev. 11:17). God's salvation will be glorious. Satan will never again throw the sin of believers into God's face and point out every failure to hurt and cut God. The believers will use three weapons to gain and defeat victory over Satan:

1. They used the blood of the Lamb Col. 1:13, 2:14-15).

2. They used the word of their testimony (Acts 4:20,

    2 Tim. 1:8, 1 Pet. 3:15).

3. They used their supreme love for Jesus.

Verse 12

All creation is out of sync because of sin. The blood of Jesus cleanses and purified all sin and curse (Rom. 8:22) on earth and the heavens. The third stanza of the hymn gives a warning from God, those left on the earth will face terror:

1. Because people's godlessness, evil, idolatry, murder, sorcery, immortality, and thievery will worsen, humanity will turn to the Antichrist for a promise of utopia upon the earth.

2. Satan knows that he only has a limited time before the eternal plan of the Lord is finished. He knows that he is facing judgment. Since he can no longer vent his anger toward Heaven and God, he turns his hatred earthward and attacks the people living upon the earth.

3. He will create the worst devastation ever seen upon earth.

4. Satan will be defeated during the Tribulation, but he will not be destroyed, not yet. God is going to judge the world and finally place Satan in prison, where he belongs.

Verses 13-17

Satan realizes that he was cast into the earth. He realized he had lost the war in Heaven. He will cast a war to persecute the woman, which brought forth the man's child. The man child is Jesus, born to a devout Jew named Mary (Lk. 1:26 – 33). Satan is staking and killing God's people. The woman symbolizes God's people. The woman will flee into the wilderness for three and half years and be protected from the serpent during the Tribulation. God will protect his people as He did with the Israelites (Exod. 19:4 Matt. 24:22). Satan will launch a terrible attack against the woman to destroy God's people:

1. The woman (Israel) will be severely persecuted and all believers who refuse to deny Christ. The world will witness a worldwide slaughter.

2. The knock on the door by the Antichrist secret police will frighten Jews and believers hovered in the corners of their homes.

3. The arrests and jailing will be efficient (children and adults).

4. Trains will carry Jews and all believers to execution camps to be slaughtered.

5. The word *"persecuted"* means "to chase or to pursue". Satan goes after Israel with a vengeance. He pursues them with violent destruction on his mind.

6. God will deliver his people on the wings of an eagle home to Heaven and others to safety upon the earth. The persecution continued for three and a half years in Verse 6 (Exod. 19:4, Duet. 32:11 – 12).

7. The image of the eagle's wings is symbolic of God's protection of His chosen people. Exodus 19:4 tells us, "Ye have seen what I did unto the Egyptians, and how I bare you on eagles' wings and brought you unto myself." God brings Israel into a place of safety that He has prepared for them.

8. The serpent, the devil, will attempt to flood Israel and believers with trials and Tribulation during the Tribulation (Ps. 18:4, 32: 6, Isa. 43:1 – 2).

9. There will be great help coming from the earth. The earth will be used to swallow up the flooding waters of attacks of the devil and his Antichrist.

10. The devastation and catastrophes of the earth will require the attention of the Antichrist. Some nations will not go along with Antichrist and escape to their shores (Rev. 6:3 – 8; 6:12 – 17; 8: 6 – 9:11; 8: 6 – 12; 8: 13 – 9:11;9 12 – 21).

The Dragon will launch an all-out attack on the rest of the woman seed. The earth will include barren areas and wilderness areas to which many will flee. The attack from Satan has always been devastating. We must remain steadfast. Jesus will provide divine protection from Satan. He is the only hope of deliverance for believers today from the destruction of Satan (2 Cor. 11:3, Eph. 6:10 – 11, Heb. 2:14 – 15, 1Pet. 5: 8 – 9, James 4:7).

Verse 18

Satan recognizes that the battle is lost. He will turn his attention to the woman's offspring and has declared war against them (the Church). John sees the beast arrived. He stood on the edge of the sea (the abyss), ready to call out those who would help him pursue God's people. The sea represents evil in the ancient world. When we get to Heaven, the sea no longer will exist (Rev. 21:1). The Dragon will begin an assault against the woman's offspring and declare war against individual believers.

God's people will always be in a battle with Satan. Satan brings more into his ranks each day because many have become defectors of Jesus Christ. Satan wants your soul. There is little time left to seek a decision. Today, you have not received Jesus as your Savior. Come to Jesus, and He will forgive you and save you. He will protect you from Satan, and you can receive the rewards of everlasting salvation.

# CHAPTER 13

## *Rise Of The Antichrist*

---

Chapter 13 continues to expand on John's vision. We are dealing with things that shall come past. He introduces Satan (the Antichrist and his cohorts). Then we get to Revelation 13 and 14 which we are looking at the time that you cannot buy and cannot sell. The Book of Revelation is unfolding before our eyes. We spoke of the fact that something will come forth from the depth of the sea and will take center stage in human history.

John saw a beast rising from the sea as the six of seven major figures described in this part of Revelation. He is the false Messiah. The man of the sea. The son of perdition known as the antichrist. We did briefly mention the second beast that will come from the death of the earth. John stands on the seashore and sees a mysterious beast rise from the sea, representing humanity's masses. Two individuals will come from among men in evil times (the Antichrist (verses 13:1 – 10), and the false prophet (13:11 – 18). The rulers will be savage and cruel. The beast refers to "a wild animal." It is used as a metaphor for a man who is "brutal, savage, and ferocious".

Satan will empower the two beasts who will gain control of the world. The Beast:

1. His origin: the sea (the abyss) Verse 1.

2. His great political power. Verses 1 – 2.

3. His dramatic rise to power. Verses 2 – 3.

4. His mention of securing world government. Verses 4 – 8.

5. His adversaries, the genuinely saved. Verses 8 – 10.

Satan is cast down to earth, which will be his main battleground and operation. He blinds and darkens the minds of God's people. Satan gives power and authority to the two beasts to forge war against humanity.

The word of God had fallen, and the blood of the saints ran like water on the earth. Evil had to triumph over good. The beast blasphemy God and dictated political and religious policies. He will persecute the faithful, "There shall be no flesh be saved except God shorten the days" (Matt. 24:22).

Verse 1

The Antichrist gives power to the two beasts. He will be a mirror image of the dragon, called forth from the people of the world as a partner in the war against the saints. Terrible things will take place:

1. The world will be full of violence, conflict, terrorist activities, wars, and rumors of wars will increase.

2. The world will suffer from natural catastrophes such as famines, and earthquakes, and diseases will increase (Rev. 6:3 – 8, 6:12 – 17, and 8:6 – 12, 8: 13 – 9: 11, 9: 12 – 21).

Humanity will be clamoring for a leader who can offer them hope and help. They will be political leaders that give humanity hope. Daniel's last half of the seventeen weeks of the seventy weeks sheds light on what shall come to pass upon Israel and the latter days (Dan. 10:14). Satan will give these two beasts power and authority, and they will be the mastermind of evil and destruction. The appearance of the first beast:

The Antichrist will have seven heads, meaning he will have enormous ability—about seven times a leader's ability. Seven mean the complete process of knowledge and wisdom:

1. He will think, plan, act, respond, and react to situations quicker than any human.

2. He has seven heads, and ten horns that represent the ten nations he will rule over.

3. He will have power, a throne, and authority.

The Antichrist will have ten horns, which means he will have power over tribes, tongues, and nations. He will pierce, rip, and tear the cruelest way:

1. He will strike terror on the world. He will be a political world dictator.

2. He will rule with a frightening terror.

3. He will have ten blasphemous names on his seven heads. He will represent the embodiment of blasphemy.

4. He will be the abomination of desolation standing in the holy places in the Temple in Jerusalem, demanding that people give him loyalty to the state (Matt. 24:15).

5. He will oppose all religions, called God, and all who worship Him (2 Thess. 2:4).

6. He will speak the great and boastful and terrible words against the highest God (Dan. 7:25).

7. He will demand worship to the state (Rev. 13:4).

8. He will control the three most powerful empires of the world: The Leopard, Bear, and the Lion (Rev. 13:2).

9. The Beast will have a body like a Leopard. His rise to power will be swift. His feet are like bear feet, meaning he will crush his opponents.

His mouth will look like a lion's mouth, meaning he will devour all who dare stand in his way.

10. His reign will last for seven years, with 42 months of terror during the last half of the Tribulation.

11. His government will be under the ten kings. He will be supreme.

Verse 2

John sees a description of the beast. Daniel 7 matches the visions of Revelation 13. His vision is the combined world empires of the Antichrist as he describes the four beasts—lion, bear, leopard, the Beast of the Antichrist combines all the world empires (Rev. 13:1 – 2). What empires do these animals represent? The age of the Gentile world dominion and Babylon. Daniel 7:4-7 speaks of the empires.

A lion was a symbol of the Babylonian Empire. A lion was a mighty beast, fearsome, and had a ravenous appetite for domination (Rev. 13: 1 – 2). It represents the first world Empire: Babylon under Nebuchadnezzar (Dan. 2: 36 – 38, 7:4)). The Antichrist will have a roar that will sweep worldwide, shouting blasphemies that will strike fear in humanity. A lion's teeth are sharp and drive deep into the flesh of prey. Babylonian Empire will have strength like a lion tearing, chewing, and eating up the nations and people of the world.

The bear speaks of the Medo-Persian Empire. Silver is the second world empire, the Medo- Persia (Dan. 7:5, 8:20). The empire possessed incredible power, like a bear crushing its enemies. (Dan. 7:5) The bear represents that the Antichrist will have feet like a bear. Big and tough feet will cover a large area and pursue its prey of people and nations without giving up. Strong claws grip the prey of nations and people without letting them go and possessing the power to rip them apart.

The bronze represented the Greece Empire. The leopard speaks of the Greek Empire (Dan. 7:5, 8:20). It is called a leopard that is quick to dominate the world (Dan. 2:39, 7:6, 8:21 – 22; 10:20; 11: 2 – 4). The

Antichrist will have nature like a leopard: sleek body, beautiful, full of spots that symbolize evil, sneaky, ferocious, and wild nature.

The fourth beast speaks of the Antichrist as the iron and the terrible beast with Rome's ten horns. He will be the dreadful, terrible, and strong beast (Rev. 13: 1, Dan. 7:7-8, 23 – 24; 9:26; Dan. 8: 21, 2:39).

The Beast of Revelation 13:1 will revive the old Roman Empire and has the characteristics of the three preceding empires combining all their strengths. The spirit of this empire will return before the end times.

The interpretation of the dreadful, terrible, and strong Beast of Revelation 13:1 will have seven heads, ten horns, and ten crowns. The seven heads will be full of blasphemy. The Antichrist will have ten horns, representing the power of ten governments. He will be the heads of state and the ten governments who will blaspheme the name of God.

The metals image of the four beasts matches the combined traits of the Antichrist. The Antichrist will combine all the mental traits of the four empires:

1. Gold (the head) represents the Babylonian Empire, is valuable and desired, which means he will be attractive and appealing like gold. He will be unaffected by the sufferings of the environment and the people. He will be volatile, wrathful, and vengeful.

2. He will possess silver, which represents the Medo-Persian Empire. Soft and easily beaten into shapes and forms, which means that he will have a remarkable ability to compromise and give and take. Silver is easily tarnished, which means that the Antichrist will be easily corrupted. Silver is the most superior of all metals in conducting heat and electricity. The Antichrist will be a strong commentator, able to pass on his ideas and wrath to others.

3. Bronze is more complex than most alloys (except steel) and strongly resistant. It is often used in bearings and fittings. Which means the

Antichrist will be brutal and indifferent to others. He will resist and stand against his opponents.

4. Iron is easily magnetized. The Antichrist will have a magnetic appeal; people and nations will willingly follow him. Iron is easily combined with other metals, combining others into a Confederation of states, one-world government.

The dragon (Satan) will give a leader (man or personality) power to do things for him as he attempts to destroy Israel again. He will be given power, authority, ability, persuasion to influence the world. He will be Satan incarnate, and humanity will follow the Beast:

1. He will be a man (2 Thess. 2:3).

2. He will stand in the temple of God in Jerusalem and proclaim himself as God (Matt. 24:15. 2nd Thess. 2:4).

3. The Antichrist will become a false leader even as other antichrists have become false teachers (1 Jn. 2:18).

We see a future reference to the ten-nation confederation to destroy God's people. As the dragon looks over the sea of nations and then implements the system of the Beast to carry out his desired goals, we see Israel's persecution (Rev. 13:2b).

Verse 3

The world will worship the Beast, but he will be defeated. His wounded are healed (Rev. 13:3, 13:12, 13:14, 17:8, 17:11). There are three interpretations of this:

1. The death of the beasts refers to the political death of the Roman Empire. The clay will crumble, and the iron will continue some of the traits and elements. The Roman Empire will be revived during end times, and the spirit of Rome will dominate in the world again.

2. The Antichrist will be the return of some evil ruler who has lived through history. He will be emperor, king, or president, whatever the world him. The devil will raise him and send him back to earth to destroy God's people (Rev. 17: 11).

3. The mortal wounds are an assassination attempt or some accident that happened to the antichrists, at the beginning of his rule. The false prophet (the 2nd beast) performs a miracle and heals the Antichrist. It will be a miracle that helped him gain credibility and support of the world's masses (Rev. 13:14).

4. Now the beast is the head raised to life again by the Antichrist consisting of ten federated kingdoms. During the Tribulation, a leader rules again in the spirit of a revived Roman empire.

Verse 4

The world will worship the dragon. The Antichrists will gain governmental and religious control of the world. Many will think the Beast will bring world peace. They will refuse to accept Christ because they are overwhelmed by his miracles and power. They look to him as a God (Rev. 13:3-4). Blasphemy claims to be God when this is false. Satan will copy the work of God and deceive humanity.

Worldly and ungodly people will worship the dragon (devil) and give him power. People will become more sinful in the last days, live worldly, evil, and ungodly (Rev. 9: 20 – 21, 2 Tim. 3: 1 – 5, 13). Worship means giving loyalty and allegiance to the Antichrist. The citizens of the world government leaders will follow this man who has all the answers to the world problems. There are methods he will use to get the world to follow him:

1. The world will be amazed at his wonders, and they will admire the beast (Rev. 13: 3).

2. He will be full of the ability to understand mysteries and solve problems (Rev. 13:1, Dan. 8:23).

3. He will secure power by military and economic strength. He will conquer all nations described as having seven heads and three horns.

4. The Antichrist will have the military power he has ever known. Nation will peacefully surrender to him and give their loyalty.

5. Other nations will fear him (Rev. 13:4, Dan. 11: 38, 43; Rev. 17: 12 – 17).

The Antichrist will speak and demonstrate "great things," and they will believe him. He will secure power through speech, oratory, persuasion, and blasphemy. He will speak encouragement that brings the world hope. He will be wealthy to help solve the economic problems mentioned above (Dan. 11:38, 11:43).

Satan will empower a world dictator who is revived as the Roman Empire leader. Humanity will be swept off their feet. Nations under his control will be wealthy, and people will ask who can make war with him? They will declare that no one can fight against the beast (Dan. 7:8-14). No man in history will match the power of the Antichrist or defeat him. His power with words will make others seem like babbling idiots! God always will come out victorious. He will be no match for Jesus Christ and will be defeated with no problem. He and his cohorts will face one who has all power (Matt. 28:18).

Verses 5-6

The Antichrist will offer world peace the three and a half years. God will still have control over Satan's activities. He will utter words blasphemy that is bold. God He is given a mouth to exercise his authority for forty-two months. He will hate God. He was slandered and blaspheme God's name, his dwellings place, those who dwell in Heaven (angelic being), anything that has to do with God and his Son. He will position himself in the temple, claiming himself to be God (2 Thess. 2:4). Confessing faith in Jesus Christ as Lord will result in death. He will call them evildoers (1 Pet.'s 2:12). Daniel had seen a little horn boasting arrogance (Dan. 7:8, 20; 11:20 – 39).

Whether you believe in pre-Tribulation or post-Tribulation theory, the text clarifies that believers will be on earth during the Tribulation. The beast will secure power through humanism, rejecting and denying God (Verse 6). He will push the idea that humanity can solve its problems through technology, denying God as the creator. Many will applaud his idolatrous behavior (Dan. 7:25, 11:36, Rev. 13:6).

He will gain world authority through war and military might, but most nations will follow willingly and peacefully their allegiance and loyalty for economic aid (oil and its wealth). The Antichrist marches into Jerusalem and declares that the state is the first object of worship (2nd Thess. 2 – 4, Rev. 13: 4, 12, 14, 14: 9 – 11, Dan. 11:36). God receives the worship of humanity through Jesus Christ. Satan will attempt to get Jesus to worship him but will be denied and defeated. Heaven rejoiced when Satan was cast out of Heaven to earth. Revelation 12:10 tells us, "The "*earth dwellers*" give their worship to Satan."

Verse 7

The beast will destroy saints on earth. His mission will be to seek out and destroy anyone who worships God and Jesus Christ during the Tribulation. Ungodly people will deny God. Anyone on earth who refuses to bow to the beast or Antichrist in worship will be put to a martyr's death. The martyrs killed here refers to the saints in Chapter 6. They are told to wait until their fellow service is killed in like manner. The beast becomes dictator over all kindreds, tongues, people, and nations.

God's grace will continue in action for all that dwell upon the earth. The word "*dwell*" means "to settle down." The phrase refers to people who have chosen to make this world their home. They have decided that they are not interested in Heaven or in anything God can offer them. They have staked all their hopes and futures in this world. The earth dwellers have refused God and His Messiah, and they have chosen Satan and his false messiah (2 Thess. 2:11-12).

Verse 8

The beast is given control over the earth. The coming battle will be fought between those who worship Satan and against those who worship God. Many will worship the beast except those names written in the Book of Life. It is to register those who will receive eternal life, in contrast to those destined for the Lake of fire (Rev. 17:8). Four statements made about the believer:

1. They are secured and the Lamb's Book of Life (Rev. 3: 4-6; 5: 6 – 7).

2. They become hearers of this message, the ones who have repented and turn to Christ.

3. They are the ones who know God will judge evil and ungodly. They know:

4. What if he led others into captivity? He can lead them out of captivity.

5. They will never be condemned for their sins; they would rise to eternal life if they died in Christ. Those who have committed evil will rise to judgment, judged by God, him playing and put to death eternity. (Jn. 5:24, 24 – 29).

Who will you choose to lead you in the world as your Savior? Will you allow Jesus Christ? Alternatively, will you allow Satan? Are you born again? You can be saved in Jesus Christ today (Rom.:10 9– 13), and your destination will be Heaven. Your second choice is to live in the world and worship the Antichrist. Your destination will be a real place called Hell.

Verses 9-10

A day is coming when God's wrath and judgment will be upon the ungodly. The opportunity to be saved will cease. God wants you to make it a top priority to come to Jesus today. God's grace is still sufficient. Many will accept the mark of the beast, and they will drop in Hell. Some people will not accept the beast's mark and will endure to the bitter and bloody end. A believer during the Tribulation should understand that God is still in control. Anyone without Jesus should have ears to listen and believe (Roman 10:9 – 13). Those who receive the mark of the beast go to Hell.

Galatians 6:7-8 tells us, "That people reap what they sow". If you live for the devil, you will reap the devil. If you reject Jesus, you will be rejected by Jesus. The time to make a choice is today! Are all your hopes and dreams locked up in this world? Or have you secured citizenship in Heaven? The day His coming when it will be too late.

Verse 11

John saw a beast rising from the sea, as the six of seven significant figures describe in this part of Revelation. He is the false Messiah. The man of the sea. The son of perdition is known as the antichrist. We did briefly mention the second beast that will come from the death of the earth.

The first beast that comes out of the sea is the Antichrist, and the second beast that rose out of the earth is the False Prophet. He will have two horns and the voice of a lamb. These two Beasts will be dictators in the political and religious world. When the second beast appears, he will gain his power in religion, being an imitator of Jesus Christ (2 Cor. 11:14) like a harmless lamb, look like a lamb, and speak like a dragon. He will be deceptive. The differences between the two beasts:

1. The first beast is a secular power completely rebellious against the true God. The second beast is the mouthpiece of the first beast. He posing to be a prophet and to direct people to worship the first beast (Verses 12 - 14).
2. The first beast is Gentile; the second beast is a Jew.
3. The first beast has ten horns; the second beast has two horns. The two horns symbolize three things:

He will appear innocent, and harmless, mild, meet, and attractive, and lovable. Nothing appeared to be frightening:

1. He will appear on the world stage as a gentle, meek, loving, and kind religious leader like the Pope. He will attract the world through his personality and pleasing words.

2. He labors to put all religions in the hands of Satan.

These beasts will appear to be one of God's little lambs or sheep and followers of Jesus Christ. He appeared to be religiously clean, free from evil, violence, and ungodliness:

1. People think he will do no wrong or at any severe wrong. One of the most famous names in the world never mentions (the name of Jesus), nor does he mention sin. He tells a few stories and builds everyone up. He will not be concerned with separating the wheat from the chaff or interested in the Word of God.

2. The beast will speak as a dragon. His voice is going to betray him. What he says will reveal a false prophet.

3. The first beast will have civil authority; the second will have religious authority and be subordinate to the first. He will use the military power of the first beast to enforce his demands and his dictatorship.

4. The second beast is a lieutenant to the first. He appears after the first beast. They both do not appear at the same time.

5. He comes out of the earth. Meaning he comes from ordinary people of the earth. He will be the second most powerful man in the government of the last few days.

John saw another beast. The second beast, the seven dominant characters described in this part of Revelation, has two horns like a lamb and he spoke like a dragon. This beast was rising from the earth. Most scholars suggest the first beast is deceive as the antichrist and most agree that the second beast is the false prophet. Neither beast is specifically named in the Book of Revelation. So, this destination is not crucial, and no one should be dogmatic about identifying them. But we do know they both are against Christ. People will be looking for someone to bring peace and order to a disordered world. Satan will give the second beast something the world needs—a spokesperson. He will become the sidekick of Satan. He gives to the beast what is offered to Jesus in Lk. 4:6 – 7 and Ps. 2. The second beast will become a copycat to be able do the same as the two witnesses of God can perform (Rev. 11:15), which references the miracles of Elijah (1 Kgs. 18:36 – 38).

Revelation 13:11-12, notice the mission of the second beast. Verse 12 tells us the beast came to cause the earth and those who dwell in it to worship the first beast. The job of this beast is to make the people worship the first beast. Note the word "worship" that is the real message here that we must hold onto as we study this passage. The second beast caused people to worship the first beast. Revelation 13:16 through 17 reveals that the center of attraction is worship. This warfare is a basic battle of who we must worship reads – 16 – 17. The beast whose name is to promote the interests of the devil will compel everyone to receive a mark by which they will be identified as of the beast. This is not going to be optional as many that will refuse to accept the mark of the beast will be able to buy and sell. The central issue is that all worship.

The two beasts will want all the humanity to focus on them so that they can become the object of worship. The beast wants to restrain everyone from worshipping the one and only true God. The Christians who will be living during this period be required to hang on; they will be required to place their faith in God even if faced with impossible odds like these. People will be face to face with the option of having to choose who exactly they will serve, God or the devil. At this point, no one can pretend to be serving God why he or she is not, because you will have to choose between two options which will clearly reveal your stand. It's all about worship.

Verse 12

The objective of any false prophet is to secure the world's devotion, loyalty, and allegiance to himself. Let us consider some facts about a prophet in Revelation 13:

1. A false prophet will be a man who exercises the power of the Antichrist. Satan will give the false prophet the right to speak and act for him with the power of healing and miracles.

2. A false prophet will use his ministerial position and influence to represent the Lamb of God.

3. He may hold some high position in religion.

4. He may be very influential and already known by many in the world.

5. He will be very charismatic, able to speak and communicate with people face-to-face in all settings effectively.

What are the objectives of false prophets?

1. To secure devotion, loyalty, and allegiance to the state

2. He will use his high office in religion to rally people to support the Antichrist and the state.

3. He will focus on worship, the devotion, and loyalty of people.

4. He will influence or force people to devote their loyalty to the state. Everyone will be forced to show their support and loyalty to a utopic state that the Antichrist has wrought.

5. His first loyalty is to the state. He will not attempt to bring peace in Jesus Christ. He will use universal religion to secure the loyalty and devotion of the people to himself. People will follow his policies and programs.

6. The world has been blessed with peace and economic recovery under his leadership. He will bring a kingdom of utopia to earth and provide people with their needs.

7. He will use religious persecution to secure loyalty. Anyone who does not worship the state and the beasts will be slaughtered. True believers with strong religious faith and others will be slaughtered in the Holocaust of the Antichrist: Christians, Jews, Muslims, and Hindus (Rev. 7: 9 – 17; 11:1,2; 11: 3 – 13).

8. The false prophet was set up the image to the beasts in the temple of God (Rev. 13: 15, 15: 2, 19: 20, 20: 4).

9. His power and his miracles will deceive them, and they will fall in the worship of the beast and his image. Exciting and mighty miracles will mark the ministry of the False Prophet. His miracles will deceive the world.

The false prophet will not appear to be what he is supposed to be. He will be deceptive like some preachers today. Attend Sunday School, church services, revival meetings a few times, and you will know where they stand. Just listen to their words and they will reveal their hearts. Money and prosperity are among the most popular subjects preached.

No one is afraid of a little lamb, but no power on earth can withstand his tremendous power. God's power will finally put him down (Rev. 19:20). We cannot lose with God. The second beast will solve the problems of religions in the world. He will solve the situation in the Middle East between Islamic, the Jews, the Arabs, and the Muslims. He will find common ground that will allow all the world's religions to exist during the Tribulation. They are the devil's duo. They will work to accomplish the devil's will here on earth during the dark days of the Tribulation Period. Some preachers are like false prophets. They limit mentioning the name of Jesus, nor do they mention sin. Many tell a few sobbing stories and build everyone up. It is easy to separate the wheat from the chaff if you know a little about the word of God. Jesus Christ warned this would happen (Mark 13:22). He also encouraged believers not to be swayed or deceived by the great miracles the beast will perform.

Verses 13-15

The second beast will be an imitator. He will be powerful, mighty, and full of miracles. He makes fire come down from Heaven on the earth (Rev. 13:13) like Elijah in the sight of humanity. He will be worse than the first Beast because he will lead humanity into blasphemy and idolatry (2 Thess. 2:4).

We do not have miracle workers on earth today who advertise that they will pull fire down from Heaven. The Antichrist advertise that he will do it. Some men claim to cast out demons, raise the dead, heal the sick, cause the lame to walk, and cure all kinds of diseases. They draw attention to themselves, and I believe in miracles. I have not seen men having such power, but I believe that God is still in the miracle-making business through the power of their prayers. Some preachers use this method to make merchandise out of sick people. Elijah prayed, and God sent fire (1 Kings 18:38 – 39).

Jesus came in the Father's name, but the false prophet comes in his name to do his own will (Jn. 5:43). Humanity will receive the beast as their messiah. The beast is called by various names in the old and New Testament:

1. The King of Babylon (Isa. 14:4)
2. Lucifer (Isa. 14:12)
3. The little horn (Dan. 7:8; 8:9 – 12)
4. A King of fierce countenance (Dan. 8:23)
5. A prince that shall come (Dan. 9:26)
6. The willful king (Dan. 11:36)

In the New Testament, he is called:

1. The man of sin (2 Thess. 2:3 – 8)
2. The son of perdition (2 Thessalonian 2:3 – 8, Jn. 17:12)

3. The wicked (2 Thess. 2:3 – 8)

4. Antichrist (1 Jn. 2:18)

5. The Beast (Rev. 13:11)

Many people globally will receive the mark of the beast on their forehead or the right hand. Many people will be bowing down to worship an image of Satan. It is difficult to see the world falling before a statue to worship idols in advanced technology and sophisticated society. When the Antichrist appears, the world will think he has the war answers, hunger, and every problem known to humanity. He will die and be resurrected at the height of his power, and the world will mourn his passing. Then, he will rise from the dead! God will send them strong delusions (2nd Thessalonian 2:8-12). He will allow the world to be deceived as part of the judgment for their ungodliness and evil (2nd Thess. 2:10 – 11).

Verses 16-17

The false prophet will use economic control to secure loyalty to the Antichrist and the state. Food and supplies, resources purchased will depend upon the mark. There is a purpose behind the mark. Those who refuse to receive it cannot buy or sell, and they will be killed refusing to worship the beast. People will have to worship the beast to be saved from persecution inflicted upon God's followers. The mark of the beast is 666 (Verse 18). The three sixes have been saved to represent many things, including the unholy trinity of Satan, the first beast, and the false prophet (Rev. 16:13).

God worked six days and blessed the seventh day and He rested from all his work (Gen. 22-3). Seven represents divine completion. Humanity was created on the sixth day and was created in the image of God (Gen. 1:26). Six is short of seven. Therefore, the number of men is 666 and says that there is a Trinity, we have not one six, but three sixes. The devil has counterfeited everything God has that is good and great. Jesus ministered for three and a half years and was crucified. The last hand of the Tribulation will be three and a half years. The Antichrist announces in the temple that he is God Almighty. He imitates God using a mark to seal his own. Every child of God has a seal (Eph. 4:30). The devil marks his children during his earthly reign.

Some believe that we will be marked with some barcode system tattooed into the skin to access their money to buy and sell. You pass through an ultraviolet lamp, and the mark becomes visible. Tiny microchips, eye retina scan, Social Security number, and your driver's license number may be used for identification.

Humanity depends upon numbers, computers, and machines. Most of us are already marked with credit cards, Social Security numbers, but this is not a mark of the beast because we are part of the Church, and we will be rapture out of here before the Tribulation.

The world's motto today is wine, women, money, but there is coming to a Superman one day that will receive the saints of God. The saints of God will be caught up with Jesus in the air and above the terrible judgment and indignation. God will pour out His wrath on the ungodly (Dan. 7:25) who receive the mark of the beast.

The ungodly will compromise their faith in Christ, and they can never be saved or forgiven. Those who receive the mark will benefit economically for a brief time before God's cup of anger is on the way (Rev. 14:9 – 12; 20:7 – 15).

Many will flee into the wilderness, forest, mountains, and dens to hide for safety and survival (Rev. 14: 9 – 11; 20:4). There will be rationing of food for people (Rev. 6:5 – 6). They will beg, borrow, steal, eat out of the rivers in the woods until they are caught and killed. Every rank of people must bow to the false messiah or pay with your life. It is what is happening on the earth during the Tribulation. God will protect the saints with a seal (2 Cor. 1:22, Eph. 1:13, Rev. 7:2-8).

Satan marks those who give themselves to him. God seals those who come to Him through Jesus. He seals them for Himself. The redeemed will bear a seal on their forehead and are exempt from all earthly suffering (Rev. 7:9).

Verse 18

The Book of Revelation is given to John by the Holy Spirit and is not men's work. It is the wisdom God who gives understands what the mark will be. God is saying here is the wisdom given to John for understanding.

Ninety percent of the people in the United States who read this Book of Revelation have several numbers and cards representing them. Social Security numbers are not the mark of the beast, but it is educating people on the earth the mark of the beast. Satan always marks his people. He marks their bodies, their souls, and their minds (Verse 18). The antichrist's number of the beasts is 666. What does it mean? In Scripture, the perfect number is seven. Therefore, since man number is six, man is incomplete and short of God's glory and perfection. The number of the beasts is the same. His days are numbered. He and his followers will die and pass on to face the judgment of God.

You can have the seal if you put your faith in him, or you can have the number of Satan. If you have God sealed on you, there is a place in Heaven when you leave this world. If you receive a Satan number, you will go to Hell forever. Which do you want today?

The two beasts will want all humanity to focus on them to become the object of worship. The beast wants to restrain everyone from worshiping the one and only true God. The Christians who will be living during this period will be required to hang on; they will be required to place their faith in God even if faced with impossible odds like these. People will be face to face with the option of choosing who exactly they will serve, God or the devil. At this point, no one can pretend to be serving God why he or she is not because you will have to choose between two options that will clearly reveal your stand. It is all about worship.

# CHAPTER 14

## *The Lamb To Come*

Chapter 14 gives a refreshing sight of the Lamb standing on Mount Zion with 144,000. They symbolize all faithful saints and the remnant sealed and spared during the Great Tribulation. They are identified with Jesus Christ and the sea of kingdom power in Jerusalem (Rev. 7:1-8).

In the previous chapter, Chapter 13, truth has fallen in the streets, and the saints' blood will run like water because Satan attempted to banish God's people from the earth (Ps. 4:6). The beast proclaimed to be God and dictated both political and religious policies. John will answer two questions: What will become of those who refuse to receive the mark of the beast? They are killed (verses 1– 5)

The faithful will go through persecution because they accept Jesus Christ as their Savior. He will shorten those days. They cannot operate without the mark of the beast, and they refuse to accept the beast's mark. God will seal them because they refuse to worship the Antichrist. God will repaint the landscape with His grace. He will take a horrible situation and turn it into a thing of glory.

Chapter 14 is a picture of the victory of the Lamb of God. The Lamb will be standing on Mount Zion accompanied by 144,00 in contrast to the beast standing on the shifting sands of the seashores. God will prevail, and the beast will be destroyed. Humanity will face the darkest hour and the most grotesque hours in human history. John is given seven visions of incredible things happening:

1. The 144,000 will be sealed on their foreheads like Mount Zion is the same group in Chapter 7. It is a place come that symbolizes where the Messiah comes to deliver Israel and where He will gather His people (Ps. 48:1f; Isa. 24:23; Joel 2:32; Rom. 11:26).

2. God gives a closing testimony of the everlasting Gospel.

3. Babylon is fallen.

4. Terrible doom will come to the beast-worshipers.

5. All saints will be blessed.

6. The harvest of the earth is reaped.

7. God's wrath and vengeance are poured out on the unbelievers.

Verse 1

The first vision of triumph concerns the redeemed, who are seen as victorious. John is seeing and looking to the future triumph of the saints; the 144,000 were selected and sealed in chapters 7:3-4. They are sealed between the sixth and seventh seals because they preached during the darkest days of the Tribulation. They survive the Antichrist's attempt to get rid of them. God preserved them during the Tribulation to serve His purpose. The Antichrist will kill the 144000. They will join the Lamb of God in Heaven.

The 144000 will be redeemed from the earth and are no longer part of the ungodly world system. They are pure because their attributes spell perfection. They represent the truth amid untruths. They who had taken a vow to stand up for Christ (Rev. 7:2 – 3). Their commitment is rewarded

(Matt. 13:43, Rom. 8: 17, Lk. 23:43, Jn. 12:26, Jn. 14: 2 – 3, 2 Tim. 4:6 – 8). They stand blameless before God and sealed with God's name. They will refuse to take the mark of the Antichrist (Rev. 13: 13 – 17).

Humanity will suffer a significant loss of people. The Antichrist will kill and destroy the faithful, but he will be powerless to kill those that God has sealed and bound for glory. Today, the unbelievers' bodies, hearts, and minds are marked with the scars of their sins. Satan marks all those who follow him. God seals the believers with the Holy Spirit (Titus 2:14; 2 Cor. 1:22; Eph. 1:13; 4:30). We have been "sealed unto the day of redemption" (Eph. 4:30). Not a single believer given to Him by His Father will be lost (Jn. 6:37-40). We are sealed for Heaven as if we are already there (Rom. 8:28-30; Eph. 2:6). The believers who trust Jesus for their salvation will secure eternal life and security. All of God's children will be at the Marriage Supper of the Lamb; there will not be an empty seat at the table!

We are told that these men meet the Lamb on Mount Zion, an ancient name for the city of Jerusalem (2 Sam. 5:7; Ps. 48:2). It is the heavenly Jerusalem (Heb. 12:22). The picture of this ultimate victory is describing the New Jerusalem, "Enter thou into the joy of thy lord" (Matt. 25:23, Rev. chapter 21).

Verse 2

John heard a sound from Heaven like roaring mighty waterfalls or the mighty rolling thunder. It is a description of the voice of God. When we hear his voice, we know it is God speaking. That will be a relaxing time:

1. His voice is like the sound of thunder: deep, rumbling, arousing, stirring, and distinctive. His voice will demand full attention. We have a problem today listening to the world instead of God.

2. The voice of God is like the sound of many harps: restful, calming, soothing, relaxing, and fulfilling. The voice of God needs to be heard in the Tribulation.

3. The 144,000 will be rewarded with the privilege of hearing the voice of God. They will be victorious in playing musical instruments.

4. The presence of harps points to some exciting possibilities in Heaven: God will create new learning opportunities to expand our joy, and some of us will learn how to play a musical instrument.

Verses 3-5

The 144,000 are spiritually undefiled, pure as virgins, meaning those who have not been involved in the pagan world system. All will be singing new song in praise to the Lord for some great, amazing things He has done (Ps. 98:1). The new song mentioned here could only be sung by people redeemed from the earth and purchased by the blood of the Lamb. I may not have a new song each day, but I have considered my favorite, *Amazing Grace* by John Newton.

Believers are those who have been purchased with the death of Christ. We secure four things regarding redemption in Christ:

1. The agent of redemption is Jesus Christ (Eph. 1:7; Col. 1:14; Rom. 3:24).

2. We are purchased with the blood of Christ (1 Cor. 6:19-20).

3. The object of redemption is that humanity's sins are forgiven, and the relationship with God is restored (Eph. 1:7; Col. 1:14).

The angels, creatures, and elders cannot sing it, for they have not experienced redemption from sin. It was a victory song. The host of Heaven was the audience:

1. We do not know what the words will be on the glorious day of redemption. The redeemed will be given a particular song of victory. The glorious victory is because of Jesus Christ (Ps. 9: 1, 67: 3, 1 Pet. 2:9).

2. They will be Jews. No falsehood was found in these believers, and they are blameless because of their faith in Jesus Christ. They are called *"virgins,"* which does mean no contact with men but spiritual chastity and devotion to Christ (Duet 22:14-24).

The Israelites were to be different from their neighbors in all aspects of life to show their separation to the living God. We are to live blamelessly and stay separated from the world (Phil. 2:15, Rom. 12:1-2).

They will be virgins. They will have committed their lives to Christ:

1. They are subject to violence to be the ministers of the people (Rom. 15: 1, Lk. 18: 29 – 30, Phil. 3:8).

2. They will follow the Lamb and commit to him (Lk. 9:23, 14:26 – 27, 1 Pet. 2:21, 1 Jn. 2: 6). To be committed to Jesus Christ requires daily application of God's word.

3. They were redeemed from among men, the first fruit to God the Lamb. The first to be saved in the Tribulation.

4. There will be on the day of truthfulness many who take a vow to serve the Antichrist (Jn. 8: 44, Ps. 32:2, 1 Jn. 2: 22).

5. They will be blameless: unspotted, undefiled, and unpolluted, and without blemish before God. Set apart unto God.

Imagine being blameless before God, unspotted, undefiled, and unpolluted, and without blemish. What a challenge. We need believers like that today (Rom. 6:13, Rom. 12:1 – 2, 1 Cor. 6: 19 – 20, 1 Pet. 1: 18 – 19).

Verses 6-7

The messenger of the Gospel will be an Angel. He will have the Gospel to preach to humanity at the end of the Great Tribulation. Remember, God's people are going to be scattered all over the world. God's grace will still be executed for the unbelievers. When the time comes, God will divide sheep from the goats (Matt. 25:31 – 46).

The message will be about judgment, not salvation. It will be good news for Israel and the saved nations. When the end times come, evangelism will be a time of witnessing. They will proclaim to people the message of salvation in Jesus as Savior of the world (Lk. 19: 40). The message of God is called the everlasting Gospel, Gospel of grace, ageless grace, but in end times is called good news that He is speaking about His Son. The Gospel is preached:

1. It is good news because of what it announces.

2. It is an eternal message meaning "age-long or ageless."

3. It is universal in the scope containing a warning to all humanity of God's judgment.

4. Its content is about Christ and salvation through His work of the cross from sin's penalty.

5. We have three commands and two causes.

6. "Fear God" refers to His holy reverence, sovereignty, and power to deal with humanity.

7. Give Him glory refers to giving God praise and honor as the Creator of the Universe.

He desires to worship, and respect displayed as obedience, prayer, and singing. Humanity must reject the beast and his image, fear God, give Him glory, and worship Him.

The Gospel must be proclaimed to every nation, tribe, language, and people (Matt. 28:19 – 20, Mk. 6:15, acts 1:8, 1 Pet. 3: 15). It is now dealing with humanity's needs of righteousness and establishes God's sovereignty over the world. The angels will proclaim the message of the Gospel in the Great Tribulation flying above the earth, proclaiming the Gospel:

1. There will be a message to fear God.

2. Fear God and keep his commandments. Give glory to the Creator, for that hour of His judgment is come (Rev. 14:7).

3. God gives us a chance of the coming judgment, and we must repent and worship Jesus Christ (Matt. 10:28, Duet. 10:12, Ps. 31:19, Eccles. 12:13).

4. There will be a message to worship God and praise God (Matt. 4: 10, Rev. 14:7, 1st Chronicles 16:29, Ps. 95:6, 96: 9).

5. The same message was preached by the Church, Paul, and the Apostles for the last 2,000 years. The message the Angel delivers is salvation through the finished work of the Lord Jesus Christ.

6. Those who refuse repentance will populate hell (Matt. 25:41-46; Rom. 6:23; 1 Cor. 6:9-11; 2 Pet. 2:4; Rev. 20:10, 15; 21:8, 27).

Jesus Christ preached a message of love (Jn. 3:16); of hope (Jn. 6:37); of eternal salvation (Jn. 6:47, 10:28; and peace with God (Rom. 5:10). The same message was proclaimed in Eden (Gen. 3:21), pictured in the Law; and purchased on Calvary (Jn. 19:30). It is a message as fresh as the need of today, yet it is older than creation (1 Pet. 1:18-20; Rev. 13:8). It is the only message that will save the human soul from the wrath of God and an eternity in Hell (Jn. 14:1-6; Acts 4:12).

When the end comes, it will be too late to believe the Gospel. Today is the day of salvation (2 Cor. 6:2). If you have never believed the Gospel and received Jesus as your Savior, you need to do that today. Waiting will be forever too late.

Verse 8

The first Angel is preaching judgment to those who live on the earth. The second Angel announces, "Babylon is fallen," meaning "come to rein." It falls religiously, politically, and commercially (Rev. 18). It is a great universal fellowship of distinct personalities: English, German, Italian, Greek, Turk, Hindu, Arab, Chinese, and Japanese. The third Angel preaches judgment to anyone who worships the beast and his image.

Babylon is the name given to the civilization that was seduced by the beast (Rev. 17:1-9). It is mentioned in the Old Testament and is spoken in the New Testament (Rev. 17 and 18). Babylon was the center of idolatry and immorality. It is a system that represents rebellion against God. Sometimes it is compared with the name for Rome (Rev. 18:9, 10, 1 Pet. 5:13). It represents a world system filled with idolatry, corruption, and sexual sin. Babylon is an ungodly nation, government, and economic system known throughout history. Each time it is mentioned shows evil resistance to God. The climax comes in Chapter 14, when God's judgment, the bowls, plagues, and intoxicating wine are poured out on her. It was the great enemy of Israel (Isa. 21: 9, Jer. 50: 2, 51:8, Rev. 14, 6-13). History reveals a war between Babylon (the evil city) and Jerusalem (the city of God). The very name:

1. Babylon was a corrupt political system that stood against God.

2. It was a corrupt economic system that stood against God.

3. It was a corrupt religion that stood against God.

John saw a world that defiled God. The Antichrist establishes Babylon as the world's capital for the second beast's political, economic, and religious system. Both systems will be destroyed at the end (Isa. 21:9, Jer. 50:2, Jer. 50: 22 – 25, Rev. 18:2).

Babylon is described as a great prostitute who enticed men into the bed by giving them wine to intoxicate them (Rev. 17:2, Jer. 51:7). Babylon represents a system of unbelief. She is seen seducing the foolish sinners of this world. She leads them away from God with her lies, and she is about to pay a terrible price.

Humanity will drink her wine, which leads to pleasure. Babylon represents everything the world desires. Babylon represents everything that stands opposed to God. His judgment is coming upon her and her heresies, and none can stay His hand of judgment. The philosophy behind all of humanity's religious heresies and rebellion against God will be destroyed. The wrath of God will shatter their foundation.

The city will be destroyed for several reasons: Babylon will make all nations drink the wine of her fornication. Those who drink will drink the wrath of God:

1. Babylon is a picture of a world system of lusts and passions. God will destroy them. Nations will no longer resist our seduction. They will be unable to rest day or night from eternal doom (tortures from the beast on earth). The believers receive eternal rest forever.

2. She will induce governments of the world to join her in her corruption. What will corruption be? (Rev. 9: 20 – 21).

Idolatry will corrupt the world:

1. The living conditions will be secular and humanistic (Rom. 1:20 – 22, and 25, 1 Jn. 5: 21, Lev. 17:7, Ps. 106: 36 – 39).

There will be the corruption of murder:

1. A spirit of senseless killing and lawlessness will be sweeping on the earth. There will be the slaughtering of millions who refuse to place the state before God (Matt. 5: 21 – 22, Matt. 19: 18, 1 Pet. 4:15, 1 Jn. 3:15, Rev. 14:6 – 13).

2. There will be corruption by sorcery: horoscope, astrology, witchcraft, and demons in the world (Rev. 9:21, Isa. 8: 19 – 20, Mic. 5:12, Gal. 5:20).

3. There will be the corruption by fornication: the immorality of end times will run wild, even more than today (Rev. 9:21, 1Cor. 6:18, Eph. 5:3, Col. 3:5).

4. There will be the corruption of thievery: stealing in both high and low places in the world (Rev. 9:21, Exod. 20:15, Eph. 4:28, Titus 2:10).

The world will be corrupted with evil and murderous days because of a secular society in the last days. Babylon will have great religious and political significance in the last days (Rev. 18). Humanity is evil and will remain evil until God's Son creates a new creature to live in a new heaven and earth. God gives His Son to die on the cross to keep you out of Hell. You can go to Heaven or Hell. The choice is yours. God's wrath will destroy the nations and the people who follow the Antichrist (Matt. 25: 31 – 32, Roman 1:18, Roman 2:8, 2 Pet. 3:7, Jude 14 – 15, Job 21:22).

Verse 9

The Angel speaks, "With a loud voice," the bad news of God's judgment would be eternal to those who have the mark of beast, worship him and his image. Here is another manifestation of God's grace seeking to get humanity to respond to the good news. God does not wish to perish but to come to repentance and the truth (1 Tim. 2:4; 2 Pet. 3: 9b).

Disbelief runs through society today about God and the Savior of humanity. God's wrath will fall on people in the end because of religious loyalty to the state. Anyone who rejects Jesus Christ will be subject to wrath (Jn. 1:12; 3:16). The word "*wrath*" translates the word "*thumos.*" It is a word that pictures «an explosion of wrath; a sudden outburst; a passionate display of hot anger" (Heb. 10:31; 12:29).

Verses 10 and 11

God's wrath awaits those who receive the mark:

1. The ungodly and evil will drink the wrath and anger of God. The judgment of God is a significant fact: God must keep Heaven perfect.

2. The ungodly will be excluded from the new Heaven and earth.

3. Those who cursed, denied, and disbelieved, and rejected the messages of the Gospel.

4. Those hostile to God and His righteousness will drink His wrath.

5. Those who do not want his control and restraint upon their lives?

6. Those who reject the righteousness of God's Son and refuse to believe in Christ will die for their sins.

God has no choice but to keep the unbelievers out of Heaven. Remember, every man will have a chance to receive Jesus Christ. God has shown his perfect love to those who trusted him. He will execute perfect justice:

1. Wrath and anger will fall upon the ungodly and evil world:

2. The ungodly will drink the cup of God's wrath.

3. The ungodly will drink the entire cup of God's wrath without God's love, sympathy, regret, or compassion.

4. The ungodly will suffer a double portion of God's judgment. A cup of wrath and a cup of his anger (Jn. 3:36, Rom. 1: 18, Eph. 5:6, Jer. 49: 12).

5. The ungodly and evil will be tormented with fire and brimstone like the city of Sodom and Gomorrah (Rev. 14: 10, Gen. 19:23 – 24). The most terrorizing judgment has fallen on earth at this time. Jesus has already confirmed the fact (Matt. 10:15,11:24, Lk. 10:12, 17:29).

6. The enemies of God will spend eternity suffering in a bed of fire and brimstone.

7. Scripture does not tell us that the judgment of Hell will be like suffering fire and brimstone.

8. We can heed this warning and repent and turn to God (Rev. 19:20, 20:10, Ezek. 38: 22). Those who worship the Antichrist, and the beast will experience eternal punishment.

9. The ungodly will be tormented by the presence of the Holy Angels and Christ (Rev. 10). Christ will be there for every eye to see. They will know who he claimed to be.

10. The Messiah has come to save the world.

11. He now stands as the judge of the world to rid the Universe of all the ungodly and evil.

12. He is the exalted Lord who brings godliness and righteousness to the Universe (Matt. 24:30, 25:31 – 32, Rev. 1:7).

The ungodly and evil will be tormented forever (Verse 11). It is a picture of duration: punishment, torment, agony, and misery; that wrenching and twisting and pain and sufferings of never being relieved, of never having peace or rest, not even for a single night on the day. There is no peace in Hell; there is no rest in hell. There is only torment and horror, unbroken punishment, and suffering. The agony and misery, the pain and suffering of the fire and brimstone, never ends:

1. The smoke of their torment ascends forever. The torment of the ungodly and evil will never end.

2. We must all face this one fact if we reject Jesus Christ, we are doomed to punishment. A great day of separation is coming. You will live with Christ or in Hell forever, a world of everlasting punishment (Matt. 25:41, 46, Mark. 9: 47 – 48. Matt. 3:20, 13:41 – 42, Rev. 21:8).

God promised that sin would be punished (Rom. 2:6-11; 12:19). The wicked will be punished and thrown into Hell. Nobody wants to suffer this fate. God gives humanity time to repent. The only reason you are not in Hell today is due to the good grace of a merciful God. At any moment, He could sever the golden thread of life, and you would plunge into a Christless eternity, where you would be lost forever. Do not let that happen! Here again, is the promise and the call of the Gospel (Jn. 3:16; Jn. 7:37; Jn. 11:28). Come to Jesus and be saved! Come before it is too late (Prov. 29:1, Gen. 6:3).

Verse 12

What a contrast there is when we come to verse 12! We leave the wrath and judgment of Verses 6-11, and we are exposed to the sweet fragrance of

God's grace. The saints will have a fantastic future, those who keep God's commandments will receive God's blessing and care (1 Cor. 10:13). They are the ones who remain obedient, refuse to worship the beast, or receive his mark, or worship idolatry of the beast.

Verse 13

The dragon realized he has lost the battle in Heaven and has been thrown down to earth, and he pursued the woman who gave birth to the child. The woman symbolizes God's people. Satan is stalking and killing those who believe in Jesus, hoping to do as much damage as possible.

Many saints will die in the Lord. These people gave up a lot for their faith in Jesus Christ. They will give their life to Jesus Christ. That means they live for Christ or die (martyr) because they have accepted Jesus as his Savior. Who are the believers? To be in Christ means that a believer walks and lives in Christ day by day. It means that he does not walk after the flesh but after the spirit (Rom. 8:1, 4). It means that he should live soberly, righteously, and godly in the present world (Titus 2 – 12). It means that we bear the fruit of the spirit (Gal. 5:22-23). It means that we abide in Christ. Becomes connected and attached:

1. We are connected and attached to the body of Christ (1 Cor. 12:12 – 27.

2. We are branches connected and attached to the vine (Jn. 15:4 – 7).

3. Having lived in Christ when Christ lived upon the earth, the believer is counted sinless and righteous because Christ was sinless and righteous.

Having died in Christ, therefore, the believer never has to die (Jn. 3: 16):

1. The penalty and condemnation of his sins have already been paid for in the death of Christ.

2. Having been raised in Christ, the believer will receive the new life (Rom. 6:2 – 5, Rom. 4:22; 5:1; 6:14 – 15).

When the believer is living or dying, God will transfer him into Heaven, into His presence (Rom. 14:8, 2 Cor. 5:8, Phil. 1:21, Ps. 116:15). The believers will receive eternal life:

1. There is the reward of rest from earthly labor. One is exhausted and worn out.

2. There will be rest for the believer who witnesses and ministers for Christ.

3. The way the believer is to stand up against all the temptations and trials of this life.

4. The believers stand up for Christ and refuse to follow the beast and accept his mark.

5. When a person is faithful to Christ, when he is truly in the Lord, then he dies in the Lord. The Lord has taken him to Heaven. Rest means refreshed, revitalized, restored, recharged, and rejuvenated. It means free trials and temptations in a corruptible world (Job 3:17, 2nd Thess. 1:7, Rev. 14: 13, 2 Tim. 2: 10).

Heaven is not going to be in inactivity:

1. People think:

2. It will not be floating around on a fluffy cloud playing the harp.

3. The saints will not be standing around singing and praising God all the time. We will have unbroken fellowship and communion with him. Our Lord is worthy of more than songs and praises, words, and music.

4. Heaven is going to be full of both worship and service.

The physical world is corrupted, decayed, deteriorating, and passing away. God is going to destroy the old Heaven and earth and make a new heaven and earth. It will be transformed into a spiritual world that is eternal (2 Pet. 3: 10– 13) without blemishes. We will rule and reign with Christ as kings and priests under the leadership, direction, and supervision of Christ in Heaven (Rev. 19:7 – 8).

Satan will kill those who believe in Jesus Christ. His anger against God will increase, but it will be directed at God's people. We are reminded, "Do not be afraid of those who kill the body but cannot kill the soul. Instead, fear the One who can destroy both soul and body in hell" (Matt. 10:28). He saved us by His grace. He gave us His Spirit. Anything we have ever done for Jesus Christ; we are going to be rewarded:

1. The saints of God will be adopted as sons of God (Gal.4: 4 – 7; 1 Jn. 3:1).

2. The faithful will stand in God's presence one day and receive rewards (1 Cor. 3:10-15).

3. They are being made blameless and harmless (Ph. 2:15).

4. Receive eternal life (Jn. 3:16; 1 Tim. 6:19).

5. Being given an enduring substance (Heb. 10:34).

6. Receive a glorious body (Phil. 3:11, 21; 1 Cor. 15:42 – 44).

7. The saints receive eternal glory and honor, and peace (Roman 2:10).

8. The saints receive eternal rest and peace (Heb. 4:9; Rev. 4:13).

9. Being given the blessings of the Lord (Prov. 10:22).

10. Being given the knowledge of the Lord (Phil. 3:8).

11. Been given durable riches and righteousness (Prov. 8:18).

12. Being made priests of God (Rev. 20:6).

13. Being given a crown of glory (1 Cor. 9:25).

14. Being given a crown of righteousness (2 Tim. 4:8).

15. Being given a crown of life (James 1:2).

16. Being given a crown of glory (1 Pet. 5: 4).

17. Rewards dealing with work, position, or rule.

18. Being made an exalted being (Rev. 7:9 – 12).

19. Being given the kingdom of God (James 2:5; Matt. 25:34).

20. Being given a position of rule and authority (Lk. 12:42 – 44; 22: 28 – 29, 1 Cor. 6: 2 – 3).

21. Being given eternal responsibility and joy (Matt. 25:21, 23).

22. Being given rule and authority over the cities (Lk. 19: 17, 19).

23. Being given thrones and the privilege of reigning forever (Rev. 20:4, 22:5).

24. Being given the privilege of surrounding the throne of God (Rev. 7: 9 – 13, 20:4).

25. Being made kings (Rev. 1:5; 5:10).

After you die, there is no more opportunity to call on the name of Jesus. Judgment is sounded out to those who receive the mark of the beast and worship the image of him. The word of God tells us, "They will be tormented in Hell" (verse 11). Pain will be tormenting because God will add holy heat to the furnace, which will last forever. Every day and night, no rest from being tormented. The wicked will burn in the everlasting Hell. The beast and the false prophets will be cast into the lake of fire (Rev. 20:19). They are still burning and will burn forever (Lk. 16). If you do not accept Jesus Christ as your Savior, you will find out that Hell exists on the other side of the grave.

The word of God is here before you heard it and will be here when you are gone. If you died right now, are you saved? Are you troubled at the thought of going to the graveyard, your body you will go there in your spirit of God back to God gave it (Eccles. 12:7) Are you content with your choice of where you will spend eternity? Would you go to Heaven or go to

Hell? Jesus promises that he will reward you with more grace (1 Cor. 2:9; Eph. 4:7 – 11; Rev.14:13). Those alive will be changed and meet Jesus in the air (2 Cor. 5:1 – 8; Phil. 1:21 – 24; Lk. 16:22).

Verse 14

John views a picture of the coming judgment. He shares the Lord Jesus Christ's position in the coming days of His terrible judgment. When Jesus came the first time, He is the Savior who came to give His life on the cross so that sin is paid for, and sinners might be set free. Jesus comes the second time as a Judge, to destroy sin, Satan, and all those who stand in defiance to God. When Jesus returns, He will come in power, glory, and judgment, and none will be able to withstand Him! There will be no cross for Jesus the next time He comes. There will be a crown! There will be no tree for Him to hang upon, but there will be an earthly throne. Jesus Christ is sitting on his throne; it represents that he has been victorious. In this vision, Christ may be waiting for the angelic message to announce the time of the harvest or judgment.

The world today hates God's people. Many nations want to destroy the believers. When the Rapture comes, God's people are gone, the Antichrist will have little mercy on Israel. The last three years of the Tribulation will be a bloody death. God will send His judgment upon a wicked world because it is ripe for harvest.

The earth is suitable for a harvest, and the results will be worldwide. He will ride on the clouds, which will be His chariots. He will judge the quick and the dead (2 Tim. 4:1, 2 Thessalonian 2:8). Jesus Christ will clear the earth of all the hellish seeds sown by the Antichrist and his followers. Jesus is coming back to judge the nations (Matt. 25:31 – 32). The judge is going to call his court to order. He is going to be victoriously over all the ungodly and evil of this world. He will have a golden crown on his head, and he has a sharp sickle in his hand, representing his kingdom coming. Jesus will be reaping a harvest with a reaping instrument. The sickle is a two-edged instrument used in harvesting grain. The instrument will proceed out of His mouth as judgment to separate the tares from the wheat.

The world is going to know the one who sits on His throne:

1. He is worth forsaking the world and its pleasures and possessions.
2. He is worth standing up for his Father.
3. He was well worth dying on His behalf.
4. He was worth dying for humanity.
5. He was deserving being the righteous sacrifice.
6. He was well worth suffering persecution.

When Jesus returns in judgment, the world will know who he is and claim to be an ideal man, representative, perfect, and embodiment of humanity and divinity. The world will know the Man Jesus, the carpenter from Nazareth, and the Savior of the world. He will return on a white cloud: white symbolizing the purity of Heaven. White is a symbol of righteousness or holiness. It symbolizes the presence, majesty, and glory of God. The one sitting on a cloud is Jesus Christ.

Jesus Christ shall return wearing a golden crown. The word "crown" translates the word for "a victor's crown." It refers to the laurel wreaths that were given out to victors in the ancient Olympic Games. The fact that this crown is "golden" identifies the wearer as a King. It symbolizes royalty, rule, dominion, and sovereignty to bring perfect peace to the Universe.

Nothing is more valuable than God upon the earth. It will be a valuable experience imaginable. Jesus Christ shall return with a sharp sickle in his hand, returning to judge the world (Mark 8:28, Acts 7:56, Jn. 5:26 – 27, 2nd Thess. 1: 7 – 8, Jude 14 – 15, Rev. 1:7). He will either be a judge or Savior. The choice is yours.

Verses 15-16

Another angel comes out the temple, crying with a loud voice, speaking to him sitting on the cloud and saying, "Thrust is the sickle and reap, for the time is come for a harvest of the earth is ripe. The Angel comes from the heavenly temple, from the very presence of God (Matt. 24:36; Acts 1:7) to deliver the command of judgment." It will be a time to separate the wicked, the righteous, and it will be God's final dealings with humanity:

1. The world is pictured as a field of wheat that is ready to be harvested. The Lord takes His sickle, and He reaps the field (Matt. 13:24-30).

2. Jesus has perfect righteousness to judge the world. The earth's harvest will be a separation of believers from the earth's ungodly and evil. Jesus Christ's will be hovering over the earth with a sickle in his hand, and in a moment, every eye sees him because the hour to reap has come (Heb. 10:12 – 13; Ps. 2:7 – 9).

The harvest of the earth is ripe:

1. The word "*ripe*" means "to be dry or withered." It speaks of a crop that is "overripe." The Greek word for ripe is "*akmazo*," meaning to be fully ripe (Rev.14:18).

2. What a picture of the grace and longsuffering of God! The harvest of sin has been ripe since the first sin was committed in Eden. God in His grace, love, and mercy has withheld judgment, giving humanity time to repent. One day His patience will be exhausted, and His judgment will come on sinners. You need to search your heart and "give the diligence to make your calling and election sure" (2 Pet. 1:10.)

3. Another angel is bringing the same message of God. What is the message? The harvest of the earth is ripe. The time for Godson to reap has come. Therefore, the shout of the Angel is, trust in your sickle and reap. It is time for Christ to separate his own follows on the ungodly and evil. He takes the servants home to Heaven.

4. When the Lamb of God thrusts his sickle into earth's harvest, plagues never seen before will immediately come on the earth (Rev. 16:13). The great whore, the beast, is stripped of her pride and haughtiness. She will suffer from plagues, tormented, burned, sorrow, anguish, woe, and misery saw before.

The harvest takes place in Verse 16:

1. Jesus Christ thrust in the sickle on earth: and the earth is reaped. The believers are harvested: they are taken out of the world and away from its ungodliness and evil. They are deliberate to Heaven.

2. Never again will a believer suffer due to the mistreatment of an ungodly person.

3. Suffer due to hungry or cold or heat.

4. Suffer due to diseases or accidents.

5. We are suffering due to toil and exhaustion.

6. Suffer due to temptations and trials.

7. Suffer due to sin and ungodliness and evil and death.

8. Never again with the believers shed a single tear. Jesus will take believers from this world and into the new Heaven and earth. All believers are to be citizens of the new Heaven and earth as servants who oversee the operations of the Universe of God.

9. A picture of the believers of the end times being harvested (Matt. 13:30, 49; 25:32, Lk. 3:17, 16: 26, Prov. 13:21).

10. God is bringing an end to earth's ungodliness and the reign of the Antichrist. (2 Tim. 2:19).

Verses 17-18

An angel appears out of the temple with a sharp sickle to destroy the world with fire. It is the third picture of the coming judgment. First, there was the cup of unmixed wine to be poured out (Rev. 14:10), the second was the grain harvest (Rev. 14:15 – 16), and third was the great harvest (Rev. 14:17 – 20).

The Angel speaks to the Angel with the sharp sickle and commands him to harvest the ripe grape clusters from the poisonous vines on the earth. The picture here is that all the false religions of humanity are fully ripe and ready for harvest before returning the victorious Christ (Rev. 19:15).

The world has rejected Jesus the True Vine (Jn. 15:1-8). They have attached themselves to the vine of this world, and they have drunk deeply of the wine of sin and have rejected God and His Son Jesus. Jesus is coming back, and the world system will crush under His feet like grapes. It is the image Isaiah shows of the coming King (Isa. 63:1-6). Jesus is coming in wrath and judgment, and there will be no escape! The enemies of God will be thrown into "the winepress of the wrath of God," and they will be judged!

Jesus Christ treads the winepress, and the blood comes out. It refers to the city of Jerusalem when God's wrath will pour out in the battle of Armageddon. Blood will run two hundred miles (Rev. 16:14; 19:19). It is here that the wickedness of the earth will be concentrated. The beast and the false prophet will meet their doom (Ezek. 38 and 39).

The Angel will have the power to destroy the world with fire and refer to the Angel with authority over the fire on the altar that plays a part in this final drama of judgment (Rev. 8:3 – 5). The Angel answers the cries of the martyr under the altar (Rev. 6:10).

Verses 19-20

The angels obey God's commands across the earth and gather grapes which are the unbelievers. They will be placed into God's winepress. A winepress was a trough where grapes were collected and smashed until the juice ran into a holding container. The unbelievers will be collected and trampled in the winepress for their evil at the end of the Tribulation.

The unbelievers will be "*trodden*". The word means "*to crush with the feet*". Jesus will do to those who have despised and rejected Him like a man crushing grapes in a winepress. He will crush the enemies of God under His feet (Matt. 5:13, 7:6; Lk. 8:5, Heb. 10:29).

The gathering armies of the nations to Megiddo in the north of Jerusalem will gather in a final attempt to defy Jesus Christ. The blood-iest battle and carnage of human flesh the world has ever known will be seen. Blood will flow like bait used from a winepress, from the north of Palestine at Megiddo some 175 miles south down the Jordan Valley, the land of Palestine (Isa. 63:3 – 6). Megiddo is the name of a city in Manasseh. God overthrows the Canaanite kings by a miraculous aiding Deborah and Barak (Judg. 4). The name comes from a Hebrew word meaning to cut off and thus means "slaughter" (Joel 3:2, 12, 14).

Jesus will crush them like grapes in the winepress. Like crushing grapes under his feet to force them to release their juices, so the Lord Jesus will crush this world under His feet, and He will crush all the life out of every opponent of righteousness against God. It will be a terrible day!) Hundreds of millions of soldiers will die in a catastrophic battle (Rev. 19:11-21). Men have rejected the precious, saving, life-changing blood of Jesus, and now they will wallow in their blood! The Bible says it is coming! The Old Testament prophets wrote about these very events (Zech. 14:1-4; Joel 3:11-14). This battle will take place, and God will be victorious.

The believers are saved from Satan because of the bloodshed of the Lamb on Calvary. Jesus's blood saves you from the judgment and Hell! What about you? Are you under the blood today? Has the blood of Jesus been applied to the doorposts and lentils of your heart? Have you trusted Jesus as your Savior? Come to Jesus right now! One day Jesus will call His court to order; you need to be sure that you are saved before that day comes. His is coming back again (Rev. 1:7; 1 Cor. 15:52; Acts 1:11).

# CHAPTER 15

## *The Seven Angels*

---

God continues to offer His mercy and grace to humanity for repentance. The choice is God or Satan. The wrath of God is coming because the world has chosen Satan, and there will be no more mercy for all those who have rejected Jesus Christ. The door of the Temple is open, and the judgment of God will come from the holiest place. God sends forth his final judgment upon the Antichrist and his ungodly followers. The last plagues will visit the earth and bring a final judgment upon the unbelievers. They come in rapid succession after the seal and the trumpet judgment.

John looked at the scene in Heaven preparations and described several angels who had the seven last plagues. These plagues were in golden bowls and called the bowl judgments directed against the land, sea, rivers, lakes, sky, and beast (the Antichrist).

God is getting ready for the execution of the judgments described in Chapter 16. They are described as the seven last plagues and then as seven bowls full of God's wrath. The seven plagues are incredibly severe and occur in rapid succession. The plagues are culminated by the return of Jesus Christ and the final phase of Armageddon.

The series of bowl judgments constitute the third woe announced in Revelation 11:14 as "coming soon". The first two woes occurred under the fifth and sixth trumpets. The third woe involves seven plagues as unfolding during the sounding of the seventh trumpet, when the mystery of God will be finished (Rev. 10:7).

John's vision takes him to Heaven, and he is given a picture of end times. Jesus Christ will be victorious over the ungodly and evil of this world. Jesus is taking his believers to Heaven with him and judging unbelievers (Rev. 14:1 – 20).

Now, the seven angels with the seven plagues, the seven trumpets blast forth its judgments. They come fast and furious. Why? Because they are the last judgment. God has decided to end human history in two periods. The first period will be three and a half years and is called the beginning of sorrows. The last period will also be three and a half years and is called the Great Tribulation:

1. When the Tribulation begins, there will be seven seal judgments upon the earth (Rev. 6: 1 – 7, 17).

2. In the final three and a half years, there will be seven trumpets judgments that will take place on the earth (Rev. 8:1 – 14, 20) which includes the seven bowls judgments. The bowls in human history as we know it.

Revelation 15 is the shortest chapter in Revelation. John's vision in Revelation 15 is heavenly preparation for the judgment. We witness scenes of joy in Heaven and the scenes of judgment on the earth. In Heaven, we see scenes of worship, and on the earth, the scenes of wrath. When the angel appears, he symbolizes the prayers of God's people are about to be answered for millions martyred in the end time. God prepares for the final judgment of the Tribulation on earth. The earth has already suffered from the judgments God has unleashed, and they will serve to increase the agony on the wicked.

Verse 1

John saw another sign. The word *"sign"* is the same word translated as "wonder" in Revelation 12:1 and 3. It stirred people to bow before God, who is love, but His wrath is ready to be executed on the ungodly. The word *"great"* speaks of something that is "important and astonishing". The word *"marvelous"* has the idea of "something to be wondered." Everyone shall see Jesus when he comes to finish the judgment against the ungodly and evil of the world. His works will be great and marvelous against the evil in the world. John calls our attention to this vision because of what is happening in Heaven and on earth.

John sees a final judgment scene, the seven last plagues or seven bowl judgments. The word *"plague"* means "a hitting or a wound". When the seven angels emerge from God's Temple, they will pour out the bowl judgments of the Tribulation Period on the earth. They are complete, final, and full of the wrath of God. God's judgment began to fall on the earth and inflicted those who rejected the Gospel. The seven "vials" or "bowls" are full of God wrath and ready to be poured out upon the earth. The actual pouring of the vials begins in Revelation 16:1.

The word *"full"* means *"to be swelled"* and refers to the wrath of God that has reached the bursting point, and the dam breaks. God's wrath, the water of judgment, is going to drown both sin and sinner, and there will be no escape (2 Kgs. 4:6, Rev. 14:10). Every eye shall see him when he comes in person to finish the judgment against the ungodliness of the earth (Matt. 26:64, Rev. 1:7).

Verses 2-4

John sees a sea of glass mingled with fire, which symbolizes wrath and judgment. Those who had gained victory over the beast are standing with harps denotes victory. Can you imagine the music coming from these victors? They are standing as the true believers:

1. They will not follow the Antichrist policies and will be slaughtered for their actions. The enemies will falsely accuse them of the states. God is going to stop the evil rule of man.

2. The martyred believers will be victorious.

3. The believers will not worship his image (Rev. 13:15).

4. They will not receive his mark (Rev. 13:16 – 17).

5. Will not receive the number of the Beast, the number of 666 (Rev. 13:18).

6. The martyred believers will process harps. The harps are symbols of being soothed and given rest and of praising and worshiping God.

7. The martyred believers will sing great songs of victory: the lamb and the song of Moses that was sung by the children of Israel when they crossed the Red Sea celebration of God's power and judgment (Exod. 15: 1 – 19).

8. They sing to the Almighty God (Amos 4:13), praising His works in power and moves in glory - Verse 3a (Exod. 15:11; Ps. 80: 10; 139:14).

9. They sing to the King of saints or nations, whose ways are always right, and the truth is His ways (Duet. 32:4).

10. They sing to the Lord. His name is worthy of receiving worship and praise from humanity – verse 4a (Ps. 99:9).


Verse 4

God is Holy and just God, for all nations shall call to worship him (Ps. 86:9; Malachi 1:11; Rev. 14:6 – 7) because He will judge the earth – Verse 4b. He alone is worthy of judging sin and sinners because your righteous acts have been revealed (Ps. 98:2). They shall fear him:

1. The Nations have given praise to the beast, but now they fear God.

2. All the nations will bow at his feet (Isa. 2:2 – 4, 56:6 – 7, Ps. 100, 148).

3. The world will be judged. The word "judgment" signified the righteous acts of God in these terrible, horrible judgments contained in the vials of wrath.

Today, the believers who stand up for Jesus Christ look back at the cross and celebrate the victorious shedding of His blood. Without the blood, there is no salvation (Heb. 9:22; 1 Jn. 1:7b). We accept Jesus Christ as our Savior and will receive rewards in Heaven. He will carry us home to be in His presence, and we will lift our voices in songs all praises to the God of salvation.

We must never accept the marks of this world or be identified among the number of unbelievers. We must be diligent and bear only the marks of Christ (James 1:12, 1 Jn. 5: 4 – 5, Rev. 2:7, 3: 5, 3: 21).

All saints go through terrible times, but the judgment in these vials is terrible for the sinner. The pain, the woe, the anguish, the misery will be unspeakable. We should fear the Lord and glorify his name.

Verse 5

John saw "the Temple of the tabernacle is God's residence in Heaven." His testimony in Heaven was opened. The word *"testimony"* refers to the law handed down to Moses on Mount Sinai. The law set God's standard for living and gave humanity an understanding of God's holiness and what He expected. The testimony was openly denied by the Antichrist, who claimed to be God. He is about to be defeated in his ungodly systems because:

1. The doors to the Temple or the tabernacle are open – Verse 5. It refers to the inner sanctuary of the tabernacle in the Old Testament, the holiest of holies or the holiest place. Measuring the Sanctuary. https://www.endtime-insights.org/2020/03/measuring-of-the-sanctuary.html (Accessed on March 2021). It pictures the judgment of God will come from the holiest place, from the very present and heart of God himself. God will send His judgment upon the Antichrist and his ungodly followers.

2. The angels who come out of the Temple are dressed to show freedom from corruption, immorality, and injustice. They oversee God's bidding.

Verse 6

The seven angels of the holiest place are fantastic creatures out of God's presence:

1. The scene is terrifying, for:

2. They hold the seven plagues in their hands.

3. They are dressed in pure white linen, the symbol of the wholeness of Heaven and God's holiness. His righteousness, justice, and how to be exercised, rule, and reign over the whole earth.

4. They have gold belts that symbolize royalty, authority, and power.

God will equip these seven angels, and they are given seven golden bowls with the wrath of God in them (Verse 7). The apparel signifies the character of the angels' mission with the vials clothed in "pure and white linen". It signifies their holiness, reflecting the holiness of the One they serve. They wear "golden girdles" around their chests, which signifies divine righteousness in their actions (Isa. 11:5; Rev. 1:13). It speaks of the majesty and glory of the God they serve.

They will be poured out on the earth the seven last plagues. These beasts give the angels seven bowls of plagues filled with God's wrath, signifying that the Tribulation plagues will be carried out against sin and sinners:

1. The throne is the source of God's trumpet judgments (the vials).

2. They will pour out upon the earth God's wrath upon the evil systems of the world and those who refuse to drink the cup of his salvation.

3. There is the cup of salvation (Ps. 116: 13).

4. There is the cup of wrath and judgment (Ps. 75:8).

5. The door to the Temple of God, to Heaven and salvation, will be close. Not until the seven judgments for completed. God will withdraw prayers; mercy will do no good. The door to Heaven and salvation will be close.

6. The glory and power of God will consume the evil of the world. No man will be able to enter the Temple of God's presence and stop it. It will be too late (Jn. 3: 36, Rom. 1:18, Roman 2:8, Eph. 5:6). The Millennium can begin for 1000 years of peace.

Jesus came to do the finished work of God, offer grace and mercy to the lost. However, the believers are expected to live holy lives for the glory of God as redeemed saints are seen as righteous!

Verse 7

The four beasts give the angels the golden vials full of God's wrath. The beasts in Revelation 15:7 do not refer to heavenly creatures. God has commissioned them, seven angels, to do the job of casting judgment never known on the earth. God has no alternative, for they have rejected Jesus Christ, and that demands righteous judgment.

God's wrath had been building against sin from the beginning. His anger will boil over, and absolute justice will be the result. Whether it is now or in that coming day, the only refuge a sinner has is the blood of Jesus Christ.

Verse 8

The scene indicates that God's mercy is passed. The door has been closed, and God will judge sinners, and there is nothing they can do to stop Him. It is too late to pray, repent and change. There is no more hope, grace, and opportunity to enter the Temple and be saved. The door of temple will not be opened again until the seven plagues are fulfilled.

There are three steps, and the judgment of the seven angels came out of the Temple of God:

1. They are commissioned and equipped in the presence of God, the Temple.

2. One of the living creatures gives each angel a golden bowl or vial to pour out on the earth God's wrath.

3. The angels cannot act until God gives the command to move and pour out his vengeance.

One of the living creatures gives each of the angels a golden bowl or vial. The angels cannot act until they receive the command from God (Rev. 6:1). When the bowls are poured out, no one escapes the judgment. When smoke filled the Temple, it manifests God's glory and power (Rev. 4:6; 5:6; 6:1; 7:11; 14:3; 15:7; 19:4). John saw that God's glory filled the Temple, appearing like smoke. God set in motion the final phase of judgment against humanity. That at this time, praise and worship were suspended.

God is longsuffering, patient, reasonable, and kind, but He is a consuming fire (Duet. 32:39-43; Ps. 7:11; Nah. 1:3; Heb. 12:29). Today, God is offering salvation to whosoever will come to Jesus. On that day, He will offer salvation to no one (Isa. 28:21). All He will give then is judgment, wrath, and damnation.

It will make a difference in what you believe, have heard, what you have been taught. God's word speaks of hell filled with fire and brimstone. You need the blessed assurance, Jesus is mine! Oh, what a foretaste of glory divine. Your acceptance of Jesus will save you (2 Tim. 1:12; 1 Jn. 3:14; Rom. 8:16). The door is open now.

# CHAPTER 16

## *The Seven Vials Judgments*

---

The seven trumpet judgments have been different from the seven bowl judgments. John sees the trumpet's judgment constituted a call for repentance and the bowls judgment constituted a call for the execution of total judgment when there is no more hope for repentance.

As Chapter 15 closes, the temple is filled with smoke from the glory of God. Nothing inside could be seen, and no one could enter the temple. There was a heavenly blackout, and there was no place for mercy. God is hidden in his glory, inside His temple. In biblical Scriptures, God's presence was in the temple for dedication or inaugurations, and no one could enter (Exod. 40:34 – 35; 1 Kings 8:10 – 11).

Chapter 16 opens with a great voice heard out of the temple, from the inner shrine of the temple in heaven, from God himself, saying to the seven angels, "Go ye and pour out the seven bowls [or vials] of the wrath of God into the earth" (Rev. 16:1). They were to go their separate ways and pour out the vials of the wrath of God on earth. In obedience to this command, each angel empties his vial into, or upon, an appointed object. There is no mistake regarding the contents of the vials that are to be poured. We have in this chapter the glory of God in judgment.

In the modern sense of vial, the original sense of the word Greek is the source of the English word "*vial*," which means a shallow cup or bowl. The pouring out symbolizes the execution of God's wrath, which finally falls upon humanity. The first three vials are poured into the objects named, while the last four are poured upon them, as indicated. Judgment is coming to the earth, the horror that staggers human imagination during the last days of human history:

There will be the seven bowl judgments:

1. The judgment is called the beginning of woes before the Tribulation.

2. There will be the seven trumpets judgment that take place during the Tribulation.

3. There will be the bowl judgments of this passage right at the end of the world, at the very end of the Great Tribulation.

4. The first bowl is on the earth. Horrible malignant sores break out on everyone who has the mark of the beast. Physical pain comes to those who have not repented.

5. The second bowl poured out on the sea; it becomes blood, and everything in it dies. With the death of the sea, all ecosystems are affected.

6. The third bowl is on fresh water. Inland waters turned to blood. With the death of the inland waters, there is no water to drink.

7. The fourth bowls is on the sun, which scorches people. People burned by the heat curse God for it.

8. The fifth bowl is on the beast's seat, throne, or kingdom. Darkness covers everything. People are in anguish because of the darkness, but they curse God and refuse to repent. They still have the sores from the first plague and the burdens from the fourth plague.

9. The sixth bowl is on the Euphrates River which dries up to provide a way for the armies of the East to march west without hindrance and gather at the battlefield of Armageddon.

10. The seventh bowl is in the air. An earthquake more significant than has ever occurred changes the face of the earth. Then comes a terrible hailstorm. The great city of Babylon is destroyed, islands are engulfed, mountains are flattered. People continue to curse God.

### Verse 1

God has always tempered His wrath (Hab. 3:2). The time for judgment has come, and there will be no mercy any longer. God's final wrath is about to be poured out on the earth. John writes, "*He* shall drink of the wine of the wrath of God, which is poured out without mixture into the cup of His indignation» (Rev. 14:10). In these verses, the world is about to experience the wrath of an offended God.

The seven angels are commanded to go your way and emptied the seven bowls of God's wrath on the earth. The great voice from the temple is the voice of God himself, who gives the command. The seven angels stand ready to move upon God's command. Empty your vials to the last drop on every square inch of the earth (Zeph. 3:8; Ps. 69:24; Jer. 10: 25).

It immediately tells us two things God is and He is righteous:

1. Therefore, we can have confidence that God will right all the wrongs and injustice upon the earth.

2. God will not allow ungodliness and evil to continue without being stopped.

### Verse 2

The outpouring of the bowls happens in rapid succession. What is the first bowl judgment? Humanity has attached itself to the company of the beast, bears punishment to the fullest, and it is poured upon the earth by divine authority. Ulcerous sores will be harmful and malignant, open, and foul, painful and purifying, repulsive, humiliating, and embarrassing. The word "*sore*" means an ulcer or break in skin tissue. It has the idea of an open, running, ulcerated place on the skin. It refers to an oozing boil.

They will cause agony and torture, giving no rest day or night from the pain. There will be no cure (cream, no poultice, or no drug) to relieve the suffering from the boils and the pain. The ulcerous sores are like the boils that fell upon the Egyptians and Job suffering (Exod. 9:8 – 11, Duet. 28:35; Job 2:7, Rev.16:10-11).

The antichrists will murder and shed the blood of millions. God's judgment is poured out only upon the Antichrist and his followers, who have the mark of the beast and worship him and his government. God is going to punish them with an equal punishment: cancerous sores. The believer will be protected by the seal Christ they have received in (Rev. 7:3) and a promise of protection (Rev. 3:18).

Verse 3

The second bowl judgment poured out judgment upon the sea. God is faithful and righteous. His love for his people will be offended. Therefore, God will punish the evil by allowing a bloody red substance to pollute the sea and the earth's fresh water. The seas will become infected will blood-red contamination, and all sea life will be killed:

1. The fishing industries and commercial outlets will go bankrupt, and the effects upon the economy will be catastrophic caused by evil the ungodly of the world.

2. The seas will become vast cemeteries. Beaches will no longer attract sun worshipers and pleasure seekers. Instead of being thronged with crowds of sunbathers, the world's beaches will be choked with the rotting carcasses of billions of dead sea creatures.

3. After the second trumpet sounds, a third of the sea creatures will be killed (Rev. 8:8 – 9; Exod. 7: 20 – 21).

4. The ocean supplies an abundance of their daily food; millions will face starvation without the seas and oceans. The socio-economic impact of this plague will devastate the earth.

### Verse 4

The third angel poured out his bowl on the freshwater where the Antichrist and his policy concentrated where little water already exists. This time the rivers and springs will turn to blood like the Nile River rivers of Egypt were polluted by God with blood-red pollution (Exod. 7: 17 – 25). Not one drop of freshwater will be left for drinking, washing, and bathing. Water is a necessity for human life. Have you ever been thirsty? People will go to their refrigerators and will not find food. The Lord is removing every prop, every comfort, everything humanity leans on for support and survival.

### Verses 5-7

The angel of the waters was in perfect agreement with God's divine judgment. He justified God's acts. Our human minds cannot comprehend the judgments of these verses. We shrink back from them and think that they are horrible. We recoil when we think about people having to suffer as people will suffer during the Tribulation. We might even feel that there must be a better way. We will understand that the time for judgment has come. We know that God's grace has held back the judgment until every soul has had a chance to repent.

Another angel from the altar of God says, "Even so, Lord God Almighty, truth and righteousness of God judgment'" (Rev. 16:7). The angels are saying, "Amen! Let them drink blood, the shed blood of saints! When judgment comes, we can rest assured that God will judge individuals in the right way. God stretches His hand out to humanity, and they pay little attention. They will not listen to his reproof. God will pour out his wrath upon humanity, and they will live in calamities (2 Thessalonian 2:8 – 12; Duet. 32:29 – 43; Isa. 28:21). Genesis 18:25 says, "Far be it from You to do such a thing, to kill the righteous with the wicked, so that the righteous and the wicked are treated alike. Far be it from you! Shall not the Judge of all the earth deal justly?"

### Verse 8

The fourth bowl judgment was poured out on the sun. In Revelation 8:20, the heavenly bodies were affected. One-third will blacken out. God will push the sun so near the earth, its rays will scorch the back of the evil inhabitants on the earth (Verse 8-9). The sun's rays scorch and burn like a blowtorch on the backs of humanity. God will take the beautiful, like giving, earth-warming sun and turned it into a giant ball of tormenting fire. Can you imagine your body burn with intense heat?

Heat waves never seen before will occur. People will be scorched, causing misery and torment. The weather will be so hot that it will burn like a hot oven. The pain will be so unbearable that humanity will gnaw their tongues and curse God. Moses and Malachi speak of the days God will use His mighty hand against humanity (Duet. 32:24; Isa. 24:4 – 6, 60:2; Malachi 4:1).

Verse 9

You would think that humanity will fall on their faces and cried out to God for mercy. The ungodly will not repent because they are sinful and have accepted the beast's mark and continue to worship him instead of Christ. They will do the same as usual: curse and blaspheme the name of God. They knew God and refused to glorify him as God (Roman 1:18). The most dangerous thing in the world is not knowing God, the truth, and refusing to follow God. They will not repent any more than they do today (Acts 7:51, 1 Cor. 24:19; Zech. 7:11).

It is incredible that people know the truth and what is happening; they stand defiantly to Him and His will. The Bible tells us in Verse 9, "They *blaspheme*" the name of God. That word means "to revile; to speak evil of". They shake their puny fists toward God and revile His holy name!

They dare to blame Him for their troubles and suffering. Of course, that has been the human way since the dawn of time. Even in Eden, Adam and Eve sought to blame their problems on others (Gen. 3:11-13). That trend continues today.

The problem is not with God. The problem is stated in Verse 9, "They repented not to give him glory." They refused to repent of their sins to the glory of God, and they are paying a heavy price for their choice. They have no one to blame but themselves!

Do not fool around with repentance. The time for repentance is now. If you are not saved, you need to come to Jesus today. You need to be saved today! If you carry a burden for those headed to this horrible time called the Tribulation, the time to pray for them is now. If you are saved and want to praise Him for delivering your soul from death, Hell, and judgment, today would be a good time to do just that. Listen to His voice and come as He calls you.

Verses 10-11

The fifth angel poured out his bowl on the seat of the throne of the Antichrist (Rev. 16:10). They will be in darkness. There will be no moon, sun, and stars, only total blackness. The last time the earth was blacked was when Jesus hung on the cross, paying the sin debt.

Jesus tells us, "In those days" (Mark 13:24 – 25). The army will be destroyed, and their government and cities at Armageddon because they are ungodly and evil. This judgment could be worldwide because the world will cooperate with Antichrist (Joel 2: 1 – 2).

Christ predicted that the sun and other light sources would be darkened, stricken with pitch-black darkness (Matt. 24:29; Exod. 10: 21 – 23). Humanity does not fall on their faces and begs God for mercy. The darkness represents sin and evil that has always engulfed the world. God sends them strong delusions, believing in the Antichrist; they are damn and doom for Hell. God lets the Antichrist, and his followers know what is waiting on them because they have rejected Jesus. Once, when speaking of Hell, Jesus said this, "And cast ye the unprofitable servant into outer darkness: there shall be weeping and gnashing of teeth" (Matt. 25:30). Here, we see a small glimpse of what those who reject Jesus will face when they go to Hell.

If you have never been saved, you need to pay attention to what the Bible is saying! There is a real place called Hell, and real people will spend eternity in judgment there. Do not turn your back on the Light! Come to Jesus and be saved, or you will find yourself in a horrible place called Hell one day!

Verses 12-16

God has always prepared the way for his people in the wilderness after leaving Egypt. He rolls back the Red Sea and the Jordan River. God prepares the way for the world to be delivered from sin when he sends his only son to the Calvary's cross. God also prepares the way for the destruction of all evil.

The sixth angel poured out his bowl upon the Euphrates River, and it sets the stage for the battle of Armageddon. (Rev. 9:13 – 21). The judgment is prepared for the nation and armies of the world for the great battle of Armageddon (verse 16). Why was the Euphrates a vital river?

1. The Euphrates River has played an essential part in human history. It served as the dividing line between the Roman empires of the West and the Parthians from the East, who had defeated the Roman Empire twice. If it dried up, nothing could hold back the invading armies. Some facts about the Euphrates River:

2. The Euphrates is the longest and most crucial River of Western Asia. The Euphrates begins in Turkey at Mount Ararat and flows south, through Iraq, and into the Persian Gulf. It is 1780 miles and ranges from 300 to 1200 yards wide. How could such a river dry? Up? It is not mentioned how this will happen. Scripture clearly says that the river's water will be dried up (Rev. 6:1 – 8; 12 – 17; 8: 6 – 12; 9:12 – 21, 13: 11 – 18).

3. The river poses a problem for a modern mechanized army, but God will remove every obstacle and prepare the way for a massive invasion

of the Middle East. God will speak, and the Euphrates' waters will cease to flow so that a massive army can pass.

4. The river drying up would allow the tremendous armed Confederation of nations to march against Israel and exterminate the Jews (Rev. 14: 20, 19: 17 – 21). This Federation is called the kings of the East. Remember some facts:

5. No matter how sophisticated weapons get, it takes a soldier to set foot on land to conquer it.

A foot soldier is needed to conquer a nation when the conquerors want to preserve the land. Atomic bombs will destroy the land and resources for decades.

1. They want to preserve Palestine for its wealth. Therefore, they march against it with foot soldiers and weapons. God will help advance the troops passing when the great Euphrates River is drive up when they march.

2. The place of the great battle (Rev. 19: 17 – 21, Matt. 25:13, Lk. 12: 37, Rev. 16:15).

Other nations of the world will become nervous. The reason may be:

1. The fear of a military move to conquer the world by beginning in Palestine.

2. The Middle East resources such as oil may be destroyed or taken.

3. The insanity of exterminating a whole people and nations like the Jews (Rev. 16:12, Joel 3:9 – 16, Zech. 9:10, 20, 12: 1 – 9).

4. The Confederation of nations of the earth is going to be involved in the great battle of Armageddon.

5. The kings of the East: all the nations East of Palestine, involving the Arabs, China, and other Eastern nations. The Antichrist will head these.

6. The intention of this army is the destruction of Israel. The phrase "*kings of the east*" means "the kings of the rising sun". This reference has caused many to speculate that China and her allies will be the army source. In Revelation 9:16, the Bible speaks of an army that numbers some 200 million. Only one nation on earth could raise an army of that size: China.

7. The East refers to the region of Mesopotamia (Assyria and Babylon) will dry up allowing the kings of the Antichrist to assemble. Their final goal will be the destruction of the Jews.

8. The kings of the north of Palestine, including Russia, will be involved in the war.

9. The kings of nations south of Palestine, including the nations of Africa, will be involved in the war.

10. The kings of the West of Palestine, including a Western alliance and some European nations, America, and Canada, will be involved in the war.

11. The armies will gather from every nation, with each taking sides to protect its interests.

Verse 13 tells us three unclean like frogs poured out of the mouths of the dragon, the beast, and the false prophet. Frogs are unclean creatures and are used here to refer to evil spirits of demons. The picture is of the demons working miracles to convince the world's kings to gather for battle. What kind of miracles? Scripture does not say, but the idea is that will be deceptive dreams of glory.

12. The dragon will strike fear within the heart, arousing bitterness and hatred among nations:

a. Paul warns that in the last days seducing spirits will come, teaching lies (1 Tim. 4:1 – 6).

Armageddon is the last great war on the earth that the Antichrist and his government will instigate. *"Armageddon"* means "the hill or city of Megiddo." *Armageddon* means Mount of Megiddo, which is in the "Plain of Esdraelon." This location is the site of some famous biblical battles. It was here that Barak and Deborah defeated the Canaanites (Judge. 4-5). It was here that Gideon defeated the Midianites (Judge. 6-8). King Saul and his son Jonathan were killed in battle (1 Sam. 31). King Josiah also met his death in the valley of Megiddo (2 Chronicles 3). The great valley runs through the middle of the Holy Land from the Mediterranean Sea to the Jordan River. It is approximately 200 miles long and 10 miles wide (Rev. 12:9, Rev. 16: 13 – 14). The kings of the earth set themselves against the Lord (Ps. 2:1 –4).

God will congregate all the kings and their armies in one place at one time for the last great slaughter. The detail of this battle will be considered when we come to Chapter 19. God is doing two things:

1. He drives up the great Euphrates River that would hinder their movement toward Jerusalem.
2. He allows three demonic spirits to go out and draw the kings and their armies to Jerusalem for the battle (1 Kings 22:20 – 22).

The scene is called the great day of God Almighty or the day of the Lord. It means several things:

1. It can mean the end times (Christ's birth and continue into the present). It will be a time when God defeats all the forces of evil. It pictures a time when God will intervene directly and dramatically in world affairs, including punishment and blessing (Isa. 13:6 – 12; Ezek. 38 – 39; Joel 2:11, 28 – 32, 3:2).

2. It can mean the final judgment day at the end of time.

3. The armies of the world will be destroyed. It is a day Jesus Christ will return to rule and reign over the earth. Time and history are no more as we know. God's goodness and righteousness will be brought to earth by Jesus Christ.

Christ warns the people on the earth (Verse 15) to watch and be prepared for the unexpected (Matt. 24:42 – 44, Lk. 12:39-40; 1st Thess. 5:2, 4; 2 Pet. 3:10). This verse is referring to the Second Coming. Jesus and He are telling His precious people to hang on for just a little longer. The saints of God are encouraged to keep the faith until the Lord returns. He is coming like a thief. The world will not see the signs, but He will come instantly and bring judgment with Him. A person must be clothed in the righteousness of the Lord, with their white garment ready. Jesus Christ is coming back like a thief in the night, in a totally unexpected manner. We must watch and be prepared. We must not be deceived by the miraculous signs performed by the demons of the evil Trinity. We must remain faithful and will not need to walk naked and ashamed. We must do so by resisting temptation and remaining committed to God's moral standards. We must remain as faithful workers in the vineyard (Matt. 20:1-2).

The pouring out of the seven bowls gives a picture of Jesus coming to render judgment upon the evil of this world. Final judgment cannot be poured out until every righteous one is out of range of God's fury. It was likewise on the day of the flood (Gen. 7:1 – 16). In the days of Sodom, God did not destroy the city until Lot was safely outside (Gen. 19). The Church (the Bride of Christ) would not go through the Tribulation (Rev. 3:10; 4:1 – 3). The six bowls will bring all the kings of the earth, with their armies, to this valley of slaughter. It has already been a great battlefield (Judg. 5:19; 2 Chronicles 35:22). It will become a valley of slaughter, two hundred miles of blood six feet deep and ten miles wide (Rev. 14:20).

Verses 17-18

The seventh angel poured out his bowl into the air or atmosphere. The very air that man breathes is affected; it is poisoned. The angel wants to show John the great judgment upon them to come upon the great prostitute. The great prostitute is Babylon, representing the early Roman Empire with many gods that killed Christians (Rev. 17:18). The great prostitute exists where there is satanic deception and resistance to God. She is a seductive government system that uses immoral means to gain pleasure, prosperity, and deception. A prostitute in the Old Testament describes a harlot, a nation that is a religious apostasy. An apostasy is falling away and abandoning religious truth.

God's thundering voice announces. The judgment of God wipes out all the armies of the ungodly nation. Nature breaks loose in the terrifying devastation imaginable. The power of God is launched through violent storms and a worldwide catastrophic earthquake:

1. It will affect the whole world.
2. The great city of Jerusalem will be shaken by the earthquake and divided into three parts, destroying Babylon, the capital city of the Antichrist will collapse and break up into three parts (Verse 19).
3. It will be destroyed.
4. Entire cities and nations of the world will collapse into ruins. There will be devastation, destruction, horror, injury, death, and mass confusion.
5. The great world city, Babylon, will be remembered by God, and he will especially pour on her the cup and fierceness of his wrath (Verse 19).

A great voice speaks out from the temple of heaven, saying, "It is finished," this is followed by thunder, lightning, and an earthquake (Rev. 16: 21). Humanity has never seen fantastic events like this before in human history. History will be finished, and the end has come. With the seventh bowl, God's wrath is completed.

Jesus paid the supreme price for the redemption of sinners. Nothing more could be added; redemption is complete. In the same expression, Jesus is about to get rid of the dragon, the beast, and his false prophets. The pain, agony, calamity, confusion, chaos, discord, agitation, and cataclysmic manifestations upon the earth are over (Rom. 8:22). It is done. Glory hallelujah!

Verses 19-20

Much of the earth will break up; some islands and mountains will disappear. The Lord of hosts shall visit the earth with thunder, earthquakes, great noise, tempest, and the flame of the devouring fire (Isa. 29:6). Satan's kingdom is crumbling. The elements have turned him into a liquid fire (Ps. 50:3 – 4; Isa. 2:19 – 21; Hag. 2:6 – 7).

An earthquake will shake the city of Jerusalem into three parts, and all other major cities all over the world are reduced to ruin. Jerusalem is protected from total devastation because it is in God's hands (Zech. 14:4; 13:8 – 9).

Verse 21

Along with the lightning, thunder, and earthquakes, great hailstones severely fell on the people on earth. The hailstones fell, weighing about a talent. Talents at the writing of Revelation were 115 pounds, why others were 135 pounds. An Egyptian talent was 86 pounds, and in Antioch, it was 390 pounds. The giant hailstones I have seen were about an inch or the size of a chicken egg or softball. Whatever the weight of the hailstones in Revelation, it caused great devastation and chaos on the earth. The people cursed God in Revelation 16:21. Instead, they chose to praise the Antichrist.

Revelation 16:21 –22 tells us, "Great devastation will occur because humanity continues to blaspheme God for the plagues. There is no reaction of the ungodly around the world today to turn from their wicked ways.

They still blame and blaspheme God for what is happening and still do not repeat it. People will be rigid, stubborn, evil, and ungodly as people are today (Rev. 13:1; 16:11). They say, where is God? The born-again saint will be thankful because of Jesus we will be air with Him. He has saved your soul, and we need to pray that others may repent and receive the salvation of the Lord.

Are you saved? Repent and believe in the Lord Jesus Christ and be saved now (Jn. 5:24; Rom. 10:9-10). Your last day of living may be today; don't waste the moment if you have not received Jesus Christ.

# CHAPTER 17

## The Mother of Evil

---

John continues to see a vision of Babylon and the ten kings who made war on the Lamb, but they were soundly defeated (17:14). We also witnessed the defiance of humanity in the face of judgment, refused to repent. Evil has exemplified religion, government, worship of the state, and the Antichrist. The Antichrist or the false prophet plans to bring all world religious systems together, but they will be defeated. The Antichrist, the beast, and his followers would no longer seduce the nations. God's punishment will unfold in Chapters 17 and 18. He gives us the details of the destruction of the Babylonian system.

God releases the last plague in Revelation 16:17-21. They bring about a great earthquake that destroys the world's cities. All of humanity's accomplishments, centers of pleasure, and profit are wiped out.

In Chapter 17, John has a vision of the last days describing the prostitute and the scarlet beast trouncing. The great prostitute is Babylon. Scripture called her a political and religious system. The judgment of both religious and political Babylon comes to an end under the seventh bowl judgment. After these things are destroyed, Jesus can come to the earth and set up his everlasting kingdom of righteousness. Before he does, a few things must be done:

Evil and godliness must be destroyed – Chapter 16.

False religion must be destroyed – Chapter 17.

All the godless politics, government, and social systems must be destroyed – Chapter 18.

Verse 1

Babylon promises to bring under one banner. The whole world will come under the seduction of false religious promises of the Antichrist: life, salvation, peace, security, and hope in life. Who is Babylon?

1. An angel approaches John to show him the judgment and the destruction of religious Babylon.

2. Babylon is a great harlot.

3. Babylon sits upon many glasses of water, that is, people.

4. Nations of the world will support Babylon.

5. Babylon will receive his powers from the beasts or Antichrist.

6. It will have a rich appearance but would be corrupt.

7. It will have a unique name.

8. It will be prejudiced and have extreme power.

Spiritual harlotry stands for false gods, false worship, false religion, and false devotion opposed to God. The Old Testament uses prostitute ("harlot") to describe a nation's religious apostasy (Isa. 1:21, 23:15; Jer. 13:27; Ezek. 16:15; Hosea 1:2). The great prostitute represented the early Roman Empire with its many false gods and the blood of Christian martyrs on its hands (Rom. 1: 22 – 23, 2 Tim. 2:5, Isa. 42:8, 45:20).

The great city of Babylon will rule over the kings of the earth. Babylon is also called a harlot. The first verse tells us that we will witness "the judgment of the great whore". The word "whore" is not a decent word to use. The Hebrew word used by the Bible translates "*qadesh*" and refers to "temple prostitute or sodomite" (duet 23:17-18). It is a woman who sells her body for sexual uses; a harlot; a mother of the prostitute. It is also used to refer to a woman who is an "idolatress". Instead of being a woman of beauty and grace, she will be corrupt and make God vomit. He will call her an abomination.

Babylon, the nations were drunk with the wine of her fornication (Verse 2). What is this fornication? A system of idol worship and self-exaltation against God (1 Cor. 1:26-31). Babylon represents people committed to spiritual harlotry and prostitution.

The primary religions recognized by most people are Christianity, Judaism, Islam, Buddhism, and Hinduism. Most of the world's population observes one of these religions. When we are involved in an earthly religion, rituals, ceremonies, and teaching instead of following Jesus Christ as revealed in the Scriptures are harlotry. The Antichrist or the false prophet will one day bring these religions of the world together under one banner.

Religious Babylon sits upon many waters, represents people and nations (Rev. 17:15). Babylon will be many multitudes, and nations and languages will be caught up in the worship of false religion during end times. Today, millions are following false religions and worshiping idols around the world. Think how many profess Christ and yet do not believe or teach Christ in the word of God.

Christianity is different from all other religions because it is not a religion; it is a faith. When the Rapture occurs, all true Christians will be removed from this world. What will be left will be those who "have a form of godliness but deny the power thereof". Those people will be easy prey for the devil and demonic religion.

Verse 2

According to Verse 2, the entire world will come under the spell of this great end-time religion. It will be intoxicated by the teaching of this false system of belief. Like a slick seducer, this great harlot will seduce the world with her promises and her power. The great city will rule over the kings of the earth. Many nations will come and enjoy her pleasures.

Babylon is also called a harlot. The harlot is a manifestation of Rome (Rev. 17:9). The harlot stands for debauched worship, idolatry, and false devotion of their own making. It is a system that sets up humanistic doctrines and rituals to replace what God commands in the Scriptures (Jer. 3:6, 8-9, Hosea Chapters 1 and 2, Rev. 2:22). Humanity wants independence from God (Jer. 13:11; 33:9, Ezek. 39:13). The first verse tells us that we will witness "the judgment of the great prostitute (harlot)". These verses teach us about this system of false religion and how it will be judged someday. The angel tells John, "Come with me, and I will show you the future judgment of false religion" (Verse 1). This government will be supported by many kings, nations, governments of the world.

It becomes a worldwide religion. It will subdue the world with the wine of false teaching and create false assurance of peace and economic recovery to the earth. The government or state will become the God, and humanity will become the servants under an authoritarian state.

Verse 3

One of the angels poured out wrath on Babylon. He will enter the Jewish Temple and demand that the world worship him (2 Thess. 2:3-4). He will demand worship, and a deluded world will give him what he desires (2 Thess. 2:11). He will give this religion its power.

The angel takes John in the spirit is taken into the wilderness. The angel proceeds to show John the mystery of the woman and the beast who carries her. The beast will ascend out of the bottomless pit (Rev. 11:7) and go to perdition (Rev. 19:20).

The Bible speaks of two women in Revelation. In Chapter 12, another woman symbolizes God's people who fled into the wilderness for protection. This scarlet beast is described as having the name written all over with blasphemies against God.

They are rivals in every respect. One righteous and the other unrighteous (the mother of the harlots and abominations. One of God, and the other of Satan. One mother brought forth a son who is to rule all nations. The second is the mother of harlots. The first woman wore heavenly garments, clothed in the sun; her clothing was radiant with heavenly light. The second woman is arrayed in purple and scarlet. These are the colors of royalty and nobility. She is "decked with gold and precious stones and pearls, which speaks of her wealth and prosperity. She has the moon (the power of darkness) under her feet. The second woman hath the power to rule over the kings of the earth.

Both women will suffer and fill a great place in world affairs. One produces masculine, and the other produces feminine. Celestial wings help one, and the other is carried by dragon power. One has the crown of twelve stars upon her head and the other the name destroyer. One will live in Heaven, and the other in Hell.

Who is the woman in Revelation 17? The second woman is said to be the great harlot wears on her head "Mother of Harlots" (Verse 5). The dragon destroys the child of the first mother in the first battle by driving her into the wilderness. One of the angels shows John the judgment that is poured out upon the great prostitute. The great prostitute is called Babylon: This false religion will receive power from the beast, the Antichrist.

One of the angels shows John the judgment that is poured out on the great prostitute. The great prostitute is called Babylon. Babylon sits upon a scarlet-colored beast, meaning that all he is a government is under his authority rebelling against God. It will be the worship of the state itself. Not the religion. Two-thirds of the earth's population comprises worshippers of idols. Many live with the same spirit of Nimrod and Babylon. The government allowing business to sell produces too damn the souls will be here until Jesus returns (the spirit of Babylon).

The seven heads and ten horns represent the scarlet beast. The seven heads represent seven mountains upon which the woman sits. There are seven kings, five of whom have fallen, one is, and the other has yet to come. The ten horns represent ten kings who give their power and authority to the Beast, make war against the Lamb.

Seven heads voluntarily surrendered, and three heads he conquers. They are representative of the nation under his control. These are the primary nations preaching the false religion of Babylon, worship of the state. One of the angels shows John the judgment that is poured out upon the great prostitute. The great prostitute is called Babylon.

Verse 4

The religion dresses to draw attention to itself. It appears healthy on the outside but is filled with corruption. It is an abomination to God! It will thrive on seduction in money and power instead of holiness and godliness. It will turn humanity away from God with power, popularity, and prosperity.

It is identified as a harlot. A prostitute usually dresses provocatively to draw attention to herself, so does this false religious system. The woman wears the colors "purple and scarlet". These are the expression of royalty and luxury. The Bible speaks of two women in Revelation. They are rivals in every respect. One righteous and the other unrighteous (the mother of the harlots and abominations). One of God, and the other of Satan. One mother brought forth a son who is to rule all nations. The second is the mother of harlots. The first woman wore heavenly garments, clothed in the sun; her clothing was radiant with heavenly light. The second woman is arrayed in purple and scarlet. These are the colors of royalty and nobility. She is decked with gold and precious stones, pearls, and earthly clothing speaks to her wealth and prosperity. The first woman has the moon, representing the power of darkness under her feet, and the second woman has the authority to rule over the kings of the earth.

Both mothers will suffer and fill a great place in world affairs. One produces masculine, and the other produces feminine. Celestial wings help one, and the other is carried by dragon power. One woman has a crown of twelve stars upon her head and the other the name destroyer's and is a drink with the blood of saints and prophets. One will live in Heaven. The other will live in Hell.

Who is the woman in Revelation 17? The second woman is said to be the "the great harlot." She wears on her head "Mother of Harlots" (verse 5). The first battle destroys the child of the first mother by driving her into the wilderness.

Verse 5

The Babylonian system first appears in Gen. 11:1-9. The city was called Babel then and was founded by an evil man named Nimrod. The word *"Babel"* means gate to God, not the true God of Heaven and earth but an idol God. The people of Babel decided to build themselves a tower to reach into Heaven as some think. It was designed as a temple of Heaven. The constellations were placed on the top of this tower, and men climbed it to worship the heavenly bodies (Gen. 11:4). The tower and the religion represent false religions started by man. They were the first false religions built on humanism and pride. Many ancient rituals like Easter eggs, unicorns, the circle of life, yin yang, and Christmas trees have their origins in the Babylonian worship rituals. God judged these people for their rebellion and worship of false religions. Revelation 17 reveals what will happen to the false religions of this world at the end of the Tribulation Period.

Babylon is the great, the mother of prostitutes, and the abominations of the earth." The fact to be revealed to them is now confirmed a different religion. It will be the mother of much false religion and abomination upon the earth. It goes back to the town of Babel, gives many false religions to the world. Nimrod, man's decision to build the state a utopia.

Humanity turned away from God and set out to make themselves secure by building a tower straight up to Heaven. They left God out of the picture. Therefore, Babylon came to mean:

1. A godless religion (Isa. 1:21, Jer. 2:20, 3:1, and Ezek. 16:15, Hosea 2:5, 3:3, 4:15).

2. A godless government and society (Isa. 3:17, Nah. 3:4).

The point is this: religion Babylon stands for all false religions. It seeks after Heaven or utopia or perfect life:

1. Humanity work and self-effort.

2. Humanity goodness and self-righteousness.

3. Human rituals and ceremonies.

4. The idea of God and worship of God.

5. Religion and courteous service.

6. Humanity community and society.

7. Humanity, government, and state.

The Babylonian system first appears in Genesis 11:1-9. The city was called Babel then and was founded by an evil man named Nimrod. The people of Babel decided to build themselves a tower to leave their mark on the world (Gen. 11:3-4). The tower first represented many false religions started by humanity.

Upon her head was a name written (Verse 5). Babylon will be the mother of all false religions. Humanity's dreams for a one-world government and a one-world religion will become a reality when Jesus returns. Babylon will sweep and spread the world's abomination and filth under a world state religion. It satisfies the masses of people to achieve a utopia. Heaven is through Jesus Christ, not by our efforts. We should labor to build a society with God, not about God (Matt. 6:33, Eph. 2: 8-10).

Verse 6

The woman will be drunk on the blood of saints show her pleasures for evil. She will be drunk from the blood of saints and martyrs witnesses of Jesus Christ. She is responsible for their death down through the ages. The woman will use people of the earth for her interest. She symbolizes the head of a religious apostasy of the last days to slaughter God's people. When the scarlet woman appears, will you be saved? It depends on accepting or rejecting Jesus Christ (Jn. 1:11-13, 3:8; Heb. 2:4; Rom. 10:9-10, 13). If you are saved, glory to God.

The religious system will be fierce. Many will be killed and prosecuted for refusing to worship the state and its leaders. The Antichrist killed millions (martyrs who follows Jesus Christ (Rev. 6: 9 – 11, 7: 9 – 17, 13:13 – 17; Matt. 10: 17 – 18; 24:9-10; Lk. 21:12; Jn. 15: 20 – 21; Rev. 2:10). Every single death caused by the Babylonian harlot; God will judge her for blood-thirsty ways. Martyrdom has increased in recent years. Many Christians are killed every year since 1950 due to clashes with Christian mobs, state-organized death squads, and anti-Christians groups.

Verses 7-8

The angel had brought John into the wilderness to witness the scarlet beast. John is astonished. The angel asked him, "Why are you astonished? The true nature of righteousness is that it cannot exist with ungodliness and evil because religious Babylon is a mystery. Many people claim to follow Jesus, yet honor leaders, government, states, doctrines, and rituals above God. It is hypocrisy. A body says they believe in Jesus Christ and yet slaughter millions of people because they do not believe.

John witnessed a picture of what false religion will look like in the last days of world history. The picture is horrifying. He saw that most of the world will be subdued by the appeal of the false religion and will worship it. Seeing this message of message on in amazement and bewilderment. While he stood shocked, Angel stepped forward and told John that he would now reveal the mystery and details of religious Babylon:

1. There is the greatness of the beasts that supports false religion – 7b – 8.

2. The beast shall ascend out of the bottomless pit and go into perdition.

3. The beast is the ancient beastly Roman Empire at the height of Jesus's ministry and stood until 476 AD. Rome will come to power immediately after the Rapture under a ten kingdom Federation (Rev. 13:2).

4. The beast will be given leadership power and strength from the ten nations.

5. They will willingly submit to him and give him the power of ten governments.

6. There is the incredible supernatural power of the Antichrist, and he will be out of the bottomless pit, the very incarnation of evil because of evil itself or else be in the way of some powerful evil forces from the bottomless pit (Rev. 9:2, 11:7, 13: 2 – 3).

7. He shall make war with the Lamb (Rev. 17:14).

8. There is a doom of the Antichrist. The word means "to be destroyed, loosens one's well-being, waste, ruin, and give a worthless existence." It means a person will be destroyed and devastated and condemned to a worthless existence.

If a person does not know Jesus Christ will face prediction. The Antichrist and his followers will be doomed. If anyone stands as an enemy to the cross, the Church shall suffer prediction. Who is the enemy of the cross?

1. The person who rejects Jesus Christ as the Savior of the world will be punished.

2. Do not believe that Jesus Christ died for him as the only way to God.

3. Do not believe that Christ bore the penalty for the imperfection on the cross.

4. Do not approach God's claiming that he is coming by the death of Christ—that is, that he will not God to send him in the death of Christ.

5. Consider the cross of Christ to be foolishness.

6. Denies and questions that Christ died for his sins (Matt. 25:46, Mark 3:29, Lk. 3:17, Heb. 10: 29 – 30, Rev. 20:1, 21:8).

7. The impact of the Antichrist will amaze the world (Rev. 13: 4 – 8).

Verses 9-11

In ancient times, the seven mountains or seven heads said by many refer to seven-hilled cities of Rome, which symbolizes all evil in the world for 1500 years: any person, religion, group, government, or anything that opposed Christ. During the time of persecution, Rome was the focus point when John wrote the Book of Revelation. John says, "The seven heads or seven hills are the seven kings or governments the woman sits receives power for one hour with the Beast about the same time (Verse 12). The seven kings represent the number of emperors persecuting God's people throughout history. They represent seven kingdoms or empires that have complete rule and power. Scripture says, "Five have fallen, and one is, and the other one is not yet come: and when he cometh, he must continue a short time" (Rev. 17:9 – 10). The best way to look at this is in the Old Testament and note that kings or empires opposed God's people:

1. Five of the kings or empires have fallen. They no longer exist. They are Egypt, Assyria, Babylon, Persia, and Greece.

2. One of the kingdoms remains down through the centuries. Traits of the ruling body and legislatures of government, the representative government and laws of nations, and papal Rome's religion still exist.

3. One King or kingdom refers to a revival of the Roman Empire or any nations in the Old Roman Empire. The Antichrist will embrace the traits of all the empires and rule over them all. The angel mentioned

the 8th ruler in Verse 11. He will be the scarlet beast identified as Satan or the Antichrist. He is another evil ruler or King who will undergo doom.

His policies seemed to focus on peace and the good of humanity, but he eventually reveals his evil character. The same person takes on the roles of both the seven rulers and the eighth.

These kingdoms or empires represent the Antichrist's complete blasphemy of God in a quest to gain the world. Everything the Antichrist does, every move he makes, every satanic law he enacts, is directed against Jesus.

The Antichrist is headed to *"perdition,"* meaning "utter destruction." The kings of the earth will witness the destruction of the powerful system of Babylon. The downfall will seriously affect the commercial and social life of the world because of wrath upon the woman and her ungodly practices. They do not like the cross and faith in Jesus Christ. Human desires and pleasures unite, and it is intoxicated with the blood of many. God is in charge, and evil will never again control.

Verses 12-13

Even with the Antichrist's power and popularity as it may seem, the ten kings give him empowerment and allegiance. In return, he gives them great power and authority. These kings are committed to the reign of the Antichrist. The kings will be puppets, controlled by the beast. We see that the ten kingdoms and the ten kings receive authority one hour, with the beast signifying that they receive power when the Federation is set up and united. They will have one purpose—to make war against Jesus Christ.

Under the direction of the Antichrist and his kings, the nations of the world will gather to do battle with Jesus Christ at Armageddon. They are fighting a losing battle because they are foolish enough to attack the Lamb. Under the direction of the Antichrist and his kings, the world's nations will gather to do battle with Jesus Christ at Armageddon. They are fighting a losing battle because they are foolish enough to attack the Lamb.

The Lamb they attack is the "king of Kings and the Lord of Lords." He will destroy them with the word of His mouth (Rev. 19:11-21).

The outcome of the battle settled. How foolish it is for men and governments to enter the war against the Lamb and Almighty God. Jesus appears in the sky riding a great white horse, and all the heavenly saints will accompany him to crush the evil enemies of God. The Lamb they attack is the "king of Kings and the Lord of Lords." He will destroy them with the word of His mouth (Rev. 19:11-21, Jude 14; Zech. 14:5;). This verse also refers to those who are with the Lamb when He does battle with the world. These called "chosen and faithful" refer to the Bride of Christ, the redeemed saints. Called "*kletoi*," which means "to be invited." Christians have been called with a purpose to be part of God's kingdom. Faithful (*pistoi*) means those who show themselves trustworthy, dependable, and loyal.

The Roman Empire crumbled in AD 476 but will be revived in the days before the end of human history. Since he will be revived from the old Roman Empire, the city of Rome would be the natural choice for his capital. Today Russia, China, and communist nations are operating in the spirit of world dictators. They have in mind the diabolical power of the beast, wrapped up in the flesh.

Verses 15-18

The Antichrist and the government will turn against religion and destroy religion. He will turn the nations, and the harlot will lure people. She will advertise as the true Church with minor concerns for the soul of humanity. When the Antichrist sets himself up as God in the Temple, he will tolerate no competition, no rivalry for worship. Nine significant facts are notable:

1. Religious Babylon will gain power in the end times (Verse 15). Religion was set up and supported by multitudes, nations, and languages. The ideal is that everyone will be worshipping the image of the beasts or state in the end time.

2. The beast will destroy religious Babylon (He will use the ten kings (Verse 16). Why? The answer is with power and money.

3. Just imagine all the money that it costs to keep a worldwide religion going: all the control and personnel needed: offices, resources, and people to show loyalty.

4. Just imagine where in the worldwide religion will process through contributions and through the property he will hold.

5. Remember the devastation that is taking place across the world during the great tribulation, the enormous cost, and significant sums of money needed to meet the needs of cities and nations.

6. The state has a large of people committed to the state. What they will not have been the money and wealth of the religion. Therefore, it will destroy religion for its wealth and power.

7. The state will hate religion Babylon: religion will have served its purpose. The harlot will be hated. The kings and great men will despise her.

8. The state now wants complete control of the people and the wealth.

9. The state will make religious Babylon desolate religion will be wrong, and all the monies, wealth, property, and holdings destroyed (chapter 18:10).

10. The state will strip religious Babylon, make her naked: expose the corruptions to public view, showing why the religion must be destroyed.

11. The state will eat her flesh, consume her, and take anything worthwhile and beneficial for the state. Whatever will be beneficial, the loyalty, wealth will be consumed by the state.

12. Religious Babylon will be destroyed because of God. God will plant this idea in the mind of the Antichrist. God will arouse the ten other governments to support Him. It will be wiped off the earth once and for all.

Verse 18

The prostitute church thinks she controls the Antichrist, but she will soon find out that he had used her from his ends. Babylon and Rome are far more extensive, and horrible will go after her. The beast takes all he can and smashes the false Church in rage and uses the harlot to achieve power, and they will turn on her. When they have reached the pinnacle of success, they have no more need for a religious system. The woman is a worldwide system of power and influence that will prevail against God and the Antichrist. Once the purpose is achieved, there is no more need for religion.

When the Tribulation Period ends, all false religions will have been destroyed. It will pave the way for the Millennial reign of Jesus. He will usher in a one-thousand-year period when people will worship only Him.

God uses these wicked men to carry out His will against the false religion. God hates false religions. In the end times, He will use the ungodly to destroy the ungodly. When anything or anyone but Jesus Christ is the center of attention, it is a false religion, and it will be destroyed by God one day!

Every world system will come crashing down, and man is left with nothing. Babylon stood in contrast to the Church that persecuting God's people and will inevitably be destroyed. Babylon means confusion. The character is described as a whore or harlot casting dominance over humanity. She sets up as a bride of Christ (Eph. 5:25 – 25). The harlot cares nothing for Christ, nor does she bow to His authority.

It will be the last form of Gentile dominance. As this bowl is poured out, a voice from the throne says, "It is done!" This statement signals the fact that judgment has reached an end. The Lord Jesus is on His way. He is prepared to take back everything Adam lost in the fall at the cross. Jesus is about to receive the glory He is due. When Jesus was on the cross, He cried, "It is finished!" There He announced His victory. Here, He cries, "It is done!" Here He announces His verdict. There He cried out in joy; here

He cries out in the judgment. He lets us know that we have reached the end of judgment; glory is just around the corner. Every belief system in the world that does not center on the Lord Jesus is a false system of belief; it is a false religion because of Jesus Christ (Jn. 14:6; Acts 4:12; Jn. 8:24). God will destroy everything that humanity has built and glories.

# CHAPTER 18

## *The Fall of Babylon*

---

The harlot in Rev. 17 turned the hearts of kings and leaders against God. The mother of harlots is an abomination of the earth. In Chapter 18, Babylon's economic, political, commercial, social, and cultural centers, the great city of Antichrist, is destroyed. Babylon represented an actual city upon the earth:

1. The city is said to be Rome that will be rebuilt. It is somewhere on the Euphrates River at the end of the Persian Gulf.

2. Babylon represents the great city that symbolizes the godless and secular society of the world. Babylon is a symbol of the destruction of the godless government and society across the world.

3. Scripture declares that Jesus Christ will destroy Babylon - destroyed (Rev. 16: 18 – 19).

4. No human agents are mentioned, and the system of corruption will be gone.

Verse 1

An angel comes with great authority to announce the destruction of Babylon, the political and commercial capital of the Antichrist's empire. Humanity will suffer the loss of lives and wealth.

Chapter 18 tells us that an economic collapse will occur that we have never witnessed in human history. The disaster will be worldwide, and it will take away humanity's economic power to purchase merchandise. It will come late in the Great Tribulation, just before the second coming of Christ, in contrast to the description of the harlot in Chapter 17, which perceives the great Tribulation and pave the way for worship of the beast.

A great Angel comes down from heaven, coming from God himself with great authority and power. The Angel is so glorious that He blazes across the whole earth. He is about to announce judgment the world does not want to hear. John gives the city the name great prostitute. She is stripped of power and possessions.

Verses 2-3

John described the city as a dwelling place for demons, a nest for filthy buzzards, and dreadful beasts. Every demonic spirit will find a dwelling place in Babylon. It will be a place energized and controlled by demonic spirits. The reason Babylon will be destroyed is that it will represent a godless society:

1. It will not look to God.

    a. The devil chooses Babylon as his capital on earth.

    b. Every foul spirit and hateful behavior found in the city.

    c. Babylon will be a place of every unclean spirit and filth of the underworld.

2. Immorality, fornication, adultery, same-sex activity, abnormal sex, lying, stealing, and cheating will become common.

3. Lusting for more possessions and pleasures of the world will increase.

4. Sorcery, devil worship, witchcraft, palm readers, fortune tellers, astrology, secularism, materialism, and humanism will dominate the philosophies and behavior of the people. Humanity will worship himself, and the secular society will focus on technology, science, education, pleasures, recreation, and comforts.

5. There will be few who will believe and follow Jesus Christ. Babylon and society will spiritually corrupt the world.

6. The great city stands guilty of misleading people into sin, into false belief or secularism and humanism. The sins have reached heaven, and God remembers his iniquities (Verse 5 (2 Tim. 3: 1 – 2, 4:3, Gen. 6: 12, Ps. 12:1).

7. Scripture says that seven spirits corrupt man will find a place in the world at end times that works in the children of disobedience (Eph. 2:2).

The condition of Babylon will cause the great city to be destroyed because it takes the lead in persecuting God's people and the religious faith of the world. Millions will be persecuted. God's wrath and judgment will fall on them because of the inhabitants of evil, immoral, self-glory, pride, selfishness, extravagance, indulgence, and drunk with the blood of the martyrs. God will avenge the death of his followers. Babylon has fallen because the kings, merchants, the apostate church of the nations, drink from the cup of the abominations. It is an abomination in the sight of God. The world has gone to the devil and has become evil and unclean.

Verses 4-6

Before God judges the city, He warns His people, "Come out of her". The righteous will be warned to flee as God warned Lot to flee Sodom (Gen. 19:1; 2 Pet. 2: 6 – 9; Isa. 13:19 – 20). The sins of this system have "reached unto heaven". The word "reached" means "to glue, to cement, to fasten together". The ancient tower of Babel failed to reach the heavens, but the sins of this system have succeeded in reaching the throne of God. God, in His patience, has held back His judgment. The day of His judgment has arrived. God's call to His people rejects this sophisticated system and tells them to not share in her sins (2 Cor. 6:17). How can a person keep away from the corrupt system, which is a reminiscence of the world today?

1. Remember, people are always more important than products.

2. Keep away from pride in programs, plans, and successes.

3. Remember that God's will and word must never be compromised (Gen. 11:4).

4. Always consider people above making money.

5. Do what is right, no matter what the cost.

6. Be involved in businesses that provide profitable products or services that feed the world's desire.

Verses 6-7

Babylon, the great city, will receive a double reward. The word "reward" here means to pay the giveback that which is due. The city will be condemned for its sinful behavior. Her sins and punishment will be doubled (Gal. 6:7).

Babylon is a religious, political, and economic system. The kings of the earth will destroy the religious system. When the prostitute church falls, the kings of the earth rejoice (Rev. 17:16). The city will be destroyed in the middle of the Tribulation. It is described as a woman sitting on a scarlet beast (Rev. 17:3). Commercial Babylon will be destroyed by God (Rev. 18:8). When the city falls, the king and merchants cry (Rev. 18:9).

The attitude of the city is, "I am invincible". Humanity had become comfortable and felt secure, in control, and feeling no need for God. This kind of attitude defiles God and is quick to bring his wrath and judgment. The Angel asked God to give her a double punishment for all evil deeds because she spilled the blood of many saints (Rev. 13:7; 17:6). The city is doomed, and the announcement is carried out. Sin cannot win, and faith cannot fail. If your faith is in Babylon, you are following a lost cause. The city will be destroyed. It will happen and suffer destruction.

Verse 8

The quickness of Babylon's destruction will happen in one day. Verse 10 tells us, "That the city would be destroyed in one hour," which refers to instantaneous destruction. In one hour, the plagues of death, mourning, and famine will sweep through the city's streets, and then it will happen: the city will be destroyed by fire. How? The verse tells us that by God, immediate destruction fell on Sodom and Gomorrah or the forcible explosive like an atomic bomb (Matt. 11: 22; 24:30 Jn. 3: 19, 2 Pet. 2:9, 3:7, Eccles. 3:17). The city will be consumed by fire (Jer. 51:58). The ungodly will not escape the destruction. The city walls and gates will be burned to the ground. God will destroy all that you work for in one hour. Humanity will face death, famine, and plagues for its sins.

Verses 9-20

These merchants are the businesspeople and CEOs of the great businesses of the world. In an instant, their financial empires are brought to desolation. They weep and mourn because no one has any money to buy their good (Verse 12). They weep and mourn for the loss of wealth and power. All their goods, which were worth so much (Verses 13-14), are worth nothing! Verse 12 tells us that the luxuries of life are out of reach. Houses, cars, jewelry, and other fine things of life will be unobtainable. Verse 13 tells us that the necessities of life will be impossible to obtain. Spices, bread, meat, and other foods will be out of the reach of every man. Verse 14 tells us that the exotic things that men long for will be taken away too. The first item is "gold" (Verse 12). The last item is "the souls of men" (Verse 13), which is where this world system places its priorities. It elevates profits over people. The system has built its power and gained its prosperity through oppression and enslavement of humanity. The collapse of the economy will mean the end of trading income. Merchants will lament the loss of commerce and markets. Commodities the merchants of the earth enjoyed:

1. They enjoyed precious stones such as gold, silver, diamonds, rubies, and pearls.

2. They enjoyed fine clothing made of linen, purple, silk, and scarlet.

3. Furniture made from precious wood, ivory, and the precious metal was made available.

4. Items made for lecturing living included precious ointments, frankincense, cinnamon, delicate meats, sheep, beast of all kinds, wheat, flour, oil, wine, and intoxicating drinks.

5. Horses and chariots are available.

6. The merchandise was made the souls of men.

They will weep when they see the smoke of her burning (Verses 8-9). The impact of Babylon will return in the spirit of the Roman Empire before the end of history. Revelation 13:1 refers to the world empires up to the time of the Roman Empire related to the nation of Israel and her enslavements under Egypt, Assyria, and Babylon. The world will weep and mourn because this system will be destroyed by the judgment of God because:

1. Political leaders and governments will be allied with the Antichrist. Some nations will depend entirely upon the capital city. The nations will trade with the city, and the economics would be significantly affected. Simultaneously, the whole world would be undergoing disaster, and many of the world's cities will be destroyed and reduced to ashes (Rev. 16: 17 – 21).

2. Babylon is destroyed, and the world mourns over her destruction.

3. It also means that the mourning is self-centered. Babylon could have been rebuilding and getting ready for the Christ returning to rule upon the earth (Prov. 15:27, Eccles. 5: 10, James 5: 3).

Everything essential to her pleasures will be destroyed. There will be mourning by the business and commercial people over the loss of wealth (Verse 17a):

1. Babylon will enslave people all over the world. People's souls will be another piece of merchandise to benefit the state.

2. The crash of this system will be accompanied by the wailing and weeping of the world's rulers. (Ps. 49:10, Job 20: 28, Prov. 27:24, 1 Tim. 6:7).

The industrial shipping world will suffer a devastating blow by the city's destruction:

1. When God's wrath falls upon this godless society and cities in the world, they will crumble (Rev. 16:18f).

2. The merchants will weep and cried, "Woe! Woe, O great city". There will no longer be a market to sell exotic and pricey goods. We can trade no more for wealth.

3. The third group who earn their living from the sea becoming rich by delivering commodities to the city, their services will no longer be required.

4. God may use whatever method of destruction as already mentioned in the end times.

The destruction will be catastrophic and worldwide:

1. Survivors will have little left (Matt. 6:19, Duet. 8:13 – 14, Matt. 19: 23, Ps. 62:10).

2. That will be rejoicing by the heavenly hosts (Verse 20). The collapse of godliness Babylon means:

3. The ungodliness and the evil of the world are going to be conquered.

4. That righteousness is soon to be established among all the people.

5. That Jesus Christ is to come soon and set up his kingdom among the earth.

6. That there will be no more rejection and rebellion allowed by God (Jer.51:60-64).

The merchants of the earth cried when they saw the smoke coming from the city. God's people who suffered abuse and persecution would be vindicated (Roman 12:19, 2nd Thess. 1: 7 – 9, Heb. 10:30, Ezek. 25:17, Mic. 5:15, Nah. 1:2).

Verses 20-23

The event comes late in the Great Tribulation before the second coming of Christ. Satan and the Antichrist are doomed. Heaven rejoices exceedingly glad about a song of victory from the angels, cherubim, and heavenly creatures. The holy apostles and prophets rejoiced because Babylon had suffered at the hands of God. Sin cannot win, and faith cannot fail. If you are a lover of Babylon, you are following a lost cause.

The destruction of Babylon is swift and violent because material wealth is worshipped instead of God. Demons were in control, not the Lord. They use magic spells to lead the nations astray. Babylon is crushed because godly men and women were killing without mercy. In her was found the blood of the prophets and God's people (Rev. 18:24). In a splash, Babylon is gone forever:

1. It is the picture of a mighty angel from heaven taking a colossal boulder and casting it into the sea. John is given an object lesson. A picture of the might and strength of the Angel.

2. The thrust and velocity of the throw are like a stone cast into the sea.

3. The huge boulder is the size of a grinding wheel that weighed tons.

4. The colossal boulder causes a violent impact as it hits the water and disappears.

5. The violent waves begin to rush out from the boulder in every direction.

6. The violence of the whole scene is pictured as an atomic bomb wave (Mal. 4:1).

7. The massive stone in the sea represents Babylon, a big splash, then gone forever.

Destruction would be total. The boulder disappeared immediately; Babylon is found no more.

The destruction will be swift and violent reduced to ashes (Rev. 22 – 23a, Lk. 3:9, 2 Thess. 1:7 – 9, Rev. 18:21). We live in the age of big business, big politics, and prominent religion. God is going to destroy these things because of evil. The fruits of humanity lust after are departed and will be found no more. Many will express their lamentations by singing praises to God.

The voices of praise will never be heard again in Babylon. The musicians, artisans, millstones, the light of the candle will shine no more, the bride and bridegroom, merchants, sorcerers, and prophets will be heard no more.

As we look at the world today, it seems as if evil is winning. Unrighteousness is winning. The day of God's vengeance is coming. God did not create this earth and humanity to be inhabited by evil people. It is all coming to an end like a thief in the night (Rev. 16:15, Matt. 24:34-39,1 Thess. 5:2,1 Thess. 5:4,2 Pet. 3:10). Dr. Roy Branson reveals in his book, *The Hard Things of God*, a list of sins in America since 1948, which are true, and some are false views:

1. Wholesale abortion.

2. Stealing.

3. Sodom

4. They are lying (some news channels give out what most "fake news").

5. Cheating has become a valid word (most of us know that the election was stolen from President Trump).

6. Outlawing the Bible.

7. Good men like (political leaders) will have a loss of moral values.

8. Closing churches.

9. Dirty preachers are not preaching Jesus.

10. Preachers will stress prosperity.

11. Same-sex attraction and lesbianism will be openly promoted without shame.

12. Filthy music.

13. Churches will split over trivial things.

14. Drugs and alcohol continue to be society's major problems.

15. Lukewarm antinomianism that Christians are released by grace from the obligation of observing the moral law in our churches and society.

16. Blaming God for "climate change".

God points out three reasons for Babylon's annihilation: the material wealth is worship (Verse 23), demons were in control (Verse 23), and God's people and prophets were killed (Verse 24).

No matter what people think, no one is getting away with sin. God's payday is coming. His vengeance will be revealed against all false religions and evils of the world because they influence millions. They have caused suffering and death. It will be a time of great tell and suffering in the history of humanity. God's judgment will one day vindicate his people. God's voice from heaven still rings loudly against the evils of the world.

Babylon will be destroyed, with no more harlot, bloody Beast, Antichrist, and devil on earth. The great city of Babylon will be destroyed forever. God is in control. They will be in the lake that burned with fire and brimstone (Rev. 20:10). It has been a time of trouble come, but there is great hope for God's people. Everyone's name, which is written in the Book of Life, will be delivered.

John is overwhelmed by what he saw. He is excited about Jesus' return and establishes his kingdom on earth. Because He is worthy of being praised. We need to get ourselves ready. The Bible speaks of Jesus's return (Matt. 24:27, 36, 42, 44; 25:13, Acts 1:9-11, 1 Cor. 15:52, Heb. 9:28, Rev. 1:7, 11:19, 20:4, 22:12).

# CHAPTER 19

## *The Coming Christ*

---

In this chapter, we study the marriage of the Lamb and the judgment of the rebellious nations. Babylon's destruction and the Tribulation have come to an end. In contrast to a funeral, the smoke from that city ascends forever. Babylon's destruction is final. She will never rise again.

God has defeated sin and evil on the earth. Satan's days have come to an end, and God's Day begins. The oppression of the Antichrist is removed from the earth, and the victorious return of Jesus Christ is ready. The believers are given a ringside view of the war between Christ and the Antichrist.

Verse 1

The crowds in Heaven burst open with jubilation, praising God for the victory. Babylon is destroyed with all its evil spirits. It is viewed differently in Heaven. The nation's cry of sorrow and mourning, while in Heaven, praises God for being victorious. The wedding of the Lamb has come (Rev. 19:6 – 8). Heaven explodes with loud shouts of praises and honor to the one who is victorious. God's enemies will be in the lake of fire.

Verse 2

God has been praised for punishing the great prostitute who corrupted the world with her immortality. "Alleluia" represents the Hebrew word meaning "praises to Yahweh" or "praise the Lord". It calls like a roar of thunder from a great multitude in Heaven. The word is mentioned four times in the first six verses. God is praised for justice for the wicked and judgment against an unrepentant world that massacred his followers. The occasion calls for every servant of God to praise and honor Him while his enemies will be in the fire. We need to keep on praising God, small or great. The verb praise is in the present, and therefore, a command is given to keep praising the Lord.

Humanity needs to fall before his throne and shout, "Amen or Hallelujah." The words *Hallelujah and Amen* are Hebrew words meaning, *Praise the Lord*. They are used in the New Testament, giving honor and glory to the Lamb. Another word used for praising God is *Hosanna,* which means, "Save us" (Matt. 21:9). The Lord has judged Babylon the great whore, who corrupted the world with evil, and He has avenged the blood of his servant. We hear for hallelujahs in the first six verses of this chapter as the smoke would rise forever. The smoke rising is the judgment of Almighty God on the kingdom of the ungodliness and a system of evil political and religious.

Are we in tune with Heaven? We hear "Amen or Hallelujah because of what the Lord has done. He deserves the right to be praised. If something blesses your heart, if the Lord is moving in your soul, just try "Hallelujah!" It will please the Lord.

Verse 3

Babylon will physically and spiritually go up in smoke resulting in everlasting destruction from God. The judgment results from ungodliness, a system of debauchery, political and religious system of evil. Babylon is anything contrary to righteousness, holiness, and purity.

Verses 4-5

John saws this grand celebration in Heaven. The 24 elders represent the Church, and the four beasts worship God. It will be a time the bride (the Church) would be happy for her return to the earth with Jesus to bring in a glorious kingdom of righteousness. Everything in John's vision is rejoicing. We can rejoice with anticipation that Jesus Christ is coming soon. Then, we can worship God with anticipation and expectation of His coming. They will be singing Hallelujah (Rev. 5: 11, Heb. 12:22). Angels, cherubim, seraphim, twenty-four elders, and who abides in Heaven give honor and praises to God. The saints of God are filled with joy. The wicked are in terror. He is the one who has bought salvation to believers on the earth. It is God's grace and mercy upon the unbelievable.

Salvation belongs to God.

The angels have witnessed the whole scene of temptation and trials upon the earth. The angels will see the most spectacular sight they have ever witnessed, the completion of God's salvation. The Lord is being praised for Satan's victory and his evil plans (Ps. 113:1, 3; 115:13):

1. They praised him as the God of salvation at the marriage supper of the Lamb (2 Cor. 9:15, 1 Pet. 2:9, Ps. 37:39, Isa. 25:9).

2. The wicked are in terror; the saints feel with joy.

3. The marriage of the Lamb is announced; the Church has been waiting for many centuries.

Glory belongs to God. He alone possesses the glory. It comes from God to us:

1. Therefore, the agent praised God for His glory at the marriage supper of the Lamb (Rom. 16:6, Ps. 22:23, 29: 2).

2. Believers are to honor God the creator. He will honor the source and creator (Rev. 19:7, Isa. 45:12, Ps. 34:3).

3. The Lord will triumph over the ungodly and establish His kingdom.

4. The Lord will triumph over all the ungodly and evil of the earth.

5. He has destroyed the Godless politics—social, commercial, cultural, and religious systems.

6. He will avenge the persecution of evil, abusive, and murdering people on earth, treating them with justice and punishment they inflicted upon the earth.

7. He will return and establish His righteousness upon the earth.

8. He will be praised for his power (1 Chron. 29:12, Ps. 107:22, Rev. 7: 11 – 12).

9. Therefore, if the great supper of the Lamb, you will break out and praise God for the great victory. (Col. 1:12, Rev. 11:17).

Verse 6

There is a new day for rejoicing, praising, and admiration saw before. The Church has been waiting for many centuries. The marriage supper of the Lamb is about to be announced. The 24 elders, the four living creatures, will burst out in hallelujahs (Ps. 57:5, 107:32) characterized by holiness and righteousness of God.

The supper will be filled with praise and worship of God's omnipotent reign (verses 5 – 6). A voice will cry out from the throne of God to all who revere Him. He is going to reign with sovereign power in the new Heaven and earth. The prayers of God's people thy kingdom come is about to become a living reality. Heaven will be stirred to praise God (1 Cor. 15:25, Phil. 2: 9 – 11, Rev. 11:17, 12:10, Dan. 7:14, 2 Chron. 20:6).

The wedding day has arrived. The Church and the Bride are about to be married. The wedding couple have made the vow of commitment, and now comes the marriage ceremony. The Lamb's wife is identified with the heavenly Jerusalem (Heb. 12:22-23). In the Old Testament, Israel is the adulterous wife of Jehovah. When Jesus returns, she is restored (Hosea 2:1-17; Isa. 54:1-10). The bride is not Israel, but a great multitude that no one could number, from every nation, from all tribes, peoples, and languages, standing before the throne and before the Lamb, clothed in white robes, with palm branches in their hands (Rev. 7:9).

The marriage invitation has been extended throughout humanity's history. John called it the wedding supper. Who has been invited?

The Bride and Church.

The Old and New Testament believers will be invited to the wedding.

Tribulation believers who died during the seven-year Tribulation. Followers of Jesus Christ who survived the Tribulation.

The groom will be the center of everything at the wedding supper.

John is stunned by the crowd. The Lamb is taking a bribe—the New Testament church. Jesus is getting ready for the grand and glorious event when the Lord Jesus will reign. The tribe of Israel and creation waits for that blessed moment when the throne of the world can be occupied by Christ:

1. Babylon with the hellish system had to be judged and destroyed.

2. The marriage of the Lamb will be celebrated in Heaven (Matt. 13:41-43). Jesus will return to the earth and (the bride) with Him (Isa. 9:6-7; Lk. 1:31-33).

Verse 7

The marriage supper of the Lamb will focus on Jesus Christ. In most weddings and weeding suffers on earth, the attention is set up on the bride, but in Revelation, the Lamb will be the focus. The reasons are clearly stated:

1. God is assuming his royal power.

2. The Lamb is taking his Bride, the New Testament church, and himself in the marriage are about to occur.

3. It will be the Lamb who will be the cause of our gladness and rejoicing (Isa. 9:6 – 7, Lk. 1:31 – 33).

4. The Lamb deserves to be honored and praised. We would not be there if it were not for him.

5. It is His supper, the great marriage supper of the Lamb.

6. It is a Lamb who stirred the bride (New Testament church) to make herself ready.

Verse 8

The joy of the Lamb is in the prepared Bride. God saved you for Christ's sake. (Ephesian 4:30-32, 2:6-7). Note two significant points:

1. It is the marriage of the Lamb. The Lamb's wife (the New Testament Church) is identified with the heavenly Jerusalem (Heb. 12:22:23) distinguished from Israel.

2. The Bride, the Church, the followers of the Lord Jesus Christ prepare themselves. How? It includes everything that a believer does to become acceptable to God:

3. A believer prepares himself by accepting the Lamb of God as his savior. A person will not be accepted at the marriage supper unless he accepts the sacrifice of the Lamb as his sins. He does not come to the Lamb; then he will not enter the supper.

4. Many worldly and indifferent lives will have to pass through the judgment seat before being awarded faithfulness stewardship.

5. A believer prepares himself by following the Lamb to work and labor to the point of exhaustion as the Lamb worked and labored. The believer must live righteous and godly, just as the Lamb did by taking up the cross and follow Jesus.

6. A believer prepares himself by righteous deeds – Verse 8. The word "righteousness (*dikaiosune)*" here means a state of being righteous in deeds and acts.

7. The believer does the right thing; his faith is counted as righteous. Why? The person believed Jesus died for his sins, as a sacrifice, as

a substitute. The penalty sin has been paid. God counts him (the believer) as righteous in the righteousness of Jesus Christ. When the believer is ready to attend the Lord's supper, fine clothing is said to be the righteousness or righteous deeds on the saints.

8. The believer is also to do other righteous deeds. Serve the Lamb in the fullest possible degree.

The Bride of Christ (all believers, not Israel) will be in Heaven. God will give them a garment that will be clean and white:

1. It will be a garment of righteousness for deeds and acts (Isa. 64:6, Rom. 3:21; 2 Cor. 5:21).

2. The pure white garment of Bride signifies that she is spotless and without blemish.

3. The garment will show position and responsibility.

4. The garment is a reward for faithfulness, and your name will be written in the Lamb's Book of Life (Rom. 10:9 – 10).

Scripture declares that there will be positions in the new Heaven and earth, degrees of labor, service, responsibilities, and duties assigned to all of us. The half faithful will not be assigned as high a position as the faithful; they will not be significantly rewarded. That will undoubtedly be a determination where we will be sitting at the great supper of the Lamb- reward (Rev. 14:13).

The Church at end times in the Rapture will be caught up; at the Judgment Seat of Christ, will be cleaned and at the marriage supper of the Lamb, cheered up! If you have accepted Jesus as your savior, I want you to know that blessed days are ahead. If you have not accepted Jesus, I want you to know to get ready to meet the Lord's wrath. Jesus is coming again and appears in the clouds to take his people out of the world.

The rest will be left behind who has not chosen Jesus as the savior. Jesus will return visibly (Matt. 24:30; Rev. 1:7). Jesus will come in majesty (Matt. 16:27) and His angels (Matt. 16:27; 24:31; 13:39). Jesus will return with the Church (Col. 3:4; Zech. 14:5) and reign in victory at his return (Zech. 14:9).

Who makes up the bride? The bride is all the saints, born-again people, and believers, and the blood washes people between acts 2 (the beginning of the Church) and 1st Thess. 4:17 (The termination of the Church on earth). The Church is the baptized body by the one spirit (1 Cor. 12:12 – 13). The Church and the Bride of Christ passed into the loving presence of the Lamb, to become his Bride forever.

Verses 9-10

The key to being able to participate in the wedding banquet is faithfulness to God. The marriage supper of the Lamb will be a blessed and glorious event:

1. It will be the most blessed celebration in history. It will be a supper of judgment contrast to the supper of the Lamb.

2. We also hear the angels calling the fowls in Heaven to come and gather for the great supper of the Lord. It will be a supper of judgment on the earth and joy in Heaven.

3. The supper will be a blessed event for one reason: all the heavenly hosts would be there, all believers and all angelic beings, and both God and Christ. It will take place in the great banquet hall of God for the first time in history.

4. What a glorious thought. Being with our Lord and God in Heaven and eternity, and that the new heavens and earth. It will be worth it when we see Jesus (Matt. 22:4, Lk. 14: 16, 1 Cor. 2: 9, Rev. 19:9, 21:7).

5. These were the true sayings of God when he spoke to holy men and the prophets (verse 9b). In the New Testament, God has spoken through his Son (Heb. 1:1 – 2).

The marriage supper will be blessed because it is to worship God and him alone. Remember, John was still a man, and not a redeemed man:

1. John is so caught up in the majestic splendor and majestic celebration of the supper that he falls at the feet of a great Angel to worship him. He is told not to worship him, only worship God alone (verses 9-10).

2. There are two reasons given for this: creatures, even the majestic angels of Heaven, are servants of God.

3. Jesus is the one who bears testimony of truth. He alone possesses and shares the truth. The only truth Jesus alone is worthy of worship. No Angel or other creature possesses the truth (Matt. 4:10, Jn. 4:24, Rev. 14:7, 22:9, Ps. 95:6, 96: 9).

An oriental wedding lasts up to 7 days! The Lord Jesus is going to present His Bride with a celebration that will last 1,000 years! After the wedding, we will return with Him to this earth. He will put down His enemies and establish His throne on this earth. Then, He and His Bride will reign together, during the Millennium, for 1,000 years. Jesus will serve His people on that day (Lk. 12:37).

In Verse 10, we see that the messenger is a fellow servant having a testimony of Jesus. The bear witness to the resurrection, his presence in glory, and He is coming again. The testimony is the spirit of prophecy. Jesus will return (acts 1:11). We will see the Son of Man coming on the clouds with power and glory (Matt. 24:30), Rev. 1:7). Jesus will come suddenly (Matt. 24:27). He will come in majesty (Matt. 16:27). Jesus will return with angels and his Church (Matt. 16:27, Col. 3:4, Zech. 14:4). Jesus will reign with his Bride forever when he returns. No conflicts or fiction will ever separate them.

Verse 11

The greatest war of all times, Armageddon, the final and climactic battle between evil and ungodliness, is destroyed. The Greek term only found in the New Testament means a mountain. To mention the word to the Jew in the background of war suggests a horrible slaughter.

Jesus returns as the great warrior king to conqueror the army of the Antichrist and this is an incredible sight for the believers. The righteousness of God ushers in at the end of human history. The armies of Heaven are the church-age believers who ride with Jesus in victory. Note the facts:

1. The Antichrist went forth conquering humanity, demanding worship.

2. The rider of the white horse armies marched out of Heaven and defeated the Antichrist and all his foes.

3. The birds of prey will be invited to partake at the great supper of God.

4. The opposing army will be defeated with the word of God.

Heaven opened, and a rider comes forth. In Revelation 6:2, we saw a rider on a white horse giving him a bow. The rider's name was Faith and True (Verse 11). The rider in Chapter 19 has eyes like a flame of fire. On his head, many crowns, and out of his mouth was a sharp sword. John saw this person standing amid the seven golden candlesticks, identified as the Son of Man or the Son of God throughout the Book of Revelation (Rev. 1:13). He is the Lord of lords. He came first on a young donkey (Zech. 9:9), but he comes on a white horse (Rev. 19). Jesus Christ will be the conquering Christ. He rides on a white horse as the Roman generals enter the city after they had won a battle on a white stallion to celebrate his triumph. The rider of the white horse signifies victory (Acts 17:31). On that day when Jesus Christ comes, we can depend on three things:

1. Jesus Christ will be faithful and the true conqueror. He was born to be a King, put down the Antichrist, sit on His Father David's throne, and reigns in righteousness.

2. Faithful means that he can be trusted and relied upon to judge every enemy and condemn the world's ungodly and evil.

3. Truth means opposed to false. A person will be generated by what they have done and strictly condemned for what they have sown.

Jesus Christ will make war upon unrighteousness. He is the great warrior who will bring justice as a judge. His righteousness will be the criteria by which he shall judge. He will be conquered, judged, and condemned precisely upon the Antichrist and unrighteousness (The marriage supper of the Lamb is about to be announced, and Jesus is coming some (Rev. 22: 12, 20:12, Ps. 62:12, Jer. 17:10).

With the appearance on the throne, the earth and sky will flee from His presence, but they find no place to hide (Isa. 51:16; Matt. 24:35; 2 Pet. 3:10 – 12).

Verse 12

Jesus Christ will be the consuming King of kings who will conquer:

1. His eyes will be like fire and symbolize a piercing, penetrating power to see everywhere, even in dark places and behind closed doors. His eyes see into the innermost recesses of the heart. He knows all. He is omniscient and can conquer all those who reject him and do evil (Dan. 10: 6, Heb. 4:13, Jer. 23:24).

2. In ancient culture, it was worn by kings and queens representing sovereign. His crowns on His head (*Diadema*) symbolize the royal crowns of Him who will rule with authority over many kingdoms of earth. He will conquer all the kingdoms of the earth (Ps. 8). He came first riding on an ass; the second time, he ran a white horse to drain the blood and make them his footstool because He is angry with evil every day (1 Thess. 1:6-8).

3. A name will be written on his clothing. His name is called the word of God. We will see it on that day (Phil. 2: 9 – 11, Rev. 19:12).

4. He is faithful and true. He is recognized in the Bible as God, Jehovah, Christ, Jesus, Lord, and Savior, which expresses his relationship between God and his creatures. He is the fullness of his divine nature and eternal existence known by the Father (Matt. 11:27). He will do everything He has promised (2 Cor. 1:20.)

Verse 13

Jesus Christ is made flesh by the word of God (Jn. 1:1-3, 14; 8:25). His robe will be sprinkled in blood, which symbolizes that he took on a body and brought God to man (2 Cor. 5:19), reconciling the world unto Himself. How did He do it? It is the blood of judgment and justice (Rev. 14:20). When Christ rides to earth on a white horse, His robe will drip with the blood of his enemies. The Lord says, "Vengeance is mine because He is angry with the wicked" (Rom. 12:17-19). The Church-age believers will accompany him with no weapons. The only weapon is a sword protruding from Jesus's mouth. His garments are stained with the blood of His enemies (Isa. 63:1-6, Rev. 14:20). We will prepare to live and serve in the kingdom. We pray, "Thy kingdom come". The kingdom of God will come only through God's power and because he will do it. Jesus will usher in God's reign.

By the word of God, He possesses the power and energy to slaughter the ungodly and evil of the world (Isa.11:4, 63:3, Heb. 4:12). By the word He existed, the maker of all things, the revealer, we know God through him, and it is an expression of who he is to the world (Jn. 1:1 – 3, 14, 8: 25).

When the army of the Antichrist attempts to stop the King of kings, Jehovah God goes into action (Rev. 20:4-6). When the Antichrist attempts to occupy the throne on earth, God's nature demands judgment on the world's evil.

*Logos* is the word of God identified in the Gospel of John with the second person of the Trinity incarnate in Jesus Christ's prophecy is give a clear witness. (Jn. 1:1, 14). If you read Revelation and do not come to know Jesus more, you have missed the message.

Verse 14

Jesus Christ will be the heavenly war leader, and the Commander-in-chief will be full of glory. The armies of Heaven follow him. Who are they? The rider of the white horse and the believers in Heaven will be clothed in fine linen, white and clean, and will return to earth with Christ as part of His army. They will be dressed in the clothing worn at the marriage supper of the Lamb (Rev. 19:8). The army will include the believers who follow Christ through the centuries, both old and New Testament. It will include the redeemed. When the Lord Jesus returns to claim victory, we will be riding in that army (Rev. 19:11-21). In addition, it will include a multitude of angels He is going to bring with him when he returned to the earth. Jesus will destroy the armies of the world in one breath. The birds will feast on the bodies of those who have fallen (Matt. 25:31, 2nd Thess. 1: 7 – 9, Jude 14 – 15).

Verse 15

The beast and his prophets prepare for a battle that cannot be won. They will be defeated by the sword from Christ's mouth. He will be the fierce conqueror. He does not bring guns, tanks, artillery, or nuclear weapons. He merely brings His Word! Remember that His Word is "sharper than any two-edged sword" (Heb. 4:12). We see four symbols of judgments:.

1. He will have a weapon; a sharp sword will proceed out of his mouth, which symbolizes that the weapon He will use will be the power of His word (Eph. 6: 17, Heb. 4:12, Isa. 11:4).

2. He will smite the nations with a rod of iron. He will take his rightful place as a sovereign Lord over the earth and all its people (Ps. 2:9, Isa. 11:4).

3. The word "rule" means to shepherd. The enemies are defeated, the Lord Jesus will establish His Kingdom and lead the earth's peoples like a shepherd leads his flock.

4. He will execute the fierceness of His wrath against those who have rejected Him (Isa. 63:3; Isa. 11:4; Rev. 14:18 – 19, Rev. 14: 10 – 11). God uses his word, and things disintegrate. The word that could bring life also brings judgment to those who refuse to hear it.

5. He shall rule them with a rod of iron (Rev. 19:15). The term denotes that the ungodly will be brought into submission (Rev. 12:5). The winepress represents the wrath of God (Isa. 63:1-3, 6).

Verse 16

The barriers between Heaven and is ripped away, and John saw a vision of a rider on a white horse whose name is "Faithful and True, Son of God, the conquering King mounted on a white horse (19:13), leading an army to strike down the nations (19:15) and trodden them him and his winepress. He has a name written on his garment and thigh, "KING OF KINGS, AND LORD OF LORDS" (19:16). The Lord will have the power of the sword in his mouth instead of on His hip. He has all absolute sovereignty over the universe. No one exists except by His will. Everyone will see his name on his thigh and worship or be banished (Ps. 45:3; 1 Tim. 6:15, Rev. 1:5,17:14, 19:16.

Verses 17-18

The day comes for the great battle of Armageddon. Believers called the great day of Jehovah, God Day, and the day of the Lord's final battle of human history. The judgment of God is upon the godless governments of the world, ending the devil's rule upon the earth at the great battle of Armageddon. The Bible refers to this battle as the last battle of the world:

1. a day of vengeance (Isa. 34:8)

2. treading the winepress of God's anger (Isa. 63:2, Joel 3:13, Rev. 14:19-20)

3. the day that will burn like a furnace (Mal. 4:1)

4. the great and dreadful day of the Lord (Joel 2:31, Mal. 4:5)

5. the harvest (Joel 3:13, Rev. 14:15-16

6. the battle on the great day of God Almighty (Rev. 16:14)

The battle of Armageddon is an intervention of Jesus Christ into world history. His return to earth and destroying all forces of evil once and for all (Rev. 14:20, 16:12 – 16). Armageddon will be a terrifying moment in human history. A mighty angel cries with a loud voice to the birds of the air to gather for the great God supper of the great God. The supper to which he invites the birds of the air immediately follows the battle of Armageddon. God is going to destroy the godless nations and armies of this world

The angels call together all the birds of the air to feast upon the ungodly. The enemies of God are on the menu for this great supper. In life, they were separated by class and by rank. Here we see slave and freeman small and great will be slain. Money, position, power, intellect, and everything precious to will be destroyed! If you leave this world without Jesus, nothing but Hell will be your future forever. All are reduced to nothing more than food for the scavengers. Note who will be slain:

1. The flesh of kings and captains will be devoured for prey.

2. The flesh of mighty men and the powerful will be slain for the birds of prey.

3. The flesh of the riders, the horses, will be drenched of life.

4. The flesh of all men, both slaves and free, both small and great, will lie in defeat, slain by one sharp sword, the spoken word of God.

Their bodies will be lying upon the blood-drenched ground, and the birds of prey will devour the flesh from their bones. Evil humanity is destroyed by Jesus Christ (Ezek. 39:4, 17-20).

Jesus is coming! There is an old legend about a man who made a covenant with Death. The contract stated that Death would not come to him unannounced and without warning. The years went by, and at last, Death appeared before the man. The old man said, "Death, you have not been true to your promise. You never gave me any warning." Death replied, "Not so! Every gray hair in your head is a warning. Every one of your lost teeth is a warning. Your eyes growing dim and your natural power and vigor abated is a warning. Oh yes, I have warned you and warned you continually." With those words, Death swept the man into eternity. You have been warned! The King is coming. Are you ready for His coming? Are you saved?

Verse 19

John is allowed to see that the day of the Lord has finally come. He witnessed God setting the stage and preparing for the Millennium reign of our peace on earth (Isa. 65:17 – 19, 66:22; 2 Pet. 2:13; Rev. 21:1). The world's armies will be mobilizing against the commander-in-chief of Heaven (rider of the white horse) to make war. Note they are gathered, and Satan is behind the plan:

1. The Antichrist is there.

2. The kings or leaders of the earth are there, a place called Armageddon.

3. The armies of the nations of their to wage war.

The battle is going to be fought with foot soldiers when there are so many sophisticated weapons. The reason is to preserve the land and its resources. The Antichrist will be armies to exterminate the Jews take over the rich resources for himself. Remember, the Jews have been saved at this time (Rev. 7:4 – 8, 11:3 – 13). Jesus Christ is there. The Antichrist cannot use atomic weapons but may call a retaliatory strike from some of the world's other nations.

How did all the armies of the world get to Palestine? God has summoned them to battle to defeat them. They get there:

1. The same way they would today. They marched. All we know is this (a future event): they will be gathered in Palestine in the end times. The point is this: when the Antichrist and the Confederation of nations under his power began to march against Israel, the world's other nations become edgy and nervous.

2. The reason is fear of a military move to conquer the world beginning in Palestine.

3. The resources of the Middle East will be threatened (such as oil).

4. The insanity of exterminating a whole people and the nation like the Jews (Rev. 16:12, Ezek. 38 – 39; Dan. 7: 19 – 27, Isa. 2:4, 11:4, Joel 3: 9 – 16, Zech. 12: 9, 12:1 –9).

5. The world's armies will gather in Palestine because there is an evil spirit behind the Confederacy of nations (Rev. 16: 13 – 14). All the nations and alliances of the world will be involved in the great battle of Armageddon:

The kings of the East and the nations east of Palestine, involving the Arabs, China, and other Eastern nations, will head up the Antichrist:

1. The kings of the north and the nations north of Palestine, including Russia, will be involved.

2. The Kings of the South and the nations south of Palestine, including Africa, will be involved.

3. The kings of the West and the nation West of Palestine include a Western alliance, and some European nations, including America

and other powerful nations of the Americas and Canada, will be included.

The enemies of God will gather from every nation, with each taking sides to protect its interest. The point of the conflict may be over oil. It may be some other interests. They will join forces within the borders of Palestine at Meggido, which runs through the middle of Palestine from the Mediterranean Sea to the Jordan River. It is about 200 miles long and 10 miles wide (Rev. 12:9,16: 13). Isaiah speaks of when the land shall be soaked in blood (Isa. 34:1 – 8; Zech. 14:1 – 3). What is behind the whole scene is an evil spirit. It started in Heaven when Satan brainwashed some of the angels to overthrow God and was thrown out of Heaven (Ezek. 28:1 – 19; Isa. 14:12 – 17).

Satan maintains the power to deceive and influence and gives the Antichrist and his false prophet power to work miracles. What kind of miracles?

1. Deceptive dreams of glory.
2. Glorious triumphs.
3. The vision of grandeur.
4. Setting passions aflame.
5. Striking fear within the heart and arousing bitterness and hate among nations.

The order of events concerning this episode are:

1. The return of the Lord in glory (Matt. 24:29- 30).
2. The beast and his hosts will be destroyed. The kings of the earth, their armies, and the false prophet are "great and terrible" (Rev. 19:11 – 21).
3. The judgment of the nation (Zech. 14:1 – 9; Matt. 25:31 – 46).
4. The thousand years of peace, the Kingdom age (Rev. 20:4 – 6).

5. Satan will be released after the Millennium to try them on earth (Rev. 20:7 – 10).

6. The second Revelation is the resurrection of the wicked and the final judgment of the wicked (Rev. 20:11 – 15).

7. The day of God—the time when the earth will be purged by fire (2 Pet. 3:10 – 13), and we will have a new Heaven, new Earth, and the Pearly White City.

Verse 20

Armageddon will be the quick and straightforward defeat of the Antichrist and the false prophet (2 Thess. 2:8). Those who receive the mark of the beast and worship will be tossed into the lake of fire eternal. The term "beast" refers to the Empire. The Lord shall slay the Antichrist with his mouth. What is the spirit of Jesus's mouth? It is the spirit of truth, holiness, and unlimited power.

When Jesus speaks, what he says is of God. The Antichrist and the beast will counterfeit God. Satan will give the false prophet the power he offered Jesus (Matt. 4:1 – 11; Lk. 4:1 – 6). The plan will be so convincing that the world bowed down to them. The forces will be the last movement against God. There has never been a battle like this one, and it depicts the separation of the wicked from the righteous (Rev. 14:18 – 20). Satan will be defeated at the battle of Armageddon (Rev. 16:16).

Christ will speak a word, and the Antichrist will be slain. It will be like blowing a little breath on a dust particle, and it is removed, never to return. The Lord of glory will destroy the Antichrist with the brightness of his coming. The word "brightness" (*epiphaneia*) is a unique word that refers to the coming of the Lord.

It refers once to His coming (2 Tim. 1: 10). The whole idea of His brightness is splendor, radiance, glory, and splendor that the explosion of every star in the universe could not amass the power of the Lord. When Christ appears, the energizing of a laser beam of glory zeroes in on the

Antichrist, and he shall be immediately destroyed by the radiance of the Lord's glory and light (2 Thess. 2:1-12). The word "destroy" makes the Antichrist's evil works powerless.

At the end of the Millennium, Jesus will test humanity, Satan will be released for a little while, but eventually, he will be cast into the lake of fire forever with the wicked (Rev. 20:10). The wicked do not burn up. The beast and the false prophet are still in the lake of fire. Fire and brimstone denote torment. Satan's plan was so convincing that He wants all the world to bow in reverence to him, and that is unspeakable (Isa. 30:33). The work of the false prophet causes millions to worship the beast. Remember, the word "worship" is significant because the beast desires worship. He wants to be worshiped like Christ. The devil is jealous of Jesus and will always be that way. Everyone whose name is not recorded in the Book of Life will be cast into the lake of fire (Rev. 20:15).

The Antichrist and those who have rebelled against God will be cast into the lake of fire. The evil destination will be a fiery lake of burning sulfur for unbelieving men, fallen angels, demons, and the devil. The word of God makes it clear, at the final judgment of unbelievers, the lake of fire is the bowl judgment to which all the wicked shall be judged and condemned. The judgment is eternal (Matt. 13:41-42, 18: 8, Rev. 20:10, 11 – 15, 21:8).

Verse 21

The armies of the Antichrist will lay in ruins in the dust of the earth. The remnants of the Antichrist were slain. They are butchered without conventional weapons like fighter planes, bullets, rockets, or atomic bombs. Jesus will use no physical weapons or materials. The only weapon He ever needs is the sword of his word. The voice of fury of the King of kings shall strike suddenly, immediately, instantaneously thoroughly, and finally. In this battle, there will not be a battle fought. The Lord will speak, and every soul of the godless nations and armies present will drop dead. There will be enough flesh for all the birds of prey to devour because they choose to reject, deny, curse God, and slaughter millions in a godless world. It will stop at Armageddon (Heb. 4:12, Eph. 6:17, Isa. 11:4).

Without firing a single shot, Jesus will prove Himself greater than any opposing army the world militaries together are capable. Satan and a vast army will lay waste (Rev. 14:9 – 11, 20:11 – 15). Zechariah gives us a clue how the armies will be slain (Zech. 14:12-13). What a horrible day that will be for all the enemies of the Lord! What a glorious day it will be for those who love Him, look for Him, and for those special ones who ride with Him!

Peace of heart will come with being saved, or doubt and fear come with being lost. The way to escape God's wrath is to accept Jesus (Ps. 2). You can be saved right now believing in Jesus Christ as your savior. Today come and accept Jesus into your heart and life.

# CHAPTER 20

## *The Bounding of Satan*

---

Revelation 20 begins with those who were reign with Christ for 1000 years after his second coming. In the previous chapter, Jesus had defeated the agents of Satan. The beast, the false prophet, and armies had gathered to defeat the kingdom of Jesus Christ. They and all the followers are thrown into the lake of fire. This chapter reveals the binding of Satan for 1000 years. We have seen the fall of Babylon (13:14; 20:3). During this period, John sees souls reigning with Christ, who were martyred for their faith in Jesus Christ and the Word of God. They will be rewarded a special blessing for their faithfulness as Tribulation martyrs. In Chapter 20, four remarkable things happen:

1. The binding of Satan. He will be placed in God's penitentiary for one thousand years (Verses 1 – 3).

2. The saints will reign with Christ for one thousand years (Verses 4–6)

3. Satan will be released a little while to test those born during the Millennium. He met his last effort to all of God (Verses 7 – 10).

4. In the last part of the chapter, we see the judgment of the wicked dead.

The Book of Revelation has emerged into four views among Christians:

1. The Premillennial view holds that Jesus will return and defeat the Antichrist, establish a literal kingdom on earth, and reign here for 1,000 years. It is sometimes called the kingdom age. Satan will be confined, the curse of sin will be lifted, peace and prosperity will cover the earth.

2. The Postmillennial view holds the view that the world has reached the proper stage of imperfection. Jesus will return after the Millennium and the end of human history. Jesus will reign over the Church and in the hearts of the believers.

3. The Amillennial view denies the literal reign of Christ on earth. He will rule from Heaven. The prior version says that there is no literal millennial kingdom. Jesus will reign over the Church in the hearts of the believers. Many believe that Satan is bound right now, the Tribulation has already occurred, and Jesus has already returned.

The term "millennial" is a Latin word meaning "1000 years" and refers to an earthly kingdom. Chapter 20 has controversial and bewildering arrays of diverse interpretations. The Millennium will allow Jesus to accomplish some goals:

1. He will fulfill the Old Testament promises of a savior coming to save the world from sin.

2. He will answer the prayer, "The Kingdom come".

3. He will fulfill the promise that the saints will reign.

4. Bring about the complete redemption of nature.

5. He will give humanity a final test under the sovereign rule of Jesus.

Satan's dominion will be removed for 1000 years and release for a short time (Rev. 20:3). Jesus Christ is going to eliminate the ungodly and evil. He will remove all unbelievers and the earth (Matt. 24:39 – 41). It is not about the Rapture but the harvest of the unbelievers (Ezek. 36:24 – 28, Matt. 13:41 – 43). Every follower of the Antichrist will not survive the Tribulation. The believers will enter the kingdom. His kingdom will establish upon the earth, and He will rule and reign upon a new heaven and earth forever. The day is coming when there will be:

1. No more sin or evil or unrighteousness upon the earth.
2. No more rejection or denial or cursing of God or Jesus Christ. He will destroy every enemy against Him and his people.
3. No more savagery, murder, or war.
4. No more sickness, disease, or ill-health.
5. No more pain and suffering or death.

Whatever view you may hold, the kingdom is coming to earth. The earth will be better when Jesus Christ rules and governs the world's affairs, known as the Millennium, which means the 1000 years' rule of Jesus Christ upon the earth. The Latin term "*mille*" or one thousand, is used to identify the 1000 years' rule of Christ with his saints. The view called 'amillennialism' is symbolic and refers to the time between Christ's first and second coming, not a literal 1000-year period. The millennium is the time of earthly harmony when Satan has been bound. Postmillennialism teaches that Christ will return until after the millennium. There will be a period when the world will experience joy and peace because of its obedience to God. Christ has bound Satan. The premillennialism teaches Christ to return before the millennium. He will descend to earth to set up a literal 1000-year earthly kingdom with the headquarters in Jerusalem.

The evil nations and armies of the world have been eliminated from the earth at the battle of Armageddon. Christ removed temptation and evil and bound Satan for 1,000 years. Old Testament believers and Tribulation believers who died before Jesus's ascension into Heaven will be resurrected when (Acts 1:9– 12). All the believers from Abel to the very last of saints of God in the Tribulation will share in the triumph of God's victory, won at Calvary, but he shares with all the redeemed saints.

Verse 1

John sees an angel coming down from Heaven to usher in the millennial reign of Christ. The angel comes down out of Heaven, having the key to the abyss and holding in his hand a great chain (Rev. 20:1). The word "*abyss*" means boundless or bottomless pit; the place of imprisonment of demons and the devil known as Satan. The abyss is where the beasts and fallen angels (demons or unclean spirits) come from (2 Pet. 2:4; Rev. 11:7; 17:8). The angel carries a chain he will use to bind Satan for a thousand years. No peace will exist if Satan roams the earth.

God will remove Satan from the earth to stop the deceptions of leading people away from God. The angels come out of Heaven from God's presence. God can bind Satan anytime. He has the keys to Hell and death:

1. The key to the bottomless pit is that he has the power to cast Satan into the abyss, away from the earth.

2. A great chain means that he can bind Satan and keep him from attempting and leading people into sin and ungodliness.

3. God locks, handcuffs, and seals the door until he decides to let Satan out. The sealing denotes that God has sentenced Satan to prison, and he will not escape until the omnipotent God releases him.

The earth will enjoy a time of peace and goodwill toward all men. Who is Satan? His name tells us:

1. He is the dragon, serpent, and the devil who causes people to behave evilly like beasts and destroy property (Rev. 12: 9, Rev. 20:2).

2. He is the dragon symbolizing cruelty.

3. He is that old serpent that deceives, seduces, beguiles, and indulges in treachery. He will kill people and lead them into sin and evil. He

disobeys, ignores, and neglects God (2 Cor. 11:3, 11: 13 – 15, Gen. 3:4, 14). Like a serpent, he is ever seeking those he might deceive.

4. He is the devil, the tempter of man who leads people to slander, lie, and murder (Jn. 8: 44, 1 Pet. 5:8). He is a false accuser, always looking for someone to defame and destroy.

5. He is Satan, the opponent, the enemy of Christ, and His people who accuse and oppose God and his followers. He is the accuser pointing out sins and failures of believers of God. He does this to cut the heart of God and to arouse God's justice against them (Matt. 4:10, Jn. 13:27, Acts 26:8, Roman 16:20).

6. Satan is behind all evil and ungodliness in this present age (Lk. 22:3; acts 5:3; 2 Cor. 4:4, 11:14; Eph. 2:2, 6:11 – 12; 2 Tim. 2:26; 1 Pet. 5:8; Rev. 12:3 – 4, 12:9).

Verse 2

How long will Satan be removed? At the end of 1000 years, the time is clearly stated that there will be no ungodliness and evil running wild upon the earth. The time is known as the Millennium. Christ will come to earth and reign upon the earth as sovereign Lord and King. It will be a glorious time:

1. No more war or killing will exist.
2. No more assaults, abuse, or crimes will go unpunished.
3. No more hunger or homelessness, or unemployment will exist.
4. No more laziness, lethargy, or unconcern will be allowed.
5. No more drug pushing or enslavement to drunkenness will be tolerated.

All the wrongs, ills, and evil will be removed. A perfect government, society, utopia, and life will be brought to the earth. All things righteous will be established for 1000 years. The earth will be blessed with:

1. All wars will cease, and peace will exist. (Isa.2:4; 9:4-7; 32:17-18; 33:5-6; 55:12; 60:18; Eze.28:26; 34:25, 28; Hos.2:18; Micah 4:2-3; Zech. 9:10).

2. The King's subjects will be happy and full of joy (Isa.12:3-6; 14:7-8; 25:8-9; 61:7,10; 65:18-19; 66:10-14; Jer.31:18-19; Zeph. 3:14-17; Zech. 10:6-7)

3. The kingdom will be a holy kingdom. There will be no rebellion. King Jesus will rule with a rod of fire on (Rev. 19:15, Isa. 31:6-7; 35:8-9; 60:21; 61:10; Eze.36:24-31; 37:23-24; Zech. 8:3; 14:20-21)

4. The kingdom will be a glorious kingdom, with the glory of God in full display. All the world citizens will travel to Jerusalem and see the glorified Savior face to face! (Isa. 4:2; 35:2; 40:5; 60:1-9)

5. Jesus will minister to every need so that there will be no want anywhere on the earth. (Isa 12:1-2; 30:26; 40:1-2; 49:13; 51:3; 66:21-23; Jer.31:23-25; Zeph. 3:18-20).

6. Perfect justice will be administered to every individual. (Isa. 9:7; 32:16; 42:1-4; 65:21-23; Jer.23:5).

7. An increase in the teaching ministry of the Holy Ghost will result in enhanced mental capabilities. (Isa. 11:1-2, 9; Isa. 41:19-20; 54:13; Hab.2:14).

8. Jesus will instruct His people in the ways of God. (Isa. 2:2-3; 29:17-24; 32:3-4; Jer.3:14-15; Micah 4:2).

9. In Genesis 3:17-19, God cursed the earth. The curse will be removed, increasing the productivity of the earth. In the wild, animals will lose their ferocity and ability to injure or kill. (Isa 11:6-9; 65:25).

10. Sickness and death will vanish from the earth. Death will only exist as a punishment for extreme sin. (Isa 33:24; Jer.30:17; 33:6).

11. All deformities will be healed. (Isa.29:17-19; 35:3-6)

12. There will be supernatural preservation of life during the Millennium. (Isa.41:8-14; 62:8-9; Jer. 23:6; Joel 3:16-17; Amos 9:15; Zech. 9:8; 14:10-11).

13. There will be no social, political, racial, or religious oppression on that day (Isa.14:3-6; 42:6-7; 49:8-9).

14. There will be no mental retardation or dwarfed bodies; extreme longevity will also be restored. (Isa.65:20).

15. The living Tribulation saints and believing Jews who enter the Millennium will reproduce. The population of the earth will soar. All children will be born with a sinful nature and will therefore need salvation. (Jer.30:20; 31:29; Eze.47:22).

16. A perfect economic system in which all needs will be met by men's labor under the direction of the King. It will be a fully industrialized world. (Isa. 62:8-9; 65:21-23; Jer.31:5).

17. The perfect labor situation will produce economic abundance so that there will be no want. (Isa.35:1-2, 7; 30:23-25; Jer.31:5; 12; Eze 34:26; 36:29-30; Joel 2:21-27, Amos 9:13-14; Zech. 8:11-12).

18. An increase in solar and lunar light will produce longer growing seasons, accounting for increased productivity. (Isa.30:26).

19. All language barriers will be removed. (Zeph. 3:9).

20. The entire world will worship God through the Lord Jesus Christ. (Isa.45:23; 66:17-23; Zeph. 3:9; Zech. 14:16; 8:23; Mal.1:11).

21. All who are subject to the King will experience divine enablement and presence. (Isa.44:3; Eze.36:26-27; 37:14; Joel 2:28-29.

Verse 3

The angel coming down from Heaven will cast Satan into the bottomless pit (Rev. 20:1). He will not deceive people for 1000 years. He cannot deceive people and nations anymore. Sins feel good, look good, and taste good. Things like food, sex, honor, recognition, vehicles, money, pleasures, power, clothes, houses, possession, stimulation of the flesh, popularity, position, comfort. The craving and lusting for them are evil because they desire these things above the Spirit of God because we:

1. lust after more and more food.

2. lust after another person.

3. lust after power over others.

4. lust after more and more pleasures and possessions.

5. lust after more and more position and money.

It is time for Satan to get what is coming to him. Scripture says that when the 1000 years end, He will be released for a little season (Rev. 12:12; 17:10) only three and half years. (12: 12-14; 13:5).

Israel will be back in her homeland in natural bodies. They will build homes, plants vineyards, and multiply by the millions. Those born during the Millennium will not be tempted. Satan will be let loose for a little while to offer the people an opportunity to worship. Many will accept Satan and his last attempt to take over the Holy City, to crush God's people that had been living in peace for a thousand years.

Verses 4-5

Who will be living in the millennial kingdom and reign with Christ? Again, John gives us insights into what he sees. John saw people sitting upon thrones given the authority to rule (Matt. 19:28; 1 Cor. 6:2-3). He saw believers beheaded during the Tribulation, those who refuse to worship and receive the mark of the Antichrist. They are the Tribulation saints who lived (were resurrected) and reigned with Christ for 1000 years. What can be determined is that Jesus chooses a particular group to help Him rule. In Verse 4, this is also the time when Christ gives believers their duties and responsibilities, their assignments and service for eternity when He creates the new Heaven and earth (Rev. 14:13, 21: 24 – 27).

The day is coming when the saints of God will rule with the Redeemer. All these Tribulation saints join with the Bride of Christ, and we reign with Jesus for 1,000 years. Daniel 7:27 promises that the Old Testament saints will reign during this time. The believers will live in a world where there is no devil. It will be a world filled with the redeemed saints until God loosened Satan for a little while.

John saw two groups in Verses 4 – 5:

1. He saw people sitting upon thrones with the authority to judge or rule (1 Cor. 6:2).

2. In the Spirit, he saw the souls of the martyrs during the Tribulation (Rev. 6:9 – 11).

3. He saw these living again: they were resurrected in the first resurrection (verse 4).

4. The unbelievers will not live again until after the 1000 years were finished ((Rev. 20:12 – 15; 21: 8). Jesus will return with the saints raised at the Rapture.

John says, "The unbelievers are described as the rest of the dead who come to life until the thousand years are over". Only the righteous will rise Christ on the Rapture. It takes place right after the step of the Lamb, just before the Millennium begins. We learn the intervals between the two resurrections—a thousand years. The second resurrection will occur at the end of the Millennium when the unbelievers will be resurrected and judged to go to Hell. It will include those who died without receiving Christ as their Savior before the Millennium and those who rejected Christ during the Millennium. The resurrection of life is mentioned in Luke 14:13 – 14. The resurrection to damnation is mentioned in John 5:29. When they are judged, the believers will go to Heaven.

Verse 6

Life in the Millennium will be blessed. The resurrected believers will be highly blessed with heavenly things. Humanity has always sought the pleasures of the earth: position, money, possessions, fame, power, and worldly pleasures. The only blessedness is found in Jesus Christ. He can raise a person in the first resurrection. He can give a person the right to rule and reign with him in his millennial reign (Matt. 6: 19 – 21, 2 Cor. 6:17 – 18, 1 Jn. 2:15 – 16, Rev. 14: 13, 16:15, 19:9). They will be separated from the world, set apart unto God, and never worry about being about them again (Rev. 20:14). They will never be touched by the second death or be separated from God forever. It means to live in Heaven with God forever. In the millennial reign:

1. Life in the Millennium would be governed by righteousness.
2. Christ is going to appoint believers as priests.
3. Christ will prevent evil from being done by one nation to another nation (Zeph. 3:13).
4. There will be national obedience (Jer. 3: 19).
5. The citizens of Jerusalem will be called holy (Isa. 4:3 – 4, Jer. 3:19).
6. Life in the Millennium will be a life of true worship. All nations, kings, and people of the will worship Christ (Ps. 22: 27, 66:4, 86:9, Jer. 4:2, Zech. 8:23.5).
7. The nation will bless Christ and glory and him (Jer. 4: 2, Ps. 22:27).

The believers will be in resurrected bodies and the unbeliever on earth in their earthly bodies. There will be mingling among the two. Therefore, during the Millennium, humanity will have fellowship with Christ. Life upon earth will be entirely different from what it is now. Jesus Christ returns to earth. His presence and power change everything.

Verse 7

A shocking message comes from this Scripture at the end of the Millennium; Satan will be let loose from Hell for a season. Why?

1. Humanity must show humility to Christ or else face destruction. Some folks will choose to follow Satan because they have longed for lusts (Eph. 2:1-2).

2. It will be a time of separation and destruction for all rebels, including Satan. The hour is coming when no one knows when Heaven and earth are about to be renovated, but it comes at the end of the I of the Millennium (Jn. 5:25 – 27).

3. Satan will be released to vindicate the justice of God and to show that people deserve to be judged and condemned (Isa. 24:22).

4. Satan and his host are released to go throughout the earth to deceive the nations who reject Christ (Eph. 2:1-2) and lead some angels astray.

5. Satan's career is doomed, and humanity total inability to save itself, even in a perfect world.

Satan will be released from the abyss to deceive the nations again for a season (Rev. 20:3). All the nations destroyed at Armageddon:

1. Survivors of Armageddon will return home and witnesses the glory of Christ (Isa. 66:15-16,19; Zech. 14:16-19).

2. Some people will survive the bowl judgments and catastrophic earthquakes (Rev. 16:16-21).

3. People will be saved during the Millennium (Ps. 87: 3-6, Isa. 53:10, Jer. 33:22, Ezek. 47: 22-23).

4. Many who are defiant and rebellious to the Lord during the Millennium will turn to Satan (Eph. 2:1-3; Rom. 3:10-23).

5. Satan will be cast into the lake of fire forever (verse 10).

Verse 8

Satan will continue his tactics against God to destroy the nations after his release during the Millennium. He again set out against the camp of God's people. Humanity will begin to think of Christ as a mere man.

Too many people will think He is just a mere ruler. Many who follow the deception of Satan will be numbered as the sand of the sea. They are called nations: Gog and Magog symbolize the nations from the north to fight against God's people (the Jews). Gog was the King of Magog (Ezekiel chapter 38 and 39). Satan's army gathers, no shot is fired. No battle is fought. Fire falls from Heaven and consumes the army which gathered in the battle against Jerusalem.

Verse 9

Gog and Magog are where Satan will find his vast army? The world is perfect! There is no poverty, no disease, and no war until Satan is released. It has been a perfect world! Why would anyone fall for Satan's lies and rebel against God? It is a battle between the unbelievers and the believers. Before a battle can ensue, God sends down fire from Heaven, only attacked the armies and consuming them (Ezek. 38:22; 39:6). God destroys the army, and not one sinner is left on the earth. Satan will be the only one left, and God deals with him (Verses 20:10).

Satan is condemned forever. He will be taken and cast into the lake, Verse 10. The unbelievers will be tormented day and night forever along with Satan (Matt. 25: 41, 2 Pet. 2:4, Jude 6, Rev. 19:20, 20:10). The lesson we learn from these verses is that with God, you will experience tremendous victory with Christ. The power is available to all believers. We must know and trust God now. We can rekindle a desire to live with God and not give in to Satan's desires. Are you saved? Have you received Jesus as your Savior? If you want victory in your life, choose Jesus.

Many people who entered the Millennium were tribulation saints. They will enjoy good health and longevity. Children will be raised in a perfect environment and still rebel against God. All those little children were born into this world with a sinful nature and needed to be saved. They will travel to Jerusalem, see King Jesus face-to-face, and refuse to bow down to him in faith and repentance. Many people in Jerusalem will be characters from the Bible, glorified saints from the Tribulation, and many will not be saved. Some folks in their hearts will remain rebels and sinners in need of a Redeemer.

Remember, millions of people entered the Millennium in flesh and blood bodies. Some were believing Jews; others were Tribulation saints. These people married and had children. In fact, because of perfect health and perfect living conditions, the earth's population will explode. People will live to be 1,000 years old again! The children born during the Millennium will be raised in a perfect environment, and still, they will rebel against God.

Every one of those little children was born into this world with a sinful nature. Every one of them would still need to be saved from their sins by faith in the finished work of Christ at Calvary. In a world where they will travel to Jerusalem and see King Jesus in person, they will still refuse to bow to Him in faith and repentance. They will live in a world inhabited by the characters from the Bible, the glorified saints of God, and with those who endured the Tribulation Period, many millions will not be saved. They will keep the rules because they will be forced. In their hearts, they are still rebelling and in need of a Redeemer. They are still sinners in need of a Savior!

Satan will raise his vast army and lead them in one final assault against King Jesus in Jerusalem. The rebels are destroyed in a moment, and they all drop off into Hell to await judgment. Satan himself is cast into the Lake of Fire, where he will spend eternity being tormented along with the Antichrist and his false prophets. When the smoke clears, and the dust settles, the Lord God Almighty will have the last say in this matter! God wins, end of story! Are you standing on the side with Jesus? Or have you enlisted in the Satan army? Right now, the devil is winning the battle. The day is coming when God will be in complete control.

Verse 11

A great white throne appears, and John saw the one sitting on it (Dan. 7:9-10). Some suggest that it was Jesus (Matt. 25:31) because the father leaves His judgment to his Son Jesus (Jn. 5:22). They occupy the throne as one (Jn. 10:20). I believe the one sitting on the throne is Jesus (Rev. 4:2, 7:10, 19:4). The earth and the sky fled from his presence, but they found no place to hide (Rev. 20:11).

These verses tell us about that terrible day when every lost sinner will face the Lord in judgment. There will be nowhere to hide on that day. No one will hide behind excuses, ignorance, and false professions. Everyone will face Jesus Christ as Lord and Judge, and they will all receive a just sentence for their sins. Those who have died in sin lived not again until the end of the thousand years was finished. Now comes Judgment Day. Jesus warned us of this day (Matt. 12:36).

The Great White Throne Judgment is where believers and unbelievers from all ages will stand before God and be judged by God. No one will be able to hide from God. Every human small and significant, shall stand before God and give an account. They will see what John saw. There will be no place to flee (Ps. 139:7, Isa. 51:6, 2 Pet. 3:10 – 12). The judgment in Matthew has to do with the nations (Matt. 25:31), and the White Throne Judgment has to do with individuals (Rev. 20:11).

Those who died without Jesus Christ as their Savior will be judged. The Judge who occupies this bench is infallible. He cannot be tainted by sin or prejudice, but He renders judgment in perfect righteousness and fairness to all humanity. John describes whom he sees on the throne, but it is:

1. Jesus sits upon the throne, and it is more significant than any high court on the earth. It is the highest court in the universe! He speaks and issues a decision based on your accepting Jesus as Savior:

   a. The decision is final and fair.

   b. The decision He makes is for eternity. You will spend the rest of your life in Heaven or Hell.

   c. The decision will never be an appeal, not even once. All human courts are tainted by sin, prejudice, and fallibility.

From this throne, a decision is determined according to your salvation.

2. All humanity will stand before the great white throne to determine whether you have rejected Jesus Christ or accepted Him. The only acceptable person who will go to Heaven is those who reject Jesus Christ as their Savior will go to Hell. The only salvation that will save is faith in Jesus Christ (Heb. 2:3, 12:25).

3. The throne of God is white because it represents God's purity, holiness, and righteousness. Our imperfections must be removed before we can stand before a perfect God. How can this be done? Jesus Christ is perfect and sinless, and He takes away our sins because of Calvary.

4. We stand before God sinless because we believe He is the Son of God, and He bore our sins for us.

Humanity will stand and bear the judgment of their sins. They will not be able to trust in their purity and righteousness except that of Jesus Christ. Unrighteousness, a problem of the unbelievers, will be condemned by God's righteousness (Ps. 96:12-13, Matt. 24:30, Matt. 8:38, 2nd Thess. 1: 7 -8). Where is Israel? The Scripture is silent; God takes care of His people.

All the earth's security, accomplishments, wisdom will not help. Money, houses, land, position, power, fame, popularity, drugs, sex, alcohol, pleasure, possessions, and comfort will be gone. There will be no place for them (Matt. 24:35, 2 Pet. 3:7, 3:10 – 13, Rev. 20:11, Isa. 34:4, 51:6, Isa. 65:17). The only thing that will count is your faith in Jesus.

The Bible tells us that a person occupies this throne. His identity is not revealed here. I believe it is Jesus Christ on this throne:

1. The man on this throne is none other than the Lord Jesus Christ Himself (Jn. 5:22, 27, 30; Acts 10:40-42; 2 Tim. 4:1). The *Savior* will be the *Sentencer* on that day!

2. He is no longer a lowly Nazarene, poor, humble carpenter. He is now the King of kings and the Lord of lords (Dan. 7:9-10).

3. His presence is so terrible and powerful that the heavens and the earth flee.

The Lord's grace is still sufficient for lost sinners. It is still time for repentance and to accept the salvation of the Lord. It is still time to receive the mercy of Jesus. The White Throne Judgment is just a twinkle away. One more second, minute, the hour is not guaranteed; come now, and receive the salvation of Jesus Christ. Nothing will be hidden from the Lord. You are bidding your life. He knows everything about you (Psa. 33:13-15; Psa. 44:21; Pro. 5:21; Pro. 15:3; Pro. 21:2; Heb. 4:13), and those sins will come back to haunt you (Num. 32:23; Gal. 6:9).

Verse 12

The events take place when the earth and Heaven flee away.

Fire will result in a new heaven and new earth (2 Pet. 3:10; Rev. 20:7 – 10; 21:1-22). A new heaven and earth will be prepared for believers, those who kept Jesus as their Savior. The unbelievers will witness the destruction of the earth. They will have no place to flee when a chain reaction destroys the old heaven and earth. Both heaven and earth are destroyed by God, destroyed by fire (2 Pet. 3:10-12). Those who are defectors, rebels, and defendants against the salvation of Jesus Christ will be judged. Both the small and the great will be judged:

1. Ordinary men and women will be judged who have not received Jesus Christ.

2. Great men and women, and ordinary people of the earth, the blue-collar worker, employee, and worker of the earth; slaves and servants; managers, supervisors, officers of corporations, owners of businesses, rulers, and kings will be judged.

3. Those who have lived a life of sins society considers unlawful.

4. Those whose names are not found written in the Book of Life will be thrown into the lake of fire.

5. The believer would be exempt from going to Hell but judged to receive their reward in Heaven.

The White Throne Judgment involves the consultation of two books: the Book of Life and works. The only thing that will count is that your name is written in the books that are opened. Preachers, deacons, church members, popes, priests, nuns, choir members, drunks, prostitutes, drug addicts, pimps, pushers, grandmothers, teenagers, moms, and dads will face that great day of the Lord. We all stand together with Cain, Judas, Hitler, and every other person who chose wickedness over righteousness will stand before God and face their judgment. The books record all the sins of every human being on this earth (2 Corinthian 5:10). When a person refuses to accept Jesus Christ, his name is erased from the Book of Life, and he loses the right to live as a citizen of Heaven with God (Exod. 32: 32 – 33, Ps. 69:28, Lk. 10:20, Dan. 12:1, Ph. 4:3, Rev. 20:12, 15; 22:19):

1. In the Lamb's Book of Life, the name of every human being who has ever lived is written. It is a book that includes the name of everyone who has ever lived or ever will live upon the earth. The book contains the names of those who are redeemed by the blood of Jesus. When a sinner repents, their name remains written in this book. Their names are erased from the books (Rev. 3:5,17:8). Jesus told His disciples to rejoice (Lk. 10:20).

2. The Book of Deeds records and maintained the deeds of all men. Every deed, both good and evil, will be mentioned. Every sin will be read aloud: Sins of commission, sins of omission, flagrant sins, secret sins, sins of the heart, and sins of the mind—all will be brought out into the open on that day.

3. There is no place to hide, no clouds to stand on, or rocks to hide behind. The earth had fled away. Everyone will face God. The fallen angels will be judged (Jude 6).

4. Verse 12 makes it clear that the lost will be judged according to their works.

Jesus will say on that day, "Well done, good and faithful servant good or the words that will condemn you to eternal life or everlasting torment! Imagine hearing Him say, "Depart from me, ye cursed, into everlasting fire, prepared for the devil and his angels" (Matt. 25:41). "I never knew you. There is no record of your saving birth. Depart from me!" (Matt. 7:21-23).

Verse 13

Whenever a man dies, the elements that make up the body disintegrate. God will resurrect a person from anywhere on the earth. The dead saints of the Church, those killed as martyred for their testimony. Hell will give up those who died without Christ as their Savior. The sea will give up bodies buried at sea, and the grave will give up their bodies to come before the Great White Throne Judgment.

The word "hell" in the second phase is the Greek word *hades,* which means the grave. The decayed bodies, the unsaved, will still stand before God and be judged at the White Throne Judgment for his or her deeds (Rev. 20:11-15). Bodies may be decayed, but God will put the pieces back together again to face the final judgment. The phrase "dead, great, and small" refers to all people, believers, and nonbelievers. No one will escape the final judgment, both the living and the dead (1 Pet. 4:5). The believer's souls will be united with the glorified bodies appropriate to their eternal existence and paradise. The nonbeliever souls are united with their bodies suited for their eternal Separation from God.

Verse 14

Then John saw a vision of "a great white throne, and him who sat on it, from whose face the earth and the heaven fled away. There was found no place for them. I saw the dead, the great and the small, standing before the throne" (20:11-12). The books opened, and according to their works, they were judged out of the things written in the books (20:12). "Death and Hades were thrown into the lake of fire. The second death, the unbelievers were thrown in the lake of fire. If anyone was not found written in the Book of Life, he was cast into the lake of fire" (20:14-15).

Wherever the bodies have gathered comes judgment day will lose their usefulness. The first death is experienced by all human beings, except Enoch and Elijah (1 Thess. 1:7-9) and those alive when Jesus returns on that day. The second death is to be separated from God forever. Death and Hades will be thrown into the lake of fire. God's judgment was finish (1 Cor. 15:26). John 21:40 explains that in Heaven, there will be no death. Isaiah 25:8 foresaw this day. The lake of fire will be the ultimate destination of everything evil.

Verse 15

The Lamb Book of Life contains the names of those who are redeemed by the blood of Jesus. Based on the evidence found in this book, when a sinner repents, their name is written in this book. The Lamb Book of Life is read, and those names do not find in the book are sentences. All sinners are judged not to merit life but to see if they deserve life. They appear before God is judged and justice is render. The first death is the physical separation from the body. The second death, the righteous Judge will sentence those to an eternal lake of fire and eternal separation from God for rejecting Jesus Christ (2 Thess. 1:6-10). It will be a death where there is no death! There will be no end to the torment in Hell, for the sinners will face the eternal fire for all their evil. It is where Satan, the beasts, the false prophet, the demons, death, Hades, and any name not recorded in the Lamb Book of Life, and those who did not put their faith in Jesus Christ will be ushered into Hell.

Humanity will die the first time physically, and without accepting Jesus the second time, they will die spiritually. The worst death is to be separate from God forever, it is spiritual death. Paul writes, "The last enemy to be destroyed death (1 Cor. 15:26). This time the unbeliever's death is spiritual. Death and sin will not be found in the new heaven and earth. John shares a complete view of what is going to happen to the unbeliever. He also tells us, "There will be no death in Heaven (Rev. 21:4, Isa. 25:8). Paul says, "The whole world will be held accountable to God" (Rom. 3:19). God's gracious gift of salvation is accessible to everyone, and they will have opportunities to believe but consistently reject. It would be best if you were watched in the precious blood of Jesus to be saved.

# CHAPTER 21

## *The New Heaven and Earth*

The days of the Lord will come as a thief in the night (2 Pet. 3:10). Chapter 21 will reflect upon events before the end of human history. Humanity gets a picture of our new home (new heaven and earth). We will have the opportunity to live in a mansion with the Lord. John gives us in Chapter 21 the following sections:

1. Background: the last vision given to (Verses 9 – 10).

2. The glory of the city (Verse 11).

3. The city walls: perfect security (Verse 12).

4. The city 12 gates (Verses 12 – 13).

5. The city of twelve foundations: the names of the apostles are inscribed in them (Verse 14).

6. The city's shape and size (Verses 15 – 17).

7. The city's materials are precious and priceless (Verses 18 – 21).

8. The city worship is the focus upon God himself a Lamb (Verse 22).

9. The city light is provided by God's glory and the lamb (Verse 23).

All bad things of the world are gone; ungodliness and evil, suffering and pain, corruption and death are gone. Revelation 22 tells us, "No more bad leaders, corrupt government, corrupt religion, sin, and temptation has reached an expiration date. Satan's evil of the world is destroyed" (2 Pet. 3:12-13). God will make a new heaven and earth where there would be no more tears, sighing, or dying. No hospitals or graves. Satan will be at the bottomless pit chained with his fallen angels. There will be no more aging wrinkles. The fountain of youth will be in Heaven. Nothing will ruin, rot, or rust. There will be no thirsting, all hungering. No itching, no blindness, no deafness, no diabetes, no cancer, heart attacks, false gods, no witchcraft, no drugs, no alcohol, or tobacco. No divorce, child abductions, accidents, and no more bills to be paid. No more sorrow, crying, pain, or death. There will be seven new things:

1. The new heaven

2. The new earth

3. The new peoples

4. The Lamb's wife, the New Jerusalem

5. A new temple

6. The new light

7. The new paradise and the rivers of water of life

John saw a vision of "a new heaven and a new earth" (21:1a)—the first Heaven and earth have passed away (21:1b). He "saw the Holy City, New Jerusalem, coming down out of heaven from God, prepared like a bride adorned for her husband" (21:2). The New Jerusalem denotes a new place. It comes from heaven and is distinct from earthly Jerusalem, the former capital of Israel. It is the city Abraham looked for, with foundations, whose builder and maker is God (Heb. 11:10). Paul called it the above city (Gal. 4:26).

God promised that "he will wipe away from them every tear from their eyes. Death will be no more" (21:4) and "Behold, I am making all things new" (21:5). The faithful will receive water "from the spring of the water of life" (21:6-7), but the faithless will be "in the lake that burns with fire and sulfur, which is the second death" (21:8).

We no longer will deal with Adam's sinful race, but we will be in God's Utopia and the Holy city, New Jerusalem with the redeemed of the ages. What began in Genesis ends in Revelation:

1. Heaven and earth were created (Gen. 21:1). In Revelation, a new heaven and earth will be (Rev. 21:1).

2. The sun is created (Gen. 1:16). In Revelation no need for the sun (21:23).

3. Night and day are established in Genesis (1:5). No more need for a natural light source. The Lord Jesus will be the light (Rev. 22:5).

4. The sea is created in Genesis (1:9). In Revelation, there will be a river of the water of life (Rev. 21:1). No more seas.

5. The curse of sin is announced in Genesis. Satan is victorious, serpent, soil (Gen. 3:14-17).

6. Man is driven from Paradise in Genesis for sin (Gen. 3:24). Man restored to paradise Revelation (Rev. 22:14).

7. Sorrow and pain began (tears are shed, with sorrow for sin) (Gen. 3:17), and in Revelation, no more tears of pain (all sin, tears, and sorrow are gone) (Rev. 21:4).

8. Death enters history (Gen. 3:19). No more death (Rev. 21:4).

9. Human history began in a garden and ended in a city.

Heaven is where billions of people want to be. The saints of all ages, the nation of the world, but those who do not believe in Jesus Christ will not be there (Ps. 102:25-27). The old song that says everybody that is talking about Heaven is not going to be there. Heaven is for those who do not believe in Jesus Christ. The believer is going to be a new creation, and old things have passed away. Heaven is a prepared place for prepared people (Isa. 65:17-19).

Satan's kingdom is filled with evil, and the very air is filled with demons. The heaven of heavens, God's new dwelling place, will never undergo any changes. His house is perfect and unscarred by the enemy. He never invades God's new heaven and earth (Isa. 62:22, 2 Pet. 3:13).

The more you may go through down here, the sweeter it is going to be in Heaven. The suffering of this present time is not worthy of being compared with the glory which shall be revealed in us (Rom. 8:18). God is about to establish His eternal kingdom and destroy the universe. He is about to establish a new heaven and earth, and the capital city will be Jerusalem. Jesus said, "I go to prepare a place for you there you shall also be (Jn. 14:2).

Many people talk about pie in the sky when we die. I want you to know that I love pies. Every Christian is looking forward to going to Heaven. Some folks say Christians are so heavenly minded that you are no earthly good. (Col. 3:1-2).

The new Heaven and earth will have a capital city where the presence of God will be there. Jesus Christ will be living there. All overcomers will be living there. Scriptures give the name New Jerusalem:

1. The New Jerusalem (Rev. 21:2, 3:12).

2. The heavenly Jerusalem (Heb. 12:22).

3. The new Holy City (Rev. 21:2, 22:19).

4. The new city of God (Rev. 3:12).

5. The great city (Rev. 21:10).

The New Jerusalem will be indescribable. How can humans describe the city? John did all he could. What stirs hearts is that we can be part of his glorious future, the city of God (Rev. 21:2). What will the city be like? What stirs our hearts is that we can be part of the New Jerusalem, the city of God (Rev. 21:2). The world we live in today will not end in a holocaust, natural disasters: global warming, wars, famines, plagues, and the sun burning out. God created the heavens and the earth, and He will bring it to an end.

Verse 1

What John is seeing is that the first Heaven and earth have passed away (Rev. 20:11). It will take place in a melting process (2 Pet. 3: 10). Here is a new heaven and earth. God is preparing a place for the saints, a place without sin. What John sees corresponds to what we see today. The world is filled with violent and evil. After God spent six days of creation, there were some great beauties in the earth, became it is cursed. The butterfly, the rose, the stars and planets, and man became cursed when Adam and Eve disobeyed God, causing every human to be born with a sinful nature:

1. All the heavens above the sun, moon, stars, and planets will be destroyed and remade. God is going to make new Heaven.

2. There will be no more violent thunderstorms, typhoons, hurricanes, or destructive reign and weather.

3. No more stars, solar systems that are burned out.

4. All of heaven above will be remade, created new, and made alive. Think how beautiful this will be when God created man in the glory and magnificence of a perfect universe. It will be a universe full of living plants and stars and solar systems. We cannot imagine beauty (2 Pet. 3:10).

5. There is going to be new earth because the old is defective; it is cursed. It suffers from earthquakes, destructive eruptions, storms, floods, scorching heat, deserts, famines, diseases, and death. The day is coming when God will make it. Think of what this will mean:

   a. No more disaster or destruction.

   b. There will be no more working unfertile barren soil to farm.

    c.  No more hunger and thirst.

    d.  There will be no more diseases, decay, and erosion, or death.

The new heaven and earth will not be tainted with a curse. All things will be made new:

1. The new earth and earth will flourish and be fruitful, bearing all the good that can be imagined.

2. The new earth will be a beautiful green, lush, productive, and fruitful. It will be peaceful, serene, and comfortable.

3. It will be secured, provision, the abundance, and overflowing of every perfect gift.

4. The sea that causes destruction will be created anew. Scripture declares it is going to happen. God is going to do it (Matt. 5:18, 24:35, 2 Pet. 3: 10 – 13, Rev. 21:1, Ps. 102: 25 – 27, Isa. 34:4, 51:6, 65:17, 66:22).

5. It will be a world free from decay, destruction, and degeneration. It will be a place "*incorruptible*". It will be a world never invaded by enemies (Matt. 6:19-20). It will be "undefiled" and cannot be spoiled with evil and sin.

6. The new heaven and earth will not decay, wear, or fade away. It is a place reserved, guarded, and kept under lock and key for the believers! Heaven is there to stay (Ps. 145:13).

We will have bodies like Jesus in the new heaven and earth. It will be the new home for the believers of Jesus Christ. Every stain of sin and evil will be removed when the old earth is destroyed. Nothing in this world will last except the spiritual investments (souls) we give to Christ. The removal of the sea yields more land and no divisions between people on the new earth.

Verse 2

The new Heaven and earth coming down are what John sees. The place is a city of God, the Pearly White City or New Jerusalem, where God will live with his people. It will be a magnificent place; a paradise God will provide to make life complete and abundant. It will be a giant paradise meaning a "Garden of pleasures". The Lord will walk with His people. There shall be no more curse, no night, perfect administration, subordination, transformation, identification, illumination, exaltation, and restoration.

"*Holy city*" is used three times in Revelation (Rev. 11:2, 21:2, 2219). The Church is also referred to as the New Jerusalem (Rev.3:12). Revelation 21:2 – 10 contrasts with the literal city of Jerusalem in Palestine. The term "new" is used three times: the new heaven, the new earth, the New Jerusalem. Heaven is a place of newness, physical, spiritual, and moral.

Jerusalem will be the capital city in the new heaven and earth, two of the several things. It will be the place where the very presence of God is symbolized:

1. Heaven is the home of God among his people (Rev. 21:3, 22:4).

2. No more death, sorrow, crying, or pain. A place of eternal joy (Rev. 21:4, 26 – 27).

3. For those who trusted Christ, the blessing will be an inheritance to be called the children of God forever (Rev. 21:7).

4. Nothing but the best and the finest will be given to God's people (Rev. 21:11).

5. Heaven will symbolize perfection and completeness (Rev. 21:15 – 16).

6. No temple, sun, moon, darkness will be needed. The people will experience God's glory constantly, for time will cease to be (Rev. 21:22, 23, 25).

7. Worship of God will be daily life (Rev. 22:3).

8. God will give constant refreshment from the river of life and meet every need of his people according to His riches (Rev. 22:1-2).

God will prepare his capital city to sit upon the earth to rule the universe and require believers to visit and report on their work (Rev. 21: 24 – 27). The Lord's throne will sit in the New Jerusalem where he will rule from them throughout eternity. It will be beautifully prepared as a bride is for her husband.

Verse 3

The new people will occupy Heaven. God's tabernacle will be with them. They will have close fellowship with God (Exod. 6:7, Duet. 7:6, Jer. 31:33 – 34, Ezek. 37:27, Zech. 8:8). They will have an asset to the Pearly White City. There will be no need for a mediator. It will be like the tabernacle of the Old Testament, the worship center of Israel, the place where the very presence and the glory of God dwell uniquely. What does this mean?

1. The tabernacle God, the very presence and glory of God, will be with men (Exod. 40:34-35, 1st King 8:10-11).

2. God would do well with them.

3. They shall be his people (Lev. 26:11-12).

4. God himself shall be with them, and He shall be their God (Gen. 3:8).

Think how excellent it is going to be in the presence of God. Will be able to talk and share with God face-to-face, fellowship and commune with him, laugh and rejoice with him, praise, and worship him, and serve and work for him—all face-to-face. God is going to take over the management of our lives face-to-face. The presence and glory of God will be living and dwelling with us here on the new earth.

Verses 4-5

Utopia will become a reality, and life will be different from what it is now. Troubles, trials, tribulations, and the graveyard will not follow us to Heaven. God will wipe away every tear from the eyes of believers (Rev. 21:4). Imagine a world so beautiful. Never again would a tear be shed:

1. Death, aging, murder, killing, all war (Rev. 21:4), will be no more. No more miscarriages, dying children, and no more parents who have passed away.

2. There will be no more funerals or cemeteries or burial grounds. Everyone will have a spiritual body, a body that will be perfected, made incorruptible and immortal, perfect in strength and honor.

3. There will be no more death in heaven or earth. God will wipe away the tears of death.

4. There will be no more sorrow: no brokenness, disappointment, regret, guilt, failure, weakness, inferiority, inadequacy, or incapability.

5. There will be no homelessness and starvation, hunger, or thirst. There will never be a regret of failure. Will be comforted and secured. We will serve the Lord without shortcoming whatsoever.

6. There will never be regret or failure to make a sorrowful. no more crying: no more disappointment, arguing, fussing, cursing, divisiveness, drugs, and evil, and immorality, and separation, bitterness, and burden, or headaches—no more bad things that can cut the heart and eyes to cry.

7. There will be no more pain: no more diseases, and accidents, and distress, pressure, abuse, beatings, fights, afflictions, or agony, or emotional or physical pain. No more anything that causes pain of any kind.

God declares the whole creation, humanity, and things are made new. The former things are passed away. How do we know that God is going to make things new? God commands all believers and things will be made new (Rev. 7: 17, 21: 4, 2 Cor. 4:17, 1 Cor. 15:26, Isa. 60:20, 65:19). God assured us that he is going to make all things perfect. He gives us three assurances:

1. God himself assured us that he is going to make all things new (Rev. 21:5).

2. God's word assurance it. It required that his word be faithful and true. We all can count on his word, it is true. God instructed John to write (Rev. 19:9). God cannot lie, and these things will indeed happen.

3. God has willed new heaven and a new earth. It will be done. The clock is set, and the event is fixed. Time is ticking away and set for his arrival (Matt. 5: 18, Lk. 21:33, 1 Cor. 1:9, 1 King 8:56).

Verses 6-7

God's sovereignty assurance it. How? By his power, He declares that He is Alpha and Omega, the beginning, and the end. All creation, promises, problems, predictions, prophecies, love, testimonies, grace, salvation, and mercy have their source and will end victorious in Jehovah God. God is expresses as being the first and the last. John saw it as an indisputable fact in the Spirit, but it is as accurate as living in the moment. He represents fullness, comprehensiveness, and all-inclusiveness. He will bring all things to an appointed end.

God's promise that he would give water as a gift from the springs, the water of life. The water of life is salvation freely given), and it cannot be bought (Isa. 55:11, James 17). It is the reward given to those who thirst for salvation in Jesus. Water came to represent Israel's deliverance in the wilderness when they were dying of thirst. God says he will give the water of life to all of those who thirst after it. He is going to give a fountain of the water of life and give it freely. To thirst afterlife means:

1. To know the life that God wants man to live.

2. The life that God gives.

3. The believer will be rewarded with an opportunity to eat from the tree of life (2:7).

4. The believer will escape the Lake of fire (2:11).

5. He will have the opportunity of the nations (2:26).

6. He will receive the things of God (2:17).

7. His name will be written in the Book of Life (3:12).

8. He was sent her price on his throne (3:21).

9. He will share in the fullness of life that is God himself.

10. The hope of a life that God has planned for man.

11. The perfection of life that God longs for man to live.

Jesus provides the water of life in the New Testament as we look to the eternal destiny He promised (Jn. 4:10). The person who thirsts after God will be a citizen of the new heaven and earth. Water is a picture of salvation. Water pictures the reward of those who have been victorious (Rev. 21:7). In the New Jerusalem, God promises the water of life will be no more. The believers' needs will be met entirely by God throughout all eternity.

The citizens of a new heaven and earth will be the overcomers. The overcomer will be believers who overcome the world and remain faithful and loyal to Christ. They will conquer all temptations and trials of life. Great promises are made to the overcomer:

1. He will inherit all things, all that the new heaven and earth offer.

2. He will be a son of God (Jn. 1:12, Roman 8:14 – 17, Gal. 4:7, Ph. 2:15).

Heaven is opened only to those who have a relationship with the Lord Jesus Christ. He is the "water of life" (Jn. 7:37-38; Rev. 22:17). It is faith in Jesus that makes us "overcomers" (1 Jn. 5:4). Those who enter heaven will enjoy a perfect inheritance (Roman 8:17; 1 Pet. 1:3-5); and profound intimacy (1 Jn. 3:1-3) with their Heavenly Father. God has already done these things through his Son Jesus Christ.

Verse 8

Right in the middle of this beautiful description of heaven, God gives us a list of those who will not be allowed to enter the new heaven and earth. God is showing that sinful people will not enter the new heaven and earth:

1. The fearful and cowardly are those who do not confess Christ because they fear what others might say. They are those who are afraid to give up the world and deny self; those who fear to fellowship or become identified with Christian people (Matt. 10: 32 – 33, Roman 10:9, 2 Tim. 2: 12).

2. The unbelieving is those who do believe in Jesus Christ as the Son of God, the Savior of the world, those who reject Jesus Christ and his death upon the cross for their sins, those who profess Christ but live hypocritical lives, those who do not believe him (Jn. 3:18, 8:24, 12:48, 2 Cor. 4:4, 1 Jn. 2: 22 – 23).

3. The abomination of polluted: those who live worldly lives and taste the impurities and lusts of the world; those who are contaminated and polluted with sin; those who refuse to separate from the world and refuse to turn to God will receive His judgment and wrath (Lk. 21:34, Rom. 12:2, 2 Cor. 6: 17 – 18, James 4:4, 1 Jn. 2: 15 – 16).

What are some abominations?

1. They are acts of same-sex attraction (Lev. 18:22).

2. An abomination is anyone who believes and practices astronomy and horoscope (Duet. 17:3).

3. A person who is a fortuneteller, a wizard, and communicates with the dead (Duet. 18:9-11).

4. A murderer who kills and takes away the lives of others includes all forms of homicide and infanticide (Exod. 20:13, Matt. 19:18, Roman 13: 9 – 10, 1 Pet. 4: 15, 1 Jn. 3:15). If you like murderers for your next-door neighbor, do not go to Hell.

5. The whoremongers, or immoral: those who are sexually impure; those who commit fornication or have sex before marriage; those who commit adultery and same-sex activity and all other sexual acts that God forbids, those who look and lust, read and lust, think and lust (Matt. 5: 27 – 28, Rom. 1: 27, Eph. 4:19, 1 Pet: 4: 2 – 3).

6. The sorcerers: those who engage in astrology, witchcraft, devil worship, spiritism, séances, palm reading, fortune-telling, and all other forms of a false belief that claim to reveal that control one's fate, life, and destiny (1st Chronicles 10:13, Isa. 8: 19 – 20, Mic. 5:12, Galatian 5: 19 – 20).

7. The idolaters: those who worship idols, with idols made with one's hand or just conceived in one's mind: those who have an image of what God is like and worship follow that image instead of following the God revealed by the Scriptures; those who put the things of this earth before God; those who give their immediate attention and devotion to someone or something other than God (1 Cor. 10:14, Gal. 5: 19 – 21, Eph. 5:5, Col. 3:5 – 6, Rev. 21:18, 22: 8).

8. The liars: those who tell falsehoods and do not tell the truth; those who deceive and mislead others; those who are gossipers and tale barriers and pass rumors along (Ps. 63:11, Prov. 19: 5, Isa. 44:25, Rev. 21:8).

Those mentioned are partakers of the second death (Lk. 21:34-36). Any person who does not repent and turn away from these things and turns to God for forgiveness will not enter the new heaven and earth. He will not be a citizen (Rev. 20:11-15). Believe in the Lord Jesus Christ, and thou shalt be saved (acts 16:31, Roman 10:9, 10). If you reject His offer, there is nothing for you but the flames of Hell forever. You will beg, roast, fry, sizzle in Hell because you did not believe in the Lord Jesus Christ, and I shall be saved (Acts 16: 31, Roman 10:9 – 10, Jn. 5:24). The person who believes in Jesus Christ and remains faithful receives the promises of Revelation 21. Heaven would not be a boring place. We are promised eternal life, a place that satisfies every human desire. The person who believes in Jesus Christ and lives faithfully will receive his mercy and grace.

Verse 9

God gives John the most glorious of visions. God carries John away in the Spirit to a great and high mountain (Verse 10a). In both the Old and New Testaments, mountains are places where people encounter God or experience Revelation from God. Moses met with God on Mount Sinai and received the tablets of the law there. Jesus went up a mountain to teach his disciples what we now know as the Sermon on the Mount.

The angel carries John away "in the spirit" (Verse 9). This phrase, "in the spirit," is used often in the New Testament by several authors (Acts 19:21; Rom. 8:9; 1 Cor. 14:2; Eph. 4:23; 6:18; Phil. 2:1; Col. 1:8; 1 Pet. 3:18; 4:6; Rev. 1:10; 4:2; 17:3; 21:10). There are three meanings. We cannot be sure which John intended in this verse. The first possibility is that the Holy Spirit inspired this vision and accompanied John on this journey. The second possibility is that John went on this journey "in the spirit" as over against "in the body". The third possibility is a combination of the first two.

John is shown the Holy City, Jerusalem, coming down out of Heaven from God (verse 10b). The righteous do not ascend to the new heaven; instead, the new heaven descends to earth in the form of the New Jerusalem.

God shows John the New Jerusalem, the great city of God. One of the angels, which had the seven vials full of plagues, carried John away in the Spirit to a high mountain and shows him the glorious city of God. He is shown that the bride, the Lamb's wife, is the Church. The angel told John that he would show him the bride, the wife of the Lamb, referring to the Church believers (Revelation 19:7 – 8) in the New Jerusalem (Rev. 21:2).

Who are these believers? They are the elect, the saints, the sons of God, the royal priesthood, the woman clothed with the sun, him to overcomes, the New Jerusalem, the tabernacle God, and the body of Christ. A description of the believers includes:

1. The elect signifies members of the wife of the Lamb being chosen from the creation of the world.

2. Saints are those who feel with the Holy Spirit of God.

3. Sons of God indicate that those born of God the father are offspring of the bride.

4. Royal priesthood shows nobility. It speaks of those who stand before God throughout the ages to come. They are God's servants who were reign with Him in the new earth.

5. The New Jerusalem portrays a great city that is the capital of the new creation. The bride represents those who remain faithful and those ready to join him.

6. The tabernacle of God is the throne of God from which he will rule the universe. It will be His dwelling place of rest.

7. The Wife of the Lamb is referred to as Christ's bride. They are believers brought into complete union with Christ.


Verse 11

John described the city as being radiant like a rare jewel, like jasper stone. John is carried to a high mountain and sees the new city shine brilliantly like God's glory and with the quality of precious stones. Jesus said, "I am going to prepare this place for you" (Jn. 14:1 – 6), and we will live there. John saw a city shaped like a cube or a pyramid. It shines with light coming from Jesus Christ. There will be no temple there:

1. The glory of God will shine throughout the city like a sparkling sheen.

2. The light of the city shines like the green of a jasper, radiating and reflecting light.

3. The light is crystal clear—everything glitters off the most beautiful green of the jasper.

4. Nothing on the old earth can compare to Heaven's new city (Lk. 2: 9, Acts 7:55, 2 Cor. 3:18, Ps. 19:1).

The light that comes from the city is crystal clear. The light that comes from the churches today is not clear. It is clouded with sin and self-seekers who call on the name of the Lord with false claims.

Verses 12-13

The New Jerusalem provides protection and perfect security for the saints of God. When the believer reached the heavenly Jerusalem, they will be behind the walls of protection. An angel will be at each gate. Why do you need guards at the gates? People and angels will have thoughts and imaginations; sin and rebellion remain possible to guard against intruders. The event happens before in Heaven. The saint of God will be secure from evil and enemies of the physical world (Jn. 17:11, 2 Tim. 1:12, 4:18, 1 Pet. 1:5, Jude 24 – 25).

We may have gates in the new city, but there is only one gate to Heaven, and it is through Jesus Christ. There are three literal gates on all four sides of the city. Three things are mentioned about the gates:

1. The gates have the name of the 12 tribes of Israel inscribed upon them.

2. Three gates are on each of the four walls of the city, 12 gates altogether.

3. The gates symbolize the only way into the city. It also means that we come to God through the Messiah, the Lord Jesus Christ. The number 12 is symbolic of God's elect. Therefore, the entrance into the heavenly Jerusalem is only through the Messiah of the Jewish nation. No one can come through the gates of salvation provided by

God unless you qualify (Jn. 4:22, Jn. 3:16, Jn. 6:35, Jn. 6:67 – 68, Heb. 9:15, 1 Tim. 2:5, Heb. 9: 24).

4. Twelve angels guard the gates: this symbolizes that the entry to the city is protected. No person enters the city unless God approves them. Salvation through his Son, the Lord Jesus Christ, is the ticket to enter. Twelve represents the number of governments, and humanity will have its perfect governments.

Everyone on the new earth is invited to enter the city into the presence of God. There is a wall that faces everyone. Everyone on earth can enter the city through the gates. There are nations of saved people, the earth, the elect, the Israel of God, the Church, and the Body of Christ. There is no discrimination, or prejudice, or partiality, or favoritism shown by God. All can come live as citizens in the city. The only requirement is that they come to Messiah, Savior of the world, the Lord Jesus Christ (Acts 10:35, Roman 1:16, Roman 10:12, Gal. 3:28).

Verse 14

In the New Jerusalem, there are 12 foundations of the city. Why the 12 foundations? The city's foundation is built on the 12 apostles and testimony that declared Jesus Christ is the Lamb of God. The names of the walls have the apostles inscribed upon them. The city's walls will be 1500 miles high and make an excellent foundation to support such a wall. The walls are 200 feet high and like a giant pearl. The 12 disciples are identified as the apostles on the Lamb.

Jesus Christ sacrificial death as the Lamb of God makes the city available to people:

1. Unless Jesus had taken the sins of man upon himself and sacrificed his life for those sins on the cross, no person will ever be free of sin and made acceptable to God. No person could enter the city bearing sins.

2. Unless a person believes in the Lamb of God and believes that Jesus Christ sacrificed his life for his sins, that person is not acceptable to God. He will never be allowed to enter the city.

The city's very foundation is the testimony of the Lamb declared by the apostles and prophets (Eph. 2: 19 – 20, 1 Tim. 6:19, 2 Tim. 2: 19). Paul tells us, "We are a (God's) house built on the foundation of the apostles and the prophets, and the cornerstone is Christ Jesus himself (Eph. 2:20).

Verses 15 – 17

The one talking to John had a golden reed to measure the city. Measuring in the Scriptures indicates judgment. It is the applying of a fixed standard against something, event, a person. The written word of God is a golden reed. The city is measured against God's word. The world has its standards by which they are measured. The saints are filled with the Spirit of God measured according to His standards.

The city has length, breadth, and height measure with the golden rod is 12,000 stadia converts to 1400 miles. The depth of it is in the love of Christ for all saints. Every human being is born with a personality that is satanic, hellish, pure, and rebellious. Christ provided redemption with the shedding of his blood on Calvary that has created a personality of saints. The victorious saint throughout all ages will enter the new city forever because the nature of Christ has been created in them. They are without fault before the throne of God, and Christ is living within them (Gal. 2:20).

The city's shape and size are given the angel was using:

1. The city foursquare Verse 16. There is one side, each facing north, east, west, and south.

2. The city is enormous, and, concerning the heavenly city, its size is beyond anything we would ever dream - Verse 16. The measurement was twelve thousand furlongs. One furlong is 582 feet. Multiply 582 x 12,000, then divide by 5,280 feet in 1 mile, and you will get the

exact size of the city—1500 miles wide, 1500 miles high. It is 1500 miles long and wide and high. It towers 1500 miles high. There are 2,250,000 square miles or 3,375,000,000 cubic miles (almost 4 billion cubic miles). If you picture a huge spaceship, building two orbits around the earth may take two centuries. Remember, the one who created the universe will be in the city.

3. The thickness of the walls and gates is 144 cubits or 266 feet thick - Verse 17. Him Bruce B. Barton

4. The city is large enough for everyone. The city covered the distance from New York to Florida and from the Mississippi River to the Atlantic Ocean.

5. The city will be large enough to include all saints. There will be room for all who come to God through his Son, the Lord Jesus Christ (Isa. 45:22, 55: 1, Matt. 22:9, Jn. 7:37, Rom. 10:12, 1 Tim. 2: 4, Rev. 22:17). If we do not become part of the Holy City is by our own choice. A lack of faith is responsible.

Verses 18 – 20

Heaven is indescribable. Sadly, I do not possess the vocabulary, the intelligence, or the insight to do that. What John has given us God made available to John in a vision. I want to spend eternity in the new heaven and earth.

The New Jerusalem is built from materials worthy of Heaven. The precious material used in the construction of the city manufactures beauty and glory. The stones mentioned are different from the ones that we know today. They provide spectacular beauty in a variety of colors never seen before. The foundation walls will be garnished with priceless, precious stones. The twelve gates are open in all directions to all the people. The sparkling colors represent the virtues that have been created into the personalities of the saints:

1. The walls are made of jasper, which is hard as quartz. It is a crystal-like rock that is green in color. The crystal green walls sparkle with the most beautiful as a reflection of God's glory beauty. Wealth vanishes when we compare the materials used to build the city.

2. The city is made of pure gold that is as clear as glass. There is no gold on earth as transparent glass. Imagine a major city made of pure gold that will be crystal-clear. Imagine how Jerusalem will look. God's elect is pure gold refined by the fire until the dross has been removed.

3. The 12 foundations of the walls are decorated with every kind of precious stone (Verse 19 – 20). The foundations are built on a solid Rock-Christ (1Corithians 3:10-11, Eph. 2:20, Ps. 11:3, Heb. 11:10). God will use precious stones. He owns Jasper, gold, rubies, diamonds, and others.

God will design the new heaven and earth for the faithful, believers, and saints:

1. The first foundation is Jasper: green rock-like crystal. Green is the color of the life of the earth. We expect to find grass and trees in heaven.

2. The second foundation is sapphire: a sky blue spotted with gold (Exod. 24:10). Blue symbolizes heaven.

3. The third foundation is chalcedony: a green stone like the green only peacock's tail.

4. The fourth foundation is emerald: a green, the greenest of all greens.

5. The fifth is sardonyx: a stone with different shades of color, white layers of red and brown breaking the white background. Brown symbolizes the earth, and white symbolizes righteousness.

6. The sixth is sardius: a blood-red stone. Red, as used in the Old Testament, and is linked to the lady, Adam. The life of man is in the Christ that was offered as atonement for the world's sins.

7. The seventh is chrysolite: a shining stone the gold radiance.

8. The eighth is beryl: a sea blue or green sea stone.

9. The ninth topaz: a greenish-gold stone that was transparent (Job 28:19).

10. The tenth chrysolite: a yellow stone the yellow recalls him the spiritual beauty of a Holy Lord. Gold represents the divine nature of God. Yellow reminds us that the New Jerusalem is the presence of God and the Lamb on the earth.

11. The eleventh jacinth: a violent, bluish-purple stone.

12. The twelfth stone is amethyst: also, a violent, bluish-purple stone, but more brilliant than the jacinth. Purple is the color of royalty.

13. The 12 gates or 12 giant pearls are magnificently beautiful.

14. The streets are made of pure gold, but the gold is transparent, as transparent as glass.

The foundation's stones reflect God's glory. There is a meaning behind each beauty (Matt. 13:44, Matt. 6:20, 19:21, Ph. 3:8, 1 Tim. 6:19, Rev. 3:18). The image of these stones comes from the high priest's breastplate, indicating that the High entered the Holy Place to make atonement for the nation of Israel. In the New Jerusalem, all of God's people will be in his presence. Nothing will ever again separate them again from Him.

I am sure that these stones speak of God and His character in some fashion. We cannot understand all they represent, but we "will know even as we are known" (1 Cor. 13:12) when we arrive there. Imagine, if you will, a city that gleams with the brilliance of God's glory. Imagine that pure light as it shines through the diamonds, the gold, and all the multi-colored precious stones of that Heavenly city. It will be a glorious sight to behold!

Verse 21

Each gate of the city is a giant pearl. Pearl is formed out of pain. A grain of sand is trapped in an oyster. The oyster begins to build up layer upon layer of calcium around a grain of sand. After a long while, sand forms a pearl. It is a slow process. We developed patience as we seek the help of Christ according to the pains and problems of life on the earth (Rev. 1:9).

The pearl is the only gem made by a living organism. The pearl is the oyster's answer to its pain. The stones used in the foundation walls are formed under heat and pressure. It takes time for them to form. Christ is formed in us was like a pearl. We were in the world eating and drinking our pride. We were self-seekers and doing selfish things. When we accepted Jesus Christ, it took time to develop compassion and love for God. We became victorious saints. It took time.

Those gates will remind that while salvation is free, neither was cheap! Everything we have was born out of the pain of our Savior on the cross of Calvary. Every time we enter that city, we will be reminded of the price He paid to redeem our souls. Heaven is our Lord's answer to the pain of His cross! The street of Heaven will be glorious to behold. We will walk about on a paved street made of the purest gold clear as glass (Rev. 21:21).

The way (street) of God is the way of refined faith. The righteous man walks in faith (1 Pet. 1:7). Walking in faith means we trust God for all about the needs. We will be tested, but it is the faith working in us that overcomes the world. We will enjoy a city prepared for the redeemed when this life is over.

Verse 22

The focus of worship in New Jerusalem, there is no temple in the heavenly city, for both God and Christ will be there. Their present will be so manifested:

1. No temple will be seen. God Almighty and Christ are its temples.

2. The atmosphere will be filled with God's presence.

3. Every person will be perfectly filled with God's Spirit.

4. Every person will be perfectly conscious of God's continuous presence everywhere.

No believer will be without complete and perfect knowledge of God's Spirit and presence. There will be no unbroken worship, communication, and sharing with God and Christ. Whatever the person may be in the new city, there will be unbroken fellowship. Therefore, there is no need for a temple, ceremonies, and rituals to pull the human mind into the worship of God (Jn. 4:24, 2 Cor. 10:5, ph. 4:8, Rev. 19:1–7, Ps. 1: 2, Isa. 26:3). The people in New Jerusalem will have immediate access to God and the Lamb without a priest, mediator, or the tabernacle. There will be no need for the meeting place. God will be everywhere throughout every inch of this city. People will be able to worship anytime, always, anywhere, and under all circumstances.

The veil that separated humanity from God has been removed through the transforming work of Jesus Christ on the cross and the Holy Spirit. Every saint becomes the fullness of Christ. The goals of salvation are to be like God, go to Heaven, and live with Him forever. We will enjoy the presence of God and Jesus Christ forever.

Verse 23

The sixth thing described the city as having no need of the sun and moon to shine on it, for the radiance of God's glory is his light. That will be no more noon and night, but one long day of eternal life, eternal glory, and eternal bliss. The shekinah glory of Christ and God will be the light (Isa. 60:19-21). Evil and sin cannot exist in the presence of a holy God. The city will be without sin and evil.

When Adam and Eve sinned, the light left the world. Spiritual darkness came upon the earth. Then men began to call on the name of the Lord (Gen. 4:26). Jesus Christ came as the true light and the only light men would be able to see. Christ created in us light fitted for the kingdom of God and the New Jerusalem. The New Jerusalem is a city consisting of resurrected holy, one made new through Jesus Christ. It will be a fantastic time when men, angels, glorified saints, and the Godhead come together in that city.

Verses 24-25

The gates of the city will never be closed. The perfected people who live on the earth will come in and out of the New Jerusalem, bringing glory and honor to God and Jesus Christ. They will acknowledge Heaven as the seat of authority and government. Ancient cities shut their gates for security and protection. Evil has been eradicated, and the gates of the New Jerusalem will never shut. It is a picture of great activity coming and going from the city.

Verses 26-27

God will reward those written in the Lamb's Book of Life in eternity (Rev. 21:1 – 22:21, Matt. 16:24-27, 19:28 – 30; Rom. 6:8, 8:17; 1 Cor. 15:42 – 58; 1 Thess. 4:13 – 18). The Book of Life is mentioned on several occasions in both Old and New Testaments:

1. Moses asked God to forgive the Israelites for their golden calf—but if God were to refuse, Moses requested, "Please blot me out of your book which you have written" (Exod. 32:32). The implication was that God recorded the names of the redeemed in that book.

2. The Book of Daniel pictures a judgment scene in which "the judgment was set, and the books were opened" (Dan. 7:10).

3. The prophet Malachi mentions, "A book of memory (that) was written before him, for those who feared Yahweh and who honored his name" (Malachi 3:16).

4. Paul mentioned his fellow workers, "Whose names are in the Book of Life" (Phil. 4:3).

5. The Book of Revelation mentions the Book of Life in five passages (including our current verse)

6. Jesus promised the Church at Sardis, "He who overcomes will be arrayed in white garments, and I will in no way blot his name out of the Book of Life, and I will confess his name before my Father, and before his angels" (Rev. 3:5).

7. John saw a vision of a horrible, blaspheming beast, and said, "All who dwell on the earth will worship him, everyone whose name has not been written from the foundation of the world in the Book of Life of the Lamb who has been killed" (Rev. 13:8).

The grace of God has recreated the new Heaven and earth. The millennial kings, nations, and Israel will walk in the bright light of the glorious city. They will bring tribute into the city and present to the Lamb and God. Anyone who enters Heaven and the new earth names must be written in the Lamb's Book of Life. It is God who loves us and has raised us together to sit in heavenly places (Eph. 2:1-7). God will reward those who endure to the end (Matt. 16:24-27, 19:28 – 30, Rom. 6:8,8:17, 1Cor. 15:42 – 58, Col. 3:3 – 4, 1st Thess. 4:13 – 18, Rev. 3:21).

God has exhausted the riches of Heaven to make it possible that salvation shall receive to enter the city. The Church has paid a great price. God is working through the believers who make up the New Testament church. When the Rapture takes place, God is not through with the Church. The New Jerusalem will be the king's capital, occupied by the King of kings and his spotless Bride, the Church.

Heaven is a prepared place for prepared people (Jn. 14:2). Jesus has cleared the way and made ready the place. It is a Perfect Place (Rev. 21:4; 9-21). Sin and evil will enter there. (Sea, v. 1; Tears, v. 4; Pain, v. 4; Sorrow, v. 4; Crying, v. 4; Sin, v. 8, 27; Satan, v. 8, 27; Temple, v. 22; Sun, v. 23; Night, v. 25; Curse, v. 22:3). It is a pleasant place of glorious proportion in size and appearance (1500 miles on each side; walls of Jasper 216 feet high; gates of pearl foundations of twelve precious stones; streets of pure gold (Rev. 21:22-27). it is a permanent place that is not going to fade away (1 Pet. 1:4).

As we looked at a horrible place called Hell, it represents the opposite of Heaven. Hell is a prepared place for the unrighteous. The Bible describes it as a place of weeping (Matt 8:12), wailing (Matt 13:42), gnashing of teeth (Matt 13:50), darkness (Matt 25:30), flames (Lk. 16:24), burning (Isa 33:14), torments everlasting (Lk. 16:23). Hell is not a pleasant place (Matt. 13:42). Hell is a permanent place forever for the unrighteous, and it will not fade away (Lk. 16:22-28, Rev. 20:15). Satan will be the Lake of fire, his eternal prison forever.

If you have never trusted Jesus as your Savior, please come to Him today and be made ready for Heaven. What is keeping you waiting? Come to Him today and commit to living for Him until He comes to take you home. Every individual must make a personal decision (Rom. 10:9, 13; Lk. 13:3; Prov. 9:12). No one can walk that path for you. You must take the step of faith for yourself. I took that step one day, and so should you! Your time is running out. Jesus died for me on the cross will be there, and I will see Him when I get there, and that is enough for me!

# CHAPTER 22

## *A Paradise Restored*

---

As we come to the last chapter of Revelation, an angel continues to show John the grandeur of God's new paradise. The Garden of Eden was supposed to fulfill the first paradise, but when Adam and Eve sinned, it caused the fall of humanity, and God put them out. God has remade Heaven and earth. It is going to be a perfect place for perfect people. Jesus encouraged us with some of his last words:

1. On the cross, "Father into your hands I commit my Spirit" (Lk. 23:46).

2. He encouraged His disciples, "Go into all the world and preach the Gospel to all creation" (Mark 16:15).

3. Before he ascended into Heaven, "You will receive power when the Holy Ghost comes on you; and you will be my witnesses in Jerusalem, and in all Judea and Samaria, and to the ends of the earth" (Acts 1:8).

4. To the Church before the Rapture, "Whoever has ears lets them hear what the Spirit says to the churches (Rev. 3:22).

Verse 1

The angel showed John a river. A pure, crystal river flows from the throne of God and the Lamb. The river is pure with no chance of germs, disease, and pollution. It is clean and crystal clear and the source of life that flows from the throne of God and the Lamb. A river in Heaven symbolizes pleasure and prosperity. What does this mean? It reminds us that Christ is the living water:

1. Who quenches our thirst for life: Jesus Christ?
2. He will satisfy our thirst for life.
3. He fulfills our thirst for life.
4. He completes our thirst for life (Jn. 4:10, 4: 14, 7: 37 – 38, Rev. 22: 1 – 2, 17).

The river is filled with *"the water of life"*. It flows down the middle of the city's great streets, giving an unending flow of everlasting life to those who have earned their rewards in Jesus. It is a picture of God's eternal blessings that come when people believe in him and allow him to satisfy their spiritual thirst (Rev. 22: 17). The river symbolizes the blessings of God. A heavenly city will be the place of peace, prosperity, and pleasure.

Today the water from saints is muddy. People come to drink spiritual water, but it is muddy with self-seeking ministers and fake saints seeking glory for themselves using the gifts of God to become wealthy. Those who continue to manipulate people spiritually are going to Hell. It is time to repent. Spiritual water is to be given freely. The time is short, Jesus is coming back again for the Church, and he offers you an opportunity to overcome the burdens of sin and come home to Heaven. "Let him who thirsts come. Whosoever the signs, let him take the water of life freely" (Isa. 51:1, Jn. 14:6, Rev. 22:17).

Verse 2

In New Jerusalem, man will have access to the *"Tree of Life."* It is the same tree of life in the Garden of Eden (Gen. 2:9). The tree of life was the first plant in the garden of Eden. If Adam and Eve had remained sinless, they would have been allowed to eat of the tree of life; but they were not allowed to eat its fruit as soon as he sinned. God drove them from the garden to keep them from eating the fruit of the tree of life and continuously live in sin. In our heavenly bodies, we would enjoy the taste of food and drinks (Matt. 26:29).

The fruit nourished life. It would have infused Adam with eternal life (Gen. 3:22 – 24) in their fallen state. The earth died at the hands of Adam and Eve. The earth will return to life at the hands of a Spirit-filled people as Christ lives in them and directs them. God's curse is removed forever in the New Jerusalem. Everything will be perfect (Rev. 22:3). There are descriptions of the tree of life:

1. The tree is referred to as a single, but there are many trees. John saw rows on the side of the river. The tree of life will always bear twelve fruits. It reminds us that Heaven will be a place of plenty.

2. The tree of life will bear twelve crops of fruits year-round. The trees will bear fruit monthly for continuous life.

3. Those who eat from the tree of life are nourished by its fruit eternally. We will live forever and will bear the fruit of the spirit eternity.

4. The leaves of the tree of life are for the healing of the nations (Rev. 22:2). They provide a perfect life. The leaves prevent sickness, suffering, and diseases are all banished from Heaven. They will make life more pleasant (Rev. 22:2, Rev. 2:7, Gen. 2: 9, 3:22, Ezek. 47: 12, 20).

5. Scripture seemed to indicate that we will not have to eat, but we will be able to eat. After Jesus' resurrection, he ate food, and I believe the tree of life is God's pleasure and enjoyment for the saints.

6. It suggests abundant life and everything necessary for life, including perpetual health.

Verses 3-4

The curse involved in the rebellion in the Garden of Eden will be removed forever (Ezek. 36:33 – 36; Zech. 14:11). Everything will be perfect. The curse put humanity out of God's presence and in the presence of weeds and thorns that brought sickness, violence, chaos, and death to the world. The earth is cursed with aging, corruption, deterioration, decay, death, suffering, evil, disturbance, division, disasters, and others. It is cursed because man rejected God.

Consequently, a man brought death and evil into the world. There is nothing perfect for him to enjoy. His rejection of God cursed humanity. In eternity, this curse is lifted (Gen. 3-9). The earth will be restored will no weeds, thorns, sickness, violence, war, chaos, or death in that world! The heavenly Jerusalem has no curse, and it is free of evil and death. It is perfect and will last eternally. There is no curse of evil in the city. The citizens of the new earth are free from the curse, and His name shall be on their foreheads. They are perfect forever (Gen. 3:17, Gal. 3:10, Zech. 14:11).

There is the throne of God and the Lamb in the city. It means:

1. The Lord servants will serve God and Christ, operating out of the city. The idea is that we will receive instructions from the very throne of God and Christ. It is where His throne will be located. We will enjoy perfect fellowship unbroken. Matt. 4:10 will be fulfillment.

2. The Lord servant will see his face – Verse 4.

3. We will see him face-to-face: talk with, and share with, discuss, worship, pray, offers thanks, and we would have the right to see him throughout all of eternity.

4. We will have glorious privileges (Matt. 5:8, Jn. 17:3, 1st Jn. 3:2, Ps. 17:15).

The name of God is written on the forehead of the believers (Verse 4). It means possession and ownership. We shall be the holy property of God and possessed by Him as his servants and be enabled to serve him. We shall belong to him under his care, love, direction, guidance, security, and safety for eternity (2 Cor. 1:22, Eph. 1: 13 – 14, Rev. 14: 1).

Verse 5

Sin and evil will be banished from this world. No more darkness will exist for the "*prince of darkness*" to do his wicked works in the land (Rev. 21: 23– 27). Lord Jesus Christ will be the light of all God's creation forever and ever. There will be no need for the sun. The glory of Jesus will be the light of God's creation forever. His glory will light the city.

Verse 6

Speaking to John, the angel said, "These things are faithful and true" (Verse 6). Jesus Christ has sounded forth a message that will happen during the last years of human history. John has seen some fantastic things. We have seen God's ability and power over the ungodliness and evils of this world. Witnesses are testifying to the authenticity of this message. The first witness to testify of this message is God through His angels and the prophets. Let's review some things John have seen:

1. God is holding the great book of destiny in his hand and Jesus walking or taking it and open to reveal the world's future.

2. The world will experience an increase in natural catastrophes—all so destructive that whole world areas will be devastated.

3. A great charismatic leader will rise on the world scene and become so evil that he can only be described as a beast. He will be the Antichrist of man who will have the answer to peace and some of the world's terrible problems.

4. The world would turn to him because of his answers and that he will bring peace and solve some of the massive problems of society.

5. Once the Antichrist has consolidated his power over many nations, he will institute a worldwide loyalty to the state—what might be called the state religion. Every citizen will be required to give his loyalty to the state. We see that he will turn from good to launch

the worst evil the world has ever seen. He will instigate a world of Holocaust ever feared by man, slaughtering millions, and millions of people.

6. The world's government, society, and religion will become so evil under the Antichrist that God will decide to go ahead and judge the ungodly and evil of the world and end world history.

God's seal judgments will bring fame and diseases that will kill one-fourth of the earth's population:

1. The trumpet judgments will bring violent storms, volcanic eruptions, meteorite mass, astronomical happenings in space, all so devastating that one-third of the earth's vegetation, seas, and water supply destroyed.

2. There were plagues of locust-like creatures that will torment all the ungodly and evil of the earth.

3. There will be a plague of demonic military riders, which we kill one-third of the earth's population.

4. At the end of the seven bowls, an ulcerous judgment sore struck humanity.

5. The freshwater supply of the earth and the death of all sea life destroyed.

6. The sun's rays would hit the earth with scorching heat; then, pitch-black darkness will strike the earth.

7. The Antichrist will launch the most massive military buildup and the largest army ever witnessed by the earth.

8. The Antichrist and his massive army will be destroyed in one moment at the last hour of history, Armageddon.

9. The Lord Jesus Christ will usher in the millennium, a period of 1000 years when He will rule and reign upon the earth.

10. The Lord Jesus Christ will destroy Satan and the present Heaven and earth and judge the dead at God's great white throne judgment.

11. Finally, we saw that the Lord Jesus Christ would create a new heaven and earth. Christ will reign with the believers. It is the highlight of the Book of Revelation. There is a better world coming, and God is warning humanity.

John assures us that the word of God is faithful and true (Rev. 1:3, 22:7). We must depend on what is written in the Book of Revelation despite what is said by liberals, conservatives, Democrats, Republicans, extremists, and haters of God (2 Pet. 1:20-21, Eph. 4:11-16, Jn. 17:17, Rev. 22:18, Prov. 30:5-6). The Revelation close when the angel explained what John has written. It is the truth:

1. The message of Revelation is faithful and true.

2. The messages are faithful and can be trusted. They are trustworthy and reliable.

3. The message is true: it is not a lie, not a message created by the imagination of men. How do we know that the message of Revelation is trustworthy and true? Note the verses: Ps. 22:27-31, Ps. 67, Isa. 9:6-7, Ezek. 39:21-29, Zech. 14:1-9, Rev. 19:15–16).

Verse 7

The message of Revelation will bring a blessing to the person who studies and obeys the book's prophecies. It will happen "soon", which means imminent and implied certainty (Matt. 24:42, 44). The person who studies Revelation will be blessed:

1. He will be given a deep awareness of God's presence.

2. He will know and be better prepared until the Lord comes on the earth in the end times.

3. He will understand the evil of this world and how God will conquer all the evil and bring righteousness to the earth.

4. He will understand Heaven more and more strongly stirred too long for Heaven.

5. He will be drawn by the Spirit of God into more and more fellowship with the Lord in preparation for the glorious days of redemption.

The Lord said, "Behold I come quickly" (verse 7). Therefore, we must be prepared and witness to a lost world that the final days of human history are upon us (Jn. 8:51, 14:15 – 16, 14:23, 17:6, 1 Jn. 2:3, Rev. 3:8). There are many blessings to those who obey God by heeding the warnings of this prophecy (Rev. 1;3, 14:13, 16:15, 19:9, 20:6, 22:7, 22:14).

Someone is saying, "It must be a mistake, Jesus is not coming, and things will continue as they have always been" (2 Pet. 3:8). I share that hope that He will come soon. Wille Morganfield is correct in his song, *Serving God Will Pay Off After A While.* Serving God begins with our faithfulness to him now (Eph. 6:7, Col. 3:17).

Verses 8 – 9

The second witness to the message of this Book is John. He writes down reminds the reader of the things he saw and heard. The message of Revelation stirs worship. When John heard the prophecies of the Revelation, he was so astounded that he was gripped with the Spirit of fear in worship. He felled prostrate at the feet of the angel (Rev. 19:10). The angel told John to worship God and God alone. The point is that the message of Revelation should stir your worship, but make sure it is God and Him alone. God is a jealous God and refuses to take second place. He wants our love, heart, soul, strength, mind, and body. Whatever we do, it should all be done for the glory of God.

The great tragedy of Americans today is that many worships false gods and not Jehovah God. They are religious and have been baptized; they attend Church and sometimes serve in the Church. But they:

1. Reject Jesus Christ, the son of God who died for their sins.

2. Refuse to live godly and righteous lives.

3. Reject the Scriptures, the word of God.

4. Reject the Revelation of the prophecy of the Lord, the prophecy that reveals what is to happen in the end times (Matt. 4:10, Jn. 4:24, Rev. 14:7, 1 Chron. 16:29, Ps. 95:6, 96: 9).

The first commandment tells us, "You should have no other God before me (Exod. 20:3, Matt. 22:37). The angel told John to worship God because He is worthy of being praised. He is above all creation, including the angels (Heb. 1:4-14). The final word of Revelation is that we should, with clarity, worship God and him only. To worship is the will of God.

Verses 10- 11

In Daniel 12, the Lord instructed Daniel to seal the book until the time of the end. Daniel is told to conceal (Dan. 12:9), and John is told to reveal. Daniel saw the end from the beginning, and John sees the beginning of the end. The Book of Revelation now needs to be opened to understand the prophecy and Scriptures, understand the coming of Jesus Christ, and prepare for His return. The third witness is the witness of the angel. It is a relevant message for contemporary believers, and it is not to be kept secret from later generations. It is to be revealed until the coming of the kingdom. The instructions of the Lord are clear:

1. Because the time for the event is at hand, we can never be prepared, nor can we prepare unless we understand what is coming and get ready for their coming.

2. Because the time is coming when it will be too late to prepare (Verse 11), we must repent, turn away from the world of sin and turn to God. We cannot be stubborn or develop a hearten heart:

   a. We will be unjust so that we will remain unjust.

   b. We will be filthy so that we will remain filthy.

    c. We will be holy and remain holy (Heb. 12:17, Ps. 36:2, Prov. 24:20).

John's revelation of Jesus is open so that we could read and understand the message until the return of Jesus Christ. The righteous (Church) will be caught to meet Jesus in the clouds. He will: sheep separated from the goats, the wheat from the tares, and the just from the unjust. If you have not accepted Jesus, there will be no further opportunities to change in any way. All choices made are fixed, all conditions are permanent. The eternal day has emerged. The unrighteous will be separated from the righteous, the sheep from the goats, the wheat from the tares, and the just from the unjust (Matt. 13:25, 25:31-46, 1 Pet. 3:18). People will have reaped what they have sowed. Those who have done wrong will face hellfire and brimstone, and those who have done good and have been holy will be rewarded (Verse 22:11).

Verses 12 – 13

The fourth witness to this message of Revelation is Jesus. Revelation forces upon humans that God's judgment is coming quickly. The Lord declares, "Behold, I come quickly to bring a reward to give according to what each has done. The reward will not be the basis of good deeds but because of God's gracious promise (Lk. 12:31-32). The Alpha and Omega, the beginning and the end, the author and finisher of faith, the first and the last, is coming quickly to reward those who have accepted Jesus Christ as the Savior. None can claim these titles. Jesus Christ is coming soon, and His judgment will be based on three things:

1. It is based upon the works of man, based upon what we have done (Rev. 20:12; 14:14 – 16, 14:17 – 20).

2. It is based upon the person of Jesus Christ as Alpha and Omega, the beginning and end of all things. None can claim this title means that he is both the universe's creator and finisher (Rev. 1:8, 1:17, 21:6).

3. He is omniscient, omnipotent, and omnipresent. He makes all things that were made. All judgment will be committed unto Him, and He is everlasting. If we tried to explain, we could not understand all we know about God.

4. Jesus spans all over the universe. He begins all things, and he finishes all things. Therefore, he will judge all godly and ungodly (Ps. 62:12, Jer. 17:10, Matt. 16:27, 2 Cor. 5:10, 1 Pet. 1:17, Rev. 20:12, 22:12).

Verses 14-15

The Greek manuscript says, "Blessed are those who have washed their robes, not blessed are those that do not keep His commandments. The only way a person can eat of the tree of life is to wash his robes in the blood of Christ (Rom. 10:4) and live spotlessly, consecrated, and dedicated lives to Jesus Christ. Humanity cannot be saved by keeping the commandments. Believers must keep the commandments of God; they keep his commandments because they love Christ and want to follow him. They do not keep the commandments to be saved. They believe in what Jesus Christ did on the cross to be saved. We then should serve him and keep his commandments. The person whom God accepts is a person who has washed his robes in the blood of the Lamb. That is the person:

1. Who has the right to the tree of life? (Rev. 22: 1 – 5)

2. Who enters the New Jerusalem, the heavenly city of God? (Rev. 21: 9 – 23, 21: 24 – 22: 5)

3. There is a reward for the believers in Heaven who must live consecrated Spirit-filled lives (2 Jn. 8). They will be blessed and have the right to the goodness of Heaven (Isa. 53: 6 – 7, Jn. 1:29, Heb. 9: 12 – 14, 10: 11 – 13, 1Pet. 1: 18 – 19, 2: 24, 3:18).

The message of Revelation tells us who will be rejected by the Lord. Some people were not allowed to enter the heavenly city of God. Who are they?

1. The dogs of society. In ancient days, the wild dog was a symbol of roaming about, being mean and savage, dirty and immoral. Those living a mean and savage life or indulge in dirty and immoral behavior will never be allowed to enter God's heavenly city.

2. The people who are described as dogs live dirty lives (Isa. 66:3, Matt. 7:6). They are cruel (Ps. 22: 16, 20, Jer. 15:3), profane (Duet. 23:18, gross and disgusting (1 Pet. 2:22). People who put a 'beware of dogs' sign in their yards are quoting Scripture (Phil. 3:2).

3. The sorcerers, the immoral, the murderers, the idolaters, and the liars have already been discussed (Rev. 21:6 – 8, Matt. 5: 20, Mk. 10:15, 1 Cor. 6:9, 15:50, Rev. 21:27). Scorchers are described as those who use portions, spells, and drugs to enhance. Whoremongers are those who indulge in sexual lust far beyond the normal.

4. The murderers produce the character of Satan and unjustly kill people without a good reason. (Jn. 8:44).

5. The idolaters refuse to give God worship and give it to another person, things, or objects. Jehovah God is replaced and rejected. Oliver Greene

Verse 16

Jesus Christ proclaims to be the prophet and now speaks as The King of kings, the Lord of lords, the King of the Jews, and the bright and morning star. In Revelation 16, He sends an angel to testify these things to the churches. Jesus testifies these things:

1. Jesus is the root and the offspring of David. He is the promised Messiah, Savior, and King from the seed line of David, who is to sit on the throne of David. He is the son of God himself.

2. Jesus was born King of the Jews (Matt. 2:2); He died as King of the Jews (Matt. 27:37. He shall reign as Kings of the Jews (Zech. 9:9). He is the King of kings, Lord of lords, and the bright and morning

star. Come, Lord Jesus! – Henderson's First Baptist Church. https://fbchenderson.org/sermons/come-lord-jesus/ (Accessed on October 1, 2020).

3. Revelation helps us to see that Jesus Christ is the author of the book. He is the promised Messiah and will give life and has the right to judge life. He knows the future, gives a warning, and tells us how to prepare for the devastating events of the end time (Jn. 15:15, 1Cor. 2: 9 – 10, Eph. 1: 9 – 10, Dan. 2:22, Amos 3:7).

Verse 17

The fifth, sixth, and seventh witnesses to the message of Revelation are the Spirit, the bride, and him who hears. Jesus Christ offers the most incredible invitation extended to humanity in Verse 17. Everyone who is spiritually thirsty needs to come. Those who need the refreshment, satisfaction, and renewal from a parched, scorched, empty, craving, burning, laboring, and sweating life need to come. Jesus told the Samaritan woman to supply her spiritual thirst (Jn. 4:10-15,7:37). Jesus Christ is the water of life. He invites everyone to come and take the water of life as a gift if they have not accepted the invitation (Isa. 1:18, 55:1, Matt. 11:28, 22:4, Lk. 14:17). Jesus Christ has paid for the cost of salvation on the cross. Whosoever will let them come freely. We have the last invitation given in the Bible.

Verses 18 – 19

The message of Revelation is a warning that is solemn and emphatic:

1. A person must not add to the word of this book. God shall add unto that man plagues. Revelation 1:3 promises a blessing to all who read it, hear it, keep it, and obey it.

2. A person must not take away from the words of this book. Revelation 22:18 – 19 warns that judgment and fury shall be poured out upon all who tamper with Revelation.

3. Any person who is a Spiritual-filled, born-again believer will have his rights canceled for eternal life and the joy of Heaven taken away (Jn. 1:1, 14, 2 Tim. 2:15).

What happens if a person tampers with the word of God? If he adds to the words, he is going to suffer the plagues covered in the book. If you take away from the words of God:

1. He will take away your share in the tree of life.

2. He will take your share from the Holy City, the heavenly Jerusalem.

3. He will take your share of all the glorious promises of the Book of Revelation.

When we are born again and do not understand part of God's word, pray, and let the Holy Spirit explain all that we cannot understand (1 Cor. 2:1 – 5, 1 Thess. 2:2 – 5, 2: 13, Rev. 22:19). Do not worry about what you do not understand, ask God for understanding.

Verses 20 – 21

The message of these verses points back to all the things contained in this book. We have the last promise and the last prayer of the Bible to the Church. We have the last words from Heaven until Jesus returns to call the Church to meet Him in the clouds and the air. The Old Testament closes with the first promise of Jesus' coming. The New Testament closes with announcing His glorious second coming at the beginning of the Millennium (1Thess. 4:13 – 18, Zech. 14:1 – 4). Jesus will come as a thief in the night and at a time when every eye shall see Him (Rev. 1:7). The Old Testament closes with these words, "I will come and strike the land with destruction" (Malachi 4:6). The New Testament closes with these words, "The grace of our Lord Jesus Christ be with you all. Amen" (Rev. 22:21).

The Book of Revelation closes with the greatest of all assurance. The assurances are twofold:

1. Jesus Christ testified to John, who dictates the things written in Revelation. They are not the imagination and words of men. They of the words of the living God, the son of God himself.

2. Jesus Christ declares, yes, it is true. I am coming soon.

The human heart needs to shout out, Amen! So be it! Even so, come, Lord Jesus (Rev. 22:21, Phil. 4:5, James 5: 8, Rev. 3:11, 22: 20). God cares for humanity (Jn. 3:16). He cares because of the works of His son (Rom. 5:8). God had demonstrated His love for humanity when Jesus came into this world to die for us on the cross. Jesus made a promise that He is going to return to reward the faithful (verse 12). He continues to extend an invitation to those who do not know Jesus Christ as their Lord and Savior (Jn. 16:7-11; 6:44, Mark 16:15; Matt. 28:19-20). Everyone who grasps the message is to have a chance to be saved.

The Book of Revelation has warned that Jesus is coming again someday (Acts 1:8-11, 1 Thess. 4:16-18; 1 Corinthian 15:51-52; Titus 2:13, Rev. 1:7). The gift of salvation is free, and it offers the recipient benefits the world cannot provide:

1. every sin is immediately forgiven (Psa. 103:12 1 Jn. 1:7)

2. adopted into the family of God (Rom. 8:15)

3. becomes a child of God (1 Jn. 3:1-2)

4. receives eternal life (Jn. 6:47)

5. given the promise of eternal salvation (Jn. 10:28; 1 Pet. 1:5)

6. made a citizen of Heaven (Phil. 3:20)

7. promised a mansion in Heaven (Jn. 14:1-3)

8. indwelt by the Holy Spirit (1 Cor. 12:13; John 14:23)

9. promised His presence in this life (Heb. 13:5; Matt. 28:20)

10. promised His provision in this life (Matt. 6:25-34; Phil. 4:19)

11. given peace with God (Jn. 14:27)

12. made a new creature (2 Cor. 5:17)

13. given a new life (1 Cor. 6:9-11)

14. name written in the Lamb's Book of Life (Lk. 10:20; Phil. 4:3)

15. seated with Christ in heavenly places (Eph. 2:6)

16. received the blessed hope of the Rapture (Titus 2:13)

Humanity will receive these gifts and benefits, come to Jesus, and He will save you. If you would like to thank Him for the gift, you can come around this altar and thank Him for all He has given you in Jesus today. If you have wasted this gift and you would like to get some things settled with the Lord, you can do that today. Revelation is Jesus' final offer. It is also a final word to a faithful people! We learn the future of the saints is settled, and the sinner's fate is sealed to everlasting fire.

Revelation 3:14 tells us that *"Amen"* is one of the names of Jesus! It identifies Him as *"the faithful and true witness."* His word verifies the truth of what is about going happy. A*re you watching and ready?"* If you are not saved, you need to accept Jesus! He came to this world and died for your sins. He rose again from the dead, offered you salvation from your sins, and offered eternal life in Heaven. If you do not know Him, you can today.

John has been allowed to see to the end of time. He knows what is waiting on him and the rest of God's children. John also remembers what it was like to be with Jesus (1 Jn. 1:1). He remembers the day Jesus saved his soul and being at the cross and watching Jesus as He died (Jn. 19:28-30). John remembers the thrill of going to the tomb three days after the crucifixion to find that Jesus had indeed risen from the dead (Jn. 20:1-8). He remembers standing there on that hillside, watching as Jesus ascended back into Heaven (Acts 1:9-11). He remembers, and he longs to be with Jesus once again. So, when he hears Jesus say, "Surely, I come quickly," John cries, "Amen!" This word means, "So be it; let it be it is so!" John is using the word as an exclamation of excitement! He is saying, "Amen! Let it be! Come on, Jesus, I am looking forward to your return!"

Jesus is coming back again! No one knows when... We are not to get caught up in watching the signs and trying to figure out when Jesus will come. Those of us who know Him are to be laboring until He returns to claim His people. Some folks may quit their job, sell their homes, and give away their possessions to go out on a hillside because their pastor said Jesus is coming on a particular day. We are to be engaged in His work of worshiping Him and sharing His Gospel until He comes.

You need to know that Jesus Christ died on the cross and shed His blood so that your sins might be forgiven and so that you might be saved from your sins. He is calling you; come to Him today. Jesus is coming back soon!

The study of Revelation has taken us from the days of the early Church to eternity in the future. John has faithfully shared his vision and completed his assignment. God gave unto him, "The Revelation of Jesus Christ, which to show unto his servant's things which must shortly come to pass; and he sent and signified it by his angel unto his servant John" (Rev. 1:1).

God reveals his plans to John, "Write the things which thou hast seen, and the things which are, and the things which shall be hereafter" (Rev. 1:19). The Book of Revelation has revealed some amazing things. The Lord has shown us how the church age will end. It will end with the Church in apostasy, cold and dead, with Jesus on the outside. We are steadily moving in that direction of Revelation today. John has shown what will follow when the Church is removed from the world:

1. There will be a terrible tribulation period that will engulf the world.

2. Billions will die from war, disease, and the tragedy of divine judgment.

3. Revelation will end with the Antichrist, and Satan judged and sentenced to an eternity in the Lake of Fire.

Revelation is a glimpse of Heaven where wars, death, disease, famine, plagues, sin, and Satan will be prohibited. We have been extended an invitation to accept Jesus as our Savior and go and live with Him forever.

As the Book of Revelation closes, God has the final word, and he controls future events. Humanity has not lived up to its expectations, and God will destroy the old Heaven and earth and rebuild a new Heaven and earth. John assured the believers that everything he has seen is both "*faithful and true*" and not a single falsehood has been said (Rev. 3:14; 19:11). Jesus is trustworthy and worthy of being praised.

The Lord has fulfilled all the promises He has made, and they will come to pass. When He issues a prophecy, it will be fulfilled. God has tied the truth of His Scriptures to the integrity of His Name (Psa. 138:2). Every prophecy made in this book will come to pass in the Lord's time. Every word in this book is "God-breathed" (2 Tim. 3:16). You can trust the Bible!

Jesus said, "Behold, I come quickly." Do not let go!" "Hang on!" "Hold fast which thou hast, that no man takes thy crown" (Rev. 3:11). The Lord comforts and encourages us with His promises until He returns. John hears the promises God in Revelation has given to him through the angel, and He is told to "Worship God!" God and God alone are worthy and deserving of our worship!

We have the Lord's promise that He is coming again. Revelation gives us an account to be prepared when he returns, or we will suffer the wrath and judgment of God:

1. First, He will return in the clouds above the earth to claim His redeemed Bride and take her home to Heaven (1 Thess. 4:16-18).

2. Then, He will return in power and glory to claim this earth for Himself.

3. He will defeat all His enemies, establish His kingdom, and rule in righteousness in this world.

The saints of God are encouraged by the hope that the Lord's return will offer everlasting peace and hope. The world will not enjoy peace and hope. They will not be able to enjoy leaving this world in the future Rapture. In the end, all humanity will stand before the Great White Throne Judgment and be rewarded for faithfulness and bless those for their service. Many faithful saints of God will hear Him say, "Well done, thou good and faithful servant: thou hast been faithful over a few things, I will make thee ruler over many things: enter thou into the joy of thy lord" (Matt. 25:23). Those who missed the mark of accepting Jesus Christ as their Savior will receive eternal doom. I will make sure that I have received Jesus Christ as my Savior.

He is the "bright and morning star". To be called a "*star*" in that culture was to be "*elevated*". The "*morning star*" signaled the advent of a new day. Jesus is reminding us that He will return to destroy the darkness of this world forever. He will sit on the throne and reign when He comes again!

God desires Jesus to return so that He might defeat His enemies and occupy His rightful place on the throne of the universe (Jn. 16:14). The Spirit desires the glory of the Son of God. Therefore, the Spirit says, "*Come!*"

The last pages of Revelation offer one last invitation to lost sinners to come to Jesus for salvation. They can drink the water of life and pass from death unto life (Jn. 5:24). The Lord has a curse on those who add or take away from the words of God. It is a warning that runs through the pages of Scripture (Deut. 4:2; 12:32; Pro. 30:5-6).

1. Humanity is warned not to add or take away from the Bible. The world needs no more Revelation of Jesus Christ. It is enough for humanity to know God.

2. Anyone guilty of doing so will bring divine judgment upon themselves.

God is serious about how we handle the word. I would rather offend you by preaching the truth than offend God by diluting and changing the truth. We must preach the Gospel as it is written. We should study it, meditate over it, and present it in the power of the Holy Spirit, then we stand and proclaim, being careful not to add to or take away from its divine message!

The word of God is to be spoken so that the lost will come and accept Jesus Christ as their Savior. The word of God does not discriminate against anyone:

3. God does not show partiality to any person.

1. The saints will walk in the light of a new heaven and a new earth.

2. The citizens of Heaven and the new earth will walk in the light of the glory of God.

3. They walk in the light of the knowledge of God, the complete and perfect knowledge of God.

4. The citizens of Heaven and the new earth will walk in the light of perfection, purity, righteousness, and wisdom, knowing precisely what to do and how to do it.

5. Believers will bring their glory, honor into the heavenly city, and give all their honor to the Lord. They praised giving them great salvation, and all kings will bring their glory and honor into the city (Verse 24).

6. Believers rule and reign, with Christ overseeing the universe. Scripture teaches this (Rev. 14:13, 20:4 – 6).

7. Each person will have a responsibility (Matt. 19:28, 25:23, Lk. 12: 42 – 44, 19: 17, 19, 1 Cor. 6: 2 – 3, Rev. 1 – 5).

8. The citizens of Heaven will have constant, unbroken access to God's presence (Verse 25). We will have perfect bodies with excellent strength. There will be no unbroken fellowship and communion and worship of God.

Revelation is no doubt about Jesus:

1. I am Alpha and Omega, and everything starts and ends with me.

2. I am the first and the last, and I will resolve history.

3. I am the beginning, meaning, the author and finisher of everything.

4. I am the root and offspring of David. I am the Messiah, who is the giver of promises given to David.

5. I am the bright and morning star, meaning I will signal the dawning of a new day and a perfect world for eternity.

Anyone who reads the Book of Revelation cannot say that they do not know Jesus. He is the son of God. Jesus assures us that He is coming back to this world to establish His kingdom of peace (1 Cor. 16:22 (Rev. 22: 20). To be a part of a kingdom, you must accept him as the author and finisher of faith. Revelation does not mystify, but it enlightens us to understand the fascinating things about Jesus Christ. The Book of Revelation is not a mystery. It is a blessing to those who have read and conveyed his understanding to a lost world.

Let us finish the book by asking you, are you saved? Have you accepted Jesus Christ as your Savior? I did not ask for the religion you prefer or your church membership. If you have not received Jesus as your Savior, you can say about you. Right now, I received the Lord Jesus Christ as my Savior. God's grace will keep you, to present you faultless for his glory. Believe in the Lord Jesus Christ, and thou shalt be saved (Acts 16:31)

# NOTES

ACKNOWLEDGEMENTS

INTRODUCTION

1.  Earl Radmacher, Ronald B. Allen, H. Wayne House, *Nelson's New Illustrated Bible Commentary* (Nashville, TN: Thomas Nelson, Inc., 1999), 1746.

2.  God's Revelation Sermon by John Kapteyn, Revelation 1:1-3, https://www.sermoncentral.com/sermons/god-s-Revelation-John-kapteyn-sermon-on-apocalyptic-21701 (Accessed on July 15, 2020).

3.  Tony Evans, *The Tony Evans Study Bible* (Nashville, TN: Holman Bible Publishers, 2019), 1510.

4.  James Moffatt, *The Revelation of St. John the Divine*. In The Expositor's Greek Testament, 5 (1910):281-494. 4th ed. Edited by W. Robertson Nicoll. 5 vols. London: Hodder and Stoughton, 1900-12.

5.  Earl Radmacher, Ronald B. Allen, H. Wayne House, *New Illustrated Bible Commentary* (Nashville, TN: Thomas Nelson, Inc., 1999), 1734.

6.    Leon Morris, *Apocalyptic* (Grand Rapids, MI: Eerdmans, 1972), 34–61.

7.    David Jeremiah, The Revelation of Jesus Christ, https://www.gty.org/library/bible-introductions/MSB66/the-Revelation-of-jesus-christ (Accessed on July 29, 2020).

8.    Apocalypse | Definition of Apocalypse by Merriam-Webster, https://www.google.com/search?q=apocalypse+means&rlz=1C1GCEA_enUS928US928&oq=apocalypse+means&aqs=chrome..69i57j0l-2j0i10l7.16133j1j7&sourceid=chrome&ie=UTF-8 (Accessed on January 7, 2019).

9.    Merriam-Webster, s.v. "subtle," http://www.merriam-webster.com/dictionary/subtle (Accessed January 2, 2021).

10.   Fireside, *The Holy Bible, Catholic Parish Addition* (Wichita, K: Catholic Bible Publishers, 1994 – 1995), 7.

11.   Douglas Connelly, *The Book of Revelation Made Clear* (Grand Rapids Michigan: Zondervan Publishing, 2007), 13.

12.   Growing in Grace, Daily Devotional, http://www.parkgatebaptist-church.com/daily_devotional.html (Accessed on February 4, 2017).

## CHAPTER 1. The Revelation Of Jesus Christ

1.    Why all the 7s in Revelation? | Biblword.net. https://www.biblword.net/why-all-the-7s-in-Revelation/ (Accessed on September 9, 2019).

2.    Fireside, *The Holy Bible Catholic Parish Addition* (Wichita, KS, Catholic Bible Publishers, 1994–1995), 39.

3.    Douglas Connelly, *The Book of Revelation Made Clear* (Grand Rapids Michigan: Zondervan Publishing, 2007), 16.

4.   Bruce B. Barton, *Life Application Bible Commentary* (Wheaton, Ill: Tyndale House Publishers, Inc., 2000), 4-6.

5.   Douglas Connelly, *The Book of Revelation Made Clear* (Grand Rapids Michigan: Zondervan Publishing, 2007), 18.

6.   #1 – He Is the Almighty – Rathdrum Bible. https://rathdrumbible. org/2021/02/17/he-is-the-almighty/ (Accessed on May 11, 2020).

7.   Richard E. Simmons, III, *Reliable Truth* (Birmingham, AL: Union Hill Publishing, 2013), 108-109.

8.   Bruce B. Barton, *Life Application Bible Commentary* (Wheaton, Ill: Tyndale House Publishers, 2000), 9-11.

9.   Father E.S. Berry's Notes on Revelation 1:9-13, 17-19) https://stjoeo-foblog.wordpress.com/2016/03/31/father-e-s-berrys-notes-on-Revelation-19-13-17-19/ (Accessed on March 5, 2019).

10.  Earl Radmacher, Ronald B. Allen, H. Wayne House, *New Illustrated Bible Commentary* (Nashville, TN: Thomas Nelson, Inc., 1999), 1735.

11.  John MacArthur, *The MacArthur Bible Commentary* (Nashville, TN; Thomas Nelson, 2005), 1995.

12.  An Argument of the Book of Revelation (Part 1) | Bible.org. https://bible.org/article/argument-book-Revelation-part-1 (Accessed on May 17, 2020).

13.  What are the seven lampstands/candlesticks of Revelation? https://www.compellingtruth.org/seven-lampstands-candlesticks.html (Accessed on June 8, 2020).

14.  End Times CompellingTruth.org., https://www.compellingtruth. org/seven-lampstands-candlesticks.html (Accessed on August 8, 2020).

**CHAPTER 2. Message To Ephesus, Smyrna, Pergamos, and Thyatira**

1.  W. E. Vine, *Vine's Expository Dictionary* (Nashville, TN: Thomas Nelson Publishers, 1997), 47.

2.  John R. Stott, *What Christ Thinks of The Church* (Grand Rapids: Eerdmans, 1958), 20.

3.  Unto the Angels of the Churches, Buried History 10:4 (1974), 13.

4.  James W. Knox, *The Book of Revelation* (THE BIBLE Baptist Church, 2014).

5.  Richard Mayhue, *What Would Jesus Say About Your Church?* (Scotland: Christian Focus, 1995), 52.

6.  Ibid., 52.

7.  Insects Mentioned in the Bible - ULC. https://www.ulc.org/ulc-blog/insects-mentioned-in-the-bible (Accessed on June 20, 2019).

8.  Sermons and Outlines - Sermon Notebook. https://www.sermonnotebook.org/revelation/Revelation%2012_7-17.htm (Accessed on June 5, 2019).

9.  JEWELS FOR THE SOUL – Jewels For The Soul Blog is the Holy... https://jewelsforthesoul.blog/ (Accessed June 15, 2019).

10. Finis Jennings Drake, *Drake's Annotated Reference Bible*, (Lawrenceville, GA: Drakes Bible Sales, Inc., 1992), 304.

11. Open to the Work of the Gardener - Ekklesia Project. http://www.ekklesiaproject.org/blog/2019/03/open-work-gardener/ (Accessed on May 1, 2020).

12. Sermons and Outlines - Sermon Notebook. https://www.sermonnotebook.org/new%20testament/Revelation%202_1-7(b).htm (Accessed on May 1, 2020).

13. Chuck Missler, *The Book Of Revelation* (Koinonia House Inc., 2005), 32-33.

14. Gold = royalty; Frankincense = deity, priesthood; Myrrh = suffering, death. Chuck Missler, *The Book Of* Revelation (Koinonia House Inc., 2005), 34.

15. Revelation Verse-by-verse / Rejoicing in Revelation, https://www.bible-prophecy.com/Revelation/rev002008.htm (Accessed on June 5, 2020).

16. Worship Christ Sermon by Christian Cheong, Revelation 1:9 .... https://www.sermoncentral.com/sermons/worship-christ-christian-cheong-sermon-on-worship-benefits-117430 (Accessed on June 7, 2020).

17. The Martyrdom of Polycarp, *Richardson translation, Early Christian Fathers, Vol. 1.*

18. John Fletcher Hurst, *Short History Of The Christian Church* (New York, NY: Harper and Brothers, 1893), 39.

19. David Jeremiah, *Agents of the Apocalypse* (Carol Stream, Ill: Tyndale House Publishers, 2014), 4.

20. Earl Radmacher, Ronal B. Allen, H. Wayne House, *Nelson's New Illustrated Bible Commentary* (Nashville TN; Thomas Nelson, Inc.) 1738.

21. Faithlife Sermons: Sermon Preparation, Presentation, and .... https://sermons.faithlife.com/sermons/292631/tone (Accessed on July 15, 2020).

22. A.T Robertson, *Words Pictures In the New Testament, Vol. 6* (Nashville, TN: Broadman Press, 1933), 305.

23. THE COMPROMISING CHURCH - Faithlife Sermons. https://sermons.faithlife.com/sermons/210934-the-compromising-church (Accessed on June 7, 2020).

24. Dear Dave, I asked what the white stone refers to in .... https://resources.christianquestions.com/en/BibleQA/CQ%20Meaning%20Of%20The%20White%20Stone.pdf (Accessed on June 7, 2020).

25. Merriam-Webster, s.v. "tessera" http://www.merriam-webster.com/dictionary/ tessera (Accessed on June 2, 2021).

26. Allan Carr, The Church That Married The World, The Sermon Notebook, https://www.sermonnotebook.org/revelation/Revelation%202_12-17.htm (Accessed on July 1, 2020).

27. White%20Stone.pdf (Accessed on June 7, 2020).

28. Prophecy - Part 34 - Obedience - Open Bible Ministries of .... http://openbibleministries.net/multimedia-archive/prophecy-part-34-obedience/ (Accessed on August 12, 2020).

29. Revelation, PART VIII, (The Church at Thyatira) a Devotion .... https://aocinternational.org/Revelation-part-viii-the-church-at-thyatira-a-devotion-for-5-october-2017-anno-domini/ (Accessed on June 4, 2020).

30. Sermons and Outlines - Sermon Notebook. https://www.sermonnotebook.org/revelation/Revelation%202_18-29.htm (Accessed on June 10, 2020).

31. Revelation CHAPTER TWO – THYATIRA, http://www.apostle.org/lectures/rev2thy.htm (Accessed on June 16, 2020).

32. Fireside, *The Holy Bible, Catholic Parish Addition* (Wichita, KS, Catholic Bible Publishers, 1994 – 1995), 7.

33. W. E. Vine, *Vine's Expository Dictionary* (Nashville, TN: Thomas Nelson Publishers, 1997), 47.

34. Earl Radmacher, Ronald B. Allen, H. Wayne House, *Nelson's New Illustrated Bible Commentary* (Nashville, TN: Thomas Nelson, Inc., 1999), 1739.

35. Merriam-Webster, s.v. "seduce," http://www.merriam-webster.com/dictionary/seduce (Accessed January 2, 2015).

36. THE CHURCH THAT COMPROMISED WITH THE WORLD - Faithlife Sermons. https://sermons.faithlife.com/sermons/656297-the-church-that-compromised-with-the-world (Accessed on August 7, 2020).

37. I Am the Same Yesterday and Today and Forever.... https://omny.fm/shows/conversations-with-cinthia/cwc-8-16-20-final (Accessed on December 2020).

38. Vance Havner, *Repent Or Else* (Westwood, NJ: Revell, 1958), 50.

## CHAPTER 3. Message TO SARDIS, Philadelphia, and Laodicea

1. Sermons and Outlines - Sermon Notebook. https://sermonnotebook.org/revelation/Revelation%203_1-6.htm (Accessed on August 25, 2020).

2. 04/10/11 CPR in Progress! - Outer Banks Community Church. http://outerbankscommunitychurch.org/sermons/04-10-11-cpr-in-progress (Accessed on January 7, 2019).

3. AN AUTOPSY OF A DEAD CHURCH, Part 3 - Faithlife Sermons. https://sermons.faithlife.com/sermons/683737-an-autopsy-of-a-dead-church-part-3 (Accessed on September 4, 2020).

4.  Sermons and Outlines - Sermon Notebook. https://sermonnotebook. org/revelation/Revelation%203_1-6.htm (Accessed on September 4, 2020).

5.  https://www.reddit.com/r/quotes/comments/1u0jbd/the_greatest_ tragedy_in_life_is_to_be_alive_and/ (Accessed on June 25, 2020).

6.  The Church Hell Cannot Handle (Rev 3:7-13 Philadelphia .... https:// ezrachimts.wordpress.com/2016/02/09/the-church-hell-cannot-handle-rev-37-13-philadelphia/ (Accessed on June 22, 2020).

7.  #41 – Hold Fast – Rathdrum Bible. https://rathdrumbible. org/2021/04/15/41-hold-fast/ (Accessed on June 22, 2020).

8.  F. N. Peloubet, *Peloubet's Bible Dictionary* (Philadelphia, PA: The John C. Winston Co., 1947), 509.

9.  The Mystical Teachings.... https://askrealjesus.com/no-one-can-keep-you-out-of-heaven[AR2] / (Accessed on June 24, 2020).

10. The Black Mannequin. https://theblackmannequin.com/ (Accessed on July 7, 2020).

11. The Raptured Diaries - WordPress.com. https://harveybtee.word-press.com/tag/repentance/ (Accessed on June 15, 2020).

12. The Faithful and True Witness defines the word "amen." Truth Revelation 3:14 - Grace Bible Church Baytown, Texas. http://www. gracebiblechurchbaytown.org/uploads/1/0/1/6/10165395/truth. pdf (Accessed on July 9, 2020).

13. Megan Sauter, The Church of Laodicea in the Bible and Archaeology, https://www.biblicalarchaeology.org/daily/bibli-cal-sites-places/biblical-archaeology-sites/church-of-laodicea-in-the-bible-and-archaeology/ (Accessed on August 23, 2020).

14. Definitions.net, STANDS4 LLC, 2021. "Zestos." https://www.definitions.net/definition/Zestos (Accessed on August 28, 2021).

15. John R. W. Stott, *What Christians Think Of The Church* (Grand Rapids, Michigan: Eerdmans, 1958), 116.

16. Merriam-Webster, s.v. "spit," http://www.merriam-webster.com/dictionary/spit (Accessed January 2, 2019).

17. Merriam-Webster, s.v. "emetic," http://www.merriam-webster.com/dictionary/emetic (Accessed January 2, 2019).

18. Prophecy - 49, God's Provision - Open Bible Ministries of .... http://openbibleministries.net/multimedia-archive/prophecy-49-gods-provision/ (Accessed on June 24, 2020).

19. James Strong, LL.D., S.T.D., *Strong Dictionary of Bible Words* (Nashville, TN: Thomas Nelson Publishers, 2001), 46, 209.

20. Vance Havner, *Repent or Else* (Westwood, NJ: Revell, 1958), 118.

**CHAPTER 4. The Things Hereafter**

1. Derek Demars, The Structure and Timeline of Revelation 4-22, https://derekdemars.com/2020/09/04/structure-and-timeline-of-Revelation-4-22/ (Accessed on September 4, 2020).

2. Oliver Greene, *Revelation* (Greenville, SC, 1963) 153.

3. W. E. Vine, *Vine's Expository Dictionary* (Nashville, TN: Thomas Nelson Publishers, 1997), 1146.

4. Paul Spilsbury, *Reversed Thunder: The* Revelation *of John And The Praying Imagination* (New York, NY: Harper San Francisco, 1988) 140.

5.  Study In Revelation 12 A Picture Of Things To Come Sermon .... https://www.sermoncentral.com/sermons/study-in-Revelation-12-a-picture-of-things-to-come-james-lee-sermon-on-book-of-Revelation-140408 (Accessed on July 16, 2019).

6.  Earl Radmacher, Ronald B. Allen, H. Wayne House, *Nelson's New Illustrated Bible Commentary* (Nashville, TN: Thomas Nelson, Inc., 1999), 1742.

7.  All Creation Joins in Praise" Commentary .... http://www.firstg.org/?p=1953 (Accessed on July 9, 2019).

8.  The Book of Revelation, http://www.baptistbiblebelievers.com/LinkClick.aspx?fileticket=iPPFNB5fF2k%3d&tabid=206&mid=674 (Accessed on July 9, 2019).

9.  *The Preacher's Outlines & Sermon Bible, vol. 13* (Chattanooga, TN: Alpha-Omega Ministries, Inc., 1992), 80.

10. Douglas Connelly, *The Book Of Revelation Made Clear* (Grand Rapids, Michigan: Zondervan, 2007), 66.

## CHAPTER 5. The Lamb And The Scroll

1.  wordsearchbible.lifeway.com. https://wordsearchbible.lifeway.com/products/15058-preacher-s-outline-and-sermon-bible-Revelation/sample_text (Accessed on August 1, 2020).

2.  Douglas Connelly, *The Book of Revelation Made Clear* (Grand Rapids Michigan: Zondervan Publishing, 2007), 78.

3.  Sermons and Outlines - Sermon Notebook. http://sermonnotebook.org/revelation/ Revelation%205_1-7.htm (Accessed on June 24, 2021).

4.  James W. Knox, *The Book of Revelation* (Deland, FL: 2002), 151.

5.      wordsearchbible.lifeway.com. https://wordsearchbible.lifeway.com/products/15058-preacher-s-outline-and-sermon-bible-Revelation/sample_text (Accessed on July 1, 2020).

6.      Jessica Olatunji, The meaning of dunamis in Greek, https://www.legit.ng/1173962-the-meaning-dunamis-greek.html (Accessed on May 23, 2019).

7.      THE SEVEN SEALS | Percykids' Weblog. https://percykids.wordpress.com/2010/07/15/the-seven-seals/ (Accessed on June 25, 2021).

8.      W. E. Vine, *Vine's Expository Dictionary* (Nashville, TN: Thomas Nelson Publishers, 1997), 47.

9.      J. Hampton Keathley, III, Studies in Revelation-The Prologue (Rev 1:1-8), https://bible.org/seriespage/1-prologue-rev-11-8 (Accessed on July 15, 2021).

## CHAPTER 6. Opening the Seals

1.      Lectionary Bible Studies and Sermons http://www.lectionarystudies.com/studyn/rev10en.html (November 11, 2020).

2.      False Teachers - Forward with Ron Moore - August 18, 2017 .... https://www.oneplace.com/ministries/back-to-the-bible/read/devotionals/forward/false-teachers-forward-with-ron-moore-august-18-2017-11778242.html (Accessed on July 23, 2020).

3.      Prophecy - Part 66 - Riders on The White and Red Horses .... http://openbibleministries.net/multimedia-on archive/prophecy-part-66-riders-white-red-horses/ (Accessed on July 23, 2020).

4.      Sermons and Outlines – Sermon Notebook. http://sermonnotebook.org/revelation/Revelation%206_1-8.htm (Accessed on July 23, 2020).

5.     Bruce B. Barton, D. Min., Linda Taylor, Neil Wilson, M.R.E., Dave Veerman M.Div., *Life Application Bible Commentary* (Wheaton, Ill: Tyndale House Publishers, Inc., 2000), 72.

6.     100+ Red colors images: Red is the color of fire and blood. https://www.awesomepic4u.com/2019/12/red-colors-images-red-is-the-color-of-fire-and-blood.html (Accessed on July 24, 2020).

7.     Sermons and Outlines – Sermon Notebook. https://www.sermon-notebook.org/revelation/Revelation%206_1-8.htm (Accessed on July 3, 2020).

8.     The Revelation of Jesus to John: Revelation 6 - Six Seals Broken. https://revelationofjesustoJohn.blogspot.com/2014/07/revela-tion-6-six-seals-broken.html (Accessed on July 1, 2021).

9.     Chuck Schumer: Buffett Rule Should Be Brought To A Vote .... https://www.huffpost.com/entry/chuck-schumer-buffet-rule-mil-lionaire-tax_n_969962 (Accessed on May 5, 2019).

10.    Earl Radmacher, Ronald B. Allen, H. Wayne House, *Nelson's New Illustrated Bible Commentary* (Nashville, TN: Thomas Nelson, Inc., 1999), 1743.

11.    Sermons and Outlines - Sermon Notebook. https://www.sermon-notebook.org/revelation/Revelation%206_1-8.htm (Accessed on July 10, 2020).

12.    Sermons and Outlines - Sermon Notebook. https://www.sermon-notebook.org/revelation/Revelation%206_9-17.htm (Accessed on September 1, 2020).

13.    TWO WORLDS IN PRAYER" 11-29-20. https://firstagrockhill.org/wp-content/uploads/2020/11/TWO-WORLDS-IN-PRAYER-oll-11-29-20a.pdf (Accessed on May 25, 2021).

## CHAPTER 7. The Multiple Seals

1. Finis Jennings Drake, *Drake Annotated Reference Bible* (Lawrenceville, GA: Drake Bible Sales, Inc., 1991), 292.

2. Sermons and Outlines - Sermon Notebook. https://www.sermon-notebook.org/ revelation/Revelation %207_1-8.htm (Accessed on December 3, 2020).

3. C.H. Spurgeon | Broken Pieces. https://jerfireandhammer.com/category/c-h-spurgeon/ (Accessed on June 21, 2021).

4. Sermons and Outlines - Sermon Notebook. http://www.sermonnotebook.org/new%20testament/Acts%202_41-47(b).htm (Accessed on June 25, 2019).

5. James Strong, LL.D., S.T.D., *Strong Dictionary* of Bible Words (Nashville, TN: Thomas Nelson Publishers, 2001), 46, 871.

## CHAPTER 8. The First Four Trumpet Judgments

1. 05 The Rapture Question – Prewrath; All views | BIBLE .... https://bibleresourceman.wordpress.com/eschatology-teaching-of-end-times/the-rapture-question/ (Accessed on April 7, 2019).

2. Oliver B. Greene, *Revelation* (Greenville, SC: The Gospel Hour, Inc., 1963), 232.

3. David Guzik, *The Enduring Word Bible Commentary*, https://enduringword.com/bible-commentary/Matthew-1/ (Accessed on October 13, 2020).

4. Douglas Connelly, *The Book of Revelation Made Clear* (Grand Rapids, Michigan: Zondervan Publishing, 2007), 121.

5. Finis Jenning Dake, *Dake's Annotated Reference Bible* (Lawrenceville, GA; Dake Bible Sales, Inc., 1991), 291.

6.     Bruce Morton, *Life Application Bible Commentary* (Wheaton, Ill: Tyndale House publishers. Inc., 2000), 95.

7.     Prophecy - Part 101 - The Seven Trumpet Judgments: Events .... http://openbibleministries.net/multimedia-archive/prophecy-part-101-the-seven-trumpet-judgments-events-during-the-great-tribulation/ (Accessed on May 31, 2019).

8.     Oliver B. Greene, *Revelation* (Greenville, SC: The Gospel Hour, Inc., 1972), 242.

9.     Finis Jennings Dake, *Dake's Annotated Reference Bible* (Lawrenceville, GA: Dake Bible Sales, Inc., 1991), 292.

## CHAPTER 9. The Fifth And Sixth Trumpet Woe

1.     Merriam-Webster, s.v. "star," http://www.merriam-webster.com/dictionary/star (Accessed January 2, 2021).

2.     Sermons and Outlines - Sermon Notebook. https://www.sermonnotebook.org/ revelation /Revelation%209_1-12.htm (Accessed on December 5, 2020).

3.     Prophecy - Part 79B - Trumpet Judgments - Open Bible .... http://openbibleministries.net/multimedia-archive/prophecy-part-79b-trumpet-judgments/ (Accessed on July 17, 2021).

4.     Bruce B. Barton, D. Min., Linda Taylor, Neil Wilson, M.R.E., Dave Veerman M.Div., *Life Application Bible Commentary* (Wheaton, Ill: Tyndale House Publishers, Inc., 2000), 103-105.

## CHAPTER 10. The Seventh Trumpet or Third Woe

1.     W. E. Vine, *Vine's Expository Dictionary* (Nashville, TN: Thomas Nelson Publishers, 1997), 47.

2. Oliver B. Greene, *Revelation* (Greenville, South Carolina: The Gospel Hour, Inc., 1963), 267-269.

3. Sermons and Outlines - Sermon Notebook. https://sermonnotebook.org/revelation/ Revelation %2010_1-11.htm (Accessed on August 15, 2021).

4. Finis Jenning, Dake's Annotated Reference Bible (Lawrenceville, GA; Dake Bible Sales, Inc., 1991), 302.

5. Oliver B. Greene, *Revelation* (Greenville, South Carolina: The Gospel Hour, Inc., 1963), 280-281.

6. Hugh Babour, *Men of the Bible devotional* (Uhrichsville, OH; Babour Books, 2015), 72.

## CHAPTER 11 The Two Witnesses

1. Bruce B. Barton, *Life Application Bible Commentary* (Wheaton, Ill: Tyndale House Publishers, Inc., 2000), 115.

2. Prophecy - Part 109 - The Great Announcement: Final http:// openbibleministries.net/multimedia-archive/prophecy-part-109-the-great-announcement-final-triumph-over-evil/ (Accessed on September 12, 2021).

3. Douglas Connelly, *The Book of Revelation Made Clear* (Grand Rapids Michigan: Zondervan Publishing, 2007), 163.

4. Jack W. Hayford, *Spirit-Filled Life Bible* (Nashville, TN; Thomas Nelson publishers, 1991), 1994.

5. Sermons and Outlines - Sermon Notebook. https://www.sermonnotebook.org/ revelation /Revelation%2011_1-2.htm (Accessed on September 12, 2021).

6.  Prophecy - Part 111 - The Great Destruction of Israel and ....
    http://openbibleministries.net/multimedia-archive/prophe-
    cy-part-111-the-great-destruction-of-israel-and-jerusalem/
    (August 23, 2020).

7.  Earl Radmacher, Ronald B. Allen, H. Wayne House, *Nelson's New
    Illustrated Bible Commentary* (Nashville, TN: Thomas Nelson, Inc.,
    1999), 1749.

8.  Revelation 7:1 - Verse-by-Verse Bible ... - StudyLight.org. https://
    www.studylight.org/commentary/ Revelation /7-1.html (Accessed
    on June 1, 2020).

9.  Oliver B. Greene, *Revelation* (Greenville, South Carolina: The Gospel
    Hour, Inc., 1963), 303.

10. Bruce B. Barton, *Life Application Bible Commentary* (Wheaton, Ill:
    Tyndale House Publishers, Inc., 2000), 115.

11. The Olive Trees and Two Lampstands, 2+2 witness! http.//wwwbi-
    bleinsight.com/1260p4.htm (Accessed on January 16, 2019).

12. Images of Sackcloth, https://www.bing.com/search?q=sackcloth&-
    form=ANSNB1&refig=979dc6a3d0144cb1a8b1fc58927371df&mk-
    t=en-us&sp=1&qs=LS&pq=sackcloth&sc=8-9&cvid=979d-
    c6a3d0144cb1a8b1fc58927371df (Accessed on February 25, 2021).

13. Michael C. Bere, *Bible Doctrines for Today* (Pensacola, FL: Beka
    Book, 1998), 233.

14. What is the significance of the olive tree in the Bible ...? https://www.
    gotquestions.org/olive-tree-Bible.html (Accessed on November 1,
    2020).

15. Two Witnesses of Revelation, http://www.herealittletherealittle.net/ index.cfm?page_name=2-Witnesses-in- Revelation (Accessed on February 18, 2021).

16. Bruce B. Burton, *Life Application Bible* (Wheaton, IL: Tyndale House Publishers, Inc., 1996), 124.

17. Douglas Connelly, *The Book of Revelation Made Clear* (Grand Rapids Michigan: Zondervan Publishing, 2007), 169.

18. Ibid. 291.

19. Jack W. Hayford, *Spiritual Filled Life Bible* (Nashville, TN: Thomas Nelson Publishers), 2001.

20. Sermons and Outlines - Sermon Notebook. http://sermonnotebook. org/revelation /Revelation.%2011_15-19.htm (Accessed on August 21, 2020).

21. Oliver B. Greene, *Revelation* (Greenville, South Carolina: The Gospel Hour, Inc., 1963), 303-306.

22. Prophecy - Part 117 - The Heavenly Temple of God is Opened .... http://openbibleministries.net/multimedia-archive/prophecy-part-117-the-heavenly-temple-of-god-is-opened/ (Accessed on June 21, 2020).

**CHAPTER 12 The Woman and The Beast**

1. Finis Jennings Drake, *Drake's Annotated Reference Bible*, (Lawrenceville, GA: Drakes Bible Sales, Inc., 1992), 159.

2. Oliver B. Greene, *Revelation* (Greenville, South Carolina: The Gospel Hour, Inc., 1963), 303.

3.   Sermons and Outlines - Sermon Notebook. https://sermonnote-book.org/ revelation /Revelation%2012_1-6.htm (Accessed on December 15, 2019).

4.   W.A. Criswell points this out by tracing some of the .... http://www. crosswindsfernley.com/wp-content/uploads/sermons/2021/03/ Study-of-Revelation-10-Chart-Handout.pdf (Accessed on May 2121).

5.   Sermons and Outlines - Sermon Notebook. https://sermonnote-book.org/ revelation /Revelation%2012_1-6.htm (Accessed on February 2021).

6.   Merriam-Webster, s.v. "adversary," http://www.merriam-webster. com/dictionary/adversary (Accessed January 2, 2021).

7.   Merriam-Webster, s.v. "cast out," http://www.merriam-webster.com/ dictionary/cast out (Accessed January 2, 2021).

8.   James Strong, LL.D., S.T.D., *Strong Dictionary of Bible Words* (Nashville, TN: Thomas Nelson Publishers, 2001), #3875.

9.   W. E. Vine, *Vine's Expository Dictionary* (Nashville, TN: Thomas Nelson Publishers, 1997), 849.

## CHAPTER 13 SOMETHING IN THE STRUGGLES

1.   Merriam-Webster, s.v. "dwell," http://www.merriam-webster.com/ dictionary/dwell (Accessed May 12, 2021).

2.   What Happens to Those Who Receive the Mark of the Beast .... https://lastgen.net/articles/what-happens-to-those-who-receive-the-mark-of-the-beast/ (Accessed January 20, 2021).

3.   Oliver B. Greene, *Revelation* (Greenville, South Carolina: The Gospel Hour, Inc., 1963), 342.

4.    What Is the Mark of the Beast? | Zondervan Academic. https://
      zondervanacademic.com/blog/what-is-the-mark-of-the-beast
      (Accessed on June 11, 2020).


**CHAPTER 14. THE LAMB To Come**

1.    IT IS FINISHED with Evangelist K L Rich: August 2019. https://
      itizfinished.blogspot.com/2019/08/ (Accessed on May 12, 2020).

2.    John Newton arranged Norman Johnson, *The New National Baptist
      Hymnal- Arranged Amazing Grace* (Nashville, TN: National Baptist
      Publishing Board, 1977), 132.

3.    Studies in Revelation, http://www.gutenberg.org/files/53775/53775-
      pdf.pdf (Accessed on April 18, 2021).

4.    John R. Walvoord, *The Revelation of Jesus Christ* (Chicago, Ill: Moody
      Press, 1966), 217.

5.    William R. Newell, *The Book of Revelation* (Chicago, Ill: Moody
      Press,1966), 283.

6.    Perilous Times' in the Last Days | Renner Ministries. https://renner.
      org/article/perilous-times-in-the-last-days/ (Accessed on September
      4, 2020).

7.    James Strong, LL.D., S.T.D., *Strong Dictionary of Bible Words*
      (Nashville, TN: Thomas Nelson Publishers, 2001), 46, 1144.

8.    Prophecy - Part 139 - Revelation 14:9-12 - Open Bible .... http://
      openbibleministries.net/multimedia-archive/prophecy-part-139-
      Revelation -149-12/ (Accessed on February 2: 2021).

9.    YE ARE DEAD, AND YOUR LIFE IS HID WITH CHRIST –
      Providence .... https://providencepbc.org/2018/10/29/ye-are-dead-
      and-your-life-is-hid-with-christ/ (Accessed on March 10, 2021).

10. William H. Newell, *The Book of Revelation* (Chicago, Ill: Moody Press, 1966) 228).

11. Rick Joyner: Prophetic Bulletin: "The Great Tsunami." http://www.elijahlist.com/words/display_word.html?ID=10308 (Accessed on August 2, 2020).

12. James Strong, LL.D., S.T.D., *Strong Dictionary of Bible Words* (Nashville, TN: Thomas Nelson Publishers, 2001), 926.

13. Prophecy - Part 144 - The Lamb [the Lord Jesus Christ .... http://openbibleministries.net/multimedia-archive/prophecy-part-144-the-lamb-the-lord-jesus-christ-will-be-victorious/ (Accessed on July 27, 2020).

14. Prophecy - Part 144 - The Lamb [the Lord Jesus Christ .... http://openbibleministries.net/multimedia-archive/prophecy-part-144-the-lamb-the-lord-jesus-christ-will-be-victorious/ (Accessed in August 2019).

15. Charles C. Ryrie, *Revelation* (Chicago, Ill; Moody Press, 1968), 92.

16. W. E. Vine, *Vine's Expository Dictionary* (Nashville, TN: Thomas Nelson Publishers, 1997), 1163.

17. Earl Radmacher, Ronald B. Allen, H. Wayne House, *Nelson's New Illustrated Bible Commentary* (Nashville, TN: Thomas Nelson, Inc., 1999), 1757.

## CHAPTER 15. The Seven Angels

1. Alan Johnson, *Revelation (The Expositor's Bible Commentary* (Grand Rapids, MI: Zondervan Publisher, 1996).

2.  Merriam-Webster, s.v. "sign, wonder, great," http://www.merriam-webster.com/dictionary/ sign, wonder, great (Accessed June 2, 2021).

3.  *The Preacher's Outlines & Sermon Bible, vol. 13* (Chattanooga, TN: Alpha-Omega Ministries, Inc., 1992), 203.

4.  Prelude to Pouring Out the Seven Bowls o | Revelation -of-John. https://godisstillgood.wixsite.com/ Revelation -of-John/prelude-to-pouring-out-the-seven-bowls (Accessed on February 20, 2021).

5.  James Strong, LL.D., S.T.D., *Strong Dictionary of Bible Words* (Nashville, TN: Thomas Nelson Publishers, 2001), 606.

6.  A Bible Prophecy Study on the Revelation of Jesus Christ .... http://www.amazingbible.org/Documents/Bible_Prophecy/ Revelation _part2.htm (Accessed on February 2021).

7.  Prelude to Pouring Out the Seven Bowls o | Revelation -of-John. https://godisstillgood.wixsite.com/ Revelation -of-John/prelude-to-pouring-out-the-seven-bo (Accessed on March 24, 2021).

8.  *The Preacher's Outlines & Sermon Bible, vol. 13* (Chattanooga, TN: Alpha-Omega Ministries, Inc., 1992), 203.

9.  Bruce B. Barton, D. Min., Linda Taylor, Neil Wilson, M.R.E., Dave Veerman M.Div., *Life Application Bible Commentary* (Wheaton, Ill: Tyndale House Publishers, Inc., 2000), 180.

**CHAPTER 16. The Seven Vials Judgments**

1.  Sermons and Outlines - Sermon Notebook. https://sermonnotebook.org/revelation/Revelation%203_1-6.htm (Accessed on August 25, 2020).

2.    The Revelation of Jesus Christ. http://www.baptistbiblebelievers.com/ LinkClick.aspx?fileticket=VTB7i249b5E%3d&tabid=239&mid=783 (Accessed on March 12, 2020).

3.    The Project Gutenberg EBook of Studies in the Book of .... http:// www.gutenberg.org/files/53775/53775-h/53775-h.html    (Accessed on March 21, 2020).

4.    Studies in Revelation, http://www.gutenberg.org/files/53775/53775-pdf.pdf (Accessed on April 18, 2021)

5.    Events of the Final Seven Years | Endtime Ministries with .... https:// www.endtime.com/articles-endtime-magazine/events-final-seven-years/ (Accessed March 22, 2020).

6.    Bruce B. Barton, *Life Application Bible Commentary* (Wheaton, Ill: Tyndale House Publishers, 2000), 184.

7.    Merriam-Webster, s.v. "sore," http://www.merriam-webster.com/ dictionary/sore (Accessed September 15, 2020).

8.    Prophecy - Part 151 - Third Bowl Judgments continued .... http:// openbibleministries.net/multimedia-archive/prophecy-part-151-third-bowl-judgments-continued/ (Accessed on February 12, 2021).

9.    Armageddon - Smith's Bible Dictionary - Bible Dictionary. https:// www.christianity.com/bible/dictionary.php?dict=sbd&id=408 (Accessed on February 17, 2020).

10.   Thomas Ice, *Armageddon, In the Popular Encyclopedia O Bible Prophecy, ed.* (Eugene, OR: Harvest House, 2004), 39.

**CHAPTER 17. The Mother of Evil**

1.    James Strong, LL.D., S.T.D., *Strong Dictionary of Bible Words* (Nashville, TN: Thomas Nelson Publishers, 2001), 780.

2.  Galatians Overview - West Loop Church. http://westloop-church. org/index.php/messages/new-testament/27-Galatians/100-Galalatians-overview (Accessed on June 2020).

3.  Oliver B. Greene, *Revelation* (Greenville, South Carolina: The Gospel Hour, Inc., 1963), 303.

4.  Seven Heads and Ten Horns | Revelation Logic. https:// Revelation logic.com/articles/the-seven-heads-and-ten-horns/ (Accessed on May 2020).

5.  Revelation 17 - A Study Guide by Mark A. Copeland. https://www. ccel.org/contrib/exec_outlines/rev/rev_17.htm (Accessed on June 2020).

6.  The Revelation of Jesus Christ. http://www.baptistbiblebelievers.com/ LinkClick.aspx?fileticket=aGoAGPNbAcI=&tabid=239&mid=783 (Accessed on February 15, 2020).

7.  Allan Carr, The Sermon Notebook, Revelation 17, https://www. sermonnotebook.org/ Revelation /Revelation%2017_1-18.htm (Accessed on April 28, 2021).

8.  Douglas Connelly, *The Book of Revelation Made Clear* (Grand Rapids Michigan: Zondervan Publishing, 2007), 291.

9.  James Strong, LL.D., S.T.D., *Strong Dictionary of Bible Words* (Nashville, TN: Thomas Nelson Publishers, 2001), #2822, 4103.

10. September 19, 2019 – VICTORY BAPTIST CHURCH. https://victo-rypalmetto.com/2019/09/19/ (Accessed on May 3, 2020).

## CHAPTER 18. The Fall of Babylon

1.  John Walvoord, *The Revelation of Jesus Christ* (Chicago, Illinois: Moody, 1966; re. ed., 1989), 259.

2. Prophecy - Part 166 - The Collapse of Political Babylon .... http://openbibleministries.net/multimedia-archive/prophecy-part-166-the-collapse-of-political-babylon/ (Accessed on March 15, 2020).

3. *The Preacher's Outlines & Sermon Bible, vol. 13* (Chattanooga, TN: Alpha-Omega Ministries, Inc., 1992), 222.

4. Sermons and Outlines - Sermon Notebook. https://sermonnotebook.org/ revelation /Revelation%2018_1-24.htm (Accessed on August 2020).

5. Bruce B. Barton, *Life Application Bible Commentary* (Wheaton, Ill: Tyndale House Publishers, Inc., 2000), 212

6. . John Walvoord, *The Revelation of Jesus Christ* (Chicago, Ill: Moody Publishing, 1989), 259

7. Adrian Rogers, *Unveiling the End Times In Our Time* (Nashville, TN: Broadman & Holman, 2004), 201-202.

8. Douglas Connelly, *The Book of Revelation Made Clear* (Grand Rapids Michigan: Zondervan Publishing, 2007), 291.

9. Dr. Roy Branson, *The Hard Things of God* (Bristol, TN: Landmark Publications, 2014).

## CHAPTER 19. The Coming Christ

1. THE WEDDING OF THE LAMB HAS COME REVELATION 19:1-21 Key .... https://www.chicagoubf.org/wp-content/uploads/ archive/ Revelation 2020/messages/ Revelation -19_1-21-message. pdf (Accessed on May 2021).

2. Bruce B. Barton, *Life Application Bible Commentary* (Wheaton, Ill: Tyndale House Publishers, 2000), 221.

3.   Jack W. Hayford, *Spiritual Field Bible* (Nashville, TN: Thomas Nelson Publishers, 1991), 1761.

4.   John Walvoord, *The Revelation of Jesus Christ* (Chicago, Ill: Moody Publishing, 1989), 310.

5.   Douglas Connelly, *The Book of Revelation Made Clear* (Grand Rapids Michigan: Zondervan Publishing, 2007), 16.

6.   Oliver B. Greene, *Revelation* (Greenville, South Carolina: The Gospel Hour, Inc., 1963), 450.

7.   The Four Beasts of Daniel Seven! – As The Lord, So Leads.... https://Ps.3756.wordpress.com/2019/07/17/Daniel-7/ (Accessed on March 25, 2020).

8.   THE MARRIAGE SUPPER OF THE LAMB - Angelfire. http://www.angelfire.com/nd/baptistpreacher/rev028.htm (Accessed on June 2019).

9.   Oliver B. Greene, *Revelation* (Greenville, South Carolina: The Gospel Hour, Inc., 1963), 453.

10.  James Strong, LL.D., S.T.D., *Strong Dictionary of Bible Words* (Nashville, TN: Thomas Nelson Publishers, 2001), #1343.

11.  John Walvoord, *The Revelation of Jesus Christ* (Chicago, Ill: Moody Publishing, 1989), 312.

12.  Ibid., 1761.

13.  A Marriage Made in Heaven. | Flaming the .... https://ezra-chimts.wordpress.com/2016/02/20/a-marriage-made-in-heaven-rev-191-9/ (Accessed on April 5, 2021).

14.  Douglas Connelly, *The Book of Revelation Made Clear* (Grand Rapids Michigan: Zondervan Publishing, 2007), 312.

15.     Prophecy - Part 174 - The Final Triumph: The Millennium .... http://openbibleministries.net/multimedia-archive/prophecy-part-174-the-final-triumph-the-millennium-ushered-in/ (Accessed on October 2020).

16.     F. N. Peloubet, *Peloubet's Bible Dictionary* (Philadelphia, PA: The John C. Winston Co., 1947), 168.

17.     Joel Green, *How to Read Prophecy* (Downers, Grove, Ill: InterVasity, 1984), 121.

18.     Logos definition - Google Search, https://www.google.com/search?q =logos+definition&ei=USpaYbfzNIO7tQa1lZPoCg&oq=logos+def inition&gs_lcp=Cgdnd3Mtd2l6EAEYATIICAAQsQMQkQIyCAgA EIAEELEDMggIABCABBCxAzIICAAQgAQQsQMyBQgAEIAEM ggIABCABBCxAzIFCAAQgAQyBQgAEIAEMgUIABCABDIFCA AQgAQ6BwgAEEcQsAM6BAgAEB46EQgAEOoCELQCEIoDELc DEOUCOhQIABDqAhC0AhCKAxC3AxDUAxDlAjoOCC4QgAQ QsQMQgwEQkwI6DgguELEDEMcBEKMCEJECOgUIABCRAjoL CAAQgAQQsQMQgwE6DgguEIAEELEDEMcBENEDOgsILhCA BBDHARDRAzoICC4QsQMQgwE6DgguEIAEELEDEMcBEKMC OhEILhCxAxDHARCjAhCRAhCTAjoRCC4QgAQQsQMQgwEQ xwEQ0QM6EQguEIAEELEDEIMBEMcBEKMCOgUILhCABDoL CC4QgAQQxwEQowI6DgguEIAEELEDEMcBEK8BOggILhCABB CxAzoLCC4QgAQQxwEQrwFKBAhBGABQ2BdYoz9gsm1oAnA CeAOAAY4BiAGVCpIBBBDEuMTCYAQCgAQGwAQrIAQjAAQE &sclient=gws-wiz (Accessed on September 12, 2021).

19.     Prophecy - Part 175 - Jesus Christ, His Coming as .... http://openbibleministries.net/multimedia-archive/prophecy-part-175-jesus-christ-his-coming-as-conqueror-the-great-battle-of-armageddon/ (Accessed on September 2, 2020).

20. Douglas Connelly, *The Book of Revelation Made Clear* (Grand Rapids Michigan: Zondervan Publishing, 2007), 272.

21. The Great Battle of Armageddon: The Removal and Binding Of .... https://www.sermoncentral.com/sermons/the-great-battle-of-armageddon-the-removal-and-binding-of-satan-jerry-cosper-sermon-on-book-of- Revelation -210818 (Accessed on April 15, 2021).

22. Prophecy - Part 176 - Armageddon: The Mobilizing of the .... http://openbibleministries.net/multimedia-archive/prophecy-part-176-armageddon-the-mobilizing-of-the-worlds-armies-part-2/ (Accessed on September 2020).

23. The Beast, His Armies, and False Prophet (Land Beast) Are .... https://www.sermoncentral.com/sermons/the-beast-his-armies-and-false-prophet-land-beast-are-defeated-John-lowe-sermon-on-beast-232657 (Accessed on September 7, 2020).

24. W. E. Vine, *Vine's Expository Dictionary* (Nashville, TN: Thomas Nelson Publishers, 1997), 1290.

**CHAPTER 20. The Bounding of Satan**

1. Earl Radmacher, Ronald B. Allen, H. Wayne House, *Nelson's New Illustrated Bible Commentary* (Nashville, TN: Thomas Nelson, Inc., 1999), 1746.

2. Henry A. Virkler, *Hermeneutics* (Grand, Rapids, MI: Bakers Books), 201-203.

3. Don Grey Barnhouse, *Revelation: An Expositional Commentary* (Grand Rapids, MI: Zondervan, 1971), 383.

4. Revelation 18 - A Study Guide by Mark A. Copeland. http://executableoutlines.com/rev_sg/rev_18.htm (Accessed on March 20, 2021).

5.   Earl Radmacher, Ronald B. Allen, H. Wayne House, *Nelson's New Illustrated Bible Commentary* (Nashville, TN: Thomas Nelson, Inc., 1999), 1746.

6.   Oliver B. Greene, *Revelation* (Greenville, South Carolina: The Gospel Hour, Inc., 1963), 481.

7.   Alan Carr, The Sermon Notebook, 1,000 YEARS OF HEAVEN ON EARTH, http://sermonnotebook.org/ Revelation /Revelation%20 20_1-10.htm (October 28, 2020).

8.   Millennium, Judgment, and the Eternal State. https://biblehelpsinc. org/publication/millennium-judgment-and-the-eternal-state/ (Accessed on March 23, 2021).

9.   Daniel Revelation Bible Studies: State of Man. http://Daniel Revelation biblestudies.com/stateofman.htm (Accessed on December 2020).

10.  The First Resurrection and The Millennial Reign Of Christ .... https:// www.sermoncentral.com/sermons/the-first-resurrection-and-the-millennial-reign-of-christ-satans-destiny-jerry-cosper-sermon-on-book-of- Revelation -210817 (Accessed on December 2020).

11.  Merriam-Webster, s.v. "hades," http://www.merriam-webster.com/ dictionary/hades (Accessed on January 2, 2021).

## CHAPTER 21. The New Heaven and Earth

1.   Oliver B. Greene, *Revelation* (Greenville, South Carolina: The Gospel Hour, Inc., 1963), 507.

2.   Richard Neill Donovan, https://sermonwriter.com/biblical-com-mentary-old/ Revelation -2110-2122-225/ (Accessed on April 27, 2021).

3.    Donald Grey Barnhouse, *Revelation: and depositional commentary* (Grand Rapids, MI: Zondervan Publishers, 1971), 400.

4.    Warren Wiersbe, *Be victorious* (Wheaton, Ill: Victor, 1985), 145.

5.    The Coming Again of the Lord – HIS GRACE ANOINTED .... https://hisgraceabc.wordpress.com/2018/01/10/the-coming-again-of-the-lord/ (Accessed on January 29, 2020).

6.    "Our Readers' Views." Columbian, Columbian Publishing Company, 1 Aug. 2014, p. A.6. (Accessed on July 25, 2021).

7.    A. T. Pierson, *A Revelation of Jesus Christ* (Scottdale, PA: Herald, 1961), 295.

8.    Bruce B. Barton, *Life Application Bible Commentary* (Wheaton, Ill: Tyndale House Publishers, Inc., 2000), 254.

9.    Ibid., 252.

10.   Wright, J. Edward, and Sakenfeld, Katharine Doob (ed.), *The New Interpreter's Dictionary of the Bible: D-H, Vol. 2* (Nashville: Abingdon Press, 2007), 767.

11.   James W. Knox, *The Book of Revelation* (Deland, FL), 414.

12.   Revelation: Chapters Twenty-one and Twenty-two. http://www.wor. org/book/3522/ Revelation -chapters-twenty-one-and-twenty-two KEYS TO UNDERSTANDING THE BOOK OF REVELATION – PART 8 .... https://firestormministry.com/keys-to-understanding-the-book-of-Rev.-part-8/ (Accessed on May 2019).

13.   Douglas Connelly, *The Book of Revelation Made Clear* (Grand Rapids Michigan: Zondervan Publishing, 2007), 350.

14.   Jack W. Hayford, *Spiritual Filled Life Bible* (Nashville, TN: Thomas Nelson Publishers, 1991), 1991).

15.  KEYS TO UNDERSTANDING THE BOOK OF REVELATION – PART 8 .... https://firestormministry.com/keys-to-understanding-the-book-of-Rev.-part-8/ (Accessed on March 2019).

16.  Prophecy 197 - THE NEW JERUSALEM - Part Two - Open Bible .... http://openbibleministries.net/multimedia-archive/prophecy-197-the-new-jerusalem-part-two/ (Accessed on March 2020).

17.  Sermons and Outlines - Sermon Notebook. https://sermonnotebook.org/new%20testament/John%2014_1-3.html (Accessed on September 2019).

18.  SOME CALL IT HEAVEN: But I call it HOME | Living Waters .... https://livingwatersoutreach.wordpress.com/2013/04/27/some-call-it-heaven-but-i-call-it-home/ (Accessed on September 5, 2019).

19.  Sermons and Outlines - Sermon Notebook. https://sermonnotebook.org/new%20testament/ Revelation %2021_9-27.htm (Accessed on May 26, 2021).

20.  Terry Watkins, The Truth about Hell, https://www2.gvsu.edu/pontiusd/hell.html (March 2021).

## CHAPTER 22. A Paradise Restored

1.  Douglas Connelly, *The Book of Revelation Made Clear* (Grand Rapids Michigan: Zondervan Publishing, 2007), 163.

2.  Jack W. Hayford, *Spiritual Field Bible* (Nashville, TN: Thomas Nelson Publishers, 1991), 1992.

3.  Dr. David Jeremiah, *Agents Of The Apocalypse* (Carol Stream, Ill: Biblica, Inc., 2011), 270-271).

4.  Jack W. Hayford, *Spiritual field Bible* (Nashville, TN: Thomas Nelson Publishers, 1991),1992.

5.  Eleven Facts About the Message of Revelation Sermon by .... https://www.sermoncentral.com/sermons/eleven-facts-about-the-message-of- revelation -jerry-cosper-sermon-on- revelation -168121 (Accessed October 2019).

6.  What are the Seven Blessings of the Book of Revelation? https://thirdmill.org/answers/answer.asp/file/46715 (Accessed on December 2020).

7.  Willie Morganfield, Serving the Lord, https://www.musixmatch.com/lyrics/Willie-Morganfield/Serving-the-Lord (Accessed on March 19, 2021).

8.  Journal of a Confessing Church. https://preachingchurch.wordpress.com/tag/offence/ (Accessed on June 5, 2021).

9.  ALPHA AND OMEGA Lyrics - GAITHER VOCAL BAND | eLyrics.net. https://www.elyrics.net/read/g/gaither-vocal-band-lyrics/alpha-and-omega-lyrics.html (Accessed on June 2, 2021).

10.  The Revelation of Jesus Christ. http://baptistbiblebelievers.com/LinkClick.aspx?fileticket=B-WWaLLnspo%3d&tabid=239&mid=783 (Accessed on May 22, 2021).

11.  Sermons and Outlines - Sermon Notebook. http://ww5.sermonnotebook.org/new%20testament/ Revelation %2022_17.htm (Accessed on October 2019).

12.  Douglas Connelly, *The Book of Revelation Made Clear* (Grand Rapids Michigan: Zondervan Publishing, 2007), 369.